KU-012-205

THE ROUGH GUIDE TO

Travel Online

There are more than 150 Rough Guide travel,
phrasebook, and music titles, covering
destinations from Amsterdam to Zimbabwe,
languages from Czech to Vietnamese, and musics from
World to Opera and Jazz.

To find out more about Rough Guides,
and to check out our coverage of more than
10,000 destinations, get connected to the Internet with
this guide and find us on the Web at:

www.roughguides.com

Rough Guide Credits

Text editor: Orla Duane
Series editor: Mark Ellingham
Production: Julia Bovis, Michelle Draycott, Susanne Hillen
Design and typesetting: Katie Pringle
Proofreading: Amanda Jones

Publishing Information

This first edition published April 2002 by
Rough Guides Ltd, 62–70 Shorts Gardens, London WC2H 9AH,
375 Hudson Street, New York 10014
Email: *mail@roughguides.co.uk*

Distributed by the Penguin Group

Penguin Books Ltd, 80 The Strand, London WC2R ORL
Penguin Putnam USA Inc., 375 Hudson Street, New York
10014, Penguin Books Canada Ltd, 10 Alcorn Avenue, Toronto,
Ontario MV4 1E4, Penguin Books Australia Ltd,
PO Box 257, Ringwood, Victoria 3134,
Penguin Books (NZ) Ltd, 182–190 Wairau Road, Auckland 10

Printed in Spain by Graphy Cems.

© Samantha Cook and Greg Ward 2002
448 pages; includes index

A catalogue record for this book is available
from the British Library
ISBN 1-85828-862-2

THE ROUGH GUIDE TO

Travel Online

by
Samantha Cook and Greg Ward

Contents

part one: basics

part two: themes and activities

activities

contents

part three: destinations

Acknowledgements

The authors would like to thank our editor, Orla Duane, for her patience and grace (and her editing); Katie Pringle for making it look so good; Jonathan Buckley and Mark Ellingham, for the idea; Neil Foxlee; all our friends who suggested useful sites, especially Alison Cowan, Link Hall, Nat Hunter, Ally Scott, Kate Stephenson and Jules Brown; our families; and each other.

Introduction

The Internet has swiftly become an indispensable tool for travellers, with the travel sector established as one of the mainstays of e-commerce. Much like an unfamiliar city, however, the Web can be a daunting place to explore on your own. Even if you have some idea of where you're heading, you can stumble into many a blind alley along the way.

This book is a simple guide on how to plan and purchase any trip online. As well as general advice – telling you what's out there and how to find it – it will also point you to hundreds of individual Websites, representing the cream of those devoted to specific destinations or activities. All you need to know is how to go online in the first place; if you don't know that, buy our excellent companion volume, the *Rough Guide to the Internet*.

The most obvious appeal of using the Net for travel arrangements is that if you know exactly what you want – a flight or ferry from A to B, the cheapest possible rental car, a cut-price all-inclusive package – there are great deals to be found. That's just one small part of the process, however. The Net can help you to choose a destination in the first place, using sites that cover the whole world as well as those focusing on particular countries or cities, and to decide where you want to stay and how you're going to spend your time. We'll also show you how to look up the latest news or weather reports before you leave, and even how to stay in touch with home once you arrive.

Throughout the book, we've mentioned whether sites offer "online booking", meaning that you can make your choice, and pay for it, without any contact with another human being. While that can be very convenient, it can also tempt you to rush into something you don't know enough about. On top of that, Websites can be very obtuse, and don't always tell you something unless you ask for it – such as the fact that there's another train an hour earlier that costs half as much or takes half as long. So, don't get too carried away. As a general rule, try to combine your Web research with phone or face-to-face conversations; you'll find in any case that many specialist operators insist on talking to all clients to be sure they know what they're doing.

Although security is an understandable concern for all Net users, online fraud is in fact very rare. Common-sense precautions to follow include never sending your credit card details via email, and making sure that all payments are carried out through a secure server. Your browser should advise you whether the connection you're using is secure; a useful indication is when the URL of the site you're on changes to start with "https://" instead of the usual "http://". On a broader level, don't trust sites that fail to carry full street addresses and phone numbers; that are hosted by free servers such as Geocities rather than having their own domain names; and that can't put you in touch with satisfied customers on request.

In addition, as with any business transaction, online or otherwise, it's up to the buyer to beware. Just because a site claims to offer cheap flights (and is found by search engines looking for "cheap flights", or has paid for a link from some "cheap flights" portal) doesn't mean its flights really are cheaper than any others. And the mere fact that a site looks pretty, or expensive, doesn't mean the product it's selling is any good (or even that the site does what it says it will). That's where this book comes in. We've trawled through thousands of sites to find those that are genuinely useful, whether they're beautiful, quirky, or downright ugly. We hope we're going to save you time and money, both at home and on the road, and point you towards some wonderful travel experiences.

part one

basics

Finding what you need

T he most essential skill for anyone making serious use of the Net is to know how to look for what you need. Although searching for specific information online might seem like trying to find the very smallest of needles in a haystack as large as China, various research tools can help cut the job down to size. Useful Websites, detailed both in the lists below and throughout this book, include **search engines**, **portals**, and **directories**, though the distinctions between those categories are not as clear cut as the names might suggest.

Search engines

The obvious way to start looking for something on the Net is to use a general purpose **search engine**. A search engine is a Website that invites users to specify any combination of words, and then trawls through millions of other Websites to find those that contain the closest match to those words. Contrary to appearances, however, search engines do not literally search the Web in real time. They work by reading a database of Web pages downloaded at some earlier juncture by whoever runs the site.

Some search engines contain all or most of the contents of the sites they include, which makes successful matching more likely, while others just contain excerpts from the home page of each site. To remain accurate, any search engine should be constantly updating its database, as there's always a delay between the time the information was gathered, and the moment you actually access it. Thus, the fact that a search engine finds a particular site is no guarantee that the site still exists.

The best known search engines are:

All The Web www.alltheweb.com
AltaVista www.av.com
Excite www.excite.com
Google www.google.com
Lycos www.lycos.com
Northern Light www.northernlight.com

You can find longer lists of search engines, together with detailed reviews, at both **www.searchenginesshowdown.com** and **www.searchenginewatch.com**.

In practice, surprisingly few sites function solely as search engines. Most search engines form part of larger sites, for example, as just one of the many services offered by an ISP such as AOL. For users, however, the ideal search engine should be as clear and straightforward as possible – and that's why **Google** is regarded by general consensus as the best of the major search engines. Too many of its rivals open up with cluttered, advert-filled home pages, and spend too much energy trying to direct visitors towards money-spinning sidelines. Google, by contrast, presents a clean, white screen, and gives the quickest results, with a simple choice between the standard "Google Search", which returns a list of relevant sites, and the "I'm Feeling Lucky" button, which has a remarkable knack of taking you straight to the most appropriate page. If you're only interested in finding **British Websites**, Google also offers a separate UK-only search facility, at **www.google.co.uk**.

Whichever search engine you choose to use, be sure to familiarize yourself with the techniques for **refining your search**. Different engines employ slightly different grammars, but as a rule entering the words **Diving Malaysia** will find pages that contain both the word **Diving** and the word **Malaysia**, though not necessarily together, while putting quotation marks in bold around a group of words, in this example, "Diving Malaysia", will find only those pages on which that exact phrase appears. It's also possible to search for pages that mention diving but do not also mention Malaysia, usually by entering either a **minus sign** (without a space) as in **Diving −Malaysia**, or the word **not**. Google's "Additional Search" page holds several pull-down menus that make the whole process abundantly clear.

For finding travel products, whether flights, accommodation, all-inclusive packages or simply destination guides, there's no advantage in using a so-called "**travel search engine**" rather than Google or one of the other general search engines. In fact, sites that claim to be travel search engines are on the whole indistinguishable from travel-related directories or portals, depending, in exactly the same way, on their own databases of operators and general information.

Search agents and searchbots

In order to throw up as many differing results as possible for a particular search, you may well find yourself running the same query through several different search engines. If so, it's quicker and easier to get an automated "**search agent**" or "**searchbot**" to do your searching for you, by comparing and combining the results from several search engines at once.

The most effective of these, **Copernic**, is a free, stand-alone program, which you have to download, once only, from the **www.copernic.com** site, and you can then instruct to hunt its way through search engines and directories alike, while the similar but less wide-ranging **Metacrawler** can be accessed each time you have a query at **www.metacrawler.com**. For Mac users, the machine's own "**Sherlock**" search facility performs much the same function, though as its default setting only includes a handful of search engines it currently makes for a poor alternative.

Travel-related portals and directories

Both **portals** and **directories** consist of hand-built lists of Websites arranged according to subject matter. Rather than entering a unique personal query, users are more likely to be invited to choose one or more categories from pull-down menus on the home page. Whether you key **Malaysia Diving** into a search engine, however, or choose first **Malaysia** and then **Diving** on a directory site, the results may well be the same. There's a smaller chance of completely irrelevant listings, since travel directories will only include travel-related sites, but there's probably a smaller pool of possibilities to draw on. Be warned that many directories only list sites with which they have some commercial relationship, or that pay for inclusion; it's usually easy to tell if that's the case by the entreaties on the home page to "list your site". In addition, directories are more likely to be out of date than search engines, so it's always worth trying to find out when the directory was last updated.

The precise difference between a portal and a directory is largely in the eye of the beholder, but broadly speaking a portal holds more original content, such as its own database of destination information or travel advice, and perhaps detailed appraisals of the sites it lists, than a directory.

The list below includes several excellent all-round portals and directories, while you'll find listings throughout this book of more specialized directory sites devoted to specific destinations or activities. In particular, be sure to check out the sites reviewed under "General adventure holidays" on p.119.

Remember too that most of the larger **ISPs**, such as **AOL** and **Yahoo**, double up as portals, offering their own travel-related content as well as links to other sites and operators, and so do the massive travel-agent sites like **Expedia** and **Travelocity**, reviewed under "Online Travel Agents", which starts on p.30.

Backpack Europe on a Budget

www.backpackeurope.com

The brainchild of American student and veteran backpacker Kaaryn Hendrickson, this site is a gem for any young person about to embark on his or her Grand Tour of Europe. Hundreds of reviewed links are organized into subject areas such as when, where and how to travel, budgeting, packing, where to stay, who to travel with, what to read and how to keep in touch. There's a full index of general travel information sites, special sections for women and students, and plenty on how to get to Europe in the first place. The bulletin boards include discussions on hostels, transport and travel gear, with a section devoted to finding travel companions.

Budget Travel

www.budgettravel.com

Hideous to look at and agonizing to read, this colossal budget travellers' directory is included here simply by virtue of its links. It's got thousands of them, from all around the world. Whether you're after a cheap travel agent in Riga or a ski operator in Kazakhstan, scroll down the home page to the full, scatterbrained list – then click for destination information, travel agents, maps, travelogues and message boards; for accommodation, cycling, hiking, adventure travel, camping, shopping, and transportation sites; and for pretty much anything at all related, however distantly, to budget travel.

Cities

www.cities.com

This useful directory, owned by media giant Universal, is devoted to online city guides, covering a lengthy and wide-ranging list of major world cities (4332 of them at last count). As well as specific travel information and up-to-date listings, it also offers links to current news stories; however, it has no content of its own.

GKsoft

www.gksoft.com/govt

An extraordinary online resource for travellers, serving as a gateway to almost twenty thousand official and/or governmental Websites in over 220 countries. The list is endless, including parliaments, ministries, broadcasting corporations and courts as well as tourist boards and embassies. Naturally, most of what you'll find is dry as dust, but if you need the official line on any world issue, you should be able to reach it from here.

The Paperboy

www.thepaperboy.com

The self-explanatory Paperboy site is a searchable directory of newspapers from all over the world, listed by state in the US (with 115 papers in New York and 38 in Missouri alone), and by country elsewhere (including 63 titles in Switzerland and 21 in Venezuela). Bookmark the site and you'll always be able to keep up with the latest news and weather wherever you're heading; it can even translate it for you (with variable results) if you've yet to master the local lingo.

Tourism Offices Worldwide Directory

www.towd.com

The addresses, with active Web links wherever possible, of every national tourist office in the world, and also many regional and local tourism organizations, including those of all US states and Canadian provinces.

The Travel Library

www.travel-library.com

A vast online archive of articles and personal travelogues, covering not only specific world destinations but also general topics such as sleeping in airports or how to travel light. Its main focus, in so far as it has one, is on round the world itineraries, with a plethora of individual experiences.

Although you can't search for anything specific, and even supposedly new postings tend to be several years old, it's still a stimulating source of intriguing ideas and serendipitous suggestions.

TripAdvisor

www.tripadvisor.com
Thus far, the TripAdvisor portal only covers destinations in the UK, Ireland, the USA, Caribbean, Mexico, and Canada, though plans to extend its range worldwide may have been implemented by the time you read this. The gimmick here is that for any chosen location it not only lists links to several destination guides (mostly drawn from guidebook sites), but also to an extensive archive of relevant newspaper and magazine articles.

TripSpot

www.tripspot.com
For almost any world destination, this portal can point you towards a dozen or more online travel guides. As ever, you're likely to find the guidebook publishers to be the best on offer, but at least TripSpot suggests a few alternatives.

Virtual Voyages

www.virtualvoyages.com
Although this destination directory only handles the major cities and resorts in North America and the Caribbean, and holds no appreciable content of its own, for those places it does cover it offers an amazing array of links, and can quickly put you in touch with hotels or restaurants that suit your exact criteria. For New Orleans, for example, it throws up sixty dedicated online guides plus another thousand sundry links to specific companies and establishments. Online hotel rates, reservations and confirmations are provided by **Travelnow.com**.

Guidebook sites

If you'd like to be able to turn to a single online source for consistently detailed advice on any **destination** in the world, you'd do best to bookmark the Website of one of the major **guidebook** publishers. Only the established book publishers have large enough databases to do the job properly, so most other travel sites that offer global destination guides, such as Expedia, use information drawn from guidebooks anyway. Currently the pick of the crop for country guides are Frommer's and Rough Guides, followed by Fodor's, while Time Out provides strong guides to individual cities. Lonely Planet's decision not to make its practical listings available over the Internet leaves it trailing well behind, despite its excellent users' forum. The drawback in all instances is that the online version tends to lag behind the print version, so that the information on the Web may be based on research that's already two or three years old.

Fodors

www.fodors.com

Like the guidebooks it showcases, the Fodors Website is a rather staid, middlebrow affair, with lots of gentle reassurance for nervous novice travellers. While it seldom strays far off the beaten track, however, it does provide detailed practical guides to major world destinations, coupled with a cross-section of "Rants and Raves" submitted by its readers. The busy message board is filled with tips, including advice for example on "how to manage the whole pub experience", while a useful separate section, wittily named fodors.mom, is devoted to family travel. Links to online booksellers make it possible to buy any Fodors book that takes your fancy.

Frommer's Budget Traveler

www.frommers.com

This useful, practically-oriented Website, run by the major US guidebook series, is still firmly stamped with the hand of Arthur Frommer himself, who has his own personal Soap Box from which to deliver generally sensible tirades about travel issues. The destination information is not all that comprehensive, but for those areas – mainly big-name cities – that are covered, it comes neatly structured in digestible chunks, with thorough reviews and listings. There are also plenty of general-interest articles, plus budget tips drawn from Frommer's *Budget Traveler* magazine and lots of good forums (especially strong on US destinations; see p.27), and you can purchase all the books online.

Independent Travel Stores Association

www.travelstores.com

The online members' directory of a group of North American bookstores.

Between them, they should be able to provide any guidebook or travel-related product you may require.

Lonely Planet

www.lonelyplanet.com
Although the Website of the best-selling Australian guidebook series offers thorough overviews of destinations throughout the world, the fact that it withholds detailed hotel and restaurant listings prevents it from being much use for day-by-day trip planning. However, its most popular feature is the busy "Thorn Tree" group of message boards (see p.27), packed with queries, advice and appeals from fellow travellers; many contributors are out on the road as they write, so it's great for up-to-the-minute tips. The SubWWWay section holds extensive links to other information sites, as well as reservation services, while under the bashful title "propaganda" you can buy the guides online.

Rick Steves' Europe Through the Back Door

http://ricksteves.com
North American travel guru Rick Steves made his name as an expert on European travel through his guidebook and TV series *Europe Through the Back Door*. His Website offers excerpts from the books plus general feature articles, with an emphasis on rail travel; you'll find few useful listings, but for destination overviews it's not at all bad, and it also includes the "Graffiti Wall" message board and suggested itineraries. To buy the books themselves, print and fax a form.

Rough Guides

www.travel.roughguides.com
Rough Guides haven't actually posted the entire text of all their travel guidebooks on the Web, but they still provide a more comprehensive online world guide than anyone else, with a huge pull-down menu on the opening page to get you straight to the destination you're after. Full accommodation and restaurant listings make the site particularly useful, although as they're taken

from the printed versions, like any guidebook, they do eventually drift out of date. There's also a community area, co-hosted with igougo, where you can read and post travel journals and photos, and links to online booksellers so you can buy the books themselves.

Time Out

www.timeout.com

So long as you're travelling to one of the forty or so most popular cities in the world – roughly twenty in Europe, and ten each in North America and Asia – Time Out can give you a detailed practical grounding in what to expect. The text is basically drawn from their published guides, but it's leavened with a smattering of current listings, so it's more up to date than most of its rivals. Would-be purchasers are re-directed to Amazon.

Online-only destination guides

About.com

www.about.com/travel

Like most of about.com's colossal online empire, its travel section is a wonderful information resource, and provides some of the best overall destination guides on the Web. In the first instance, it connects travellers with more than eighty subsidiary about.com sites, variously devoted to countries, continents, interests, cultures, and languages. Each area has a named host (complete with photo, for that human touch), and is packed with articles and additional links. At a glance, it's not easy to tell where About ends and the rest of the Internet begins, but the deeper you dig, the more likely you are to pass beyond its boundaries, perhaps to a specific operator who can sell you a trip to the destination in question, or to some learned academic journal. The one caveat is that every screen is cluttered with endless menus, adverts and messages from sponsors, making it tiresome to read the text at its core.

Away.com

http://away.com

Providing destination information is just a sideline for this massive, wide-ranging and heavily funded site, which is more concerned with selling flights, car rental, and adventure-holiday packages. Nonetheless, although working your way through its pull-down menus is a slow and cumbersome business, in the end it usually comes up with a meaty practical guide to your chosen destination, such as the entire text of the relevant Moon handbook – something you won't find on Moon's own site – as well as travelogues and message boards. Its Trip Finder facility can also pick a destination for you; specify a general region, plus details of your interests and your budget, and it will pick the perfect spot. Not only will it recommend an actual trip, it will even try to lend you the money to do it.

Bugbog

www.bugbog.com

An endearing British-produced online guide to the world for independent (and predominantly low-budget) tourists. It's far from detailed or comprehensive, and occasionally lapses into traveller-speak – of Bali, for example, it

says "the local people can be mercenary" – but it does provide lively overviews of potential global holiday destinations, and holds some great images (including spectacular photos of alien spaceships bombarding Bournemouth).

Passplanet

www.passplanet.com

General resource for budget travellers in Asia and Central America, put together as a labour of love by a French backpacker. It provides only minimal destination information for countries as a whole, and maddeningly there's no search facility, but it comes into its own with its rapidly expanding database of personal recommendations and practical listings for specific towns across the two continents.

Travel Intelligence

www.travelintelligence.net

A compendium of articles by seventy or so top-flight international travel writers. Searchable by destination, theme or author, it's designed more to inspire than to provide step-by-step practical advice, but cumulatively it forms a database of information on most countries in the world.

Maps and route planners

Adventurous Traveler

www.adventuroustraveler.com
This Vermont bookstore accepts international orders online for its extensive stock of maps and guidebooks. As well as reductions for members of their Adventurous Traveler Club, there's a Bargain Basement section offering big reductions and a fine stock of rare and out-of-print titles. Though the graphics are limited, the search facilities are good.

Elstead Maps

www.elstead.co.uk
Top-quality independent British map retailer, which uses its Website to sell around fifty thousand maps, globes, atlases, and CD-Roms to customers all over the world. If you can't find what you're looking for with a straightforward search, they also have a prompt and personal email enquiries service.

Expedia

www.expedia.com and www.expedia.co.uk
The North American version of Microsoft's massive Expedia site can produce a good-quality map of almost any world location, keying in hotels and attractions if required, and offering on-site links to make travel arrangements of all kinds. It also offers an excellent, fully illustrated route-finding facility to show driving itineraries between any two US addresses. Although it can display most of the same basic maps, the UK version is not up to the same standard, having difficulty in distinguishing London, England from London, Switzerland, and supplying all-but-useless driving directions.

Mapblast

www.mapblast.com

If you're searching for a location anywhere in the world – especially in Europe or North America, and whether you specify a town name, address or postcode – Mapblast should quickly find and display an on-screen map for you; the trouble is, it will probably be ugly and hard to use. Where the site comes into its own, however, is with its LineDrive route finder, powered by the Vicinity Corporation who also supply such sites as Alamo car rentals. For road trips in both the US and the UK, it produces simple, accurate and carefully timed driving directions, beautifully schematized in a hierarchy of maps.

Mapquest

www.mapquest.com and www.mapquest.co.uk

Invited to search for any location on the planet, Mapquest will swiftly deliver a reasonably attractive online city plan or regional road map, which you can print, email, buy, or download to a handheld device. Both the North American and European Websites also offer good Road Trip Planners for their respective continents; the initial response is just a thick purple line across a continental map, but you can zoom in for as much detail as you require.

Maps Worldwide

www.mapsworldwide.co.uk

British online retailer that sells maps on paper and CD-Rom, including road maps, historical maps, specialist maps showing waterways and cycle paths, and full atlases. Though they specialize in maps of the UK, the scope extends to the whole world. All prices are reduced to some extent, with a general twenty percent discount on UK Ordnance Survey titles.

Multimap

www.multimap.com

Basically an online atlas of the UK, on which you can zoom from regional maps down to local street level, Multimap even knows which streets are one way. Each new screen brings up an extensive list of links, including local sights and attractions and even star-marked properties for sale. There's also an adequate route finder, plus an interactive map of London's tube system.

Shell GeoStar

www.shellgeostar.com

Available in half a dozen languages, Shell Europe's site is a largely success-ful bid to meet the needs of anyone planning a European driving itinerary. As well as plotting a route between any locations in 16 countries, it can provide details of accommodation and sites of interest along the way. It's also better than most such sites at allowing British travellers to specify their ferry crossing to the continent. In addition, it sells travel guides, printed maps and motoring accessories.

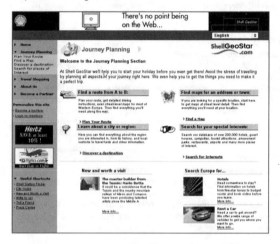

Terraserver

www.terraserver.com

Terraserver displays and sells not maps, but aerial photos from all over the world. Both North American and British customers should find they're able to zoom in for a close-up view of their own home, though for the finest res-olution, you have to buy the printed version; prices start at around $25 plus postage.

University of Texas Library Online

www.lib.utexas.edu/maps/

The University of Texas has put together a compelling Website that centres on the map collection of its Perry-Castañeda Library, which includes more than 250,000 maps covering all areas of the world. Around five thousand public-domain maps are available online for free downloads, and there's also a great set of links to "other map-related sites", which range from the very earliest attempts at cartography, dating from 6000 BC, up to the latest images of Mars.

US Maps.com

www.maps.com

Well-designed site selling high-quality downloadable digital maps, along with printed conventional maps, atlases, globes, wall maps, travel guides, antique maps, books and travel gear. It also offers a reasonable route-finding facility, as well as entertaining sidelines such as interactive historic maps, showing, for example, the progress of the US Civil War, and even online jigsaws.

Via Michelin

www.viamichelin.co.uk

The Website of French tyre-and-guide company Michelin suffers slightly in English translation, but for travel in continental Europe it's a tremendous resource. Its extensive range of road maps and city plans are interlinked with its database of hotels, attractions and general information, so when asked to plot a driving route it can suggest accommodation and pit-stops along the way. In Britain itself it's less comprehensive; you can't specify individual addresses in London, for example.

Newsgroups, forums, email lists and ezines

For many people, **online discussion groups** are every bit as useful, if not more so, than Web pages. Discussion groups epitomize the original concept of the Internet; a global community based on freedom of speech. The first such groups were established through a network called Usenet, set up in 1979 as a collection of academic bulletin boards or **newsgroups**. Today there are tens of thousands of newsgroups, each devoted to a topic or theme – eating disorders, camper vans, baked beans, Satan – subscribed to by users from all walks of life. Don't be misled by the name; these groups don't exist to send out news as such, but act as forums where anyone can swap information, queries and opinions. They're useful tools for travellers, who can post questions about anything from airline safety to how to find a cheap hotel in Borneo, and who often find the honest responses a welcome relief among the minefield of advertorial, fly-by-night dotcoms and sheer bad travel writing on the Web. How seriously you choose to take the opinions of someone you have never met, however, and whose tastes may be completely unlike your own, is down to you.

Finding newsgroups

First you'll need access to a **newsreader program**. Most browsers, including Internet Explorer and Netscape, come with such programs built in; to get them rolling, consult your ISP's technical help pages, or look at the **Rough Guide to the Internet**, which talks you through the process of subscribing to newsgroups step by step. Alternatively, you could choose a specialist news provider, such as **Agent** (for PCs; **www.forteinc.com**) or **MT Newswatcher** (for Macs; **www.smfr.org/mtnw**), many of which have extras over and above the inbuilt programs, and which are usually free to download.

You can also use the Web to access newsgroups, by going through superfast search engine **Google** (see p.23), but while this is great for searching old posts, it doesn't offer as many options as the specialist providers. With most newsreaders, you can mark messages you've read, and save messages to read later. You can choose to see only messages you haven't read, sort messages by date or subject, select all messages by a certain author or keyword, or skip unwanted subjects or authors. Google offers fewer features.

Ideally (though not always), newsgroup **names**, which are laid out in chunks separated by full stops, should make it clear what the group is about. Most crucial are the three- or four-letter abbreviations at the start of the name. Known as **hierarchies**, many of these are undecipherable, but the best-known are clear enough, telling you the general concerns and tone of the group. Of these, **alt.** ("alternative" topics), **misc.** (miscellaneous), **rec.** (recreational) and **soc.** (society and culture) all hold groups useful to travellers. Thus **rec.travel.australia+nz** will concentrate on travel to and around Australasia, while **alt.travel.greece** is the group to join if you're off island-hopping around the

Dodecanese. Don't assume, however, that the alt. group will be full of counter-cultural drop-outs, or that the rec. group is the domain of carefree folk out to play. Newsgroup naming isn't an exact science; there is a lot of crossover between groups, and within each group messages cover a broad range of topics. Most people subscribe to a few groups relating to similar interests.

Using newsgroups

Within each group, individual messages are known as **posts**; an ongoing string of posts is a **thread**. Whether you're using a news-reader or Google, posts and threads are listed by their subject title, in date order, with the newest at the top. Clicking on the subject title opens that message, followed directly in a thread by its **fol-low-ups** (responses posted for the group, as opposed to **replies**, which are emailed direct to the original poster). While the longer threads may be the meatiest, they are also the most difficult to trawl through. As follow-up follows follow-up, each message becomes more unwieldy, with text copied from earlier postings and overlong email signatures appended with quotes and annoy-ing ASCII graphics. Regular users soon **learn how to decipher these postings**, scanreading to find the final point, and skipping messages from anyone they've learned to avoid. There tend to be hundreds of **questions** and rather fewer answers in each group; even if you post a question of your own there is no guarantee that anyone will reply, or if they do, that the answer will be of any use. It can be more productive to **browse** debates that have already taken place. This is known as **lurking**, and is perfectly acceptable.

To "delurk", and post your own messages, you need to **sub-scribe**. This is usually simple enough, but varies according to your ISP. (Posting to a group via Google is slightly different; see below.) Once you've subscribed, your personal choice of news-groups will appear automatically every time you open the pro-gram. It's as simple again to unsubscribe.

Travel newsgroups

These groups are unmoderated unless stated otherwise.

alt: (Vaguely) offbeat groups
alt.rec.camping
alt.rec.hiking
alt.travel
alt.travel.canada
alt.travel.eurail.youth-hostels
alt.travel.greece
alt.travel.marketplace
alt.travel.road-trip
alt.travel.uk.air Buying tickets,
  jet lag, DVT, flight delays ...
alt.travel.uk.marketplace
  Cruises, home exchanges,
  online street maps ...
alt.travel.usa-canada

rec: Recreational topics

Destinations
rec.travel.africa
rec.travel.asia
rec.travel.australia+nz
rec.travel.caribbean
rec.travel.europe
rec.travel.latin-america
rec.travel.usa-canada

Travel topics
rec.backcountry Bear attacks,
  tent debates, mountain biking
  in the US outdoors ...
rec.bicycles.off-road
  (moderated)
rec.bicycles.rides
rec.boats.cruising

rec.boats.paddle
rec.climbing
rec.food.restaurants
rec.outdoors.camping
rec.outdoors.national-parks
rec.outdoors.rv-travel
rec.parks.theme Safety warnings, theme park queries,
  rollercoaster reviews...
rec.scuba
rec.scuba.locations
rec.skiing
rec.skiing.alpine
rec.skiing.backcountry
rec.skiing.nordic
rec.skiing.resorts.europe
rec.skiing.resorts.misc
rec.skiing.resorts.north-america
rec.skiing.snowboard
rec.travel.air Booking flights,
  airline food, good fares, disas-
  trous airlines...
rec.travel.bed+breakfast
  (moderated)
rec.travel.budget.backpack
rec.travel.cruises
rec.travel.marketplace Tour
  guides, ticket agents, B&B
  owners, home exchangers ...
rec.travel.misc Travel tips, couri-
  er flights, luggage reviews ...
rec.travel.resorts.all-inclusive
  (moderated)
continued overleaf

21

Travel newsgroups continued

soc: Social and cultural issues

Most messages posted to the groups in the (selective) list below are written in English. There are many more groups where debates are conducted in the language of the home country, and others, not listed here, concerned with specific regions and peoples – Basque, Breton, Hmong and so on.

soc.culture.african
soc.culture.asean [sic]
soc.culture.australian
soc.culture.baltics
soc.culture.british
soc.culture.burma
soc.culture.cambodia
soc.culture.canada
soc.culture.caribbean
soc.culture.china
soc.culture.costa-rica
soc.culture.cuba
soc.culture.egyptian
soc.culture.europe
soc.culture.french
soc.culture.greek
soc.culture.haiti
soc.culture.hawaii (moderated)
soc.culture.hongkong
soc.culture.indian
soc.culture.irish
soc.culture.israel
soc.culture.japan (moderated
    and unmoderated groups)
soc.culture.jordan
soc.culture.kenya

soc.culture.laos
soc.culture.latin-america
soc.culture.malaysia
soc.culture.mongolian
soc.culture.nepal
soc.culture.new-zealand
soc.culture.pacific-island
soc.culture.palestine
soc.culture.portuguese
soc.culture.russia
soc.culture.singapore
    (moderated and unmoderated
    groups)
soc.culture.south-africa
soc.culture.soviet
soc.culture.sri-lanka
soc.culture.syria
soc.culture.thai
soc.culture.ukrainian
soc.culture.vietnamese
soc.culture.zimbabwe

misc: Miscellaneous topics
misc.kids.vacation

Spam

Freedom of speech has its downsides. Many of the most popular groups are inundated with **spam** (junk mail), and **MMFs**, illegal "Make Money Fast" schemes. Some groups are filtered or **moderated** to reject unwanted messages before they are posted, but many more are not. When you do post, note too that your email address is made available so that newsgroup members can **contact you direct**. To avoid being inundated with spam, many people type in invalid addresses – **nojunksam@nospamaol.com**, for example. Other users recognize the dummy phrases (in this case, no junk and no spam) and disregard them when replying (to **sam@aol.com**), while the spammers, who tend to do blind mailshots, will be foiled. This ruse, which entails a bit of untangling on the part of a potential respondent, is frowned upon by some groups. If that bothers you, you could set up a **separate email account** for newsgroups alone. You might prefer to do this anyway, if you're secretive about your email address.

Google

With **Google**, the queen bee of the search engines (see p.4), it's possible to search the entire Usenet archive – that's thousands of newsgroups – dating back to 1995, and to post your own mes-

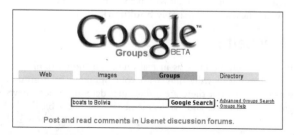

sages. The service is as user-friendly and convenient as you'd expect from Google, and great if you're looking for something specific. Anyone who wants sophisticated preferences, however, will do better with a newsreader (see p.19).

Typing in **groups.google.com** brings up a list of the major categories (**alt.**, **misc.**, **rec.**, and **soc.**). Click each to see a full list of groups in that hierarchy, along with an indicator to show how active they are, and keep clicking to get more specific until you find the group you want. Outside these major hierarchies the thousands of other groups are organized alphabetically via drop-down menus. It would take days to browse them all, which is where Google's search facility comes into its own. You can **search** for a group by typing in keywords – skiing, Graceland, whatever – and quick as a flash the engine will pull up all the messages, in a variety of groups, that include those words. You then click to read the full message – and all its follow-ups, if there are any – and from there you can get to that particular newsgroup's main index. Keying "lesbian guesthouse", for example, links you to messages on **alt.travel.marketplace**, **uk.gay-lesbian-bi**, and **soc.women**, among many others, while from "Paris restaurants" you could visit dozens of groups including **rec.travel.europe**, **alt.cities.paris**, and **rec.food.restaurants**.

To **post a follow-up**, or to start a new thread using Google, you have to log in, giving an email address and password. Messages turn up on screen within a few hours. To fast track back to your chosen groups, simply **bookmark** them.

Netiquette

In virtual communities, as in real ones, you should think twice about barging in willy-nilly with your opinions. Each group is self-regulating, but there are a few rules defining general newsgroup **netiquette**, and while members will cut a bit of slack when it comes to "**newbies**", they tend not to suffer fools gladly. As well as heading straight for the **FAQs**, or Frequently Asked Questions (regular postings, clearly marked, which cover the group's codes of conduct), you should ideally spend some time **lurking** before subscribing. Not only does this allow you to get to know the group, it may prevent you from making a fool of yourself – your question may well have come up before, and you will be expected to have done some work in finding the answer. You'll also win no friends by blithely turning up with queries that can be easily solved by a quick surf on the Web ("Where can I find the address of the Japanese tourist board?", for example).

Though it's by no means obligatory to buy into Net speak, with its copious use of abbreviations and **emoticons** – such as :-) or :-0, which translate as smiling, or shock – you should know that to post a message in **capital letters** is counted as shouting, and is generally frowned upon. To emphasize a word or phrase,

Just for newbies: newsgroups about newsgroups

The hierarchy **news.** denotes a group devoted to newsgroups. Though we've given each a broad review below, as ever there is a lot of crossover.

news.newusers.questions (moderated)
All sorts of questions, some of them technical.

news.announce.newusers (moderated)
Basic information, news and updates.

news.answers (moderated)
FAQs from a number of different newsgroups.

news.groups
General issues relating to newsgroup use; lots of debate about moderation and freedom of speech.

news.groups.questions
From how to reply to how to start a group of your own.

news.groups.reviews
Reviews from users about their favourite groups.

it's best to tag it with asterisks. Capitals tend to be used by **trolls**, members who are known for their **flames** (offensive messages) – if you get flamed, rather than starting a **flame war**, simply ignore the message and move on. **Cross-posting** – when you copy an article to more than one newsgroup – should be done very sparingly, and only if the message is truly relevant to each group. And, of course, you should *never* send spam, use members' email addresses for your own mailing lists, or post a personal email sent from someone else without their consent.

For the wittiest, sharpest and most sarcastic take on Netiquette, log on to **www.psg.com/emily.html**.

Online forums

Travel forums, or **message boards**, also proliferate on the Web. The biggest and best come on guidebook sites, including **Rough Guides**, **Frommer's** and **Lonely Planet**, but many of the sites we've reviewed for travel agents and specialist operators have their own. **AOL** and the major search engines also have travel forums; as with the newsgroups, however, you have to be prepared to trawl through a certain amount of drivel to glean useful information. To post your own message you usually need to **register**, a simple case of supplying email address, a "user name" (nickname), and password.

AOL travel boards

Type in keywords "Travel Boards" to access discussions on destinations, interests (adventure, casinos, food and wine, gay and lesbian etc) and advice (airlines, lodging, travel news and so on). Though many of the topics are US-dominated, and postings can be rather general, AOL does have some unusual destination forums, including Antarctica and Micronesia, where messages tend to be brief and articulate. Members can simply tap in a reply, and after a first visit choose to see only new messages.

http://frommers.com

Frommer's superb site (see p.10) has a very good range of forums, with hundreds of discussions. Click "Travel Message Boards" to see the full list, and then again to get to the individual folders. You can also do a keyword search. Forums are very well organized by region (of all the guidebook sites this is the only one that divides the US into states) and topic: in "Ask The Expert", you can post a query direct to a Frommer's author (each destination gets a couple of weeks' worth of discussion before being archived), while on the monthly "Hot Issue in Travel" debates rage on subjects such as air miles, national parks, booking holidays over the Net, and so on. There are also forums on road trips, skiing, cruising, bargains, student travel and travel partners, many with a US-bent. To register, enter your name, email address and password; after posting, you have thirty minutes' grace to edit your message.

www.igougo.com

This innovative travel journal site, packed full of personal accounts and photos, works in a similar way to a forum, providing first-hand information on places around the world from various correspondents. You can search by destination and contact community members who have been there before you. The site also offers a range of incentives for "travel club members" and is partnered with our very own **http://travel.roughguides.com**.

http://travel.roughguides.com

Click "Travel Talk" to be involved in discussions about world destinations – organized by region – and special forums devoted to finding travel partners, women travellers, gay and lesbian travellers, health and safety, round-the-world trips and travelling with kids. Registration is required if you want to post.

www.lonelyplanet.com

Lonely Planet's forum, Thorn Tree, includes discussion groups on twenty regions, plus topics including gay travellers, long-haul trips, diving and snorkelling, politics, food, the arts, and travelling with kids. There are also separate "non-threatening" spaces for male and female travellers. Though the information can be useful, especially when it comes to Asia, there seem to be more flamers on these forums than on those linked to the other major guidebooks, and many anonymous posters, which makes the longer threads difficult to follow.

Email lists

Email lists, though similar in intent to forums, are groups or communities that use email to exchange information: once you've joined a group, every email you send is received by every member, and vice versa.

There are hundreds of email lists devoted to travel topics, and several **directories** where you can find them. The best of these, **www.topica.com**, uses handy icons to show which lists are most informative or intriguing, which are available to read via the site, which insist upon approval for new subscribers, and so on. Topica's many travel-related lists are divided into categories from adventure travel to trains, with a good few devoted to particular destinations. Click on the name to find out about the list's

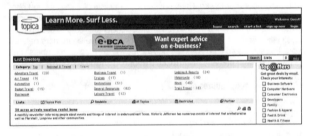

content, who runs it, how many members it has and how many messages per day you can expect. Sometimes messages are available to browse before subscribing. You can subscribe right here on the site (after submitting all your personal details); store the immediate email confirmation somewhere safe, as it will tell you how to unsubscribe. Then select whether to receive all messages as they come, digested weekly or monthly, or, in some cases, not by email at all but solely through the site (where they are listed as though on a message board).

If you don't find what you're looking for on topica, check **http://groups.yahoo.com** (travel is filed under "Recreation and Sports"), which has lists organized into more than thirty categories from dude ranches to whale watching – for most of these, however, you have to join blind, as the archives aren't viewable by non-members. Another directory worth a look is **www.lsoft.com/catalist.html**.

Incidentally, you might want to set up a **separate email account** to deal with the sheer volume of mail that many groups attract, or at least establish a special folder in your current email program.

Email newsletters and ezines

You can also sign up to receive free **email newsletters** (also known as one-way lists, or **ezines**) from a variety of companies. Many of the Websites reviewed in this book – including the guidebook sites (see p.9), which also have their own forums, and the major airlines, who will email you their latest deals – offer their own email newsletters. We've mentioned the most useful in our individual reviews. For an alphabetical directory of big-name email newsletters, a handful of them travel-related, check Netscape's "In-Box Direct" at **http://home.netscape.com/ibd**, which links you direct to the individual Websites.

Online travel agents

In addition to the sites listed below, young people and students in search of travel bargains should check out the operators reviewed on p.178. We've also listed specialist operators for most of the destinations covered in Part Three of this book.

a2btravel

www.a2btravel.com

This large British online travel agent provides information, advice, and easy bookings for anyone travelling from, to, or within the UK. As well as flights, ferries and car rentals, it offers a database of last-minute holiday bargains, a brochure-ordering service for all major operators, and links to associated sites such as the cut-price **www.bargainholidays.com** and the self-explanatory **www.ferrybooker.com** and **www.1ski.com**.

Advantage Travel Centres

www.advantage4travel.com

Website that pools the resources of Europe's biggest network of independent travel agents. You can search for package holidays of all kinds, as well as flights, cruises and city breaks, or look for last-minute deals by selecting from a long list of popular resorts. Most, but not all, of the participants offer online booking.

American Express

http://travel.americanexpress.com

The travel section of the massive American Express site doles out destination advice culled from Fodors, Zagats, and *Travel & Leisure* magazine, and has some mouthwatering 360° panoramas of major world destinations. For travel shoppers, it's probably best as a source of individual components of your trip, such as flights, car rentals or accommodation, but in association with various big-name partners it also offers all-inclusive packages and last-minute special deals, all available online. And, of course, you can also buy your traveller's cheques ...

ebookers

www.ebookers.co.uk
Having started life as the online arm of the discount air specialists Flightbookers, British all-round agency ebookers bought out its parent company to become the tail that wags the dog. Its vast database of all-inclusive packages ranges across all the continents, taking in beach holidays, adventure trips, etc; the site also sells flights, cars, hotels, insurance, and cruises.

Eurovacations

www.eurovacations.com
Impressive site devoted exclusively to selling European tour packages to North American customers. If you don't know where you want to go, its Destination Wizard will guide you step by step in choosing a vacation. Once you do know, the site is effortlessly interactive, enabling you to custom-design every detail of your trip, from flights and transport arrangements to specific hotels. Prices are very reasonable, and rail travel is a speciality. You can complete the whole booking process online, though human operators are available to answer phone enquiries.

Expedia

www.expedia.com (North America) and **www.expedia.co.uk (UK)**
That Expedia is the most all-embracing travel site on the Web is hardly surprising, in view of the fact that it's owned by Microsoft. In addition to selling flights, lodgings, car rental, packages, and cruises, it offers any number of fancy extras, including destination information from Fodors guidebooks, plus online maps, airport guides, and currency and weather information. Certain services on each site (such as car rental) are available to international customers, but to be sure that you'll actually be able to buy what you see on screen it's safest to use the site targetted at your home country. US users looking to buy all-inclusive packages can choose

from 350 destinations, none of them in Asia, Africa or Australasia. UK customers visiting the "Holiday Shop" are offered an entirely different list of worldwide resorts, with holidays from a wide range of leading operators. Most can be booked online, but you're heavily encouraged to call the operator by phone instead.

Go-today.com

www.go-today.com

Internet-only travel agency based in Seattle, specializing in cut-rate packages from the US to either Europe or South America. The primary focus is on last-minute travel, but many deals are available up to three or even six months in advance. Trips range from guided tours, city breaks and fly-drives (for which automatic cars cost only slightly extra), to cruises and barge rentals. The site itself is exceptionally easy to use, with pull-down menus making it clear which departure cities are available for each itinerary, explicit itemized on-screen prices, and full online booking.

Lastminute.com

www.lastminute.com

Legendary, in its home territory of Britain at least, as the definitive over-hyped and over-valued dotcom-boom Website, Lastminute has nonetheless survived and, within reason, prospered. More a source of stimulating ideas than of rock-bottom deals, it holds an impressive selection of off-the-wall trips, such as a day in Iceland or Morocco, as well as city breaks to Paris or Brussels by Eurostar or by air. Not everything is last minute; conventional holidays bookable a month or more in advance include plenty in long-haul destinations like Barbados or Egypt. The database is searchable by date, destination, and/or type of accommodation. Most but, oddly, not quite all trips are bookable online. If you don't fancy going anywhere at all, the site also provides current TV listings.

Luxury Link

www.luxurylink.com

Los Angeles-based site centering on a database of expensive and opulent vacation possibilities offered all over the world by assorted upmarket operators. Specify your interests or desired destination, and its simple search engine returns a long list of alternatives; asking for all-inclusive tours of Italy, for example, produces 43 options, with links to the relevant Websites. In addition, Luxury Link also sells some of its featured package deals, via a special offers page or by auction. Results of past auctions are available to provide a sense of what might constitute a winning bid, and make very interesting reading.

Orbitz

www.orbitz.com
As it's owned by five major US airlines, it's only natural that the Orbitz Website is most useful as a source of air fares, as described on p.40. It does, however, also offer its North American-only customers a reasonable assortment of discounted package vacations, not only within North America, but also to the Caribbean, Middle East, Europe and South America (although not Asia and Africa). The best bargains are in the Last-minute Getaway section, in which you search according to your departure city.

Site59

www.site59.com
Fast, efficient North American site, open to travellers of any nationality, and devoted exclusively to "last-minute weekend getaways" – the name refers to the 59th minute – from around thirty US and two Canadian cities. Specify where you're travelling from, and whether you want to go "this weekend" or "next weekend", and it comes up with literally hundreds of well-priced city breaks, with pull-down menus to choose exact flight schedules and extras such as car rental. Complete the whole process online if you like what you see, otherwise sign up for an email newsletter of future offers.

Travelocity

www.travelocity.com (North America) and www. travelocity.co.uk (UK)
The Travelocity mega-site, owned by Sabre and available in separate versions in North America and Europe, is Expedia's largest rival as an all-round online travel agency. Much like Expedia, it sells flights, accommodation and car rental singly or together, and offers comprehensive destination guides (courtesy of Frommer's in North America and eDreams in the UK). For all-inclusive packages, the North American site draws on deals from half a dozen big-name tour operators and major airlines, while the UK version uses a larger database of operators and has a separate "Late Deals" section. Succinct comparison charts make it easier to weigh up your options, but for most packages you can only complete bookings by phone.

Unmissable

www.unmissable.com
British Website dedicated to selling unusual and off-the-beaten-track holidays all over the world. Search its database by destination and/or activity, and it reels off a list of unlikely trips, both demanding and idyllically lazy, plus all sorts of useful background material. Email or phone to make a reservation, or fill in a lengthy email form detailing your interests and requirements, and they'll "tailor-make" an itinerary for you.

European city breaks

Bridge Travel

www.bridge-travel.co.uk
British travel agency that arranges short breaks in around 25 European countries plus Canada, the US, Morocco and the UAE. Beyond the eye-catching special offers to Paris and Amsterdam on the home page lies a menu of deals to lesser-known destinations like Latvia and Estonia. All hotels are fully described, and can be booked without a flight as well, but the main business is selling all-inclusive packages. An email form secures your reservation.

Inghams Eurobreak

www.eurobreak.com
This British tour company provides very much what you'd hope for from a city-break site; the home page opens with a large map of Europe, on which several dozen cities are highlighted. Click on one, or use a pull-down menu, and you're offered a brief description, with another menu of hotels, and a button to find the price and flight details. What you see is simply a JPEG of the relevant brochure page, but so long as it's more than a week before you plan to travel, you can nonetheless go on to check availability and complete your booking online. You'll even get a free *Eyewitness* guidebook thrown in.

Short Breaks

www.short-breaks.com
City breaks from London to Paris, Bruges, Brussels or Antwerp, using Eurostar trains. For each city, pick from a list or map of hotels to get a

detailed description and specific all-inclusive prices. Then use pull-down menus to specify when and where you want to go – remembering the cost, as it doesn't appear again – and someone will call you back when they've checked availability. The site also carries full timetables and a page of links.

Webweekends

www.webweekends.co.uk

UK-based site that takes great pains to point out that it's an "online distributor, not a travel agent or weekend supplier". What that means is that while the site contains a vast array of enticing, well-priced short city-break and activity packages, searchable by destination, price, timing and other criteria, actually booking them requires you to contact the individual suppliers direct – whose name you only get once you register – with no guarantee as to availability or pricing. Most trips are within Europe, though Jamaica, Kenya, the US and even Turkmenistan feature here and there; there's also a section for US customers.

Where 2

www.where2break.com

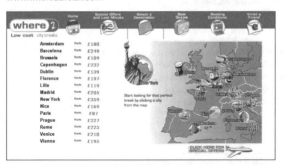

This site can be slow to load, but once its fancy opening map is in place it reveals a mouthwatering selection of low-cost city breaks, with fifteen major cities highlighted across Europe, and New York suspended out over the Atlantic. Clicking on the hotels listed for each destination brings up only minimal details, and while the prices look amazing at first they tend to be bumped up by all sorts of unexpected supplements, but if you want to book a cheap short trip online, this is a good place to start. All holidays are available to UK residents only.

Major BAM operators

In addition to the specialist Internet travel agents listed in this section, many of the large BAM operators – BAM stands for "Bricks and Mortar", to denote companies that have a physical presence outside the virtual world – also maintain useful Websites. Where appropriate to specific destinations or activities, you'll find those sites reviewed throughout this book.

UK

Club 18–30 www.club18-30.co.uk
Club Med www.clubmed.com
Destination Group www.destination-group.co.uk
Erna Low www.ernalow.co.uk
JMC www.jmc.com
Kuoni www.kuoni.co.uk
Lunn Poly www.lunn-poly.co.uk
Magic of the Orient www.magic-of-the-orient.com
Thomas Cook www.thomascook.co.uk
Thomson Holidays www.thomson-holidays.com
Titan Travel www.titantravel.co.uk
Trailfinders www.trailfinders.com
Voyages Jules Verne www.vjv.com

US

Abercrombie & Kent www.abercrombiekent.com
Contiki www.contiki.com
Cosmos Tours www.globusandcosmos.com
Maupintour www.maupintour.com
Saga Holidays www.sagaholidays.com

Buying flights

a2btravel

www.a2btravel.com
General online travel agency, which uses the Travelocity search engine to
hunt out good deals on one-way and round-trip flights between any two
airports worldwide.

Airhitch

www.airhitch.org
The "Airhitch" concept is not for everybody; judging by the Website's insis-
tence on clichés about "tourists" and "travelers", it's largely designed for
those who like to feel they're beating the "system". Restricted to US-
based users only, the idea is that you specify roughly where you're travelling from, where you're going (Europe, Hawaii or the Caribbean), and when
(within a five-day range). A few days before you set off, you're finally told
when and where you're going – and you have to accept it, even if it's
Amsterdam rather than Paris. So long as you're comfortable with the
uncertainty, you'll end up benefiting from such flat-rate one-way fares,
available even in high season, as just under $200 to Europe from the East
Coast, or $250 from the West Coast. "Usually", you even get the exact
destination you asked for.

Airline Network

www.airline-network.co.uk
British agency that sells flights from the UK only to all world destinations. All
fare quotes include all taxes and surcharges; even if they don't seem to be
the cheapest at first glance, it's worth checking the small print on their
competitors before you commit.

Airtreks

www.airtreks.com
Although it can quote you (unexceptional) prices for standard round-trip flights anywhere in the world, the Website of Californian air-ticket specialists High AdventureTravel, outperforms its conventional competitors when it comes to putting together multi-stop globetrotting trips. Start by constructing your own routing, or taking advantage of the pre-planned Around-the-World and Circle-Pacific itineraries, online; either way, you'll then need to call or email to optimize the fare.

Cheap Flights

www.cheapflights.co.uk
Cheap Flights is a superb and simple UK flights site: you just key in a destination and the airport you want to leave from and up come the range of options available - all of them, as this is not an agent, but an impartial source. You can then click through to book, or browse links to all sorts of relevant associated information.

Cheap Tickets

www.cheaptickets.com
This Hawaii-based discount agency prides itself on hunting down the lowest possible fare for any flight in the world. Its online engine certainly manages to dig out some pretty obscure airlines, and in general the prices compare well with their rivals. The only real drawback is the cumbersome log-in procedure before you can get to work.

Council Travel

www.counciltravel.com
Air fares here are available only to "student", "youth" (under 26), or "teacher". Assuming you fall within that remit, are planning a journey that originates within the United States, and are happy to use a "Flexisearch" that will suggest options a day or two each side of your preferred date, then there's a good chance you'll find an acceptable deal.

ebookers

www.ebookers.com
The online arm of the Flightbookers travel agency quotes competitive fares to and between destinations worldwide, but that's without checking avail-

ability; in order to go any further, let alone book, you have to register. Long-haul trips tend to be the best value; for European jaunts, they tend not to find lesser-known and cheaper airlines.

Expedia

www.expedia.com (North America) and **www.expedia.co.uk (UK)**
The Microsoft-owned Expedia sites provide users with the prettiest interface of all the online air ticket merchants, and they're sufficiently wide-ranging that they're always worth trying as you scout around for a deal. On the whole, however, it has to be said that it's unusual to find a fare on Expedia that you can't better elsewhere. Be warned also that it tends to suggest truly bizarre routings; scan down the list of recommendations and you may well find a much more convenient schedule for a mere $5 extra.

Flynow.com

www.flynow.com
Flynow.com, formerly known as The Travel Bug, suggests equally appealing fares for both short- and long-haul flights from Britain, and can also sell tickets for journeys anywhere else in the world. It's also unfailingly polite, wishing you "good morning" or "good afternoon" depending on when you log on.

Global Traveller

www.telme.co.uk
This user-friendly Website, run by Seaforths Travel of Aberdeen, enables you to seek out good-value fares to Europe and further afield, with easy pull-down menus, instant availability checks, and no registration required in order to book online.

Hotwire

www.hotwire.com
If you're looking to book the cheapest possible scheduled flight, Hotwire is probably your best bet. However, "Hot-Fares" come with their own unique restrictions – most obviously, you only find out the exact times of your flights, and even which carrier you're using, once you've bought your ticket, with no possibility of alterations. In addition, all flights must originate within the United States. You can specify a maximum number of stopovers, or where applicable that you won't accept a red-eye or overnight flight, but otherwise you have to decide on the basis of price

alone and forgo frequent-flyer and other such benefits. With typical transatlantic fares coming in at around $200 below other e-travel sites, you may well feel it's worth it.

1click4flights.com

www.1stnetflights.com

UK travel agency site that offers an easily searchable database of well-priced scheduled flights, arranged by destination and bookable online. They cover both European and long-haul destinations, but all trips must originate within Britain and Ireland. There's a strong selection of services from London City Airport. Separate sections sell a large array of charter flights, to Canada all year round, and to major European destinations in summer only.

Orbitz

www.orbitz.com

Jointly owned by five airlines – American, Continental, Delta, Northwest, and United – and subscribed to by several dozen more, the Orbitz Website has been controversial since it was on the drawing board. Participating airlines either have to guarantee that they're offering Orbitz their lowest Internet fares, or spend a substantial sum on marketing the site; online competitors charge that Orbitz may come to dominate the market and thus, eventually, be able to drive prices up. For the moment, Orbitz remains one among many, and the fares thrown up by its slightly slow-witted search engine – "The Orbot" – are not conspicuously better than what you'd find elsewhere. Look out, however, for the special Web fares labelled "this weekend" and "next weekend".

Priceline

www.priceline.com (North America) and www.priceline.co.uk (UK)

In the few short years since William Shatner announced its arrival in the US in 1998, Priceline has come a long way. The premise remains the same as ever; you tell them how much you're prepared to pay for a particular flight (or hotel room, or rental car), and they'll get back to you if an airline accepts your offer. Much like Hotwire, the catch is that you're buying "opaque inventory"; you're not told which carrier you're using, or the exact times of your flight, until after you've made the purchase. Although Priceline suggest that you may save "up to forty percent", prices seem to have settled down since the early days to a fairly standard twenty-five percent discount off the cheapest fare you'll find on conventional sites. The obvious strategy is to see what's available elsewhere (especially on Hotwire, if you're in North America), and then offer less.

Qixo

www.qixo.com

The "Quest for Impossibly eXcellent Offers" provides a simple twist on the standard air-travel Website. Its interface is much like the rest, and its searches take as long, but behind the scenes it is in fact comparison shopping. It trawls through twenty other ticket-purchase sites, including both airlines and agencies, so you don't have to; it displays interim results as it searches, so you get an exciting couple of minutes of screen-watching. Once you've found a fare that appeals, register to buy your ticket. They don't tell you which site offered the best bargain, and you pay a $10 premium, but if you're in a hurry it's not a bad deal. Although the flights can be anywhere in the world, you must have a US address to buy a ticket, and because only North American sites are searched you may not find the best deal on journeys commencing elsewhere.

TicketPlanet

www.ticketplanet.com

This California-based site claims to have been the first to sell consolidator fares over the Internet. For international flights – especially circle-Pacific and round-the-world itineraries – they're up there with the best, offering competitive fares and also the facility to book accommodation and car rental.

Travelocity

www.travelocity.com (North America) and www. travelocity.co.uk (UK)

Travelocity rank among the very biggest names in online travel, with a straightforward search engine for flight deals that set the standard for the rest of the pack. The fares thrown up by the Sabre system continue to match what's available on more overtly budget-oriented sites – not surprisingly, as many also use Sabre – and they also provide a huge range of other travel services, such as accommodation deals and all-inclusive packages.

European net airlines

Four budget airlines now compete via their Websites to sell cut-price scheduled flights from Britain to popular European holiday spots. Not only have they effectively created a new market in spur-of-the-moment and weekend breaks, carrying passengers as likely to have been tempted by the price as by the destination, but unlike their conventional rivals they have also continued to prosper since September 11, 2001. When the Internet boom started, **Ryanair** was already in business, offering bargain-basement shuttles between Ireland and England; **easyJet** and **Buzz** were subsequently set up by entrepreneurs keen to exploit the new potential of the Web; and **Go** was spawned as British Airways' hasty response to their brash new rivals.

Buying a flight with any of these airlines is a broadly similar experience. All offer straightforward sites, bedecked with eye-catching offers and detailing their routes and schedules. Only when you enquire about flying on a specific date are you quoted exact fares, with each leg of a return trip priced separately. What's more, that fare only applies if you book immediately; call up the self-same journey tomorrow, and it may cost double. The airlines make their money by charging exactly what the market will bear at any moment. As each plane fills up, the prices rise, while if too many seats remain unsold, they fall. Incidentally, you don't literally buy a "ticket"; when your booking goes through, you're given a confirmation number which you use at check-in to claim your seat.

So how do you find a bargain? As a rough rule of thumb, Ryanair is the cheapest, followed in ascending order by easyJet, Buzz and Go. Whatever the popular myth, you're more likely to get a better deal by booking **early** rather than late. An August flight which you could have bought for £50 in March may well be £150 if you leave it to the summer. In addition, you should keep on trying different permutations of days and times – even the slightest change can make a vast difference – and remember that travelling mid-week rather than at weekends normally pays dividends. Be sure also to check whether taxes and extra charges are included.

Buzz

www.buzzaway.com

Buzz fly from London's Stansted airport to around twenty European cities, especially in France and Germany. Most routes are served more than once per day, with flights at reasonable hours. The easy-to-use Website opens with an eye-catching list of one-way fares; searching for particular dates brings you all flights for a day either side as well, so you can choose the cheapest or most convenient option. With no hidden extras, it's usually possible to find and book a mid-week return for under £100. If desired, you can also reserve accommodation and a rental car.

easyJet

www.easyjet.com

Calling itself "the Web's favourite airline", easyJet uses an interactive on-screen map to illustrate its network of no-frills flights to eight European and five British cities from London Luton airport; four European cities from London Gatwick; seven European destinations, plus Belfast, from Liverpool; to Belfast from Edinburgh and Glasgow; and to Amsterdam from Belfast, Edinburgh and Glasgow. Amsterdam and Geneva also serve as hubs for additional flights within Europe. To keep costs down, there are no on-board meals, just the opportunity to buy snacks from the in-flight "easyKiosk". On the Website, pull-down menus make it simple to check timetables – you'll notice many flights are scheduled for antisocial hours – and then enquire about specific flights. Note that taxes and airport fees are not included, and tend to add £5–10 to a typical return price.

Go

www.go-fly.com

Go, British Airways' budget European airline, flies to destinations across the continent from both London Stansted (which has services to 15 European and 4 British cities) and Bristol (6 European, 3 British), and also offers domestic flights within Britain from Belfast, Edinburgh and Glasgow. Most services are at convenient times, and often several times per day, making them suitable for business travellers as well as holidaymakers. The rates are well below ordinary BA fares without being phenomenally cheap – think £100 each way rather than £50 – but offer a little more flexibility than online competitors, and are quoted inclusive of all extras.

Ryanair

www.ryanair.com

By far the cheapest of the online airlines, Ryanair offers astonishing special deals to a wide range of European destinations. It's nonetheless said to be the world's most profitable airline, in part because costs are kept down

both on the ground and in the air, where half the usual number of cabin staff are employed, and no hot food is served. There have also been reports of passengers, stranded by cancellations, being refused accommodation or help. Ryanair's core business remains between Ireland and Britain, with connections between a total of five airports in Ireland and twelve in the UK, and up to thirteen flights daily between Dublin and London Stansted alone. They also fly from Stansted to 33 European cities, predominantly in France and Italy. Quoted fares can drop as low as £2 for a return flight to Brittany, or just £25 to Venice; by the time you've factored in taxes and extras (there's even a £4 credit-card fee) a £40 return fare can work out at around £60, but it's still not something to be sniffed at.

Airlines

Web addresses for a hundred of the world's major airlines are listed below. If the specific airline you're looking for is not listed, then two general directory sites may be able to help you find it: **www.flyaow.com** and **www.air.findhere.com**. Wherever possible, the page referred to here is in English, but many have links to sites more specifically tailored to passengers from your home country.

Adria Airways (Slovenia)
www.adria.si
Aer Lingus www.aerlingus.com
Aeroflot (Russia)
www.aeroflot.com
Aerolineas Argentinas
www.aerolineas.com.ar
Aeromexico
www.aeromexico.com
Air Canada www.aircanada.ca
Air China www.air-china.co.uk
Air France www.airfrance.com
Air India www.airindia.com
Air Jamaica
www.airjamaica.com
Air Malta www.airmalta.com
Air Mauritius
www.airmauritius.com
Air New Zealand
www.airnewzealand.com
Air Pacific (Fiji)
www.airpacific.com
Air Zimbabwe
www.airzimbabwe.com
Alaska Airlines
www.alaska-air.com
Alitalia www.alitalia.com

All Nippon Airways
http://svc.ana.co.jp/eng
Aloha Airlines
www.alohaairlines.com
America West Airlines
www.americawest.com
American Airlines www.aa.com
American Trans Air www.ata.com
Ansett Australia www.ansett.com
Asiana Airlines (Korea)
www.flyasiana.com
Austrian Airlines www.aua.com
Aviateca Guatemala
www.grupotaca.com
Biman Bangladesh Airlines
www.bangladeshonline.com
/biman
Britannia Airways
www.britanniaairways.com
British Airways
www.britishairways.com
British European
www.flybe.com
British Midland www.flybmi.com
British Regional Airlines
www.british-regional.com

continued overleaf

Buzz (see p.43)
www.buzzaway.com
Cathay Pacific
www.cathaypacific.com
China Airlines
www.china-airlines.com
China Eastern Airlines
www.cea.online.sh.cn
Continental www.continental.com
Croatian Airlines
www.croatiaairlines.com
CSA Czech Airlines
www.czechairlines.com
Cubana www.cubana.cu/ingles
Cyprus Airways
www.cyprusair.com
Delta www.delta.com
Eastern Airways (UK)
www.easternairways.com
easyJet (see p.43)
www.easyjet.com
Egypt Air www.egyptair.com.eg
El Al www.elal.com
Emirates www.emirates.com
Estonian Airlines
www.estonian-air.ee
Eva Air (Taiwan)
www.evaair.com
Finnair www.finnair.com
Frontier Airlines (US)
www.flyfrontier.com
Garuda Indonesia
www.garuda-indonesia.com
Go (see p.43) www.go-fly.com

Gulf Air www.gulfairco.com
Hawaiian Airlines
www.hawaiianair.com
Iberia www.iberia.com
Icelandair www.icelandair.com
Indian Airlines
http://indian-airlines.nic.in
Japan Air Lines www.japanair.com
Jet Airways (India)
www.jetairways.com
jetBlue (US) www.jetblue.com
Kenya Airways
www.kenya-airways.com
KLM www.klm.com
Korean Air www.koreanair.com
Kuwait Airways
www.kuwait-airways.com
LanChile (Chile)
www.lanchile.com
Lauda Air (Austria)
www.laudaair.com
LOT Polish Airlines www.lot.com
Lufthansa www.lufthansa.com
Malaysia Air
www.malaysiaair.com
Malev Hungarian Airlines
www.malev.hu/ew/angol
Martinair (Holland)
www.martinair.com
Mexicana de Aviacion
www.mexicana.com.mx/mx2
/english
Monarch Crown Service (UK)
www.fly-crown.com

National Airlines
www.nationalairlines.com
Northwest Airlines
www.nwa.com
Olympic Airways (Greece)
www.olympic-airways.gr
Pakistan International Airlines
www.piac.com.pk
Pan Am www.flypanam.com
Philippine Airlines
www.philippineair.com
Polynesian Airlines
www.polynesianairlines.com
Qantas www.qantas.com
Royal Air Maroc (Morocco)
www.royalairmaroc.com
Royal Brunei Airlines
www.bruneiair.com
Royal Jordanian Airlines
www.rja.com.jo
Royal Nepal Airlines
www.royalnepal.com
Ryanair (see p.44)
www.ryanair.com
Sahara Airlines (India)
www.saharairline.com
SAS Scandinavian Airlines
www.scandinavian.net
Singapore Airlines
www.singaporeair.com
South African Airways
www.flysaa.com
Southwest Airlines
www.iflyswusa.com

SriLankan Airlines
www.srilankan.lk
Swissair www.swissair.com
Tam (Brazil) www.tam.com.br
TAP Air Portugal
www.tap-airportugal.pt
Tarom Romanian Airlines
http://tarom.digiro.net
Thai Airways International
www.thaiair.com
TransBrasil Airlines (Brazil)
www.transbrasilairlines.com
Tunisair (Tunisia)
www.tunisair.com.tn
Turkish Airlines
www.turkishairlines.com
TWA www.twa.com
Ukraine International Airlines
www.ukraine-international.com
United Airlines www.ual.com
US Airways www.usairways.com
Varig Brasil (Brazil)
www.varig.com
Vasp Brazilian Airlines
www.vasp.com.br
Vietnam Airlines
www.vietnamairlines.com
Virgin Atlantic Airways
www.virgin-atlantic.com
Virgin Express
www.virgin-express.com
West Indies Airways
www.bwee.com

Car rental

Renting a car is an activity ideally suited to the Internet. Most renters know exactly what they want, and so long as they get the cheapest rate they don't care who supplies it. The range of prices you're offered on the Web is quite extraordinary, so there are huge savings to be made. Searching for a week's rental from London's Heathrow airport, for example, the highest rate quoted (by Avis) was eight times the lowest (by Travelnow).

All the **major international rental chains** run similar Websites, offering online availability checks and booking. Unless you have a very strong reason to choose a particular one, however – such as a corporate discount or frequent-flyer deal – there's no point in using the chain's own sites. Most are frustratingly slow, with ponderous and pedantic interfaces that require you to state the exact minute you'll pick up the vehicle, or to tick "check all rates" as well as "check rates" before they'll give you a quote. With the exception of Alamo's impressive route-finding facility (see p.15), none provides any useful extra content, and the rates they offer never seem to be better than those you'll find, even for the same company, on more **general comparison sites**. Surprisingly few allow customers travelling in Europe to request a vehicle with automatic rather than manual transmission – something it's much easier to ensure on a general site. Note also that some offer different rates for exactly the same vehicle to customers from different parts of the world; Avis and Dollar are the worst offenders for charging British citizens more than Americans.

The major chains

Unless otherwise specified, British and North American customers enter these sites via the same Web address.

Alamo www.alamo.com
Avis www.avis.com (North America) • www.avis.co.uk (UK)
Budget www.drivebudget.com
Dollar www.dollar.com (North America) • www.dollar.co.uk (UK)
Hertz www.hertz.com
National www.nationalcar.com
Thrifty www.thrifty.com

BreezeNet

www.bnm.com

BreezeNet's online "Guide to Airport Rental Cars" is a useful tool if you want to see which car rental companies are represented at any major airport, together with a rundown of the best rates available when you're planning to visit. A link to the relevant company then enables you to secure that rate. In fact, it only really works for the larger airports in the US – where all the major companies are always represented anyway – and for North American customers only. For international destinations, it can't provide instant quotes, and it's easier in any case to use an all-in-one site on which you can complete your booking.

Cruise America

www.cruiseamerica.com
The largest North American rental company specializing in RVs
(Recreational Vehicles), those thirty-foot behemoths designed for family
touring vacations and crammed with bedrooms, bathrooms, kitchens and
even garages. Simple menus facilitate bookings for round-trip and one-way
rentals from locations throughout the US and Canada. Rates are not
cheap, however, and there's a surcharge if you drive more than seventy
miles per day. The Website also lists international agents who handle reservations for foreign visitors. In addition, Cruise America rent motorcycles,
though only Hondas, with no online booking facility.

easyRentacar

www.easycar.com
Proclaiming itself "the world's first Internet-only car rental company",
easyRentacar was created as an offshoot of budget airline easyJet, and
provides inexpensive car rental at most – but not yet all – of the European
destinations that airline serves. That currently amounts to eight European
cities and five British ones, though its three London locations do not
include the major airports. Prices are significantly lower than the standard
rates offered by its larger competitors, but not necessarily the very lowest
to be found, and there are drawbacks: you can't request a specific type of
car or transmission, and the quoted rates only cover 75 miles per day,
which for most holidaymakers is nothing like enough. In addition, Mac
users will find it impossible to key in the necessary details online.

Expedia

www.expedia.com (North America) and www.expedia.co.uk (UK)
Wherever you access it from, Expedia returns the same rate for any specific rental, and it'll be a very good rate too, in whichever part of the world
you're looking to rent a car. It won't always be the cheapest you could
possibly find, but if you let Expedia set a benchmark you'll know you're
doing well if you manage to beat it.

Holiday Autos

www.holidayautos.co.uk (UK) and www.kemwel.com (North America)
British-based Holiday Autos call themselves "the largest vacation car rental
broker in the world", and maintain probably the simplest rental Website
around. Operating from the common-sense premise – oddly rare elsewhere

– that you want to rent a car, its straightforward pull-down menus set out exactly which locations they serve and how much a car will cost. Their great strength is the sheer quantity of obscure European destinations, which tie in nicely with many cut-price flights. Unfortunately, however, an equally great weakness is the appallingly high cost, which, where comparison is possible, is regularly double what you'll find on Expedia. Only the British site offers rentals in the US, and again, they are seriously overpriced. For otherwise unavailable destinations, Holiday Autos may well be your only option; for major cities, however, you'd do much better to shop elsewhere.

Sidestep

www.sidestep.com

The much-vaunted Sidestep system, which only works with Windows, amounts to no more than the sum of its parts. Sidestep is a program which you have to download and install before you can use it; it then pops up as a sidebar on your screen and invites you to search for airlines and hotels (both of which come out too expensive, which is why Sidestep is not reviewed in those sections of this book) or rental cars, in North America only. Searching through all the big-name rental operators' sites, it comes up with the same list of prices you'd get if you trawled through them individually. So it saves time, and it finds you the best conventional deal; it just won't find any bargains.

Street Eagle

www.streeteagle.com

Take a vacation in Hog Heaven, thanks to Street Eagle, who offer an all but irresistible alternative to car rental – the chance to rent a Harley Davidson motorcyle instead. Hardly the world's most content-rich Website, it does detail fifteen US locations, from Tampa to Las Vegas, along with typical rates that start at around $140

per day including insurance. Reservations are made via email rather than online, but it's all worth it for the moment you can use the pull-down menus to order seven Electra Glides.

Travelnow

www.travelnow.com
Although the rental-car section of this North American site seems at first glance to cover only a handful of US cities, those are simply its most popular destinations; assorted pull-down menus enable you to find almost any domestic or international location. What's more, Travelnow checks rates and availability across a wider range of companies than other comparison sites, to find some truly excellent deals.

Travelocity

www.travelocity.com (North America) and www. travelocity.co.uk (UK)
As with airline tickets (see p.41), the Travelocity search engine can be relied on to work quickly and efficiently in finding great-value car rental offers, both in North America and Europe.

Woods

www.woods.co.uk
A British rental agency, run in association with Budget, Woods offers a reasonable though not outstanding flat rate for rentals in the UK only, serving London (offering all the airports plus delivery to any central address) plus 37 other UK cities. The site itself is easy to use and aimed largely at American travellers, who are most likely to appreciate the tips on driving in Britain, and the fact that there's no drop-off fee if you return the car to a different point than where you picked it up.

Trains

Accent on Travel

www.accentontravelusa.com
No-nonsense site from a highly rated Oregon-based US travel agency. Train enthusiasts Ted and Sylvia Blishak can custom design rail trips and tours throughout North America, on Amtrak and VIA, for most budgets, arranging accommodation along the way and suggesting itineraries. They also handle overseas rail tours on trains such as the Orient Express, The Royal Scot and The Al Andalus Express. No online ordering – email them to request a booking – but the site is useful for rail travel tips, links and detailed rail travel reports from the Blishaks.

Die Bahn

www.bahn.de
Using a mind-blowing database of rail stations – 150,000 in Germany alone

Note that Websites devoted to rail travel in any one country can be found in the relevant section within our Destinations chapter. These include:

Alaska Railroad www.akrr.com	see p.419
Amtrak (US) www.amtrak.com	see p.419
Business Tourism (India) http://businesstourism.com/train.html	see p.299
Indian Railways www.indianrail.gov.in	see p.303
John Steel Rail Tours (Canada) www.johnsteel.com	see p.249
Public Transport Information (UK) www.pti.org.uk	see p.395
Train Hoppers Space (US) http://catalog.com/hop	see p.421
The Trainline (UK) www.thetrainline.com	see p.395
UK Railways on the Net www.rail.co.uk	see p.395
Via Rail Canada www.viarail.ca	see p.251

– German rail network Die Bahn provides online schedules for rail (and many road and sea) connections all over Europe. Click on "International Guests" for an English-language version.

Europrail International

www.europrail.net

Well-designed and user-friendly US site selling the major European rail passes, with schedules for services to all the cities in Europe, and an easy facility for checking ticket prices between any two points. You can order passes online and download printable maps of European rail routes.

Euro Railways

www.eurorailways.com

Marvellous site bringing together information on rail travel throughout Europe. Though the English translation can be rusty, it's an astonishing venture, enabling you to plan your route and buy thousands of tickets and single and multi-country passes, including youth passes, online. There are pull-down menus everywhere you turn, and, if you're really lost, a "personal travel assistant"; simply type in the countries you want to visit and the type of accommodation you require, and they'll email you a suggested itinerary. Also online booking for hotels thoughout Europe, with a handy currency converter.

Eurostar

www.eurostar.com

Slick, visual and vibrant, Eurostar's site offers timetables and fare charts for their high-speed rides between London, Paris and Brussels, with online booking up to ninety days in advance. They also provide all the gen on trips to Disneyland Paris and the French Alps, details of special Eurostar packages, and a "Euroguide" to shopping, eating and drinking in the cities they serve. Register to receive latest offers and save time booking.

Eurotunnel

www.eurotunnel.co.uk

Eurotunnel's official Website isn't exactly a barrel of laughs, but it does its job with timetables for their Folkestone–Calais service, a fares calendar for up to a year ahead, and options for online booking. The site also provides details on local events and sights (market days and gardens in Normandy etc), with links for online route planning and travel insurance.

Great Rail Journeys

www.greatrail.co.uk

UK operator Great Rail Journeys organizes luxury escorted group holidays
throughout Europe, North America and South Africa. Choose from a pull-
down menu of train operators or click on thumbnail photos of destinations
to read details of a good range of journeys, from a tour of northern Spain to
a nineteen-day coast-to-coast USA trip. You can check availability on the
site and make provisional reservations, but to book you need to fill in a hard
copy form (downloadable in PDF format).

Leisurail

www.leisurail.co.uk

A division of Thomas Cook, this UK operator specializes in independent
train travel throughout the US, Canada, Australia, the Far East and South
Africa. Though they give some idea of their services here, you'll need to
order a brochure for full timetables and details of their many options, from
independent itineraries using rail passes to luxury tours including overseas
flights, sightseeing jaunts and swish hotel accommodation.

The Man in Seat 61

www.seat61.com

Railway fansite *par excellence*, put together by British obsessive (and former British Rail station manager) Mark Smith, and named after his favourite seat on Eurostar. The main focus is on catching trains from London to anywhere and everywhere, within the UK as well as beyond, with fares, timetables, and detailed practical recommendations. On top of that Smith's remit also extends to advice on rail (and, to a lesser extent, sea) travel the world over, making his site an invaluable resource at the planning stage of almost any expedition. Though it's all entirely noncommercial, so you can't buy or book anything here, all the necessary contact numbers and Web links are provided.

Orient Express Trains

www.orient-expresstrains.com

Basic, surprisingly static site for such a silver-service venture, with details of the various Orient Express tours through the UK, Europe, Australia, and Southeast Asia. Prices aren't as outrageous as you might expect – a nine-day/eight-night Singapore to Bangkok journey costs £1695 per person, flight included, and there are some Internet-only offers. Online booking is secure.

RailEurope

www.raileurope.co.uk

A very useful site selling point-to-point tickets and all the major passes – Eurail, Europass, Interrail, Euro Domino, etc – for rail travel throughout Europe. The site can take a while to load with its busy bunch of graphics, and its garish design makes it look more complicated than it is; once you've got the hang of it, schedule checking and secure online ordering (£5 off Interrail passes booked online) couldn't be easier.

Rail Serve

www.railserve.com

This speedy, comprehensive, and easy to use directory of rail sites is a vast labour of love managed by teenage train enthusiast Christopher Muller. Scroll down the scores of departments – antiques and collectables, clothes, books, societies, model railway clubs, and sound effects, among others – to the section on passenger and urban transit (subdivided into

Africa, Asia, Australasia, Europe, North and South America), where you can click onto literally hundreds of links. Europe brings up more than 250 sites, from the tram network of Charleroi to trainspotting sites in Wales; almost as many links come up for North America, including local train network sites from Alaska to Wisconsin.

Trains.com

www.trains.com
Nicely designed US portal encompassing everything related to railways, real and pretend. Among the model trains, train shops, and hobby magazines, there is a good little travel section, with Amtrak schedules, travel features, and a few regularly updated links to train holiday operators.

TrainWeb.org

www.trainweb.org
Searchable US portal for a vast range of railroad sites including model railroading, forums, photos and rail cams. The travel section includes links to Amtrak and VIA services along with travelogues, travel agencies, tourist railways, dinner trains and the like.

Travel Notes

www.travelnotes.org/General/eurotrains.htm
An astounding interactive database that allows you to search all the major European train timetables. Enter your departure and destination points and your ideal dates and departure times; quick as a flash you get durations, connections and prices (in the currency of your destination; you'll need a currency converter) of your intended journey, with a detailed itinerary and relevant maps.

USA by Rail

www.usa-by-rail.com
Comprehensive guide to train travel throughout not only the USA but also Canada, with details of the national networks, steam railroads and railway museums, and a USA rail guide. There are good links to North American railway travel sites, with reviews of all the major Amtrak routes, including The California Zephyr, one of the world's great trains. See p.419 for more on train travel in the USA; p.248 for the same in Canada.

Ferries

All Greek Ferries

www.ferries.gr

If you need to find and/or book a ferry trip to or within Greece, don't trawl through the many individual ferry companies that operate in Greek waters; head instead for this site, run by a travel agency on Crete. It holds up-to-date timetables for international connections with Italy, Cyprus, Israel, and Turkey as well as the myriad inter-island routes, and provides instant online booking.

Brittany Ferries

www.brittanyferries.co.uk

Brittany Ferries, who operate cross-Channel services from Portsmouth, Poole and Plymouth in southern England to Brittany and Normandy in France, and also to northern Spain, run an excellent Website on which you

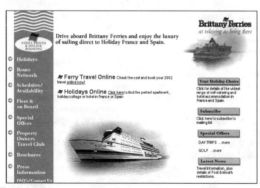

Note that Websites devoted to ferry crossings in any one country can be found in the relevant section within our Destinations chapter. These include:

British Columbia Ferry Corporation www.bcferries.com	see p.249
Caledonian MacBrayne (Scotland) www.calmac.co.uk	see p.405
Public Transport Information (UK) www.pti.org.uk	see p.395
TT-Line (Australia) www.tt-line.com.au	see p.237

can easily check schedules and make on-line reservations, choose from a huge number of all-inclusive packages and accommodation deals, or simply order their printed brochures.

DFDS Seaways

www.scansea.com
Information and online reservations for ferry routes across the North Sea from England to Scandinavia and beyond. Sailings operate between Newcastle and Norway or Holland, and between Harwich and Denmark or Germany. The site itself is surprisingly easy to use, though you may have to guess a little Danish along the way.

Ferry Savers

www.ferrysavers.com
Several British Websites claim to offer discount deals on all ferry crossings, but Ferry Savers comes the closest to delivering that promise, covering sailings to Ireland, Spain, Belgium, Holland, the Channel Islands and Scandinavia, as well as the standard routes to France, and including the tunnel for good measure. Search by time and date, and you'll be given a range of alternative fares, including any special offers that may apply, with a price guarantee that you won't find the same itinerary cheaper elsewhere. Strictly speaking, your booking is not quite interactive; you have to await email confirmation.

Hoverspeed

www.hoverspeed.co.uk
Hoverspeed's Website provides schedules, prices and online booking for their trips between England, France and Belgium (none of which is by hovercraft, despite the name). Making a booking is a very slow and cumber-

some business, however; unlike most other ferry sites, you have to know precise departure times rather than simply choose a date, and the two percent discount for reservations is pretty paltry. What's more, they can't accept online bookings for pets, but at least they also sell good-value short breaks to nearby Continental cities such as Antwerp, Honfleur, and Rouen.

Irish Ferries

www.irishferries.ie

Timetables, prices and easy on-line reservations, with instant confirmation of availability, for sailings between Ireland and both Britain and France. You can also take a 360° virtual tour of *Ulysses*, the world's largest car ferry, which plies the Holyhead–Dublin route.

Loglink

www.loglink.net/ferries.htm

You may not be interested in the multitude of academic treatises and technical specifications that are accessible from the Loglink ferry site, but it's invaluable in providing links that make it possible to plan trips with almost any ferry company in Europe or North America.

P&O European Ferries

www.poferries.co.uk

The main home page for P&O European Ferries carries links to the four separate subsidiary sites that handle sailings from Portsmouth to Le Havre and Cherbourg in northern France, and Bilbao in Spain (**www.poportsmouth.com**); across the Irish Sea between Larne and Cairnryan (**www.poirishsea.com**); to Orkney & Shetland from the Scottish mainland (**www.poscottishferries.co.uk**); and over the North Sea to Zeebrugge and Rotterdam (**www.ponsf.com**). In each case, the step-by-step online booking service is easy to use, though it doesn't go out of its way to guide you towards any special offers or bargain rates that might be available if you adjust your travel dates.

P&O Ferries and Stena Line

www.posl.com

P&O Ferries and Stena Line have joined forces to offer services on the busiest and most famous ferry route across the English Channel, between Dover and Calais. This stand-alone Website offers straightforward timetable and fare information, and a £5 discount for bookings completed online.

Sea Containers

www.steam-packet.com

Schedules, fares and reservations for Irish Sea Ferries routes such as Belfast to Heysham and Troon in Scotland, and the Superseacat service between Liverpool and Dublin, as well as the Steam Packet line between the Isle of Man and northern England. The online booking procedure is reasonably efficient, though you do have to work through the timetables to find the exact sailing you want before you can make any enquiry. There's also a two percent discount for Net reservations.

SeaFrance

www.seafrance.com

French operator SeaFrance run this straightforward Website to promote their rival Dover–Calais ferries. Trimmed down to bare essentials, it offers a simple online booking procedure from its opening page, with a £5 discount on standard returns – and little else.

Stena Line

www.stenaline.co.uk

Though maddening to use, with its tiny print and endless pull-down menus, this Website does enable you, in the end, to make confirmed online reservations for Stena's ferry routes from England, Scotland and Wales, to both Ireland and Holland, and also for certain Scandinavian services as well.

Trasmediterranea Ferries

www.trasmediterranea.es/homei.htm
The English-language version of the Website of Trasmediterranea Ferries, who operate several Spanish ferry routes. English speakers can easily make online bookings for all their services, from Barcelona and Valencia to the Balearic islands, from Algeciras or Malaga in the south across to the North African coast, and from Cadiz out to the Canaries.

Youra.com

www.youra.com/ferry
Dan Youra, an American ferry obsessive, has equipped his "Ferry Guide" with links to ferries and ferry systems all over the world, including China, Japan and Vietnam as well as most of Europe. His listings are especially strong close to his home base of Washington state, with the various Puget Sound operators well represented, and he also covers a selection of cruise lines and shipping companies.

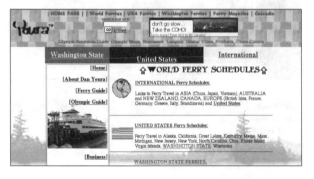

Buses

For overlanding bus trips, see p.145.

Budget Travel

www.budgettravel.com/eurobus.htm

The sprawling budget travellers' informaton site has a useful directory of European bus links. Though it needs tidying up, to say the least, scrolling down the page brings you to a variety of links to even the most obscure sites, many of them with short reviews. Whether you want to check the local schedules in Belarus or plan a coach tour around Wales, you'll find a site to help you here.

Busabout

www.busabout.com

A great idea for independent travellers – hop-on-hop-off coach trips to seventy destinations in fourteen European countries, with optional door-to-door service to a range of Busabout-recommended hostels, campsites and hotels. There are 10 passes: 6 of which give unlimited consecutive travel over fixed periods, and 4 "flexipasses", which allow you to choose how

Note that Websites devoted to bus travel in any one country can be found in the relevant section within our Destinations chapter. These include:

Green Tortoise Adventure Travel www.greentortoise.com   see p.420
Greyhound www.greyhound.com   see p.420
Greyhound Canada www.greyhound.ca   see p.249
National Express (UK) www.gobycoach.com   see p.394
Public Transport Information (UK) www.pti.org.uk   see p.395

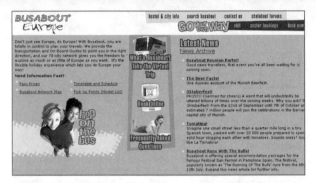

many days you travel. You're looking at spending anything from £169 for a two-week consecutive pass to £659 for a flexipass getting you thirty days travel across five months. You can also buy add-on ferry tickets to the Greek islands, Morocco and Croatia. The site has secure online booking, and as soon as you've bought your pass you can, if you wish, book all legs of your journey online. If you want to reserve Busabout accommodation, check the site's city and hostel guides, then browse the message boards for reviews and feedback.

Eurolines

www.eurolines.com

Eurolines is the umbrella organization for more than 30 companies running scheduled buses between 500 cities throughout Europe. As well as individual fares, they offer the money-saving Europass, which gives unlimited travel between 46 cities for up to 15, 30 or 60 days (from £90 for a low-season youth pass lasting 15 days, to £259 for an adult 60-day pass in high season). The site (go for the non-Flash version, unless you've got time to kill) has a table of fares and timetables for all the major destinations, and you can buy passes online (as long as you've got at least three weeks before you set off).

Wallace Arnold Holidays

www.wallacearnold.co.uk

The UK coach holiday specialists, best-known for their tours of the UK and

Europe, actually offer a huge range of holidays (more than 500 of them) including trips to North America and New Zealand – even a three-week tour of China, including a Yangtze River cruise. These are a good bet for anyone who wants an easy life: with more than 1600 pick-up points in the UK, it shouldn't be a hassle to get to one, and once you have, all your bags are carried for you right up to your hotel room. Hotels are upmarket and most of them offer full-board plans. You can browse the range by using the simple "Holiday Finder", but it can take a while to trawl through the choices, and even then the site features just a selection; for more, you'll need to order hard copy brochures. There's no online booking, but you can check availability.

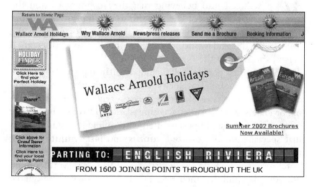

Accommodation

When it comes to booking a room, many people are seduced into believing that they're going to find the cheapest rates online. As with so much received wisdom about the Internet, this is often not the case. However, on the Web, as in the real world, research is the key to getting good prices, and for that the Net is invaluable.

The obvious first ports of call include **multipurpose mega sites** such as Expedia and Travelocity; these are efficient and fast, and offer competitive rates, although they do tend to concentrate on major chains and upmarket accommodation. **Directories** usually offer a wider range of options, often with online reservations. Sites that specialize in **discounted rooms** and **last-minute offers**, including **travel auction sites** (which work in the same way for hotel rooms as they do for flights or packages), are worth a look, but you may find that their rates are no better than those offered by the bigger sites. More importantly, they may even be higher than those you'd be quoted if you called the hotel direct.

The Web is also flooded with sites specializing in **B&Bs**, along with **villa and condo rental sites**. The vast majority are based in North America, and the condo sites in particular tend to be aimed at senior travellers who will enjoy the nearby golf courses and facilities in the sunshine resorts featured. However, booking villas online is also increasingly popular in the UK, especially for properties in southern Europe. **Home exchange sites** – where property owners swap homes or take turns staying with each other – are undeniably good if you're on a budget and really want to live like a local. However, there's so much fussing to be done before you can get going – reference checking, arranging dates, letting each other know how the hot water works and so on – that some people find the savings are simply not worth the effort.

Researching and booking a hotel online

First and foremost, be sure the site has full contact details for the property, along with a rundown of all facilities. It's always best to see **photos** (while exercizing the same caution as if you were looking at a hard copy brochure – they'll obviously portray the property in the best possible light) and it's useful to have a **map**. When booking, check if the **rate** quoted is for single or double occupancy – some places charge supplements for solo travellers in double rooms, while others will charge more for two people – and note any potential extras. If you're after a discount rate, always check the site's cancellation policy. Many companies allow no changes whatsoever to discounted rooms booked online. Then, and this is crucial, once you've done your research, log off and **call the hotel direct** to see if they can better the price. You may well be offered a lower rate than those quoted on the Net.

If you do find the best rates online, or simply decide to book on the Net for convenience, bear in mind the differences between dealing with the property direct and going through a booking site. Though it's usually more time-consuming to deal with an **individual hotel** – and you'll need to do more research than if you were simply booking a flight or even a package holiday – it does have its good points. Emailing hotels direct allows you to ask questions, make requests, and perhaps even do some bargaining – and at least you know your reservation is secure. Using **booking services or consolidators**, though fast and simple, can be nerve-wracking. Always call the hotel direct to check the reservation has been made. And however you choose

Don't forget the various **newsgroups** (see p.18) and forums on the Net – as well as the popular newsgroup **rec.travel.bed+breakfast**, many region- and country-specific groups feature discussions on accommodation, while many of the sites listed below have their own forums.

to book, always make sure to get an email **confirmation**, detailing the full cost charged to your card.

Though we've reviewed the best general sites below, many of the biggest sites concentrate heavily on properties in the US. For **country-specific accommodation** – chains, individual properties, hotel groups – turn to the destinations section of this book (where we've devoted an entire section to **UK accommodation**, by the way). Often the official **tourist board sites** (most of which we've reviewed, if they're any good at all) have sections devoted to accommodation, concentrating on the types of places special to that particular country or region.

For family **camping vacations** and family-friendly hotel chains, see p.166. And for details of holiday letting agencies that specialize in **gay-friendly properties**, see p.172.

Portals and information

About.com

http://hotels.about.com

The about.com concept – which combines links and original content on a huge variety of subjects, each masterminded by one human "guide" – works well when it comes to hotels. The emphasis veers towards the US, but there is plenty of stuff from around the world with links to online hotel directories and discount sites, plus sections on "fabulous finds", unique hotels, and the like. If you can't decide between a chateau or a ski chalet, a cottage or a cabin, a family hotel or a nudist camp, this is a good place to settle down to some research.

Cheapnights.com

www.cheapnights.co.uk

Well-composed information site. Key in the first letter of the place you're visiting, from Abidjan to Zion National Park, to see a page of links to booking sites, home exchanges, B&Bs, local chains and so on for that destination, each with a brief site review. The "Hot Deals" section, which fast tracks you to the deals on offer from various UK-based accommodation sites, is really useful, as are the links to chain hotels (see p.73) and accommodation forums (organized by continent). A growing number of city destinations feature Rough Guide accommodation reviews, with an option to browse and book online.

Discount sites

Travellers from the UK should also check the "Hot Deals" page of **www.cheapnights.co.uk** (see above), which links to all the specials currently on offer from British accommodation sites.

Expedia

www.expedia.com (North America) and www.expedia.co.uk (UK)

With its database of more than 40,000 hotels and vacation rentals (which includes B&Bs as well as apartments and villas) in all the top US destinations and major European cities, Expedia leads the way in online accommodation booking. They promise that any hotel flagged with the logo "Special Rate" guarantees you the lowest online price available; if you prove them wrong within 24 hours, they'll refund the difference. Searches – which you can refine with requests for disabled access, restaurants, pools, non-smoking rooms and so on – result in a dizzying choice; those with special rates are listed first, and can be booked immediately. Other possibilities, for which you need to check availability and prices, come lower down. (Note that when it comes to smaller destinations, while there's usually a good choice, prices are not always that low.) Though both sites work in the same way, **www.expedia.co.uk** benefits from a searchable database of rental accommodation. Click the link under "Travel Partners" and specify property size, location and theme – beach holidays, say, or camping – or simply browse their last-minute offers.

Hotel Reservations Network

www.hoteldiscounts.com

This searchable consolidator site offers discounts of up to 70 percent on more than 3000 hotels in major cities and resorts around the world, with the highest concentration in North America. Search results, laid out in an inconvenient horizontal line, give you the hotel's star rating, its general location and the lowest prices for your chosen nights (in US dollars, with a currency converter link); click for full address, facility list, reviews and photos. However, you're not told how much, if any, of a discount these prices represent. Once you know a place is available, it's worth calling direct to see if you can get a lower rate. Online booking is simple and secure, and US travellers can download a "coupon" to claim rebates of between $20 and $100 for multi-night stays.

Laterooms

www.laterooms.com

UK-produced database of discounted late availabilities on a wide range of accommodation, with sections for hotels (including guesthouses and B&Bs) and holiday rentals (gîtes, apartments, condos and villas). Most properties are in the UK, but the US, Italy, France, Germany, New Zealand, India and Spain are well represented too, and there are a few hotels each in a longer list of countries. Search by town or region and refine your choice by opting to see only big savers, budget beds, best deals, four/five-stars or hotels with disabled access. For hotels you can search from the same day to three weeks in advance of your stay and reservations are made direct with the property. Rental listings, on the other hand, can be viewed up to a year ahead and include online booking facilities.

Lodgingdiscounts.com

www.lodgingdiscounts.com

Good discounts and lots of choices, including B&Bs, on this US-based discount reservations site. Search results – for North American destinations, at least – are user friendly and up to date, quoting full address, available room types, nightly rates, booking conditions and total savings even before linking you to Websites for more details. The few European countries covered – along with Australia, the Caribbean, Central America and Indonesia – have less detail, though the discounts can be good. You can also search for printable discount coupons from individual hotels at your destination.

Priceline

www.priceline.com (North America) and www.priceline.co.uk (UK)
Major travel auction site, dealing in flights (see p.40), rental cars and hotels.

Tell them how much you're willing to pay for a room, where and when you want to go, select a star rating, plug in your credit card details and they'll get back to you within an hour. There are major catches: you *have* to buy if they come up with a match; you're not told which hotel you'll be staying in until after you've bought it (they deal mostly with chains); and all deals are non-negotiable and non-refundable. But if price is your priority and you're a gambler at heart, then it's a good option. The US site deals with cities in North America, Europe, the Caribbean and Mexico, and will only search for double rooms. Same day bookings (not usually available outside North America) are available up to 6pm on the day. Local hotel taxes are added to the price, along with a $6 booking fee. The UK site, which allows you to search in Europe and North America and to request single or double rooms, only takes bookings up to a day in advance, and charges £5.

Travelocity

www.travelocity.com (North America) and **www.travelocity.co.uk (UK)**
Both Travelocity sites work beautifully if you're looking to stay in North America, less so if you're heading off elsewhere. For the US and Canada the fast and efficient search engine has the edge over its competitors, and the "GoodBuy" rates (which require full prepayment, and carry a penalty for changes or cancellations) prove to be among the lowest you'll find – though it's still worth checking the deals offered on other sites to see if it's possible to shave off a few dollars. Note, too, that Travelocity's initial search results quote rates for the first night of your stay only – don't presume that this is the same each night, and if you're hoping to stay for a few days click again to see the nightly rates. To book hotels outside North America you'll need to visit **www.travelocity.co.uk**, where your only choice is to search for hotels near airports. Options then come up in a random and hard-to-decipher list, telling you how many miles they are from the airport.

Directories and booking sites

Accommodation Search Engine Network

www.ase.net
Currently the largest accommodation directory on the Net, with links to around 200,000 hotels, this admirable site, fuelled by a highly efficient search engine, comes up with matches in some pretty obscure locations. It also boasts some really handy extras. You can fast track from the home

page to hotels in major destinations such as London, New York and Paris, Disney World and Yellowstone National Park, or to find "activity lodgings" for adventure holidays. After selecting a destination and choosing a currency (click the "Languages" tab), you can set preferences, depending on how important it is to have a central location, or such like, to pull up a customized list of possibilities. Reviews, as well as featuring photos, maps and a rundown of amenities, provide links to as many Websites as the hotel may possess (often hosted by other accommodation sites, or local tourist boards) so you can compare rates and descriptions. Log in (you'll need a user name and password) to store your favourites and jot down notes. All this and swift, secure online booking – you couldn't ask for more.

All-hotels

www.all-hotels.com

Nicely organized, searchable directory of some 60,000 hotels worldwide. While there are listings for smaller places, you'll do best if you're looking to stay in a sizeable town or resort, especially if it's in the US. Hotels are conveniently arranged via district, in folders labelled luxury, standard, economy and specials, with their corresponding price bracket (often in local currency) – economy class folders generally yield a good selection. Within each folder

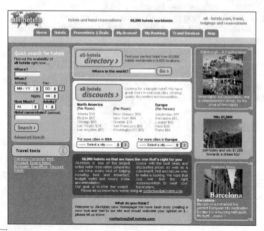

hotels come with overview, price range and links to Websites. Clicking the "Book" button lets you check availability and rates on your preferred nights; you can then choose a room and book online through the site's secure server. A separate section links you to various hotel discount sites, and you can sign up for an email newsletter alerting you to hot deals around the world. Plus a currency converter and links to Travelocity and Priceline for flights.

Hotelguide.com

www.hotelguide.com

Though the directory itself – with more than 65,000 properties in 200 countries, from golf resorts to guesthouses – isn't the best out there, neither is it the worst, and is certainly worth including for its informative email newsletter, Hotel Talk, which features articles, readers' questions and recommendations, along with news of special deals around the world. The site is efficient, if unexciting, allowing you to search by destination or in more detail by budget and facilities, business services and so on; results come as a no-frills list which you click for more details.

Leisurehunt

www.leisurehunt.com

Based in England, this speedy worldwide accommodation finder (with 100,000 lodgings on its books) is particularly good if you're looking to stay in Europe. Their booking service allows online reservations in some 31,000 hotels and B&Bs in the UK alone, and the search engine digs out places in even the smallest continental towns. Simply search for a city or region (refining by stating your budget, hotel type, and any special requirements), bang in the number of nights and dates you require, and you'll get a long list of matches in descending price order, detailing nightly rates. They also provide lists of hotels between 10km and 25km from your town of choice.

Chains

For **links** to hotel chains around the world, go to
www.cheapnights.com/general/hotel_chains.html.

Accor

www.accorhotel.com

With more than 38,000 hotels in more than ninety countries, the Accor group includes Europe's Etap and Formule 1 chains and slightly more luxurious Ibis hotels, along with the more upmarket Sofitel, Novotel, Mercure and Thalassa hotels and US cheapies Motel 6 and Red Roof. You can search by country or town, or for hotels along a driving route from one country to another (complete with door-to-door directions), or by keying in a place of interest or postal address near which you'd like to stay. Reviews come with 360° tours, but you have to have started the booking process before you discover how much they want you to pay.

Open World

www.openworld.co.uk

More than 4000 links to leading chains and hotel groups around the world – Holiday Inn, Hyatt Regency, Crowne Plaza and Intercontinental predominate – along with a number of individual hotels. Search by region or key in a city name to pull up a random list with addresses, phone numbers and links. Featured hotels include fast-track links to get you to their home page, reservations, photographs or location map.

Major US chains and hotel groups

Baymont Inns

www.baymontinns.com

The reliable US cheapie Budgetel has moved slightly upmarket to become the Baymont, with rooms at around $60.

Best Western

www.bestwestern.com

Worldwide directory of clean, affordable hotels.

Choice Hotels

www.hotelchoice.com

Major group of mid-priced US lodgings, including **Comfort Inn**, **Econolodge**, **Quality Inn**, **Clarion**, **Sleep Inn** and **Rodeway Inn**.

Days Inn

www.daysinn.com

Inexpensive US hotels that pop up around the world.

Embassy Suites

www.embassysuites.com
All-suite chain with properties in North America, Venezuela and Colombia.

Hilton Worldwide

www.hilton.com
The swanky Hilton is now a worldwide group, including the less expensive
chains **Doubletree**, **Embassy Suites** and **Hampton Inn**.

Holiday Inn

www.holiday-inn.com
One of a group that includes **Crowne Plaza** and **Staybridge Suites**.

Howard Johnson

www.hojo.com
Established, low- to mid-price chain with some 500 hotels in fourteen
countries.

Inter-Continental

www.interconti.com
Top-notch mega-hotels and luxury resorts in the world's major cities.

La Quinta

www.laquinta.com
Around 300 vaguely Hispanic-themed motels and suite hotels throughout
the US, many of them in Texas and the Southwest.

Marriott Hotels

www.marriott.com
Upmarket US chain whose "family" includes **Renaissance Hotels**,
Courtyard by Marriott, **Residence Inn** and **Fairfield Inn**.

Motel 6

www.motel6.com
The classic roadside chain, where they "leave the light on for you", with
more than 800 low-priced motels in the continental US.

Radisson

www.radisson.com
Posh hotels around the world.

Ramada

www.ramada.com
With Inns and Plazas throughout North America, Ramada runs the gamut
of cheapies to business-class towers.

Red Carpet Inns/Scottish Inns

www.reservahost.com
No-fuss cheapies concentrated in the central and eastern US.

Red Roof Inns

www.redroof.com
More than 330 motels in 38 US states. So you can indeed "always stop at
red".

Select Inn

www.selectinn.com
Few frills but good prices in the northern and western states.

Starwood Hotels

www.starwoodhotels.com
Includes **Westin**, **Sheraton** and the newer, hipper (some say pretentious)
W hotels.

Bed and breakfast

See also the newsgroup **rec.travel.bed+breakfast**, and **about.com**
(see p.68), which has a channel devoted to B&Bs.

Bedandbreakfast.com

www.bedandbreakfast.com
Comprehensive directory of more than 27,000 B&Bs around the world
(around 20,000 of them in the US). An intelligent and speedy search facility
pulls up scores of possibles, whether you key in a city name, click on a

map of the US or choose from a lengthy list of countries from Argentina to
Zimbabwe. You could also search selecting amenities and keywords, or
choose to see only places with immediate availability and online booking.
Member B&Bs are covered most extensively, but you can also find out a lot
about non-members. Though it's possible to make a reservation request or
book through the site, in most cases you can contact the owner direct.
Before booking, check the message boards for honest opinions of some of
the B&Bs featured on the site.

InnSite

www.innsite.com
Big directory of B&Bs that lets you search by country, city, keyword or from
a huge number of offbeat options (cats on site, canopy beds, espresso
bars nearby ...). Reviews come with contact details, rates and so on, and
some have star ratings calculated from visitor reports. You can make reservation requests through the site, or contact properties direct – in most
cases there are links to the B&B's site, which is where you are most likely
to find photos. Innsite's own forum is usually full of questions and fewer
answers; best to follow the hotlink to the newsgroup
rec.travel.bed+breakfast.

Lanier Travel Guides

www.travelguides.com
Published by hotel guidebook writer Pamela Lanier, this twee-looking site is
in fact a very good searchable database of more than 70,000 characterful
accommodation listings – some 40,000 of them B&Bs, inns and guesthouses – mostly in the US. Following the B&B link allows you to search for
an inn by location, keywords and amenities (pets, low prices, etc), while
other links offer less sophisticated searches for golf resorts, boutique
hotels, all-suite accommodation and condos. You can't book through the
site, but it does provide details of themed packages and special offers.

Distinctive accommodation

Design hotels

www.designhotels.com
Ice-cool site for people who believe that hotels are the new black, with a
bookable database of hip urban hotels around the world. There's not that

much hard information, just thumbnail pictures and PR reviews, but you can find out more by clicking the "Book It" link – and besides, if all you're after is somewhere to see and be seen at one of the world's coolest destinations, who wants to bother with details?

EcoRes

www.eco-res.com

Reservations at eco-lodges – a broad term, including wildlife and kayak camps, hilltribe lodges, mountain retreats and yurts, among others – around the world. You can search by destination or category (the list includes options such as treehouses, astronomy and romance) to read information on each lodge, including details of current package deals (quoted in US dollars). The site also provides itineraries, including the "Subterranean Honeymoon" in Belize, where one night is spent in a cave, or "Samoa Survival", where you build your own *fale* to live in. Bookings are made by emailing the site.

1st Travelers Choice

www.virtualcities.com

The strength of this rather old-fashioned looking directory is in the kind of place it lists – no chain hotels here, just B&Bs, country inns, boutique hotels, dude ranches and vacation rentals in North America and Mexico (with a scattering in the Caribbean, Australia and Europe). Search by state or region or by theme – the site suggests pet-friendly inns, ski resorts, good places for romantic breaks, and so on, presented state by state. Lodging details are available, but you need to contact the owners direct to book.

GoNOMAD

www.gonomad.com/lodgings/lodgings.html

Directory of unique and alternative lodgings around the world – from eco-lodges and igloos to paradores, caves and monasteries – from this excellent site. Top picks are organized by region, with detailed reviews and contact details. You can also use a pull-down menu to search by lodging type or country. Prices range from budget (a raft on the River Kwai) to expense account (a 115-foot cypress tower on Kenya's Lake Naivasha). Plus guides to farmstays, retreats, follies and home exchanges, with relevant contact information.

GrandTrunk

www.grandtrunk.com

This London-based agency, devoted to "Classic and Exotic Travel Online", helps customers reserve some of the world's most exclusive (and expensive) hotels and resorts. Simply let your cursor glide over the map on the home page, and a host of enticing destinations swim into view, from the Caribbean to the Far East, without even the need for a languid click of the mouse. GrandTrunk's team of writers and photographers describe and illustrate each property in the minutest detail, and simple pull-down menus enable you to make enquiries via email. Note, however, that these are not the kind of places that see any need to offer discounted rates.

Organic Holidays

www.organicplacestostay.com

Bare-bones but efficient site listing a good selection of organic hotels, B&Bs and farmstays around the world. Clicking on the map or the list of countries pulls up reviews with photos, contact details, and tempting accounts of the delicious food served or grown. Though the majority of listings are in the UK and Europe, you'll find fabulous lodgings in destinations as exotic as Morocco, Sri Lanka, Hawaii and Peru.

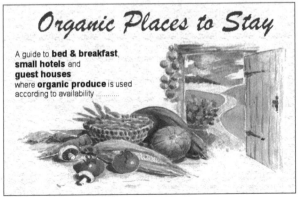

Organic Places to Stay

A guide to **bed & breakfast**, **small hotels** and **guest houses** where **organic produce** is used according to availability ....

Hostels

To ask advice from other hostellers, check the forums on
www.hostels.com below. You can also visit a number of **news-groups** (see p.18) including **uk.rec.youth-hostel**, **rec.travel.europe**,
rec.travel.usa-canada and **rec.travel.budget.backpack**.

Hostelling International (HI)

www.iyhf.org

Official HI site offering online booking at 500 of the association's main hostels through **www.yhabooking.com** (see below). Though you don't need
to be a member to book a bed, you do need to join before sleeping in it.
The site tells you how to join (which also gives you discounts on, among
other things, travel passes, currency exchange and Internet cafes), either in
advance or at individual hostels, with links to all the HI youth hostel associations around the world. Pity about the shrill colour scheme.

Hostels.com

www.hostels.com

Superb one-stop resource for anyone interested in travelling on a budget,
including older travellers and families. Independently run (which means it
doesn't necessarily endorse the hostels on the site), this is primarily useful
for its searchable database of thousands of hostels worldwide, with links to
sites where available. Some you can reserve directly from here, but there
are no reviews, so make sure to do a little more research – perhaps by
asking around on the bulletin board, or simply by emailing the place direct
– before booking. Includes well-written guides to hostelling and independent travel, news about special deals and links to sites selling tickets, rail
passes, travel gear and books. You can also sign up for their newsletter.

International Booking Network

www.yhabooking.com

Operated by Hostelling International (see above), this site allows users to
search for hostels by country, read reviews and see photos, check availability for every day over the next six months, and book online (for a maximum of six nights in any one place). Non-members can book, but need to
buy membership from the nearest YHA office or a "welcome stamp" (for a
maximum of six nights) upon arrival at the hostel.

Network of European Independent Hostels

www.hostelseurope.com

Searchable directory of more than 300 independent hostels and budget hotels around Europe, with information on rates and facilities and links to individual sites. You can book online, and order a Hostels of Europe discount card; this gives 5–15 percent discounts at most of the hostels, as well as reductions on tours, activities, transport, Internet access and museum fees. The site also has general information on budget travel around Europe, with links to providers of bus and train passes.

House swapping and hospitality

House swapping is one area where the Net comes into its own. Joining an agency offline you have to pay for a directory, send letters and make calls overseas, and sit around waiting for responses that might never come. **Internet-only services**, on the other hand, are usually cheaper, and as listings can be altered immediately online, their lists are often more up to date. They tend to lean heavily towards North American destinations, however, so anyone who wants to venture further afield may prefer to plump for established companies, such as Homelink, which use print directories as well as online services – their reputations also mean that they tend to attract the most experienced and reliable home owners.

Global Freeloaders

www.globalfreeloaders.com

Produced by an eager young Australian to harness the hospitable streak in the "travelling community", this site matches travellers in need of a bed with others willing to put them up. Enter your destination and dates to pull up a list of potential hosts, with information about who they are and what they have to offer. Once you've chosen, you fill out a form, which is forwarded by the site, and wait for the hosts to email you back. The catch, of course, is that you have to return the hospitality to other global freeloaders. The registration period is six months, during which you can block out any time you don't feel like visitors, and the service is entirely free. While members range in age from 18 to 70, apparently the average freeloader is in their mid-30s. You can specify any age preferences upon registering.

Holi-Swaps

www.holi-swaps.com

This site's amateurish appearance and spelling mistakes belie its efficient house swapping service; it's widely used, and responses tend to be fast. If you're looking for a place, browse the list of worldwide property owners offering swaps or rentals, and email them direct (via the site). You'll do better, however, making a swap if you list your own property. This costs £25/$37 for a year, and you write your own entry, which can be as long as it needs, with none of the abbreviations used in print directories. You can also update it whenever you like, adding photos or links if you want to be really flash. Once you've posted, your details are emailed to a list of active current members so you can get going quickly. You can also ask to be sent new offers as soon as they arise.

HomeLink International

www.homelink.org

HomeLink's slick site reflects its clout as the world's largest and longest established home exchange organization, with thousands of properties in more than fifty countries. The home page takes you to your country's own site, each of which has a searchable database of properties. Though you can't fast track to particular destinations, you can search for places on or near the sea, and click a checklist of facilities. You can also opt to see only properties added in the last week or 48 hours. Entries themselves read like truncated lists of amenities (a hangover from HomeLink's roots as a huge, hard copy directory), but most have colour photos. To access contact details you'll need to join; members receive five printed directories, and their listings are kept online for more than a year. American travellers can join online (and opt for a Web-only membership deal), but if you're looking at the UK site you'll need to email or call.

International Home Exchange Network

www.homeexchange.com

Internet-only site offering home exchanges, hospitality schemes and holiday rentals in more than seventy countries (around half of the swaps are based in the US). Though browsers can access the directory and email owners without having to post their own information, users who pay to list details of their property and their requirements receive benefits including email updates on upcoming swaps for up to three destinations. The search mechanism on this site is one of the best – you can opt to find exchangers who want to stay in your area, homes in places you want to go, swappers who are looking for certain dates, or by all of these, adding keywords to refine your search – but only some entries come with photos. It's easy to book online, and if you don't succeed in exchanging during your first year, your second is free.

Vacation rentals

See also the discount sites reviewed on pp.69–71, most of which have sections devoted to self-catering accommodation.

Cyberrentals.com

www.cyberrentals.com
Chunky database of privately owned vacation rentals, the vast majority of which are in the US. Click on the name of a state or a country, or enter a town name, and you'll pull up a list of matches with thumbnail descriptions including number of bedrooms and the nightly or weekly rate. Then click for more details, including links to Websites, and book direct with the owner. You can also search for award-winning properties and pet-friendly homes by clicking the links on the home page.

Holidayleaders

www.holidayleaders.com
Slick, independent Website, based in the UK, which pulls together thousands of worldwide rentals offered by a variety of leading agencies. Key in your destination and the number of travellers, specifying price range, property type (villa, cottage, chateau, apartment), and whether you need a pool. You can also use keywords to hunt for something specific, or choose to search one agency only (the site includes detailed profiles and guestbooks for each). Matches come with contact details so you can book direct, or you can register and add them to a shopping-cart style "suitcase". There is also a good selection of late offers (up to six weeks in advance), plus personal reviews and a forum – Holidayleaders withdraw from the site any property which gets bad reviews.

Holiday-rentals.com

www. holiday-rentals.com

Well-established directory of some 6000 private rental properties (from barns to ski chalets) in more than 50 countries – there are 800 in France alone, more than 600 in Spain, and hundreds more in the UK, Italy and Florida – with properties throughout the world. You can search by destination, facilities or keywords, using the advanced search to specify price, property type and suitability for kids. Under "Holiday Ideas" they've grouped properties into themes such as city centre, villas with pools and mountain properties. Matches come with full details and at least four photos. To return to a particular entry you'll need to note the property number, as there's no suitcase facility. Booking is done direct with owners, or, occasionally, through the site. They also detail special offers, and link to car rental companies and flights.

Vacation Rentals By Owner

www.vrbo.com

More than 8000 private villas and apartments around the world. Click on the name of the US state or the country you're interested in to pull up a list, then click for more details (not always including photographs). You then email the owner direct to book. Many of the properties are special, and prices aren't always that low, but the broad selection makes this site a good place to start.

Embassies and visas

Bureau of Consular Affairs

http://travel.state.gov

This government site, run by the US Department of State, provides the definitive official lists of visa and/or entry requirements both for US citizens travelling to any country in the world, and for foreign travellers coming to the United States. As well as contact details for the relevant foreign embassies and consulates in the US, it also offers links to US representatives abroad, and carries the latest travel warnings and advisories.

Embassyworld

www.embassyworld.com

Elaborate directory-cum-search-engine that enables users to find any embassy or consulate, either by the government it represents or by the country in which it is located. If you need to find the Brazilian embassy in Japan, for example, this is the place to look. However, there's no guarantee that the embassy you require will have its own Website; you may have to settle for a phone number or address.

Express Visa Service

www.expressvisa.com

Express Visa Service, which has offices in seven US cities, handles passport and visa applications for US citizens in need of urgent travel documentation, and can also deal with visa requests on behalf of non-US nationals. In addition, they offer translations and legal advice.

Passport Express

www.passportexpress.com
Commercial US agency that guarantees to obtain or renew passports for eligible US citizens as quickly as you need them; their Website holds all the necessary forms.

Travel Document Systems

www.traveldocs.com
Based in Washington DC, TDS provides an express service for US citizens who need to obtain passports and visas for travel to other parts of the world. The need for signed original documents means that you can't complete the whole process online, but the Website does enable you set the ball rolling. In addition, although it contains no information on travel to or within the US, for every other country it's invaluable, listing vaccination and visa requirements (with downloadable visa application forms) for non-US as well as American travellers, and also providing maps and general information.

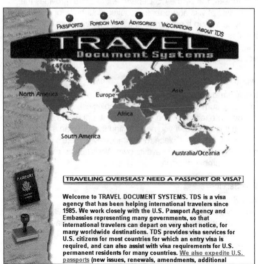

United Kingdom Passport Agency

www.ukpa.gov.uk

This official UK site enables British residents to apply online to renew, change or obtain their UK passports; the relevant form takes twenty minutes to complete and is then posted back for you to sign. The site also explains the requirements for obtaining British citizenship, details visa requirements for overseas travel, and lists all their offices, as well as offering an express service if required.

Visa Connection

www.visaconnection.com

Canadian visa expediter, with offices in Vancouver, Calgary, and Toronto, whose Website sets out visa requirements for Canadian travellers all over the globe, and provides printable forms to help speed up your application. They offer a "Red Hot" one-day service for extremely urgent cases.

Visaservice

www.visaservice.co.uk

The London-based Visaservice company processes visa and passport applications for UK residents travelling abroad, and can also help visitors to the UK both with UK immigration and visa requirements, and with arranging their onward travels. Internet customers receive a reduction on their usual fees.

Visiting Australia – Visas

www.immi.gov.au/visitors/visas.htm

The official Australian government guide to entry and visa regulations for prospective foreign visitors to Australia, which includes details of, and the ability to apply online for, the unique "Electronic Travel Authority", which precludes the need for a traditional printed visa.

Health and safety

Blood Care Foundation

www.bloodcare.org.uk

If you're travelling in places where health care isn't what it might be, you'll want to check the site of the Blood Care Foundation, a fine charity that

sends screened blood and sterile transfusion equipment to members wherever they are in the world, and offers special consultancy services for on-site medical staff. Annual membership costs £36, plus a registration fee of £30 (payable once only), or you can get short-term memberships from £8.50 for a month. You can't join online, but they provide all contact details.

Centers for Disease Control

www.cdc.gov/travel

Excellent US-based site run by the federal CDC. Though it's most useful for checking inoculation requirements, other good features include health and safety ratings for all the major US cruise ships – marks are given out of 100, with detailed reports of every dirty plate and rusty pipe. You can also get the scoop on outbreaks and trouble spots around the world, order a range of CDC books and reports, and download their useful *Health Information for International Travel*. Good links, too, to various health organizations.

Foreign and Commonwealth Office

www.fco.gov.uk/travel
The FCO provides up-to-the-minute news of trouble spots and safety issues for British travellers. The "travellers tips" are basic, to say the least (learn a few words of the language, look after your belongings, etc), but the country-specific advice notes – detailing political unrest, lawlessness, violence, natural disasters, epidemics, anti-British demonstrations, and aircraft safety – are up to date and useful. You can search for countries using a drop-down menu, and sign up to receive news by email. For an equivalent service, travellers from the US should check
http://travel.state.gov/travel_warnings.html.

Flyana.com

www.flyana.com
The Website of Diana Fairechild, US author and champion of air travellers' rights. She knows all there is to know on the causes and cures of jet lag, phobias, air rage (lack of oxygen, apparently), DVT, skypoxia (yes, really), ear agony, etc. Though you might balk at stuffing your nostrils with vegetable oil and chanting affirmations, it all makes a lot of sense, and is lively reading in a gruesome sort of way.

IAMAT

www.sentex.net/~iamat

The International Association of Medical Assistance for Travelers advises of health risks, diseases, immunization requirements and sanitary, environmental and climatic conditions around the world, and provides a list of hospitals and clinics which treat travellers while abroad. You can join online, for free (though they welcome donations) to get various useful bits and bobs, including an immunization chart which covers 200 countries, climate charts and risk charts for malaria and other diseases.

MASTA

www.masta.org

Run by the Medical Advisory Service for Travellers Abroad, based at London's School of Hygiene and Tropical Medicine, this authorative site has all the information and advice you need on potential health hazards in far-flung corners of the world, and a rundown of recommended and required immunizations. Usefully, you can buy health products online, including repellents, water purifiers and medical equipment (no orders taken yet from outside Europe). The jet lag calculator is a handy little gizmo: type in your starting place and destination, the direction you are travelling, the length of stay and your normal sleep times, and they'll advise you on how to minimize jet lag at your destination.

MedicAlert

www.medicalert.org and www.medicalert.org.uk

MedicAlert bracelets, which detail health and personal information including medical conditions or drug allergies, are particularly useful when travelling abroad. You pay a one-off fee for the bracelet, plus a smaller annual membership; there's no way to join online, but you can download an application form.

Medicine Planet

www.travelhealth.com

Drawing its information from the World Health Organization, plus the US State Department and Centers for Disease Control, along with medical journals, the slick Medicine Planet site is more successful in some places than others. Useful features include the "personal travel clinic" where you enter your destination and health information to receive customized travel health recommendations and news, and the medicine translator, which provides the local name for medications abroad. The articles are worth a look, covering subjects such as women, the elderly, students and families, with a general section detailing all the latest on DVT, malaria, cruise sanitation and the like. The information on infectious diseases is less useful, giving a list of symptoms but no prognosis, and the online travel store invariably fails to load. Register to receive email notifications about any health alerts in your areas of interest.

Travel Health Online

www.tripprep.com

This very good, user-friendly, US-based site provides detailed health profiles for more than 220 countries, comprising country information, vaccination requirements, malaria risks and the like, with a consular fact sheet for each one. Everything is covered here, from precautions around insects, food and drink, to how to avoid crime and deal with medical emergencies (the list of recommended travel health providers around the world comes with full contact details). The directory of diseases, which covers some pretty obscure ailments, is a hypochondriac's dream. All this plus maps, foreign entry requirements (for US visitors) and advice for travellers with special needs.

World Health Organization

www.who.int

Though it's not specifically geared towards travel health, the impressive, multilingual site of the World Health Organization tells you all you could ever want to know about every communicable disease under the sun, including details on vaccination requirements, up-to-date disease outbreak news, and advice on how to avoid and treat potential health hazards when travelling abroad. Along with news stories and a searchable database of reports and features on travel health, you can also access hundreds of WHO documents.

Insurance

Travel insurance is one area where you can make good savings on the Web. But you need to shop around, as rates and coverage vary widely, as does site usability; some demand reams of personal contact info before they will even hint at a quote.

Financial Information Net Directory

www.find.co.uk/insurance/NT
FIND lists more than 150 travel insurers: choose from brokers, sellers, and online-only agents. With short reviews of many of them, and hotlinks to them all, this is a good start if you're wanting to do lots of research and obsessively shop around.

GoSure.com

www.gosure.com/quote/quote.asp
Internet-only travel insurers, providing short-stay, skiing, backpacker and annual multi-trip policies on a very easy-to-use site. Key in the number of people in your party, where you're going and the duration of your trip. You can also choose extras and reduced cost options; quotes appear almost instantly, and if you want to buy, all details are confirmed before you go ahead. Their rate comparison chart shows that their prices are consistently cheaper than many of the other major providers (but it's always best to check how far the comparison dates back). Policies are emailed to you within fifteen minutes, and there's a cooling-off period of fourteen days.

Insuremytrip.com

www.insuremytrip.com
North American travel insurance comparison site offering around 30 different plans from a variety of companies. To compare policies head

straight for the quotes page; real-time ordering means that you are emailed a confirmation almost immediately, then the policy is mailed to you.

Leading Edge

www.leadedge.co.uk
Groovy polka dots greet you at this youthful site. Here the speciality is backpacker, multi- or single-trip cover for the under-40s, and you'll find some really good prices. Online policies are emailed instantly, and can be bought right up to the moment of travel.

Planet Travel Insurance

www.planet-travel.uk.com
A variety of travel insurance policies for backpackers. Rather than applying for a quote, scan their price list to choose a policy, and then fill out an online form. They have a number of reasonably priced long-stay options, and, unlike many companies, offer good single-trip policies for travellers up to the age of 80. You can buy right up to the day of travel and there's a fourteen-day money-back guarantee. Policies are both emailed and, if there is time, sent hard copy.

Screentrade

www.screentrade.co.uk
Type in your travel needs, wait a few seconds, and Screentrade will come up with a comparison of quotes from a handful of major insurers, complete with full details of cover and exclusions. You then choose the one that suits, order online, and receive confirmation by phone or email. They promise that if you can find a cheaper quote elsewhere, for an identical policy, they'll refund the difference.

Trailfinders

www.trailfinders.co.uk/insurance/split.htm
Trailfinders, known for its long-haul holidays, also handles travel insurance. If cost is the major issue, this user-friendly site is a good place to start. Key in a few details and you're immediately provided with a quote for single-trip or annual multi-trip policies. (You have to click a couple more times to get full details of the cover.) Online ordering is secure, and they'll send the policy online or by mail. If you change your mind, you've got fourteen days to let them know.

The Travel Insurance Agency

www.travelinsurers.com
Though it looks a bit rough, this fast and efficient site offers a nice variety of policies, including one for people already on the road and another for budget travellers. Quotes are given instantly, without you having to key in any personal information, and online ordering isn't too time consuming. Guaranteed 48-hour delivery, and a fourteen-day money-back option.

Travel Insurance Online

www.travel-insurance-online.com
Competitively priced policies for single-trips, long-stays, and a multi-trip "wanderer" for the under-45s. There's no shenanigans here; type in the number of people travelling, your destination and dates (it's possible to buy on the day of travel), and you'll get an instant quote. Policies are sent online and, if there's time, by snail mail, and if you change your mind within seven days they'll give you a refund. Links from this site direct you to sister company **www.annual-insurance.com**, which specializes in annual multi-trip policies available to UK residents. These come with a fourteen-day cooling-off period.

Travel Insurance Services

www.travelinsure.com
North American travel insurance that is available to nationals, green-card holders, temporary residents and international visitors. No online ordering, but the site has full details of the policies and the costs and a printable application form.

Universal Travel Protection

www.utravelpro.com
This North American company will provide insurance right up to the day before your trip. They have two single-trip plans, a multi-trip plan – covering trips taken more than 120 miles from home – and special cruise insurance, and online booking is relatively simple. You'll receive policy confirmation by email, and have three days to cancel.

Worldwide Travel Insurance

www.worldwideinsure.com
User-friendly, very fast site with a good range of policies, including options

for international departures, non-UK residents
(**www.worldwidetravellers.com** – see below) and long trips or winter
sports holidays. Prices are competitive, and you can buy off or online, and
receive policies by email or post. There's a fourteen-day money-back
guarantee.

Worldwide Travellers

www.worldwidetravellers.com

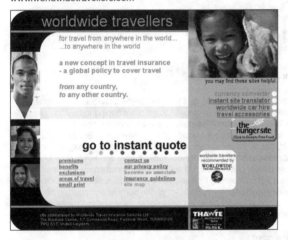

Travel insurance for non-UK residents provided by
www.worldwideinsure.com (see above).Getting a quote is speedy
and simple, without the need to type in any personal details, and you
can buy online. Cover can be bought up to one day before travel, and
only round-trips from and to a traveller's home country can be insured.
All claims are handled in England.

Currency and money

American Express

www.americanexpress.com/travel

US travellers can order up to $1000 in traveller's cheques online (plus $10 handling fee and a shipping fee); UK travellers hoping to buy cheques should log on to **http://home3.americanexpress.com/uk /personal_main.asp** for details of Amex services in Britain. For local ATMs, check the locator under **http://maps.americanexpress.com /expresscash/mqinterconnect?link=home** and key in your location. If you're in North America, you'll pull up maps and detailed directions to the nearest ATM; anywhere else and you'll get addresses only. To locate your nearest Amex office, with address, phone number and opening hours (plus mapping features for North American cities) go to **http://travel .americanexpress.com/travel/personal/resources/tso**.

Mastercard

www.mastercard.com

The ATM locator finds Mastercard/Cirrus cash machines around the globe – though only those in the USA come with small maps and full directions. To find them anywhere else in the world entails a lot of clicking, and results in a long list of addresses in random order. You can also access numbers to call in case of emergency, but again this involves a lot of clicking.

Oanda.com

www.oanda.com/channels/traveler

This huge venture quotes daily exchange rates for 164 currencies (and has an archive of daily rates stretching back to 1990). Useful features include printable "cheat sheets" – converters for any combination of currencies you like – and customizable expense reports, great for business travellers, that automatically calculate how much you've spent in your own currency. US travellers can buy cash and traveller's cheques online, with free shipping for two-day delivery. There's a message board, a before-you-go checklist, and a fast link to VISA's ATM locator (see below). And if you're curious about what currency they use in Bhutan, or in Haiti, they've produced a handy little device that will tell you (it's the ngultrum and the gourde respectively, if you were wondering). Palm Pilot users can download the currency converter and cheat sheet, and the currency converter is available on mobile phones.

This Is Money

www.thisismoney.com/tourist.htm
General money advice site from the UK, with a list of all the major rates against the pound, updated daily, and sensible advice on taking money abroad, what to look for when buying travel insurance, and how to go about claiming compensation for holiday disasters.

Travlang

www.travlang.com/money
Simple and user-friendly money conversion for travellers: click on any two currencies to draw up the current exchange rates between them, with a graph showing that same exchange rate over the last four, eight or twelve months, and a calculator that allows you to convert arbitrary amounts to and from each currency. They also produce a printable exchange rate converter for the chosen currencies, some information about them, and photos of the major notes and coins.

Universal Currency Converter

www.xe.com/ucc
Updated every minute, this easy-to-use site gives the exchange rates for some 180 currencies and features a number of useful services including the "Personal Currency Assistant" (**www.xe.com/pca**), a pop-up currency exchange window that floats on screen as long as you need it. Business travellers should check also **www.xe.com/tec**, a travel expenses calculator that takes into account dates of transactions and credit card charges to estimate how much you can claim. At **www.xe.com/ict** you can create

cross-rate tables for major currencies in the base currency of your choice, and query rates for dates as far back as 1995. All services are available on your mobile, Palm Pilot or pager.

VISA

www.visa.com
VISA's Website has a number of tools for travellers. Their VISA/Plus ATM locator is gratifyingly efficient: wherever you are in the world, simply key in your street address, or as much detail as you have, to be presented with the nearest cash machines, ordered according to distance, and a street map highlighting where you and they are. Plus advice on what to do if your card is stolen, and details of the prepaid Travelmoney card, which you can use to withdraw cash from a special travel account.

Weather guides

Accuweather

www.accuweather.com

This US site usually takes forever to load – hardly surprising when you take into account its huge visual content. With satellite maps of the world, and animatable radar maps of all the US regions, it also boasts golf maps (showing wind and lightning) and ski maps (snow, ice and rain, plus five-day forecasts for the major resorts) for resorts in the US. The "travel" section, which covers the US only, has maps for travelling by land (storms and snow, six-day interstate forecasts), by air (flight delays) and sea (wind, hurricanes). One area that doesn't use maps to best advantage, however, is the forecasting facility. Searching by destination either pulls a result or it doesn't; a map, showing all places covered, would allow you to make a second choice if you didn't get a match for your first. Forecasts themselves span five days and include "realfeel" maximum and minimum temperatures in °C and °F. Creating a local page allows you to access weather information for your home town – or wherever you choose – but climate charts (which you can use to predict conditions when planning a holiday) are only accessible to "premium users", who pay a small subscription fee.

BBC Weather

www.bbc.co.uk/weather

Educational site with a number of handy tools, including interactive maps, UK and US forecasts, satellite and radar images and shipping news. Search by postcode to create your own home page – with local weather stories, plus 24-hour and five-day forecasts that include air pollution. Under "Travel and Holiday", the destination finder allows you to read climate information for more than 500 cities – search by city, or select a month. (Cities are arranged alphabetically rather than shown on a map, so if you're checking the weather in a small resort, look at a map first and come prepared with a few back-up destinations in case your first choice isn't covered.) Though smaller places are neglected, the information itself is thorough, with monthly charts detailing maximum and minimum temperatures, rainfall, hours of sunshine and humidity. Under "Sports and Events" you can check skiing conditions around the world. For a daily pollen forecast for the UK, or flood risk bulletins, visit "Features Weekly".

CNN

www.cnn.com/weather
Five-day forecasts for more than 10,000 cities, with a good range of destinations. Each forecast includes minimum and maximum temperatures, humidity, wind, and sunrise/sunset; US forecasts also throw in pollen and air-quality indexes and allergy reports. There's a lot of technology on show here, with numerous radar (US only) and satellite maps (worldwide), and Quicktime movies showing temperatures and forecasts, weather systems and storms over a 24-hour period for the entire USA. You can also sign up during hurricane season for email bulletins on Atlantic storms.

Intellicast

www.intellicast.com
Concerning itself with "weather for active lives", this colossal US-based site is a great tool for anyone planning on spending time outdoors in the States. Groaning with radar and satellite maps, 3D and virtual features, it offers information on everything from kite-flying conditions to national park

forecasts. The home page gathers seasonal features from throughout the site – allergy reports, storm warnings, beach conditions and travel delays in summer; snow and flood warnings and wind-chill reports in winter. US four-day forecasts – click on the nationwide weather map – bring up nicely designed temperature maps; you can then access separate maps detailing particular conditions, including one which predicts how long you'll be able to spend outside during the next 24 hours. For ten-day international weather forecasts, click on the interactive map or scan a longer list. There are some glaring omissions (the whole of Turkey, for example) but it's worth trying the keyword search, as new places are being added all the time. The climatology feature allows you to search for a specific day and month to find average temperature, rainfall and weather conditions – useful when planning a holiday.

Snow-forecast

www.snow-forecast.com

Quality content, stylish design, and cutting-edge technology: this UK-based weather site is one of the best there is. Three-day snow forecast maps, updated every few hours, cover more than thirty countries, including Japan, Bolivia and Iceland, while detailed three-day ski resort forecasts – updated twice daily – show snow depths, rain, freezing levels and wind, and, usefully, real temperatures on the slopes themselves. There are hundreds of resorts detailed, and the list is growing all the time – they'll add your favourite if you ask. There's also a world snow overview, which pinpoints where snow will fall in the next two days, and you can sign up for snow alerts by email (free for one resort), or WAP forecasts on your mobile. All this plus an accommodation booking system for ski resorts around the world.

Wunderground

www.wunderground.com

Real-time weather around the world, with detailed three-day forecasts (including heat index, wind-chill, humidity and visibility) for most places you can think of. If the destination you're after doesn't show on another site, there's a good chance you'll find it here. Local US forecasts (use the fast search to find by town name or zip code) are even more detailed, spanning seven days, with radar and satellite maps, marine forecasts, allergy information, and astronomic conditions. To look up what weather you can expect when on holiday, search for the city you're interested in, choose a date in history, and read daily weather readings for every day since 1994.

Kit and gear

Bigdeal

http://bigdeal.com

This hip US site – all muted blues and khakis in cool snowboarders' style – offers good prices for skate- and snowboards, boots, accessories and clothes. Discounts are considerable, but as the goods are top quality (Vans, Da Kine and so on) you'll still end up spending quite a bit, especially for international shipping. Search using scroll-down brand menus to see pictures and written details of products, then buy online using their secure system. Registered members get special deals, but you don't have to register for them to email you updates and offers. Other features include competitions and a classifieds section where you can trade used gear.

The Brasher Boot Company

www.brasher.co.uk

Dotted with images of tranquil British landscapes and soothing reminders

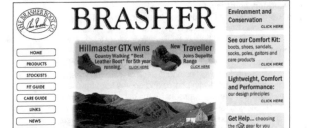

to treat your body kindly, this is not your run-of-the-mill outdoor gear site. Athlete Christopher Brasher, designer of the "boots that bring happiness to your feet" spends as much time on how to get the best fit and how to care for his remarkably comfortable footwear as on insisting you buy. Half catalogue, half mission statement, the site includes details of the Chris Brasher Trust, whereby a fee from the sale of every shoe – or sock, or pole, or whatever – goes towards preserving the wild places of Britain. No online ordering, but they'll mail a catalogue and newsletter. The search to find your nearest retailer is impressive: click in your postcode to get a long list, with the stores' full contact details, along with the distance in miles they are from your house. Customers from outside the UK can buy by mail order.

Christine Columbus

www.christinecolumbus.com

Thoughtful site selling more than 150 gewgaws for female travellers, ranging from the genteel – toilet seat covers – to the downright indispensable – wrinkle remover spray (for clothes, sadly), lightweight luggage and specialist guidebooks. The feelgood, all-gals-together ambience extends to the travellers' tales and packing tips, with useful links to authors, magazines, publishers and travel companies. There's an emphasis on security, with products that you don't see elsewhere; check out the half-slip with zippered pockets concealed under the lacy hem, for example. Based in the US, they accept international orders, but you'll need to email them to find out the shipping charges.

The Compleat Carry-On Traveler

www.oratory.com/travel

This "Compendium of Opinions and Ideas on the Art of Travel" from Canadian Doug Dyment is one of the best travellers' sites out there, a must for businesspeople and budget backpackers alike. Here you'll find everything you ever needed to know on what to pack, what to pack it in (just one carry-on bag), and how to pack it (the fine art of "bundle packing"), along with genuinely useful travel tips and dozens of reviewed links. Though it's an attractive site, peppered with photos and quotes from travellers such as Johnny Cash and Samuel Johnson, it's the content that impresses. The "essential" packing list itself is bible-sized; a bookmark menu allows you to mark the sections you need, and a downloadable checklist version is provided. Recommended products, from knives to crumple-free little black dresses and guidebooks (hotlinked to Amazon), are reviewed in detail, with supplier contact information. Get on the mailing list for updates.

Cotswold Essential Outdoor

www.cotswold-outdoor.co.uk

Detailed site from the respected UK-based firm, selling a nice range of camping gear, including sleeping bags, pots and pans and accessories, as well as clothing and shoes, and an unusually good selection of kids' stuff. Click on thumbnail photos to get a small review and a bigger picture; to buy you need to register, which is simple enough. The Adventure Directory (search by interactive map or keyword) gives names, addresses and links to thousands of activity providers and destinations, and you can also read travel advice on subjects from weather to health, with news updates and intelligent features.

Craghoppers

www.craghoppers.com

Glossy online catalogue for Craghoppers' innovative range of extra-light-weight and crease-resistant gear. The site also features skirts, fleeces, waterproof rucksacks, jackets, and a selection of walking poles, along with detailed gear reviews written by testers and editors from the specialist out-door press. No online ordering, but British travellers can enter their post-code to pull up a list of local stockists. Don't miss the table of links to out-doorsy Websites in the UK (National Trust, Ramblers Association, etc).

Eagle Creek

www.eaglecreek.com

This San Diego-based outfit produces a wide range of travel products including a particularly effective eye mask, a fantastic padded travel strap, and various handy travel packs. There's no online buying, but once you've browsed the range you can click on a link to be sent to an online dealer. Buying Eagle Creek gear you have the added satisfaction of knowing that some of the profits go to good causes, including Eagle Creek's Children of Nepal fund, an orphanage in Mexico, and an American Food Bank.

Leatherman Tools Online

www.shop-for-leatherman-tools.com

Leatherman knives have come to overtake the trusty Swiss Army Knife as the multi-function tool of choice for intrepid campers. Each of the twelve is versa-tile and ergonomic, from the Micra (nine tools including scissors, tweezers, nailfile and three screwdrivers) to the phenomenal 17-tool Wave, which has everything from pliers to screwdrivers to wire cutters, and they all come with a 25-year warranty. You can have a good look at them all, with full details and user reviews, and buy them at low prices via **Amazon.com**.

Letravelstore.com

www.letravelstore.com

This large San Diego-based travel store is a warren of luggage, guidebooks, maps, travel accessories and travel services. Their chummy site, packed with pictures of The Travel Store crew and their favourite destinations, is a good place to buy a wide range of brand products, with lots from Eagle Creek (see p.105). Online ordering is secure – or you can call or fax – with next day shipping to the mainland US and good prices on international shipping.

Magellan's Travelers' Catalog

www.magellans.com

Magellan's Santa Barbara store has got a reputation as one of the best places in the US to get state-of-the-art travel products. The site offers their full range of high-quality, low-priced luggage and travel clothing – with a wider than usual choice for women – but where they really excel is in accessories. This is the place to buy superb surgical rubber braid clotheslines, lightweight drawstring shoe bags, leakproof folding cups, modem and phone accessories, adapters and converters and much more. Check the regular clearance sales for bargains. Online ordering is secure, your goods are shipped immediately within the US (or within 48 hours for international orders, which incur shipping charges of around $30), and all products are backed by an unrestricted guarantee. If you have queries, log on to their Live Person facility, and have an online chat with a member of staff.

Recreational Equipment Inc

www.rei.com

Enormous Internet store from the US chain that specializes in sturdy gear for camping, climbing, cycling, snow sports and so on, along with clothes and boots, including several under their own brand. REI has been a co-op for more than sixty years, and though you don't need to be a member to shop here, membership (a small one-off fee) gets you an annual dividend of up to 10 percent of what you spent with them the previous year, plus savings on repairs and rentals at REI stores, discounts on REI Adventures trips and so on. Head straight to **www.rei-outlet.com**, separate from the main site, if you're after bargain prices on discontinued products. Online ordering is secure, and they detail shipping charges for international orders.

Rock+Run

www.rockrun.com

Produced by Rock+Run, the British mountaineering stores, this user-friendly site features a searchable database of top-quality camping and climbing gear, footwear, clothing, rucksacks, sleeping bags, wrist computers, navigation tools and the like. Zoom in on products, read the review, and gather them up in your basket as you go. Prices are quoted in sterling and US dollars, with a pop-up currency converter for buyers from elsewhere. A separate menu offers clearance deals on brand-name shoes, clothing and bags. Online ordering is secure, and they'll deliver to the UK within 24 hours if you email before noon. International shipping rates, calculated when you check out, are reasonable. Even if you're not buying, this is a good site for information on climbing and safety, with weather forecasts, forums and links.

SimplyScuba.com

www.simplyscuba.co.uk

The biggest online dive store in the UK has a jazzy site full of good content. Thumbs up to the detailed equipment reviews and downloadable size charts, and to the loyalty scheme whereby you save "bubbles" redeemable against all non-sale gear in the range. Online ordering is secure, and there's a phone-back facility (for UK orders only) – UK customers will usually get their stuff within 24 hours, and they ship to most places worldwide. You can also search their vast database of diving holidays, with links to rep-

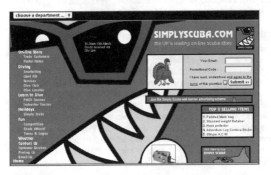

utable UK operators, pick up details of dive courses, read the latest on dive sites worldwide and trade used kit on the message board.

Tilley Endurables

www.tilley.com

This classy adventure clothing specialist, best known for floatable, unshrinkable hats, offers a selection of high-quality travel wear on a user-friendly site. Seasoned travellers swear by anything (trousers, T-shirts, shorts) made with their "Adventure Cloth", which stands up to the toughest treatment. Prices (from £32/$50 for a hat) reflect the quality, and everything comes with a lifetime guarantee. The site has separate entrances for US, UK, Canadian and international visitors, making online ordering easy and efficient as well as secure.

TravelSmith

www.travelsmith.com

US mail order site with a good range of well-designed travel clothing, including accessories and luggage, for men and women. Prices aren't bad, and the site is a breeze to navigate: clicking on "recommendations" gives you pictures and brief reviews of new stock, customer favourites, and featured gear for particular types of travel. "Shop by destination and activity" brings you to a series of packing lists, with recommended products for each one. Check the Sale section for discounts of up to 50 percent on discontinued and overstocked products. There's secure online ordering for US customers only; international customers can call, though, as ever, you should calculate shipping charges before placing an order.

Universal Packing List

www.henricson.se/mats/upl

The Universal Packing List – brainchild of über-organized Scandinavian Mats Henricson, god among packing obsessives (and there are more of them out there on the Net than you'd care to know) and founder of the rec.travel newsgroup (see p.21) – is in fact a bunch of checklists covering all you need to pack and all you need to do before a trip (remembered to shave?). In addition to the bog-standard clothes list, there are lists for hikers, photographers, campers, divers and so on, and they're being adapted all the time. Explanations and anecdotes are attached to each entry, with comments from users, and there's a set of links to other packing sites. The UPL, as it's known also comes in a Palm Pilot version.

On the road

D ay by day, the Internet is making it easier to stay in touch with your family, friends, or workplace, from wherever you may be on the planet.

Travellers have two basic options. Either you can carry your own **laptop** around with you, or you can pay to use publicly accessible computers on the road. Each alternative has its advantages and drawbacks, but broadly speaking, most ordinary travellers find it more convenient to use **cybercafes** and the like. There's no need to take your own machine just to communicate with home; it's only worth it if you're trying to keep up a more complicated working and/or social life.

In the lifetime of this book, improved global-ranging cellular phones, enabled by WAP (Wireless Application Protocol) technology to pick up email and read simplified Web pages, may provide a third approach. For the moment, however, they're not quite good enough to compete.

Cybercafes

No matter where you may go, you're never far these days from a **cybercafe** (or "Internet cafe", or "e-cafe", or any of a thousand other possible names). These come in all shapes and sizes, from rudimentary travellers' hang-outs in Thailand to slick business communication centres in Switzerland. North America, in particular, also offers a growing number of Internet-adapted payphones and kiosks, in some instances dedicated exclusively to AOL.

In every case, the basic concept remains pretty much the same. You get to go online for a certain length of time, enabling you to read and write email and check out whatever Websites may be weighing on your mind. You should also have access to a printer, so you can print out any important messages or practical details that you may receive. Expect to pay according to how long you spend online; fees are usually (though not invariably) low, and compare well with the telephone and ISP connection charges you'd incur using a laptop. It's even quite possible that you'll be given free Internet access, in museums and libraries, for example.

For security reasons, take care when you go online in public places to keep your passwords secret, and make sure to log off completely before you leave. It's also best not to send emails that contain confidential personal information such as credit card numbers.

Several Websites can help you **find your nearest cybercafe**, including directories such as **www.cybercaptive.com**, **www.cybercafe.com**, and **www.netcafeguide.com**. Alternatively, simply use an ordinary search engine, entering your desired location together with the word "cybercafe".

It is, however, easy to exaggerate the benefits of cybercafes. There's a difference between knowing that one is bound to exist in some unfamiliar city, or even having its address, and actually finding it on the ground. Your entire trip can turn into a never-ending quest to find the next cybercafe. What's more, sometimes that quest will fail, and you'll be out of touch for a few days. On top of that, if you're planning to base yourself in one spot for a while, especially if that spot is in a rural area, there may well not be a cybercafe within reach.

Web-based email and storage

Whether or not they already have email back home, most travellers now prefer to use free **Web-based email** accounts (also known as "freemail") instead. Unlike an account with an ISP – for which users pay to access the Internet and thus to be able to send and receive email – with Web-based email you need only visit the appropriate Website to read your email. There's no charge, partly because the sites carry a lot of advertising, and partly because they attract potential customers themselves.

With a conventional ISP account, your own machine saves copies of all incoming and outgoing email, and you can read it whenever you choose. Web-based email, on the other hand, is stored by whoever provides the service, and you can only access it online. What's more, they'll only allow you a certain amount of memory (and thus a limited number of messages), and they'll only keep it for a certain period; both vary according to the provider.

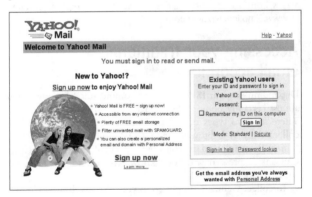

By far the best known providers of Web-based email, readily accessible from any computer on the planet, are **Hotmail**, owned by Microsoft (**www.hotmail.com**), and **Yahoo** (**www.mail.yahoo.com**). There's no great reason to choose one over the other, though Yahoo does offer its users rather more memory. Both tend to be easy targets for spammers (senders of unwanted mass-circulation emails). To set up an account, follow the simple instructions on their Websites; all you need is a unique name and password. Alternatively, both **www.fepg.net** and **www.emailaddresses.com** list countless other sources of free Web-based email accounts, ranging from Postman Pat to Manchester United.

A further refinement of the concept is to sign up for **free Web-based storage** as well, in order to be able to access any personal files you choose to store whenever and wherever you log on. Providers do tend to come and go, or to start charging for services that were previously free, so it's worth storing copies of your files in more than one place. Forty or so suppliers are listed on the Web Wizards site (**www.webwizards.net/useful/wbfs.htm**). If you simply want to store your passport and insurance details for emergency access, Lonely Planet offers a free password-protected "travel vault" at **www.ekno.lonelyplanet.com**.

Accessing your traditional email account

Depending on your ISP, once you're online at a cybercafe it will almost certainly be possible to check your usual email account. There are two types of ISP mail account, **Webmail**, which is collected by Web browsers, and **POP3**, which stands for Post Office Protocol, and is collected by email programs such as Outlook Express. If you don't know which kind you have, ask your provider.

To collect Webmail, simply go to your ISP's Website, and enter your usual details. You can obtain POP3 mail by running Outlook Express or whatever email program is available, but it's likely to involve re-configuring the program with such details as the name of your POP3 server, which you'll have obtain in advance from your ISP. Instead, it's much simpler to receive and send POP3 mail via either Yahoo or Hotmail, both of which provide straightforward instructions for users to access their usual email. Even if you have no intention of ever using a freemail account with Yahoo or Hotmail, it's worth opening one for this reason alone. Finally, the **www.thatweb.com** site promises to enable any user who tells it their email address and password to pick up their mail.

Travelling with a laptop

Most of the pros and cons of taking a **laptop** on your travels are self-evident. A computer is heavy, vulnerable to damage, and a constant security risk (be warned that airport X-ray machines are notorious locations for opportunistic laptop thefts). On the other hand, you have all your files and programs with you, and you can access them, or the Web, in privacy whenever you like.

From a communications point of view, the most obvious reason to carry your laptop is in order to access your own ISP, and thus your usual **email account**. How easy that is depends on your ISP; in fact, it's an important factor in choosing an ISP in the first place.

The central issue is whether your ISP has an **access number** – preferably toll-free, but at least local – that can be dialled from the location in which you're travelling. Otherwise, you'll have to make an expensive international phone call to your home country every time you go online. The easiest way to get round that problem is by choosing an international ISP such as AOL (**www.aol.com**), Compuserve (**www.cis.com**), or AT&T Business (**www.attbusiness.net**), all of which offer worldwide coverage.

However, many smaller ISPs have banded together to form "**global roaming**" groups, which enable their members to use shared access numbers in different world destinations. Typical groups include GRIC (**www.gric.com**) and the I-Pass Alliance (**www.ipass.com**). Check with your own ISP to see whether it belongs to such a network; if it does not, it should be able to suggest some alternative. Finally, whatever kind of ISP you're using, be warned that there will almost certainly be a significant surcharge on top of your usual fee for accessing your account from abroad.

Next comes the question of **hardware** – how you physically connect your computer to a telephone line. Ideally, you want to be able to plug your modem directly into a phone socket. Most modems these days are equipped with an **RJ-11 phone jack**, which is the standard plug used in North America, the Far East, and other countries such as Greece, Spain, and Ireland. Machines sold elsewhere, including in the UK, tend to come provided with a removable clip-on adapter to suit local sockets.

Travellers in the US and Canada should therefore have no problem hooking up to hotel-room or payphone sockets; travelling anywhere else, you'll need the relevant RJ-11 adapter. The trouble is, there are dozens of different jack designs. Several of the Websites reviewed below can tell you which jack is required for which location; some can sell it to you too. You should also be able to buy adapters in local hardware or computer stores when you arrive.

If you can't get hold of the appropriate jack; or if your hotel phone not only lacks a data port, but it's wired directly into the wall; or if you simply don't know which country you're going to end up in, it's possible to strip your modem lead down to the bare wires, and hard-wire them either to a telephone or straight into a wall socket. An easier solution is to buy an **acoustic coupler**, a device costing around £80/$110 that slots into your modem at one end and clips around a telephone handset at the other, and thus avoids the need for any wires to connect at all. Advice on both methods can be found on **www.laptoptravel.com** and **www.roadnews.com**.

Even once you've made a physical connection, the process of dialling the ISP number is surrounded by yet more pitfalls. First of all, some hotel and business exchanges use **digital** technology, as opposed to the analog technology used by computer modems; to put it simply, trying to dial on a digital system could well destroy your modem. A dedicated data port will always be analog, but with ordinary phones you can't spot the difference. Either check with the management each time; invest in a line tester, costing around £20/$30; or, once again, use an acoustic coupler. Secondly, phone systems may be either pulse or tone, and your modem has to be set to match. Depending on what computer and/or ISP you're using, that's done either by clicking a box in the software, or by flipping a switch on the machine itself.

Further potential complications include having to dial an initial number to get an outside line, and the possible inability of your machine to recognize an unfamiliar dialling tone. Both should be solvable by finding the appropriate option in the modem or ISP software.

If you're worried by the sheer cost of making long phone calls from a hotel room, you may find it possible to use a **prepaid calling card**. The trick is to program your modem with the full phonecard number and codes as well as the ISP access number, but to separate the two components with strings of one or more commas.

Finally, if you're having real difficulties, you could always try taking your laptop to a cybercafe. It might sound a little counter-intuitive, but many cybercafes allow customers to plug their own laptops into the Web, and in an unfamiliar country the staff can be an invaluable source of help and information.

Help For World Travelers

www.kropla.com
Steve Kropla's handy site contains illustrated country-by-country charts of the myriad plugs and adapters used for both telephones and electrical appliances all over the world, plus links to online retailers who can sell them to you.

Laptop Travel

www.laptoptravel.com

The Laptop Travel site provides immensely detailed advice on all aspects of travelling with computers, including descriptions of the latest accessories, and step-by-step troubleshooting instructions for anyone trying to go online via a hotel phone. The trouble is, of course, that you have to get online in order to read it.

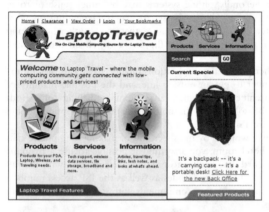

Roadnews

www.roadnews.com

Roadnews offers all the latest tips and technologies for "Laptop Warriors", reviewing gadgets and gizmos, listing adapters, explaining how to dismantle and hard-wire a telephone, and providing a forum to exchange ideas.

Teleadapt

www.teleadapt.com

Visit the sites listed above to find out which "laptop connectivity products" you need, then buy them from Teleadapt, who operate four separate online stores, for customers in the US, Europe, Asia, and Australia. All are accessed through the same Website, which contains very little advice or information apart from technical specifications.

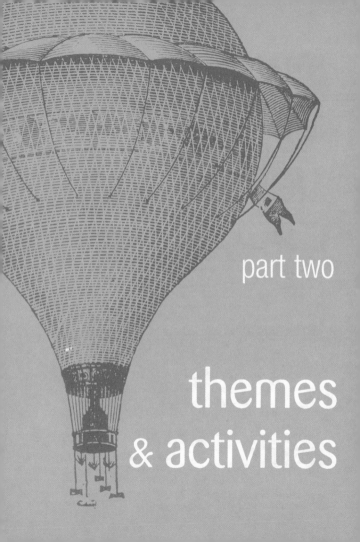

part two

themes
& activities

Activities

General adventure holidays

Adventure Directory

www.adventuredirectory.com
The Adventure Directory, a London-based adventure portal, offers users a staggering list of activities, from canyoning and cave diving to round-the-world sailing, plus a hierarchy of interactive maps. Most searches produce a long list of operators in any chosen destination, the majority of whom have their own Websites.

Away.com

http://away.com
As described on p.12, the huge US-based **away.com** site is an all-round online travel agency and information resource, but it also comes up trumps if you're simply looking for an adventure-tour package anywhere in the world. Activities on its intricate hierarchy of menus range from dogsledding in Nunavut or mountain climbing in Pakistan to sea-fishing off Venezuela, and even sailing around the world in 88 days on a freighter; simply email to request a reservation.

Backroads

www.backroads.com
From its origins as an exclusively cycle-tour operator (see p.126), San Francisco's Backroads company now arranges upmarket adventure vacations of all kinds, in every continent. Besides hiking, golf and watersports, it even offers "Active Gourmet" trips in Europe, walking between luxury inns in Tuscany and Provence. All trips are fully described onscreen, as well as being easy to find via pull-down menus, and can be booked online.

Exodus

www.exodus.co.uk

British adventure-tour operator Exodus arranges expeditions in over eighty countries, from Japan to Morocco; the travelling is definitely part of the experience, with different trips focusing on hiking, biking, overland safaris and even camel trekking. Though the Website is structured to correspond to the company's various brochures, its actual content is very detailed and often interactive, and it features full online booking. Prices are quoted according to your country of origin, and trips are sold with or without air-fares.

Explore Worldwide

www.exploreworldwide.com

The UK-based Explore Worldwide company offers a tantalizing programme of small-group tours worldwide, ranging from sailing tall ships in the South Pacific, via trekking through the rainforests of Borneo and Madagascar, to hiking in the deserts of Namibia. Whether you fancy rafting, trekking and even "ethnic or tribal encounters", you'll find it described onscreen, with up-to-the-minute availability; once you've made your mind up, email to reserve a place.

Footprint Adventures

www.footprint-adventures.co.uk

Though it's bursting with superfluous ads, links to Amazon, weather info and other whatnots, the core of this rather tricksy Website is the extensive list of wildlife and trekking holidays run by UK-based operator Footprint Adventures. It leads small groups of eco-travellers in around forty countries, with an emphasis on bird-watching wherever possible (see p.223); use either the "Geographical Index" or the "Activity Index" to find a trip that suits you. To complete a reservation, you have to email or phone, but you can make all payments online.

Geographic Expeditions

www.geoex.com

San Francisco-based tour company Geographic Expeditions aim to reveal "Inner Asia", "Inner Europe", "Inner Africa" or the "Inner Americas" to adventurous travellers prepared to join its demanding (and expensive) pro-gramme of tours. Specific trips might include mountain trekking or sea kayaking, but most fit into the general category of "rigorous exploratory

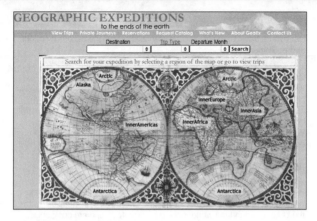

touring"; in fact it takes pains to point out the standards of mental and physical fitness expected of its customers. Book by email or phone.

GoNOMAD

www.gonomad.com

This US-based resource centre sets out to inspire and inform "alternative travellers", whom it takes pains to define as those prepared to participate and engage in the culture of whatever place they're visiting. Use its feature articles, destination guides and mini-guides to such topics as "Volunteer Vacations" or "Teaching English Overseas" to focus your interests, then search its database for companies and organizations that provide relevant trips.

GORP

www.gorp.com

The US-based GORP (Great Outdoors Recreation Pages) Website is probably the single best online resource for adventurous travellers. As well as running its own tours worldwide, sorted here according to activity, destination and interest, and all bookable online, it provides a vast amount of general information, with feature articles and Top 10 lists to whet even jaded appetites. Dig deep into its US national-park coverage and you'll find detailed hiking guides; elsewhere it holds practical advice on biking, climbing (see p.124) and other active sports. Eye-catching headlines promote last-minute travel bargains, and you can also buy all the necessary books and equipment.

High Places

www.highplaces.co.uk

High Places, a UK company with offices in northern England and New Zealand, offers small-group trekking, climbing, cycling and all-round activity holidays from Britain to everywhere from the Arctic to the Andes. The Website sets out all the necessary information with little superfluous clutter; email or phone to book whichever trip catches your fancy.

iExplore

www.iexplore.com

Run in association with National Geographic, the excellent iExplore database holds more than five thousand adventure-travel opportunities, within the US and around the world, offered by over 150 separate companies. Search by activity, destination, or both; arrange the results by price, date or other criteria; and then receive personal advice by email or phone. Prices are guaranteed to be the cheapest available anywhere. There's also plenty of destination advice and tips on specific activities, both from experts and from fellow-travellers, and you can buy books or equipment.

KE Adventure Travel

www.keadventure.com

KE Adventure Travel is unusual in maintaining offices in both the US and the UK, which makes it easy to reserve places on its expeditions to most of the major mountain ranges on earth, and especially the Himalayas. Some of the trips involve trekking and biking, others are long-distance jeep safaris in search of rare wildlife, and yet more are fully-fledged mountaineering expeditions. Separate online booking facilities cover British and North American travellers; look out for last-minute discounts.

Sierra Club

www.sierraclub.org/outings

Among its many activities devoted to raising awareness of environmental issues, the US-based Sierra Club runs its own programme of outdoors-oriented "outings" for adventurous travellers. As detailed on p.422, most are within the US, but it also has a smaller selection of expeditions in 25 widely scattered countries around the globe. These don't necessarily cover the most obvious destinations; thus in Asia it only goes to Bhutan, Iran, Nepal and Uzbekistan. Search according to region or activity, and you're instantly told how many spaces are left on each relevant trip; sign up online, then phone with your credit card details.

Wild Dog Adventure Directory

www.wild-dog.com

Whenever your cursor hovers over an active link on this appealing British-run directory of worldwide adventure operators, the Wild Dog wags its tail. Search by country or activity – or both – and it returns long lists both of tour companies that can take you to the relevant destination, and local operators who can cater for you if you arrive independently. Technically, the connections are buffered, so you can only order brochures while you remain on the Wild Dog site, or use the "Perfect Lead" facility to request emails from the various operators. However, it's easy enough to find your way onto their own sites, and complete your arrangements online.

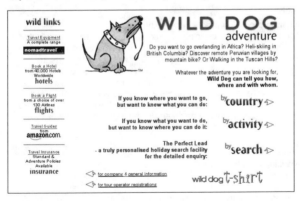

Wilderness Travel

www.wildernesstravel.com

Californian adventure-tour company Wilderness Travel offers a huge array of stimulating trips in all continents, from elephant trekking in Thailand to sea kayaking off Baja California. Some are luxurious, as with the "Palace on Wheels" rail excursion in India, others much more gruelling. Its Website is quick and instinctive, with a "Trip Finder" that can suggest vacations to match whatever dates you have free, and special Web-only discounts. To reserve, either call or download and complete the booking form.

Climbing

About.com

http://climbing.about.com

The climbing section of the huge about.com Website serves as a portal to many of the world's best mountaineering sites, but also offers plenty of its own content, with articles, book reviews, equipment sales and general advice.

GORP

www.gorp.com/gorp/activity/climb.htm

This comprehensive climbing site, run as part of the US-based GORP site (see also p.121), contains an astonishing array of information, ranging from advice for newbies, through technical tips for experts, to accounts of legendary expeditions. For North American users, it can point you to your nearest climbing club or organization, while the interactive E-quipper helps you choose and buy equipment online. Best of all, however, it sells climbing vacations all over the world. Call up the details on screen, then send an email, and a trip advisor will call you back.

Jagged Globe

www.jagged-globe.co.uk

Jagged Globe is a leading British operator of mountaineering courses and holidays. Learn to climb in Scotland or the Alps, then join an expedition – or even put together your own – to the world's highest and most challenging peaks. All trips are available to climbers from anywhere; book the whole thing online, or talk it through on the phone if you prefer.

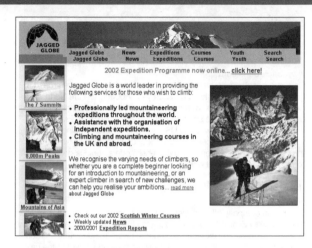

Mountain News

http://mtn.co.uk
Both the Mountain News site – which covers mountaineering, hillwalking
and trekking – and its sister site, ClimbUK (**www.climbing.co.uk**), devoted to rock climbing, share the same busy design and the same gung-ho
eagerness to cram in as much information as possible. In among all the
articles, polls, quizzes and adverts, you'll find equipment sales and advice,
destination guides and a whole lot of very busy bulletin boards, plus links to
operators of all kinds.

Rocklist

www.rocklist.com
General climbing Website, based in Arizona but offering news, features,
photography and even poetry on mountaineering all over the world. Less
male-dominated than most such sites, it includes a "learn the ropes" begin-
ner's guide to climbing, a "Data Guide" online guidebook to climbing destinations, a bulletin board and a plethora of climbing-related links. Sign up for
a monthly email newsletter.

Cycling

Backroads

www.backroads.com

California-based adventure-travel company Backroads arrange around a hundred specialist biking holidays each year. Roughly half are North American wilderness trips, with a heavy emphasis on the Southwestern deserts, while the rest are scattered all over the world, from France and Italy to Peru or Bali. A few of the US vacations involve camping, but the vast majority use the highest standard of accommodation available, and thus work out pretty expensive. The Website offers copious details of all tours, plus secure online booking.

Bike Tours

www.biketours.co.uk

This British company offers cycle tours worldwide (Europe and further afield to China, New Zealand, Cuba, Russia, the USA, Kenya, Turkey), graded to all levels of fitness and experience. You don't have to ride with the group if you prefer not to, but each day your luggage is carried ahead to the next evening's hotel or camp site. The Website enables you to select from all upcoming tours, and make reservations online. It also provides links to sister organization Cycle Rides, responsible for charity events such as the annual London to Brighton Bike Ride.

Biking UK

www.bikinguk.net

In terms of editorial content, this British-run mountain biking site concentrates on road races and events, and is aimed largely at participants. It's also bursting with small ads, for private sales of bikes and accessories. For the casual browser, however, the best feature has to be the vast quantity of links, not only to trail guides and UK tour companies, but also to biking holiday companies worldwide.

CycleActive

www.cycleactive.co.uk

British operator offering mountain-bike tours in all parts of the world, some of which involve other sports into the bargain. As well as plenty of

European and North American trips, it features more unusual destinations such as Malawi, Ethiopia and Réunion Island. The tour prices don't include international flights, so customers of every nationality are accepted. Actual booking is by email or phone.

Cycling Links

www.cyclinglinks.com

As the name suggests, this site is solely devoted to providing as many bicycle-related links as possible, covering cycling history as well as up-to-date racing news. Though originating in North America, it covers the whole world. For travellers, it's most useful for its directory of cycling shops, and the long list of international tour operators.

Discover Adventure

www.discoveradventure.com

British tour operator specializing in biking and trekking vacations. Its most eye-catching trip is a 24-day bike safari across Tibet, but as well as exotic marathons in Peru, Morocco, Chile and Nepal ("Around Annapurna By Bike"), it offers shorter European jaunts. The Website features plenty of very enticing photos and some even more enticing prices; email for availability and booking.

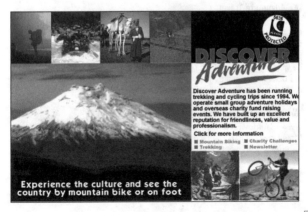

Easy Rider Tours

www.easyridertours.com

Easy Rider Tours arranges cycling vacations not only in its home base of New England and the neighbouring Canadian Maritime Provinces, but also across the Atlantic in Portugal, Spain and Ireland, including across Spain following the ancient pilgrim route to Santiago de Compostela. All tours are van-supported, while the actual cycling is just demanding enough to make you feel entitled to gourmet picnic lunches and comfortable inn-style lodging. Airfares are priced separately. Email the online form to make a reservation, and you'll be called back for your credit card number.

Inorbitt

www.inorbitt.com/home.htm

Inorbitt is a campaigning, non-profit Web group that sets out to promote the cause of sustainable transport in Asia by organizing free-to-join mass bike rides. Previous escapades include a millennium marathon ride from Hong Kong to Goa via Tibet. Its Website carries details of and suggestions for future trips, plus accounts of bike trails all over the world, with movies and photos; it also sells a few bike-related products.

KE Adventure Travel

www.keadventure.com

KE Adventure Travel, who have offices in both the US and the UK, organize trekking and mountain biking expeditions to "some of the most outlandish places on earth". Biking destinations range from Kazakhstan to Costa Rica, by way of a trans-England ride, trip lengths from one to four weeks; most are demanding, but some are gentle. Once you've checked availability by email, you can make secure reservations online.

Maui Downhill

www.mauidownhill.net

Maui Downhill fulfil the ultimate fantasy in effortless biking; a forty-mile ride down the mighty Hawaiian volcano of Haleakala, in which you barely need to brake, or even pedal, as you enjoy the stupendous views. Decide between the half- and the full-day jaunt, and make your reservation online. Rates include bike rental, and, of course, the van-ride to the summit.

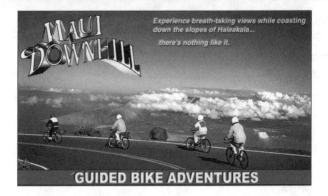

Experience breath-taking views while coasting down the slopes of Haleakala...

there's nothing like it.

GUIDED BIKE ADVENTURES

Rim Tours

www.rimtours.com

Thanks to the magnificent red-rock country that surrounds it, Moab in south-east Utah has become a mecca for mountain bikers from all over the world. Local operator Rim Tours specialize in catering for their every need, renting bikes as well as arranging tours. Its stock in trade is in day trips along Moab's own Slickrock Bike Trail, or into nearby Canyonlands National Park, but it also offers multi-day camping trips, accompanied by guides and chefs, and ventures further afield into Arizona and Colorado. Reserve by phone or email.

Rough Tracks

www.rough-tracks.co.uk

UK operator that arranges both road and mountain-biking holidays in various European countries. On the whole, the trips are relatively undemanding; luggage is carried by van, daily distances average well under forty miles, and accommodation is in small hotels and B&Bs. As well as weekends in England, destinations include rural and mountainous regions of France, Portugal and Spain. Email the online form to make a reservation.

Saddle Skedaddle

www.skedaddle.co.uk

Another British cycle-tour company, whose holidays extend from the UK and Europe to cover North America, Cuba, Patagonia and India. One intriguing itinerary follows the Rio Grande from New Mexico into Mexico itself, spending time with the Taruhumara people of the Copper Canyon. The less ambitious can enjoy a three-day weekend in either Mallorca or Spain's Picos de Europa mountains. Phone reservations only.

Suffolk Cycle Breaks

www.cyclebreaks.co.uk
Despite the name, this small-scale British cycle-touring company ranges slightly further afield than Suffolk – but only as far as neighbouring Norfolk. That means all its tours, which range from two to eight days in length, are through the flat-as-a-pancake landscape of East Anglia. Since they average less than thirty miles per day, and include transport for your luggage and comfortable inn accommodation, this makes for a gentle, easy vacation – and the prices are not too demanding either. Email for availability and reservations.

Wild Cat Bike Tours

www.wildcat-bike-tours.co.uk
Scotland's premier adventure bike tour company gained its reputation through running the coast-to-coast Scotland trips that still form the centrepiece of its brochure. These have now been joined by several more itineraries through the Highlands and islands – including some for tandems only – and a wide range of extended Morocco holidays, including off-road jaunts along ancient caravan routes in the Atlas Mountains. The Website features a busy message board for past and prospective riders. Enquire by email for availability, then book by phone or email.

Worldwide Quest

www.worldwidequest.com
American company that arranges small-group cycle tours, designed to suit all levels of fitness and experience, in far-flung destinations such as Tibet, India and Vietnam, and also coast-to-coast Cuba trips. Its "Best of China by Bike" is an 18-day tour that takes participants through the limestone scenery of Guilin as well as cities such as Xian and Beijing, while its 28-day tour of India is promoted as an "Introduction to Expedition Travel". Trip prices exclude airfare, which can be arranged separately.

Diving

Aquatours

www.aquatours.com

Under the slogan "Adventures for thinking divers", this UK-based operator sells tropical dive holidays and live-aboards across most of the world, including the Red Sea, the Indian Ocean, and the Caribbean, but not the Great Barrier Reef. It offers both BSAC and PADI training. The Website includes last-minute deals, but there's no interactive booking.

Barefoot Traveller

www.barefoot-traveller.com

This London-based dive operator specializes in the Bahamas and the Caribbean, but also offers a handful of Asian destinations including Thailand and Sri Lanka, and is experienced in catering for disabled divers. Its Website isn't hugely informative on prices, though it does claim to cover all budgets, and also lists and sells discount airfares. Complete the online form for more details.

British Sub Aqua Club

www.bsac.co.uk

The Website of the UK's official body for certifying dive schools and instructors can put members in touch with local branches and training facilities, but its most useful feature is the links page at **www.bsac.org /world/links1.htm**, which, as well as dive sites the world over, offers connections to subjects ranging from underwater archeology to marine biology and the elusive giant squid.

Dive Channel

www.divechannel.co.uk

This general UK dive site sets out to be a "one-stop dive travel shop", enabling users to search a database of dive holidays available from several different operators. The "Dive The World" section, open to all, provides general information on diving destinations worldwide, but to get very far with specific holidays you have to register with DIVEChannel. As well as making it possible to book last-minute holidays at dramatically discounted prices, this brings you regular email updates on new offers.

Dive Pacific

http://pac-aggressor.com
This American company sails its "Aggressor Fleet" of luxury live-aboard yachts to dive destinations throughout the Pacific, from Hawaii to the Solomon Islands, and also ventures into the Caribbean and the Red Sea. Its best-known vacation is aboard the *Truk Aggressor* live-aboard in Micronesia's Chuuk Lagoon, which abounds in World War II wrecks. The Website is packed with enticing video clips, and details specialist itineraries with big-name underwater photographers. Though this is the top end of the market, the prices are not as high as you might expect. Book by phone or email.

DiveQuest

www.divequest.co.uk
Online version of this UK dive operator's brochure, detailing diving vacations in the Caribbean, Southeast Asia, Australasia and throughout the Pacific, and including plenty of live-aboards. It also offers courses and tailor-made tours. Along with rave reports from satisfied customers, the site does at least carry full prices and details; booking is by email, mail or phone.

Divernet

www.divernet.com
The online version of British monthly magazine *Diver*, this general dive site holds a searchable archive of articles from its print counterpart – invaluable if you're researching a particular destination – plus links to equipment suppliers and private sales of secondhand gear, and a handy set of connections to tour operators.

Explorers Dive

www.explorers.co.uk/dive/dive_home.htm
Leading UK dive operator that arranges scuba vacations in all the major destinations, with a huge list in the Red Sea, but also such exciting Micronesian adventures as descending to the "Ghost Fleet" of Chuuk Lagoon. Yet again, most of the Website is simply an html version of its brochure, but it does offer some great last-minute deals – how about £199 for a week in Sharm-el-Sheikh? Check availability by email rather than online.

If You Dive

www.ifyoudive.com

General database of UK dive operators that asks users to select a date and a destination for their next scuba trip, and returns a selection of holidays with relevant companies. Before you commit yourself, be sure to check out the extensive reviews of specific worldwide dive sites.

Jules' Underwater Lodge

www.jul.com

What claims to be the world's only underwater hotel, in Key Largo, Florida. The "Jules" in question is Monsieur Verne, and this futuristic fantasy, perched on stilts at the bottom of a tropical mangrove lagoon, is straight out of science fiction. To reach it, you have to dive 21-feet down, then swim up from underneath. Rather than passing through an air lock, you emerge from a small swimming pool to find

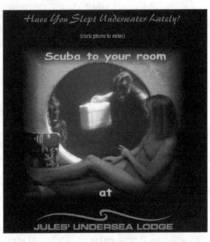

yourself in a cottage-like structure that holds two guest bedrooms, a kitchen and a lounge, but is also a genuine research laboratory. The basic package, including unlimited diving, costs around $250 per person per day, and it's also possible to train as a diver for the first time; luxury deals, with the services of a gourmet "mer-chef", work out twice as expensive.

Maldives Scuba Tours

www.scubascuba.com

Having started out as specialists in the Maldive Islands of the Indian Ocean, this British operator has expanded to cover other enticing, far-flung dive destinations such as the Galapagos Islands, Cocos Island (off Costa Rica), and especially Papua New Guinea. Among trips available to customers worldwide, it still offers two live-aboard dive boats in the Maldives, together with several local resorts, as well as charter boats elsewhere for specific dive cruises. All can be booked by submitting the online reservation form.

Maui Dive Shop

www.mauidiveshop.com

The leading dive operator on the best of the Hawaiian islands for scuba diving, running daily boat-diving excursions to the tiny volcanic islet of Molokini Crater, and regular trips to prime sites off the south coast of nearby Lanai. As well as making online reservations for all trips, users of the attractive Website can also request free booklets detailing Maui dive sites, and even a free video.

Professional Association of Diving Instructors

www.padi.com

PADI's international headquarters is located in California, though most national branches of the world's leading authority for certifying schools, instructors and individual divers also maintain their own Websites. As well as providing information on rules and regulations, the main world site is also the place to access the PADI Travel Network, through which it's possible to book dive vacations for all tastes and levels of experience in almost a hundred countries.

Regal Diving

www.regal-diving.co.uk

The straightforward Website of this British scuba specialist caters for beginners and experts alike, and offers dive trips to worldwide destinations, with a special emphasis on the Red Sea. Booking is by phone or email, but there's plenty of stimulating information to work your way through first online, with clickable maps as you choose your destination, and a handful of special offers to give you ideas.

ScubaDuba

www.scubaduba.com

Perhaps the best place to dip your first toe into the mysterious waters of the online scuba world, this general US-centred resource is determined to be "the Ultimate Scuba Diving Site On The Web". Alongside the expected chatrooms and small ads from divers selling equipment or seeking buddies, it offers such eccentric features as the ScubaDuba Top 5: A Worldwide Attempt At Scuba Humor (eg "The Top 5 Reasons Not To Dive With Your Doctor") and ScubaDuba WebLibs ("the old party game with a new, under-water twist"). The real reason to drop in, though, is for the copious, careful-ly categorized pages of links, including operators all over the world. If you're looking for someone who can take you diving in Bulgaria, they're probably here already, looking for you.

Scuba Safaris

www.scuba-safaris.com

Luxury diving holidays are the speciality for this British tour company, whose seventeen dive destinations circle the globe, from the Indian Ocean to Central America. As well as representing the Aggressor and Dancer fleets of live-aboard yachts, it also offers resort and beach-based diving holidays, with side trips to keep non-divers entertained. Reserve by phone or email.

Tropical Adventures

www.divetropical.com

Seattle operator that boasts a thirty-year record of arranging scuba trips in tropical locations from Mexico to Micronesia. Website users are challenged to match its detailed rates for any specified destination. Choosing "Honduras", for example, throws up a long list of well-priced possibilities, while if you're simply pursuing a bargain you can ask for the latest offers worldwide. You can also find a buddy for your next trip, or sign up for a live-aboard or special charter. Booking, however, is not currently possible online.

Golf

Classic Golf Tours

www.classicgolftours.com

Based in Colorado, but with additional offices in Scotland and Ireland, Classic Golf Tours arranges self-drive and escorted golfing vacations in the US and around the world. All the legendary Scottish courses are available,

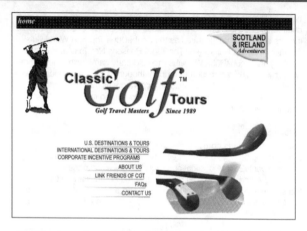

with prices depending on the standard of accommodation, and substantial discounts for non-golfing members of your party. Submit the online form to make your booking.

FreeGolfInfo

www.freegolfinfo.com
Calling itself "the world's largest golf community", this comprehensive US-based site combines a worldwide golf-course guide, sales of new and secondhand equipment, book and video store ads, online instruction, and hundreds of links. Its travel section (operated by Golfpac Travel, and accessible directly at **www.golfpactravel.com**), offers a wide range of US and international golfing vacations, all bookable via email.

GolfBreaks

www.golfbreaks.com
UK company that specializes in short golfing holidays in Britain and western Europe. Whether you simply want to play a particular course, or to take one of its standard three-day breaks, it's easy to pick your destination online and find a suitably priced trip. Email a request, and you'll be called back.

Golfonline

www.golfonline.com

Produced by *Golf Magazine*, this huge US site carries masses of tournament news, feature articles, technical advice and equipment reviews, but it's also invaluable for golfing travellers, with a huge section devoted to golfing vacations, albeit predominantly within North America. Courses and resorts are ranked and compared, and there's a weighty database of tour operators, with active links to almost everything featured.

The Golf Travel Company

www.e-golftravel.com

US tour company specializing in golf tours of Europe, with extensive programmes in Scotland and Ireland, and also an annual trip to watch the British Open. The Website sets out full itineraries and course specifications, with an online form to submit if you want to make a reservation.

ifyougolf

www.ifyougolf.com

The leading Website for British-based golfers, centering on a wide-ranging selection of over 75,000 world golfing holidays. Search by destination, or choose a particular course from its database, then look for tour operators or accommodation options in that vicinity. Ifyougolf also holds around 2000 pages of news, reviews and general golfing information, plus a bulletin board and equipment shop, and – appropriately enough – a fine set of links.

Health breaks and spas

For another range of alternative treatments, see p.207.

About.com

http://spas.about.com/travel/spas

Another huge and useful directory from the about.com stable. With hundreds of intelligently arranged and reviewed links, the site tells you all you'd ever need to know about a spa holiday. Among other things, you can search for spas around the world, check which ones cater for specific needs – including weight loss, Ayurvedic or family-friendly – and then read reviews and related articles from the world's media. Also spa news and special deals (mostly in the US), and links to relevant books and magazines.

Bath Spa Project

www.bathspa.co.uk

Having lain dormant since 1978, Bath's three hot springs are due to re-open as a leisure spa and treatment centre in 2002. Set to be the only working spa in the UK that draws on natural thermal waters, the complex will combine flashy new structures with the original buildings. In addition to a thermal pool, the elegant Hot Bath will house a medical centre offering watery treatments – spray massage, aeration baths, watsu (shiatsu in a swimming pool) and the like – along with "dry" and alternative therapies, for around £30 a go. The day spa, in the new Spa building, will feature thermal pools, steam-rooms, airbeds and massages.

Blue Lagoon Iceland

www.bluelagoon.is

Iceland's Blue Lagoon, around forty minutes' drive from Reykjavik, is a mineral-rich, milky-blue geothermal pool steaming away in the middle of a lava field. At the heart of the upmarket spa of the same name, it's particularly invigorating in the middle of winter, when you can languish in the muscle-warming waters, sipping a lurid blue cocktail, while shielding your eyes from snow-blindness. The Website tells you all about the treatments, the geothermal sauna, the various pools (including a cave pool) and the lagoon itself. There's also a restaurant, but no accommodation.

Body and Soul Holidays

www.bodyandsoulholidays.com

This UK operator is a great start for anyone planning a spa holiday. It can pack you off to luxurious resorts around the world, in places including South Africa, Indonesia and India – and at reasonable prices. Search by treatment or by resort: click on the one you fancy to read about its therapies, facilities and types of breaks, then click again for costs. Prices vary: you're looking at anything from £315 for three days in Budapest to £685 for two nights in the venerable Brenner's Park Hotel outside Baden-Baden, or £1910 for a seven-night "wellbeing and beauty package" in Monte Carlo. All costs include flights from the UK.

Canyon Ranch Health Resorts

www.canyonranch.com

Set in Arizona's stunning red-rock desert, the original Canyon Ranch spa resort is consistently rated as one of the best in the US. With hundreds of therapies, from the spiritual (breathing, Chi Gong, "Oriental vitality", yoga), to the physical (ballet, boxercise, spinning), you're also offered help with problems you may never have realized you had. Who could resist "healing heartache with humour" or "getting past the past"? All-in packages start at $1210 for four nights in summer (it gets *very* hot in Arizona); ten nights in spring or fall will set you back from $4500, based on two people sharing.

Chiva Som

www.chivasom.net

Voted the best in the world by readers of *Condé Nast Traveler* magazine, Thailand's Chiva Som spa resort is as luxurious as you'd expect, with space for just 57 people in a seven-acre beachfront setting dotted with lagoons and waterfalls. The Website is great, too, though the images and fancy fonts take a while to download: not too gushing, with articles and reviews of the treatments (which include sound healing, chakra balancing, floatation and no-knife face lifts) and even a few recipes thrown in. It costs a bomb, of course: standard packages range from $315 rising to $10,000 for two weeks in the palatial "Golden Bo" suite. Submit a form to check availability.

Daintree Eco Lodge

www.daintree-ecolodge.com.au

Fabulous Australian spa in the rainforest of Queensland, where guests sleep in luxurious treehouse villas set high in the canopy. The Website will set your mouth watering, not least when you read the restaurant menu (toothsome gumleaf-smoked kangaroo, anyone?). There's lots to read about the facilities, the rainforest and the various therapies – the signature "Julaymba Rain" combines aromatherapy massage with an invigorating blast of pure water from Daintree's waterfall, but it offers anything from Aboriginal massage to the marvellous-sounding "calm machine". It also organizes trips to the Great Barrier Reef, along with Aboriginal rainforest walks, cultural performances and art classes. You can book online, but the server is not secure; email direct if you prefer.

Grand Wailea Resort

www.grandwailea.com

The kind of thing they do so well in Hawaii: an ostentatious spa resort that manages to combine holistic "wellness" with extraordinary luxury. Clichés like tropical paradise don't do this place justice: on a white sand beach on the island of Maui, it's the ultimate in spa heaven, with a five-level swimming pool linked by waterslides, hot-tub grottoes, and a "hydrotherapy circuit", in which you wade from one water therapy to another. The site is admirably thorough, giving full details of all the rooms, with floor plans and rates (from $410 per night to $10,700 for the 5500 square-foot Grand Suite). The therapies will set you back a bit – you're looking at $150 for fifty minutes lomilomi or Ayurvedic massage – but day packages are available. Browse and dream, and start saving now.

Mer & Sante – Thalassotherapy

www.mer-et-sante.asso.fr/us/index.html

English-language site covering the history and benefits of thalassotherapy – the chic French hydrotherapy that uses heated seawater, seaweed and mineral-rich mud to cure all number of ills. The site has a selective list of locations in France, Spain and Tunisia, but only a few are hotlinked (and, of course, most of the sites are in French). Once you've read up on the benefits of being drenched in salt water, check the French site **www.thalatel.com/centres** for links to home pages of centres throughout the French-speaking world.

Rajah Healthy Acres

www.ayurveda-in.com/index.html

Spread across one hundred acres in the lush southern Indian state of Kerala, Healthy Acres offers Ayurvedic treatments for many types of illnesses and rejuvenation therapy for anyone in need of a rest. Rooms cost from $8 to $82 per night, depending on whether you want to stay in a bamboo hut or a two-bedroom villa panelled with herbal wood; each one has a kitchenette, and there's a dining room on site. Check the links page for other Ayurvedic health centres, resorts and practitioners throughout India. You'll need to email to make a booking.

Somatheeram

www.somatheeram.com

Fifteen-acre Kerala beach resort offering Ayurveda and yoga, plus courses

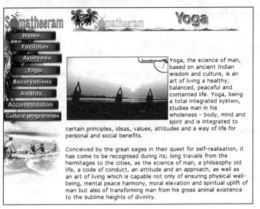

and seminars on Indian dance, music, philosophy, literature and meditation. Room rates vary widely: a Christmas break in a thatched cottage, built of mud and bricks and with a sea view, will set you back $90 per person per night (based on two sharing), though you could spend as little as $15 and as much as $200 depending upon season and style of accommodation. The many Ayurvedic treatments and courses cost extra (from $3 for a one-off to more than $1000 for a month-long programme), as do flights and meals ($5 for breakfast, $10 for lunch and dinner). Email to make reservation.

Sources de Caudalie

www.sources-caudalie.com
Healthy living with a difference: surrounded by vineyards near Bordeaux, Sources de Caudalie is a four-star "vinotherapie spa", which claims to combine grape polyphenols, grape-seed oil, wine yeast extracts and tannin with natural thermal waters to create anti-ageing and slimming treatments. So you can have red-wine baths and Merlot wraps, Sauvignon massages and Cabernet body scrubs while staying in fabulous themed rooms and stuffing yourself on gourmet French food. You're encouraged to enjoy vintage wines at the "Bar du French Paradox" – and talking of paradoxes, it's an odd sort of spa that offers a cigar bar ... Packages include four wine-soaked treatments per day. If you want to spend your holiday eating nothing but organic grapes, you'll need to make contact direct.

Horse riding

British Horse Society

www.bhs.org.uk

Visiting the Website of the British Horse Society is hardly the most thrilling experience you'll ever have online, but it's great if you need to get in touch with riding clubs or schools anywhere in the UK. It also has links to companies that offer riding holidays in Britain and around the world.

Guest Ranches of North America

www.guestranches.com

Texas-based Website that hosts home pages for guest ranches throughout the US, plus a handful in Canada and one in Mexico. Each individual ranch provides details of its rates and facilities, and can be contacted directly, but apart from the listings being arranged by state there's no overall search engine to help you pinpoint the horse-riding vacation that suits you. A separate section details job opportunities at the various ranches.

Hidden Trails

www.hiddentrails.com

Vancouver operator Hidden Trails offers horseback holidays in 18 US states, 3 Canadian provinces, and over 40 overseas destinations, with 5 percent discounts on all guest ranches. Highlights of its list include riding through Tanzanian game parks to Mount Kilimanjaro, and a week-long adventure in Monument Valley; it also has separate Best Rides and Best Deals sections. Availability for each tour is constantly updated, so you can make a reservation simply by emailing the form with such personal details as your height, weight, and, of course, your credit card number.

Holiday On Horseback

www.horseback.com

This plum address belongs to Warner Guiding and Outfitting, based at Banff National Park in Canada, who run horseback trips through breathtaking mountain scenery. Standard inexpensive multi-day excursions involve overnight camping; others, described as "roughing it the civilized way", stay overnight in wilderness lodges. Specific themes include park history or, alarmingly, grizzly bears. Day-trips and picnic excursions are also available. Only provisional bookings can be made online.

Inntravel

www.inntravel.co.uk

British operator Inntravel specializes (though not exclusively), in horseback holidays in Spain, Portugal, Italy and France as well as in Britain, with an emphasis on its home base in the Yorkshire Dales. On its three-day Normandy break, for example, participants can choose between dorms in equestrian centres or comfortable hotels; rates vary accordingly. Other trips stay in different villages every night. As there are no online availability checks, only provisional bookings can be made by email.

In The Saddle

www.inthesaddle.com

This British tour company divides its horseback vacations into three broad categories: ranch stays, predominantly in North America; riding holidays in Europe, based as a rule in equestrian centres; and riding expeditions in far-flung corners of the globe such as Botswana, Mongolia and Patagonia. It caters for riders of all levels; one trip, in Ireland, allows experts to go on unaccompanied trail rides for as much as two weeks. Email for availability and general advice, then make your reservation by phone.

Outlaw Trails

www.outlawtrails.com

Strangely enough, British company Outlaw Trails offers exactly what its name suggests; the chance for hardy riders to follow the self-same trails used by legendary Wild West outlaws such as the Wild Bunch and the Hole-in-the-Wall Gang. Long-distance trips require participants to camp en route; others, such as in the legendary "Robbers' Roost" district of Utah's remote canyonlands,

OUTLAWTRAILS.COM

Ultimate Horseback Vacations

North and South America &
Unique Western Adventure

involve stays at working ranches. Rates are remarkably reasonable, and are quoted without airfares, so all nationalities are welcome. To pursue your enquiries, send an email.

Ranchweb.com

www.ranchweb.com

The definitive Website for horseback vacations, run by Gene Kilgore, who writes (and sells online) the five-hundred-page *Official Guide to Ranch Vacations in North America*, in conjunction with US operator Equitour. A cornucopia for wannabe cowboys and city slickers alike, it lists over a hundred holidays worldwide, from Wales to Jordan, and ranch vacations not only in the USA and Canada, but even in Argentina and Mongolia. The search facility is superb, enabling you to pick a ranch according to whatever criteria matter to you – a request for Wyoming ranches available in June that also offer golf and swimming throws up 38 suggestions – or you can simply point to a spot on the interactive global map. However, you can only request a reservation by email, rather than complete one online.

Ride Worldwide

www.rideworldwide.com

This attractive site opens up to the thunder of approaching hoofbeats; then the words "Ride Worldwide" gallop into view, and skid to a halt. Sadly, however, though the British tour company runs a very impressive programme of worldwide riding and ranch holidays, from dude ranches in Wyoming to yurting safaris in Kyrgyzstan, the site itself can only whet your appetite. The only thing it actually lets you do is order or download its print brochure.

Unicorn Trails

www.unicorntrails.com

Through offices in Britain and Ireland, Unicorn Trails sells horseriding holidays in destinations worldwide, catering for novices and experts alike. It has a particular penchant for deserts, with trips to the Pushkar Camel Fair in Rajasthan and across Namibia, but also includes less gruelling options such as swimming with horses in Crete. The quoted prices do not include airfares, so independent travellers can link up with chosen tours. Email enquiries rather than actual bookings are invited; onscreen photos and biographies add to the personal touch. From time to time, there are online competitions for free holidays.

The Wild Horse Sanctuary

www.wildhorsesanctuary.org

The Wild Horse Sanctuary, a non-profit-making organization located near Lassen Volcanic National Park in northern California, invites travellers to join trail rides among the wild mustangs. It offers two- or three-day weekend pack trips, and also four- to six-day cattle drives and round-ups, with accommodation and food provided in cabins beside Vernal Lake. Email full details, including credit card, to guarantee your reservation. Alternatively, you can stay at home and simply sponsor a wild horse.

Overlanding and long-haul bus trips

For a review of America's own Green Tortoise bus company, see p.420.

Bukima Expeditions

www.bukima.com

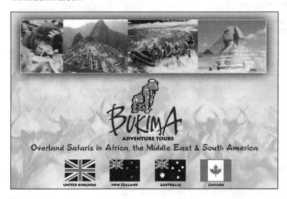

This British operator, which also has agents in Canada, Australia and New Zealand, runs trans-continental camping safaris by jeep across Africa, the Middle East, and South America (which works out a little cheaper). You can join a trip for just ten days, or by combining various segments travel for as long as 28 weeks; each jeep has its own email address for you to stay in touch with home. Once you've chosen from the Website, print off the form and fax or post it to your nearest office.

Contiki

www.contiki.com

More than a hundred overland bus tours, in the US, Canada, Europe, Africa and Australasia, for 18–35 year-olds from all over the world. Each region has its own Contiki site. Search by continent to get a list of tours with prices and then click to get a detailed itinerary, dates and rates, plus links to travellers' reviews. Check also the "great deals" for bargains. Although the largest choice is in Europe, where you can choose between budget tours, or the more expensive "Time Out" tours, the range is vast, taking in a month's travelling around Australia or on safari through Namibia, Botswana, Zambia and Zimbabwe. Accommodation, sightseeing and, by all accounts, as much heavy drinking as you can manage, is included. No online ordering; email direct for bookings.

Dragoman

www.dragoman.co.uk/index2.html

Based in the UK, Dragoman provides overland journeys from 2–37 weeks in length, in 62 different countries. Its Website allows searches not only by destination and length of trip, but also by kind of lodging (camping, hotels, or both) and degree of adventure (easy, moderate, challenging or extreme). Pop-up screens bombard you with further options at every stage. Classic overland routes include the old Hippy Trail from London to Kathmandu (albeit recast as "In the Steps of Alexander"), as well as hardier trans-Africa expeditions. The one North American trip runs from Alaska to Mexico. Prices are a little higher than elsewhere, but then the trips aren't aimed exclusively at young backpackers. Email the form to register your interest.

Encounter Overland

www.encounter-overland.com

The youth-oriented arm of Dragoman (see above), organizing trips of all lengths across Africa, Asia and South America. Its in-your-face Website opens by demanding "r u wild?", and insists that its expedition leaders "are NOT tour guides because you are not a tourist". The actual trips are as inexpensive as possible, with all park fees and extra adventures such as rafting or climbing priced separately. Despite the full details given online, however, you can only make a booking at present via snail mail.

Exodus Travels

www.exodus.co.uk

Among its many adventure-travel options, this British company arranges overland expeditions in Central and South America, Asia and Africa. Most travel in relative comfort, and are priced accordingly. Although the Website supplies surprisingly few on screen details about individual trips – download the Acrobat version of the brochure to learn more – you can, nonetheless, complete online bookings with the minimum of ceremony.

Oasis Overland

www.oasisoverland.co.uk

This relatively new UK-based company organizes overland camping expeditions, in purpose-built vehicles, for budget travellers who don't expect any pampering. As well as large-scale trips across Africa (most of which end up in Nairobi or Cape Town) and South America (including a Coast to Coast route from Chile to Brazil), it also offers shorter jaunts such as a ten-day Egypt tour. Click on any trip to obtain prices and schedules, and then reserve by emailing your personal details. Online payments aren't accepted, so you'll have to follow up by mailing a cheque.

Suntrek

www.suntrek.com

Californian tour company that offers low-budget, long-distance expeditions across North America and Mexico for participants of all nationalities, travelling in customized 4WD "maxi-vans". On the Website, trips are arranged by duration, ranging from one week up to thirteen weeks; some are exclusively camping, while pricier alternatives use hotels instead. Electronic reservations are taken, though it isn't possible actually to pay online. For details of their Mexico trips, see p.341.

Trekamerica

www.trekamerica.com

Trekamerica is a UK-based company that runs forty distinct overland camping trips across Canada, the USA, and Mexico, for small groups of travellers aged 18–38. Its Website, divided into separate sections for either British, or American and worldwide customers, and featuring an animated banner image of a van rolling through classic red-rock scenery, provides full details of itineraries and prices, and accepts credit card details for online bookings, subject to subsequent availability checks.

Skiing

Beau-Mont

www.beau-mont.com

London-based travel agency specializing in bargain Alpine skiing breaks, combining good-value accommodation with cheap flights from net airlines like Ryanair and easyJet. Check information on your chosen resort – even take a peek via Webcam – then book your weekend trip online, with a pause while availability is checked.

Bigfoot Travel

www.bigfoot-travel.co.uk

UK-based agency Bigfoot Travel run this highly informative Website to sell its programme of short skiing or snowboarding breaks on the slopes of Chamonix in the French Alps. It operates six chalets and one hotel in the region; read all the details onscreen, and take advantage of the (small) discount for online bookings.

Colorado Resort Net

www.toski.com

Representing all Colorado's ski resorts, this Website offers destination information and links to every resort and city in the state. Its "One Minute Vacation Planner" invites users to fill in a detailed form specifying their holiday requirements, which is automatically emailed to every member offering the relevant services; someone then gets back to you with the best deals, by phone if you prefer that to email. Alternatively, click on an individual resort for ski packages and a full list of online accommodation options.

Crystal Ski

www.crystalski.co.uk

Specialist UK ski operator that sells holidays in eight European countries, plus the USA and Canada. Its Website has a high standard of information, not only on the 120 resorts it represents, but also on specific accommodation options within those resorts. You can check availability and complete your booking online – assuming you're prepared to pay the relatively high rates that usually seem to be on offer.

Go Ski

www.goski.com

US ski site that provides copious information on over 2000 resorts in 37 different countries, from Lesotho to Greenland. Not surprisingly, it's strongest on US destinations, with great details on all the domestic resorts (including first-hand reports, not always positive, from ordinary skiers) and a host of bargain deals available online. Specialist interests are well catered for, and there's plenty of equipment on offer too.

If You Ski

www.ifyouski.com

Part of a small family of British Websites (others include If you dive and If you golf) designed to sell inexpensive activity-oriented package holidays. Choose from its list of ski resorts – shorter than on many such sites, and predominantly European – to summon up informative maps and written details; finalize your plans by telling the straightforward search engine where you want to go and when, plus where you want to fly from; and then book online. Other site features include a regular newsletter, complete with ski humour and equipment reviews.

Ski Central

http://skicentral.com

The premier online skiing directory is a vast compendium of ski-related sites, centring especially on North America. For destination information it's unbeatable, with links to each resort's own general sites as well as specific accommodation options and other businesses. Other categories include equipment suppliers and up-to-the-minute snow reports, plus plenty of fun stuff like snowcams, chat rooms and competitions.

Ski Club of Great Britain

www.skiclub.co.uk

Certain areas of this top-quality information site are only accessible to enrolled club members, but any skier or snowboarder can use its search facility to find a holiday to suit their needs; possible criteria include your level of skill or your favourite off-piste activities. The site covers resorts in Europe, North America, and the southern hemisphere, with snow reports, features articles and an optional email newsletter. Join the club to benefit from discounts from all the featured operators.

Ski France

www.skifrance.fr/welcome.htm

The English-language version of this French skiing portal can connect you with a hundred ski resorts all over the country, divided into seven distinct categories from "charming village" to "superfitness". It's not all that good at providing general destination information, but if you already have a reasonable idea of where you'd like to go, it will usually come up with an extensive list of last-minute bargains, and put you in touch with a wide range of specific hotels.

Ski Holidays

www.ski-holidays.com

Online database of well-priced deals offered by dozens of UK ski and snowboard operators. As well as straightforward searches by departure point and/or specific ski destination, in Europe or North America, it holds a range of last-minute bargains and a "Take a Chance" section in which you can buy a cut-rate holiday so long as you don't mind where you end up. You can't complete your booking online, however; once you've selected a holiday, you have to call a toll-free line and give its code number.

Ski New England.com

www.skinewengland.com
This companion site to the general New England travel site
www.seenewengland.com covers skiing possibilities throughout the
region, with easy links not only to each resort's own Website but also to
individual accommodation options within that resort. You can set about
finding your dream holiday either by searching for the perfect resort to
match your chosen priorities, or by using the excellent "lodging finder" to
find the ideal property anywhere in New England.

Snow.co

www.snow.co.nz
All the information you could possibly need about skiing in New Zealand,
covering every resort in the country with live Webcams, plus forthcoming
events, up-to-the-minute snow reports and details of which roads and ski
lifts are currently open. Links to each resort make it possible to arrange
your entire trip online.

The Snow Team

www.ski.co.uk
A very useful UK-oriented directory of ski- and snowboard-related Websites,
arranged (and rated with marks out of ten) according to several different criteria, including "Late Availability" and "Short Breaks" as well as the basic
"Travel Operators". It also lists resort sites, equipment retailers, and ezines,
and offer an advice service if you email your requirements for a skiing break.

Surfing and windsurfing

A1Surf

www.a1surf.com
Though it provides news and competition reports from around the globe,
the A1Surf site is primarily devoted to surfing in the UK. Its up-to-the-
minute Surfcheck relays conditions from all the country's major beaches,
while a busy bulletin board is filled with equally up-to-date reports from
surfers. British equipment manufacturers and retailers are well represented,
or you can pick up cheap secondhand boards via the small ads, and
there's a massive set of (mostly European) surfing links.

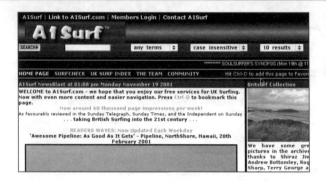

About.com

www.surfing.about.com

The surfing and bodyboarding section of the massive North American about.com site is well up to the usual standard (see p.12), packed with online resources such as articles, equipment sales, destination guides, topical forums, surf cams and weather reports, and featuring links to every imaginable surf site. If you're looking to plan or book a surfing vacation, this is a great place to start.

Las Olas

www.surflasolas.com

This irresistible specialist site is devoted to promoting an all-women surf school located near Puerto Vallarta on Mexico's Pacific coast. It offers luxurious surfing vacations for anyone from beginners to experts, in idyllic conditions, with yoga, massage and spa treatments also available. Complete and submit the onscreen form for full details.

Maui Windsurfari

http://windsurfari.com

Custom vacation packages in the world's premier windsurfing destination – the Hawaiian island of Maui. This simple site lets you put together your own "windsurfari", with flexible choices of accommodation, tuition if needed, car or board-adapted van rental, and also equipment rental – though you'll have to arrange your flights yourself. Submit the onscreen form once you've decided what you're interested in.

Surfing Australia

www.surfingaustralia.com

At first glance, the Surfing Australia Website appears to have a very heavy bias towards news and features about competitive surfing. Delve a little deeper, however, and you'll find a wealth of listings and links covering every aspect of surfing in the country, including surf schools and tour companies in every state.

Wavehunters

www.wavehunters.com

This full-service surfing travel agency, based in California, is actually a division of the giant Carlson Wagonlit group, which probably explains the high-tech resources lavished on its memory-gobbling Website. If you're in the market for an all-inclusive surf vacation, pick a destination from the interactive global map – options include little-known South Pacific and Southeast Asian spots, as well as the more famous North and Central American resorts – swoon briefly at the photos, then call or complete the onscreen booking form. You can also check out assorted world surf reports and maritime weather sites.

Windsurfer.com

www.windsurfer.com

The two main focuses of this American windsurfing portal are selling new and secondhand windsurfing equipment, and providing a searchable database to help you find and buy windsurfing vacations in North and Central America. It also provides virtual tours for the best-known destinations, with a clickable map to find hotels in suitable spots.

Walking and trekking

Note that in addition to the sites listed below, most of the companies listed in the "General Adventure Holidays" section on p.119 offer walking and trekking holidays.

Active Journeys

www.activejourneys.com
While this Canadian operator also arranges biking and canoeing trips, its speciality remains walking, with an unbeatable programme of well-priced hiking tours in all parts of the world (except the US). Its easy-to-search Website swiftly unveils a diverse range of trips, from comfortable inn-to-inn walks in Britain and Europe to high-altitude treks. Many are available both as self-guided strolls, which you can take more or less when you choose, and as scheduled, but only slightly more expensive, guided small-group expeditions. Email for full details, then download and mail the reservation form.

Headwater Holidays

www.headwater-holidays.co.uk
Family-run British firm that arranges a year-round programme of "soft adventure" walking tours in Europe and North Africa, concentrating largely on inn-to-inn hiking holidays in Mediterranean destinations. Some are purely scenic, others take in historical and archeological sites. Via its easy-to-use Website, it sells holidays to travellers from all parts of the globe, quoting prices with and without air or ferry fares. Specific dates are listed for each tour; email the onscreen form to check availability and make a provisional reservation, and someone will call you back.

The Ramblers' Association

www.ramblers.org.uk
As well as offering detailed news and advice on walking in the UK, including guides to long-distance footpaths and updates on legal issues, the Ramblers' Association Website links to the Association's sister company, Ramblers Holidays (at **www.ramblersholidays.co.uk**). This organizes walking holidays in Britain and many other destinations, from the Alps to the Himalayas, with accommodation usually in hotels, but does not offer online booking.

Sherpa Expeditions Online

www.sherpaexpeditions.com
UK company that offers trips for walkers of all abilities, from gentle self-guided hiking excursions in Europe and inn-to-inn walks in the Atlas Mountains of Morocco to guided donkey treks in the Fann Mountains of Tadjikistan or full-scale trekking in the Himalayas. Most trips are within Europe, and many within England itself, including coastal walks. The Website holds full details and itineraries, all clearly and neatly presented.

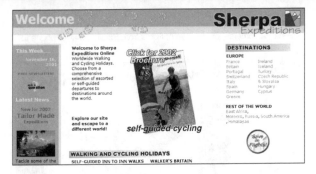

Self-guided trips can be arranged whenever you like; for guided tours, check availability by email or phone; payments can be accepted online.

Webwalking.com

www.webwalking.com/hiking.html

The home page of this American walking and hiking portal holds an extensive menu of articles, features and reviews of interest to hikers, including destination guides from about.com (see p.12) and lots of eye-catching top-ten lists and equipment bargains. Its greatest value, however, comes in its huge directory sections, with vast lists of tour operators and hiking organizations that either cover specific destinations or operate worldwide.

World Walks

www.worldwalks.com

British company that arranges both guided and self-guided walking tours in the UK and most of Europe, plus a more limited selection in New Zealand, Indonesia and the USA. Submit the online form to make your booking.

Water-based activities

Adrift White Water Rafting

www.adrift.co.uk

UK operator that runs well-priced white-water rafting trips in Turkey, Nepal,

Ethiopia, Uganda, Ecuador, Zimbabwe and Zambia. Its Website carries full details and itineraries, quoting prices either on a river-only basis – for international customers – or inclusive of flights from Britain. Email or phone to make a reservation.

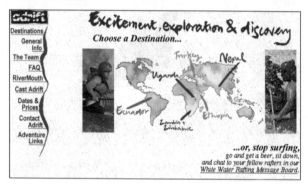

Blakes Boating Holidays

www.blakes.co.uk

Blakes began life in 1908 renting out wherries on Britain's Norfolk Broads; it now arranges boating holidays of all kinds throughout western Europe, and even as far afield as the St John's River in Florida. Vessels include yachts and cabin cruisers, but the most popular choice remains a barge (narrowboat) trip along the canals of England, France or Holland. Check it all out online, but reservations and payments are only accepted by phone.

British Waterways

www.british-waterways.org

A superbly informative site devoted to "the hidden world of Britain's inland waterways", which meticulously maps out the UK's canal network and traces its two-hundred-year history. You can search for tour and rental companies that operate on each individual segment, as well as attractions, museums and other facilities along the way. There's also a calendar of events and an online shop.

Ecosummer

www.ecosummer.com

The main speciality of this Canadian operator is providing crewed yachting trips in its home waters of British Columbia and Alaska, including wildlife expeditions in pursuit of whales and bears, but it also arranges kayaking and river-rafting vacations in South and Central America. Reserve via email or phone.

Far Flung Adventures

www.farflung.com

Specialist rafting operator with a programme of white-water trips throughout the Western US. You can join expeditions along the Colorado and the Rio Grande, but the real highlight has to be the musical jaunts near its home of Big Bend, Texas, on which participants are serenaded around the campfire by top-name country musicians such as Jerry Jeff Walker or Butch Hancock. You can check availability online but not make bookings, as it insists on customers speaking with staff first.

GORP Paddling

www.gorp.com/gorp/activity/paddle.htm

As ever, the North American GORP site (see p.121 and p.421) provides an invaluable resource on "paddling" – which covers canoeing, kayaking and rafting. As well as instructional articles, travel features, bulletin boards, links and equipment sales, it holds a database of vacation operators all over the world, searchable by both destination and specific activity, and mostly available for online booking.

The Moorings

www.moorings.com

Although based in Florida, the Moorings has set up its sailing vacations Website to accommodate customers from all over the world. Beginners can learn to sail in the Virgin Islands or join crewed charter excursions in North America, the Mediterranean, the Caribbean or the South Pacific. If you can demonstrate the necessary experience, you can also charter your own vessel. The easy "trip finder" facility shows what's available, but to get an online price estimate you have to submit all your personal details, and you can only book via email or phone.

Neilson Holidays

www.neilson.com

Thanks to its school at Brighton Marina, this British operator can teach you to sail in the English Channel, but its more enticing activities centre on flotilla and bareboat yacht-charter holidays in Greece and Turkey. Expert sailors can get cut-price trips by helping to get the fleet into position at the start or end of the season. Reservations by phone or email only.

Sunsail Holidays

www.sunsail.com

Based in the UK but offering separate Websites for American, British, German and French customers, Sunsail Holidays arranges crewed and "bareboat" yacht charters in the Mediterranean, Caribbean, Indian and Pacific, and also US coastal waters. Work through all its destinations, checking availability and receiving price quotes for specific dates, then secure a booking by submitting payment online.

Western River Expeditions

www.westernriver.com

Western River Expeditions, whose base is in Moab, Utah, launches rafting trips onto the rapids of mighty rivers such as the Salmon, Green and Colorado, with one enticing option being a four-day Grand Canyon run that sets out (by road) from Las Vegas. The Website's "trips navigator" makes it easy to check availability; as the simple key puts it, "Yes = Yes, No = No". However, you have to phone to make your booking.

Special requirements

Children's holidays and camps

See also the theme park sites reviewed on p.172.

ActionQuest Worldwide

www.actionquest.com

ActionQuest Worldwide offers summer live-aboards for teenagers, with three-week camps and courses for all levels in sailing, scuba diving, wake-boarding, water-skiing, windsurfing, and adventure sports. Kids come mostly from the US, but there are campers from South America and Europe, too, and programmes are available in the Caribbean, Galapagos Islands, Mediterranean, Tahiti and Australia. The site features lots of purple prose, with rave recommendations from past clients and idyllic photos. If you can afford it – you're looking at $3000 for a basic sailing/diving course in the British Virgin Islands to $4600 for Galapagos trips, with everything included – download an application form to book.

British Activity Holiday Association

www.baha.org.uk

The British Activity Holiday Association sets safety standards and minimum requirements for facilities and staff training in activity centres – including children's camps and family attractions – around the country. The site is simple and fast, allowing you to pull up a list of its members, with full contact details and Websites for more information.

Camp Beaumont

www.campbeaumont.com

One of the stalwarts in the children's holiday field, with seven residential and day camps in England, and one in Normandy, with lots of outdoor activities, creative endeavours and character-building for kids as young as three (day camps) and six (residential). Small groups are organized by age; in the camps where all age bands are catered for, children over 12 sleep in a separate area from the little ones. To reserve, fill in the online booking form (with space for up to four children) and wait to be invoiced for a deposit.

Camp Channel

www.campchannel.com

Searchable summer camp directory from the US, with hundreds of options including adventure camps, family camps and retreats, adults-only camps, specialist camps, camps for people with special needs, and some thirty camps outside North America. Browse the lists under each category and click for full details, including programmes, capacity, average prices and the like, following swift links to Websites where available, and the option to contact them direct for more details. You can also keep a tally of camps that interest you, in compact or expanded, printable format, and then compare them all at the end. Check the Camp Store, too, which has links to all sorts of useful outfitters for camping and outdoor gear.

Camp Down Under

www.campdownunder.com.au

More of a touring holiday for American teens than a summer camp. These three-week summer trips in Australia are just for 14–17 year olds, who travel around the country (by bus and plane) visiting Sydney, Ayers Rock, Alice Springs, Kakadu, Cairns and the national parks, snorkelling the Barrier Reef, camping in the outback, white-water rafting and making didgeridoos. Trips cost around \$US4400, including everything but transport to LA (children are met at LA airport, from where they fly to Sydney). You can read the itinerary and download it as a PDF file; to book, apply online for a registration form.

Camp Page

http://camppage.com

Comprehensive directory of North American summer camps (many of which accept kids from abroad). Either search by state, or decide if you're after a wilderness camp, boys' camp, girls' camp, or co-ed camp, then click on a map to choose a region of the US (there's a separate section for Canada). Up comes an alphabetical list, with brief reviews and contact details, together with links to the individual sites.

Cross Keys

www.xkeys.co.uk

Cross Keys runs day and residential camps in North London, Hampstead Garden Suburb and East Anglia. There are two kinds of day camps, held in the school holidays and at half-term: Cross Keys Activities, for the 4–12s, allow the kids to specialize in art, drama or sport, while Mini Minors, every Easter and summer, are for the 3–8s, and geared more towards free play. They both start from £95 per child for a week. Residential camps, held in East Anglia during the summer, are £300. These cater for 6–17 year olds, with clay pigeon shooting, cookery, woodwork, computers, fancy dress competitions and the like, plus lots of free time and day-trips. No online booking; you need to email or phone for a brochure, or download an application form.

Kids' Camps

www.kidscamps.com

Huge Internet directory of summer camps in North America, including day camps, residential camps, family camps, teen tours, sport camps, art or academic camps, special needs camps, leadership programmes, weight-loss camps – the lot. You can't browse the full list, but search by region or by keying in a few preferences. Up comes a list of the relevant camps, with logo, blurb, and contact details including Websites.

LondonExpatWel.com

www.londonexpatwel.com/KidsHolidayCamps.html
The Website for expat Americans has a selective list of recommended day and residential camps and adventure holiday companies in the UK, with reviews, Websites, and in some cases, parents' comments and ratings.

National Camp Association Inc.

www.summercamp.org
Really useful American site that will help you choose the best summer camp for your child, either in the US or abroad. First, it gives a rundown of the questions you need to ask yourself before sending your darlings off for a month or so; you can then go on to use its free advisory service. Simply key in your needs and you'll be sent a list of summer programmes that meet your requirements by email, post or fax. You will also receive information from each camp, including brochures and videos if you wish. The form is simple, but covers all the bases: you need to be as specific, and as flexible, as possible. You can also ask for an opinion on any camp that you might be considering.

PGL

www.pgl.co.uk

PGL is the UK market leader in kids' camps, offering a wide range of activity holidays in the UK and France for ages 6 to 18. The holidays – from ski trips to themed weeks such as "secret agent" and "cyber surf", all geared towards different age bands – are great: the site, unfortunately, is not. Designed, presumably, to appeal to the kids, for adults it's all but impossible to slog through the flashy, hyperactive graphics – even without the screaming colours, stripes and circles, it suffers serious Web flaws. The simplest of information, including holiday costs, dates and so on, simply shouldn't take dozens of clicks to access. You'd do better to request a brochure (even then you have to go through each section to request separate brochures on each type of holiday), which includes everything including booking form and parent guide.

Disabled travellers

Access-Able Travel Source

www.access-able.com

Amazingly useful information site, produced in the US, with links to travel resources – accessible hotels, tour operators, equipment rental outfits and so on – around the world. You can also see a list of operators – most of them in the US – that arrange trips for travellers with disabilities, and a searchable cruise section which reviews individual ships according to their accessibility. Also FAQs, trip reports, a monthly feature article highlighting a major destination, travel tips on a variety of subjects from travelling with oxygen to taking guide dogs on taxis, and a good range of disability and travel-related links.

Accessible Journeys

www.disabilitytravel.com

US operator, with offices around the world, offering a wide variety of touring holidays for slow walkers, wheelchair users and their companions. As well as fixed-base holidays in places such as Andalucia, Moscow, London and Devon, it leads trips around the national parks of the American West and as far afield as Nepal, South Africa and Kenya, where a two-week safari will set you back around $3000 (not including flight). There are also many cus-

tom-designed possibilities, from adventures in Morocco and the Philippines to boat trips down the Amazon. The travel shop links to online suppliers of medical supplies, wheelchair accessories and such like, and there's an intelligent set of links to a variety of travel sites. Unusually, the travel tips section comes up trumps, and you can subscribe to a monthly newsletter for more of the same.

All Go Here

www.allgohere.com

This UK-based site includes help for people using speech systems or who cannot see the screen clearly, and has two very useful features: the data-base of more than 2000 hotels (all in Britain), rated for accessibility and list-ed with contact details; and the directory of disability-friendly world airlines, complete with reviews covering carriage of wheelchairs, oxygen provision, boarding procedures and the like. Each has been vetted in person.

Justmobility

www.justmobility.co.uk

UK-based information service for anyone with mobility problems. The body of the site is made up of links to publications, associations and vehicle rental companies, and to travel providers, hotels and travel advisory servic-es in Britain.

Microtel Inns and Suites

www.microtelinn.com

Inexpensive American hotel chain that strives to be "the preferred chain for travelers with disabilities". You can take a 360° tour of a typical disabled access room, check each motel for facilities such as roll-in showers and hearing-impaired guestroom kits, and then finalize availability and rates before booking online.

Society for Accessible Travel and Hospitality

www.sath.org

Major lobbying organization, based in New York, whose aim is to create "a barrier-free environment (architectural and attitudinal) throughout all segments of the travel and tourism industry, in the United States and abroad". The site provides guides on how to travel with various disabilities or illnesses, with sample articles from SATH's quarterly travel magazine *Open World*, which includes trip reports, updates on accessible tours and cruises and news of regulations affecting disability. Plus travel tips and scores of useful links, organized by disability, destination, and theme.

Travelability

www.travelability.co.uk

UK-based operator and agent run by mobility-impaired travel specialists, offering accessible adventure holidays (trekking, tandem parachuting and diving, for example), city breaks, hotels and apartments. As well as the typical European destinations – Spain, France, Italy, the UK – you could also get to Cuba, Australia and New Zealand, Israel and Dubai, choose an adaptive skiing break in Colorado, or rent a villa in Orlando. There's a section on cruises, with lots of sensible advice, and a number of good disability-related links. Although there's no online booking, you can email an availability form. An occasional ezine, *Accessible Globe*, brings news stories and feedback from fellow travellers.

Travelin Talk

www.travelintalk.net

Password-protected directory of thousands of travellers with disabilities, most of them in the US, willing to offer advice and assistance – from researching hotels to recommending equipment repair shops – to other members who are visiting or passing through their home towns. Membership costs $19.95, for which, as well as a monthly e-newsletter filled with news, access information and resources, you get discounts of up to 50 percent at hotel chains and on equipment and travel publications.

Transitions Abroad

www.transitionsabroad.com/listings/travel/disability/index.shtml
This bi-monthly alternative tourism magazine has a very good list of resources for travellers with disabilities, from educational programmes to home exchanges and diving trips. Each entry gets a brief review and contact details, including URLs, but there are no links.

Family travel

For children's holidays and camps, see p.159.

British Youth Hostel Association

www.yha.org.uk/sctn_fami/intro.html
The British Youth Hostel Association offers a good deal with its "family-friendly" hostels. With kids older than three you can breeze past the dorms to your private bunk-bedded room, complete with washbasin, and for families travelling with babies there are cots and highchairs for hire. You're given your own keys and all-day access to the hostel, and can choose self-catering, special menus, or both. Most hostels have a games room, and organize activities from wildlife-watching to treasure hunts. For details of YHA's family activity packages, look at **www.yha.org.uk/sctn_acti /intro.html**; options range from pony-riding, dog-walking or dry-stone walling to stargazing, art classes and day-trips to France, with active sports for the older kids. A year's YHA membership costs £25 (£12.50 for one-parent families), with children under 18 free. You can join online with a secure server.

Butlins

www.butlins.co.uk
The classic British holiday camps (sorry, resorts) may not have quite shaken off their enduring image – all hyperactive Redcoats and hearty bootcamp activities – but they certainly know their stuff when it comes to family holidays. The resorts, in Skegness, Minehead and Bognor, have splash pools, crazy golf, funfairs, bowling alleys, tennis courts, cinemas –

even Burger King franchises – with special features for different age groups. The live entertainment isn't to be sniffed at, either, with big pop acts – Steps, Five and the like – doing the rounds. The site details a wide variety of last-minute and seasonal deals. To book online, key in the date you want, and how many people in your party, and it'll come up with a list of options.

Centerparcs

www.centerparcs.com

Centerparcs' Website has information about its woodland "villages" in the UK (Longleat, Elveden and Sherwood) and northern Europe, but is good for little else. The online booking facility, though secure, is laborious and eccentric: currently you can't book for any stay longer than a week, nor can you book more than one villa, nor the speciality breaks detailed on the site. You can, however, read about the villas, the "Aquadomes" with their "sub-tropical swimming paradises", the sports facilities, and the spas. Everything at Centerparcs is family-oriented, with play areas, adventure playgrounds, swimming classes, children's menus and the like; for a fee you can use the kindergarten (for kids older than three) and babysitting services. The only way to find out how much things cost is to set off on the online booking trail: key in your details to access a list of what's available on your chosen dates, with the price per villa per night. Prices vary widely according to season and villa type.

Esprit Ski/Esprit Alpine Sun

www.ski-esprit.co.uk and www.sun-esprit.co.uk

UK-based family-holiday specialist offering alpine holidays all year round. Both sites are clear, useful and easy to navigate, with details of all resorts, facilities and accommodation, and the holidays are great, with tons of child-care facilities. Sun-Esprit has "Alpies" clubs for kids (summer tobogganing, biking, rafting and circus skills, for example), along with nurseries, babysitting, and children-only meals. Prices include Eurotunnel crossing, chalet accommodation with breakfast, evening meals with wine, and a couple of nights free babysitting. Meanwhile, the sophisticated Ski-Esprit site details a number of resorts including Vail and Whistler, with a great range of activities, including ski classes for children as young as three ("spritelets"), and clubs for "Super Sprites", who receive instruction in skiing, snowboarding, raquetting and snowblading. Call direct to make a reservation and leave a deposit.

part two: themes and activities

Keycamp

www.keycamp.co.uk

Upmarket camping holidays in palatial four-bedroom "super tents" throughout Europe. Clicking onto the name of the site brings up a photo and all the salient details: click again for blow-by-blow accounts, with photos and ground plans, plus information about the local area. All sites have restaurants, sports facilities, games and TV rooms, and pools; the children's clubs are free, and there's an emphasis on hearty outdoor activities. Many throw in use of canoes, windsurfers and barbecues for free, and offer special offers and short break deals. A few of the French camps even offer soccer courses run by UEFA-qualified coaches. The campsite search allows you to key in your requirements to find the best matches, but there's no online booking. You can, however, email to check availability and make a provisional reservation.

Kidshols.com

www.kidshols.com

Commercial UK database of tour operators offering child-friendly holidays (with kids activities, crèches, childcare services and so on) in Europe, Florida and the Caribbean. It's a good starting point for anyone planning a family break – including a camping holiday or skiing trip – though bear in mind that operators pay to be included. In each section – Kids Deluxe, Beaches and Sun, Florida, and The Great Outdoors – you can search by destination, operator or childcare provisions to pull up a list of operators. Click each name for more details; some are linked to their own page on the site.

Thomson Family Adventures

www.familyadventures.com

A great idea: a family-owned US operator offering creative adventure holidays for families. The range of destinations is inspiring, with holidays in Alaska, Australia, the Galapagos, Costa Rica, Borneo, Africa, Turkey and Nepal, and the site covers each trip in detail, with itineraries, photos and journals from past clients, and intelligent travel tips. Everything is well-planned, from the activities – rafting, safaris, rainforest tours and snorkelling, among others – and the accommodation (family-owned guesthouses, villas, safari lodges and campsites) to the "pen pal" visits to community projects and schools where kids can hook up with local children. This company genuinely likes kids: check out the teen scrapbook and the

touching "pen pal" photos. Prices are, not surprisingly, high. Submit an online form to make a reservation; you'll be contacted direct to book.

ukparks.com

www.ukparks.com

The British Holiday and Home Park Association (BHHPA) Website is a searchable database of more than 2500 holiday and residential parks in the UK. You can search by name, town, county or type of park – and there's a separate search tool for special deals. Each park has their own page on the site, with full details of facilities, and, in many cases, photographs. The Virtual Brochure link allows you to add whichever park you are interested in as you go; you'll then be sent an email with full information on the parks contained, with hot links back to the relevant pages on the site. Special conservation award icons denote parks that David Bellamy has pinpointed as having positive eco-policies, as well as being in particularly lovely countryside – you can search for the award-winners direct.

Single parents

One Parent Families

www.oneparentfamilies.org.uk

Crisp and helpful site from the UK's National Council for One Parent Families. Click on the Helpdesk icon, then again on One Parent Families, to order a free booklet listing organizations – including some which can offer financial aid – that help lone parents to arrange holidays. Also information on house swaps, group holidays, insurance and the like.

Opfholiday

members.aol.com/opfholiday

Though the site design is pretty poor, the concept – group holidays (camping, self-catering and in hotels) for single parents and their kids, geared around the school holidays – is so good that it's well worth a look. Options include France (including Disneyland Paris), Spain, Florida (more theme parks), Australia, Singapore and Malaysia, and it even offers a world tour. Head straight for the calendar to see what's on offer when, then check the index for costs and "vacancies" for availability. It's a charitable organization, and offers good deals. US travellers can join groups in Florida and on French camping/caravan holidays.

Family holiday advice

For a rundown of the family programmes offered by the major cruise lines, check **www.cruiseinformationservice.co.uk** (see p.192). And for information on health precautions for children travelling, go to **www.tripprep.com** (see p.91).

CyberParent

www.cyberparent.com/trips

Forthright US family site with a subsection on travel. Short, focused articles emphasize the need to make family travel relaxing and spontaneous, keeping in mind the needs of both children *and* parents. The content is perceptive, covering subjects such as cruises, flying with children, and the particular problems faced by single parents. And it throws in a couple of suggestions for lifesaving travel games for good measure.

Family.com

http://family.go.com/travel

Disney-owned site with a large section devoted to family-friendly holidays throughout the US and the Caribbean. Lots of Disney ads, of course, with information about and links to the parks – which is useful in itself – but it's gratifyingly broad-focused, with good articles, destination awards, trip reports, sensible travel tips, pre-departure checklists and a wide range of links to accommodation, attractions, budget holidays and last-minute deals.

Family Travel

www.family-travel.co.uk

This stylish, independent UK site – no adverts! – deals with everything you need to know when planning a holiday with kids, whatever their age and whatever your budget. Content ranges from the fairly obvious to what, in this field, is relatively hard-hitting (pointing out, for example, that so-called "child-friendly" hotels can be a real nightmare for adults). With news on deals, offers and events around the world, along with scores of articles on immunization, independent travel, Round the world trips and the like, it also features a monthly special report. These are incredibly detailed, with readers' reports, links to operators, and so on; when their month's up they're stored in a database (there are plans to charge a fee to access this, but for now it's free). There's also a moderated noticeboard, filled with recommendations.

Family Travel Forum

www.familytravelforum.com

"Have kids, still travel!", chirrups the logo of this excellent US subscription-based site. Joining online gets you loads of discounts plus the FTF newsletter (trip reports; book, toy and travel gear reviews; resort ratings and so on). Non-members can read a selection of stories, access special deals and contact tried and tested family-friendly agents around the world. There's a good index of fifty or so family-travel links and open forums.

GoNOMAD

www.gonomad.com/family/familyTravel.html

If theme parks and French campsites don't appeal, turn to the excellent GoNOMAD site, which details alternative holidays across the spectrum. The ambitious, eco-friendly options recommended for families include swimming with dolphins and visiting the orang-utans in Borneo. See p.121 for more on GoNOMAD.

Tiny Travelers

www.tinytravelers.net

Brought to you by the same people as Family Travel Forum (see above), this slick US site specializes in the issues raised when travelling with kids younger than four. Beautifully easy to navigate, it's one to bookmark, with a range of articles subdivided into clear sections. "Trips" is devoted mostly to reviews of American and Caribbean resorts, with some general info on flights, cruising, home swaps and so on; "Tips" tackles common problems (car journeys, flights, tantrums and the like); "Health" has advice on things like preventing motion sickness and ear pain, while "Gear" not only features gear reviews and articles but also links to the Family On Board shop, which sells laptop games, strollers and air-turbulence protection vests. You can read more gear reviews on the message board ("Tales").

Theme parks

Note that the major American theme parks are reviewed in our USA section; see p.417.

Theme Park Insider

www.themeparkinsider.com
Incredibly handy site reviewing the world's major theme parks. (All but 6 of the 31 featured parks – Alton Towers, Blackpool Pleasure Beach, Disneyland Paris, Tivoli Gardens, Tokyo Disneyland and Universal Studios Japan – are American.) Each ride, restaurant and hotel is ranked and reviewed individually by site users, with comments listed on the right-hand side of the screen. There are separate sections reviewing rides for toddlers and for kids, with tips for thrill-seeking parents wanting to maximize their own fun. You need to register to log your votes and reviews, and to post a comment on the message board. It's available in a WAP form, so you can even carry it into the parks with you.

Tim Melago's Directory of Amusement Park and Rollercoaster Links

http://users.sgi.net/~rollocst/amuse.html
Hundreds of links to theme parks and water parks around the world, hooking up to official sites – including those for parks in South Korea and Egypt – and, even better, the vast range of unofficial fan sites.

Gay and lesbian travellers

For a gay guide to Australia, see p.236. And for the same writer's take on gay Thailand, see p.381.

Damron

www.damron.com

The publishers of the leading gay guides to the USA (and, to a lesser extent, Europe), have a useful, if not freely accessible, Website. You need to subscribe (around $30 per year) to access the online guides: doing so allows you to search a database of destinations, with thousands of listings for bars, clubs, restaurants, stores, helplines, Websites, community centres, magazines, and sex clubs around the world – including places not yet in the printed guides. Non-subscribers can read the online calendar, detailing circuit parties, Pride events, AIDS fundraisers, etc (all in the US), and also the vacation finder, a set of links to US operators offering men-only, women-only, and mixed holidays, in all sorts of categories. Ordering the guides online gets you a 20 percent discount.

Gay Travel

www.gaytravel.co.uk

Wide-reaching directory of worldwide travel services, all of which claim to be either gay-owned or gay-friendly. Sometimes the "gay" tag is tenuous: clicking the link for "car hire", for example, or "flights", brings up the usual big-name Websites, and many of the hotels listed mention nothing whatso-ever about gay credentials, but if you stay specific, choosing "lesbian accommodation", "gay travel weeks" and so on, you'll do OK. Categories include accommodation in the UK, Europe, USA, Canada and worldwide; travel guides; UK travel services; and worldwide tour operators. Plus links to Amazon for gay travel guides.

IGLTA

http://iglta.org

The IGLTA (International Gay and Lesbian Travel Association), based in Florida but with offices around the world, provides a directory of gay-owned or gay-friendly travel suppliers, who pay a fee to be included. The site is as much geared towards travel professionals as tourists, who should head straight for the Members page to search by city, country or business type for travel agents, tour operators, hotels, car rental companies, resorts, air-lines, and a host of other companies.

Out and About

www.outandabout.com

Online version of the gay and lesbian travel newsletter produced in New

York City. The site, which looks great, and is a dream to navigate, features the contents page of the current issue, plus a sample article – you can then subscribe online, or order from a list of back issues, organized by destination. In addition, although you can read extracts from its 65 most popular worldwide guides, you need to pay to see them in their entirety. Other tools include a calendar of gay tours, with links to operators, and ratings for airlines, car rental companies, hotels and cruise lines (all of which are mostly American, naturally). Plus good gay links, with an online travel store. One to bookmark.

Outlet

www.outlet.com

Easy-to-use site for gay-owned holiday lets in New York and London, with lots of good locations. Information comes up clear and fast, with photos, per-night rates and full descriptions. Email first to check availability, then send on credit card details to secure a booking (payment is made upon arrival).

Planet Out

www.planetout.com

Huge gay lifestyle portal, produced in San Francisco, with an excellent travel section. It's beautifully designed, and very user friendly, with travellers' tales, articles on anything from gay ski vacations to lesbian rodeos, and useful tour- and event-finders. Much of the site is devoted to the worldwide destination guides; search by region, or use pull-down menus to fast-track to the most popular US or European cities or resorts. For each place you get reviews of accommodation, restaurants, nightlife, shops, sightseeing and so on, and each category allows you to filter listings further, choosing to view only "very gay" hotels, say, or "renowned cuisine". You can also read local news for every place covered.

Respect Holidays

www.respect-holidays.co.uk

British travel company specializing in quality package holidays to popular gay resorts in Spain and Greece, including Gran Canaria, Ibiza, Mykonos and Sitges. The site features an edited version of its hard copy brochure, with lots of detail on its rather good accommodation (from basic to very luxurious), plus destination reports and travel tips, and sections devoted to last-minute and flight-only deals. You can also hook up with other travellers by registering as a member and using the forum. Bookings, however, need to be made direct.

Sensations Holidays

www.sensationsholidays.com
Established UK holiday operator offering gay and lesbian packages in Europe, Florida, Mexico, Thailand, South Africa and Australia. You can choose a holiday either by destination or theme – European sun (which offers by far the biggest choice), city breaks, alternative holidays, world-wide, and events – clicking to read about accommodation and prices (which are quoted per person and include flights, though you can also book hotels only). Call or email to make a booking, or to order a hard copy brochure.

Toto Tours

www.tototours.com
Men-only US operator, based in Chicago, that "takes Friends of Dorothy over the rainbow to experience the excitement of adventure travel". Click the red slippers to enter, then read details of its affordable, appealing holidays. It's nothing too macho, with soft to moderate activities including rafting, horse riding, trekking and sailing in great locations like the Galapagos,

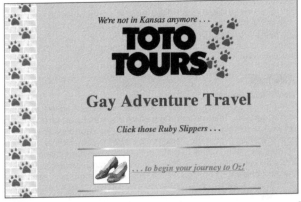

Costa Rica, Egypt, Iceland, Tanzania and Nepal. Each holiday is covered in detail on the site, with pictures of accommodation and full itineraries. To reserve, click on the scampering Toto and download a form, which you then need to send with a deposit.

Walking Women

www.walkingwomen.com/lesbians.htm

UK company (see p.185) organizing women-only walking holidays in the Lake District, Madeira, Crete, Lesbos, and Italy. Though all women are welcome, it does encourage lesbian ramblers, and a couple of breaks per year – as yet only in the UK – are exclusively gay.

Senior travellers

Elderhostel

www.elderhostel.org

This US-based, not-for-profit company offers an extraordinary range of adventure/educational holidays in more than 100 countries – open to people over 55 only. Programmes range from short stints exploring the culture of the Mississippi to jungle treks in Borneo and shipboard art classes on the canals of France. Frustratingly, though, you have to instigate a search by destination or keyword only, and nowhere can you browse a full list. You can, however, check availability and book online – if you manage to decipher the byzantine security code system. You'll need patience to get the best out of this site, but the programmes themselves are well worth it.

ElderTreks

www.eldertreks.com

Toronto-based company running small-group walking and adventure trips for the over-50s. There are exciting destinations, from Easter Island through Sarawak to Iceland, and you can choose your own pace depending on your stamina and interests. Although most trips have you sleeping in guesthouses, you could choose to camp, or bunk up in a tribal hut, and some trips involve canoe trips, bike rides or (moderate) climbs. However, even the most challenging holidays are not meant to be a strain, and each one employs local guides, cooks and porters for support. There's no online

booking, but you can browse a list of tours, with activity ratings, and submit an email form to check availability. Prices include everything but the flight; solo travellers share with others of the same sex.

Saga

www.saga.co.uk/travel
The leader in travel for the over-50s in the UK – also offering insurance and financial services – has a frustratingly slow-moving, image-heavy site divided into cruises, flights, touring, holidays, language courses, and "travel services" including hotels and car rental. You can search by destination (and there are many, from the Rocky Mountains to Sri Lanka) to read information on resorts, hotels and tours, but there's no online booking. Sadly, until the design is sorted out, you'd do best to use this site to order a brochure, as the holidays themselves are great.

Senior Women's Travel

www.poshnosh.com
Upbeat US site "for the 50+ woman with a passion for travel", offering pricey European city tours – usually including food tastings and a cooking class, literary tours, and shopping trips – for older women who don't want to go it alone (there are no single supplements and no sharing required). It

also has grandmother/granddaughter packages, and can design independent itineraries. No online booking, but you can read about the trips and email to make a reservation. Plus book reviews, trip reports and travel news, and links to the ezine *Senior-Spirit*, "dedicated to reflecting the millennium senior woman".

Student travellers

See also p.80 for hostels. For interrail and train passes see p.54, and for bus passes see p.63. And if you've come out of college with a yen to do good ... turn to the volunteering sites reviewed on p.216.

American Institute for Foreign Study

www.aifs.com

AIFS organizes educational trips, cultural exchange and study abroad programmes for American students, while foreign students can apply to live with an American family and attend high school for a year, or offer their services as an au pair while studying at an American college. The Institute also oversees summer camp programmes (the site links through to **www.campamerica.co.uk**) and employment opportunities in major US resorts (**www.resortamerica.co.uk**). You can download application forms from the site.

Backpack Europe on a Budget

www.backpackeurope.com/studentstuff.html

Bursting with useful links, Kaaryn Hendrickson's excellent budget travel site, though written mainly with Americans in mind, is perfect for any young person embarking on the "grand tour". The section devoted to students, featuring study/work abroad programmes and volunteer agencies, however, is particularly useful to travellers from the US.

BUNAC (British Universities North America Club)

www.BUNAC.org

Information site for BUNAC, the work/travel programme specialist. Best known for its US summer camps, BUNAC also offers schemes in places such as China, Argentina and Ghana, many of which are teaching programmes, and not all of which are exclusive to students. The site gives

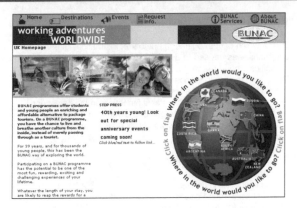

details of the possibilities, along with downloadable application forms. You'll need to become a member in order to apply.

Campus Travel

www.usitcampus.com

Campus Travel's detailed site has pretty much everything that a student traveller could desire. With information on city tours, sunshine breaks and recommended budget accommodation around the world, the main plus is the speedy farefinder – airfares are discounted for students and anyone under 26 – but you can also read useful stuff on student/youth discounts, exchange programmes and outdoor activities. Flights, Busabout passes (see p.63) and car hire (with Holiday Autos; see p.50) are bookable online; for anything else, you'll need to call direct.

Council Travel

www.counciltravel.com

This lively Website, run by North American student-travel specialists Council Travel, concentrates largely on selling airfares, discount lodging, and rail passes to bright young things heading for Europe. Its Trip-On Europe section is devoted to all-inclusive packages to a dozen of the continent's hippest cities. Simply load up your shopping basket with whatever trips take your fancy; you can even buy RTW itineraries.

International Student Travel Confederation

www.istc.org

The ISTC, which brings together a number of international student travel organizations, was devised to develop travel, study, and work exchange opportunities around the world. If you're a student, or a teacher, or under 26, you're eligible for one of its ISIC identity cards, which give discounts on travel, hotels, theatres, restaurants, shops and attractions in more than fifty countries. The site has information on the cards, and where to get them (if you want to buy online you'll be directed to your local student travel office), as well as details on work and study exchanges.

STA

www.statravelgroup.com

Worldwide specialists in under-26 and student fares, STA has a huge Website that leads you to different pages depending on which country you are in. Wherever you're looking from, you'll read about STA's deals on tickets, tours, insurance and accommodation, with offers from a number of operators and pop-up windows advertising last-minute flights. Most services are available online, including ordering an ISIC card (see **www.istc.org**) or procuring certain visas. To book a flight, however, you may do better to call your local office – the convoluted availability checking system is a nightmare. Still, with ideas for gap year and graduate travel, competitions and articles, there's a lot to read, and it's worth looking at in conjunction with the other student specialists.

Study Abroad

www.studyabroad.com

Comprehensive listings of study programmes in more than 100 countries. You can search first by subject or destination or from categories including summer schools, intern/volunteer, TEFL courses and so on; course descriptions come with email addresses so you can contact the organization direct. Elsewhere on the site you're linked to organizations offering student fares and discount cards, and there's a good set of links emphasizing budget and responsible travel. Before logging off, check Express! for special offers, news, and links to organizations that can give financial aid, and browse the message boards (one for each destination covered).

Weddings and honeymoons

www.cruiseinformationservice.co.uk (see p.192) provides a fact sheet for honeymooners and anyone planning to get hitched at sea.

About.com

http://honeymoons.about.com/travel/honeymoons

More from the monster US directory about.com, which consistently comes up with quality links and strong content. The honeymoon channel can hook you up to sites arranged into categories including planning, destinations, all-inclusives, "weddingmoons" (the destination wedding package where absolutely everything is included), beaches, budget honeymoons, cruises and train journeys, as well as lingerie, "naked escapes" and sex advice. Clicking each section might get you straight to a list of reviewed links, or to one of the specially written about.com articles, which are themselves peppered with even more links.

Absolute Asia

www.absoluteasia.com

Luxurious custom-designed tours in Asia and the South Pacific offered by a classy New York company. The site has an entire section devoted to honeymoons: look under "Special Tours" for a choice of ten. Fiji, Indonesia, Vietnam, Bora Bora, the Philippines, New Zealand, Australia – all of them sound fabulous, but few can match the "Maharaja's Honeymoon". Among other treats, this throws in a traditional Indian wedding ceremony, a horse-and-carriage ride to the Taj Mahal, Ayurvedic treatments and massage, elephant rides, and three nights at a top beach resort in Goa, all for $5000 for the two of you (excluding flights). These romantic plans are only suggestions: you have to call direct to benefit from the pampering personal service.

Destination and Specialty Wedding Page

www-personal.umich.edu/~kzaruba/wedding.html

The site is tired looking (as Karen, the host, readily and unashamedly admits) and maybe too chummy for some tastes, but overall it's a gem: devoted to unconventional, themed and destination weddings, it's well written and informed, with hundreds of indispensable links, many of which apply to honeymoons too.

Hawaii Weddings

www.hawaiiweddings.com

Unconventional wedding packages in out-of-the-way Hawaiian beauty spots performed by the non-denominational Reverend Howie and his flamboyant parrots. The emphasis here is on spirituality: no orders to "obey", no parting through death, three blasts on the conch shell and much

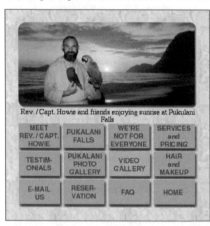

Rev. / Capt. Howie and friends enjoying sunrise at Pukulani Falls

MEET REV. / CAPT. HOWIE	PUKALANI FALLS	WE'RE NOT FOR EVERYONE	SERVICES and PRICING
TESTIM-ONIALS	PUKALANI PHOTO GALLERY	VIDEO GALLERY	HAIR and MAKEUP
E-MAIL US	RESER-VATION	FAQ	HOME

Hawaiian chanting ... though all the usual things, like photo-graphs, flower gar-lands, cakes and videos are taken seriously, and you can even get a drop-dead gorgeous make-up job (check the entertaining before and after photos). A handful of video clips allow you to see the Reverend in action, performing weddings by a waterfall, on a boat, and under the ocean.

Honey Luna.com

www.HoneyLuna.com

American wedding gift registry service that allows you to demand romantic honeymoon activities (dinner cruises, scuba and sailing trips, spa treatments, candlelit dinners), and chunks of your honeymoon (contributions to airfare, lodgings, tours), instead of the usual pillowcases and toasters. Look at the site's sample registries, and then contact HoneyLuna direct to have one designed for you. The gift payments are eventually presented as a lump sum, and none of the honeymoon excursions have to be pre-paid, so if you change your mind about that hot air balloon trip you can effectively pocket the cash and use it for whatever you like. But, of course, that would be missing the point.

The Knot

www.theknot.com

The Knot – "Weddings, Gowns, Gifts" – is a slick US information site and directory for anyone about to tie just that. Go straight to the honeymoon channel for links to the major cruise companies and all-inclusive resorts, and articles on the Caribbean, Europe, Hawaii and the Pacific, Mexico, and North America. Destination weddings are also dealt with, with real-life stories, question-and-answer lists, and practical "dos and don'ts". "Daydream Central" deals with planning, budget honeymoons, packing checklists and so on, while the glorious "Travel Smarts", in addition to dull old airline sites and hotel groups, features a flurry of frothy articles on beauty products, packable "romance enhancers", and star sign destinations for you and your sweetie.

Sandals Resorts

www.sandals.com

The big name in all-inclusive Caribbean resorts, with ten luxurious complexes, "created exclusively for couples in love", in Jamaica, Antigua, St Lucia and the Bahamas. It was Sandals that patented the "weddingmoon" (which "speaks of love forever true"), and its sun-and-sand weddings – including champagne reception, flowers, cake, photos, candlelit dinner and 'Just Married' T-shirts – are now among the most popular in the world. No online booking: North American travellers can search by their zip code for their nearest agent, while sweethearts from the UK are directed to **www.sandals.co.uk**.

Women travellers

See p.104 for **www.christinecolumbus.com**, where you can shop online for all manner of ladylike travel gizmos.

Adventures in Good Company

www.goodadventure.com

Eco-friendly tour company that arranges outdoor and wilderness trips for women of all ages. Something over half its programme takes place in the US, especially around its homebase of Minnesota, but it also offers vacations in Asia, Europe and elsewhere; a few require a high standard of physical fitness. Discounts are available for single mothers and certain last-minute bookings. Call or email to check availability, then reserve by fax, phone or email.

GoNOMAD

www.gonomad.com/womens/womensTravel.html
The alternative US-based travel site comes up trumps with its directory of "top women's travel picks" – female-friendly tours, accommodation and destinations – organized by world region. These aren't always exclusive to women – coffee tours in Costa Rica, batik-making classes in Indonesia, 4WD in Australia – but they're chosen carefully, with detailed, balanced reviews and relevant links. Plus handy articles on women's safety, adventure travel, tour operators and the like, with hotlinks.

HERmail

www.hermail.net
International directory of more than 3000 women travellers who are happy to advise others coming to or passing through their home town. There is no list to browse, you simply add your details and request a contact in your chosen destination. Email addresses are kept private, and all initial communication is channelled through the site. You'll also find travel articles, a good links page (check under "Classifieds", too), and some genuinely useful travel tips (loved the one about lavender oil and Chinese toilets) – but we could do without the site's disarming practice of using the third-person feminine at every possible opportunity ("Sign Her Up!").

Journeywoman

www.journeywoman.com
"Gal-friendly" quarterly travel ezine, produced in Canada and providing information for female travellers the world over. With a lively message board, plenty of practical tips – from how to buy tickets for Egyptian trains to where to dine solo in Calcutta – and entertaining anecdotes from intrepid adventurers, it's a really good read. There are also links to dozens of companies that specialize in women-only travel, though these tend to be pricey, and you can sign up for an e-newsletter, which pulls together highlights from the site. One caveat: like HERmail, the incessant use of the third-person feminine –"Try our search engine. You'll love her!" – comes across as a little bizarre.

Walking Women

www.walkingwomen.com

UK company organizing women's small-group walking holidays – in the Lake District, Madeira, Crete, Lesbos, and Italy – for all levels of fitness. It also offers trips that combine walking with photography, creative writing, natural history or quiet contemplation, women-only Murder Mystery Weekends, and a couple of lesbian breaks – all of them reasonably priced. The site provides full information about each of the holidays, with photos, and there's an email booking form.

Wild Rose

www.wildroseholidays.co.uk

When it comes to all-women holidays in the UK, walking holidays rule the roost. This UK operator offers women-only breaks that entail walking (for all levels), plus T'ai Chi, creative writing, visits to ancient sites, garden tours or watersports. Most are based in the sunny south of England, though there are some trips to Mallorca and Gozo. You can read details of each on the site, but brochure requests and bookings have to be made direct.

Wild Women Adventures

www.wildwomenadv.com

Don't be misled: the holidays offered by this women-owned US tour operator are not exactly wild, and they're not even all that adventurous – here, "wild" means doing your own thing; adventure means "travelling the world

Wild Women ADVENTURES

Worldwide Luxury Travel for Small Groups of Women

Wild Women Adventures is currently restructuring, so our itineraries are temporarily unavailable. We will be back soon, bigger and better than ever, so please <u>sign up</u> to become a **Webette**™ and we will keep you posted on all of the latest, exciting developments!

Restore! ----------Relax! ----------Rejuvenate! ----------Intrepid Fun Lovers Hit the Road

Getaways Galore&More! · FAQ · Horoscope · E.Mail Us!

and taking the risk to be yourself". These are luxury tours ("We consider it roughing it when there is no room service") to off-the-beaten-track destinations in Europe, Mexico, Egypt, Thailand and Tanzania, in groups no bigger than twelve, and they aren't cheap – though international airfare is included in the price. The tone is sassier than in some of the other US sites, with quizzes, tongue-in-cheek features and book reviews.

Women Traveling Together

www.women-traveling.com

American travel club offering women-only trips – from weekends in New England and New Orleans to longer stays in safe-bet destinations in the Caribbean, Europe and South America. Membership costs $35 per year and the vacations aren't that cheap (especially if you want a room to yourself), but accommodation is generally top-notch, and most tours and many meals are included in the price. Members also earn "travel dollars" which are redeemable against future trips. Each vacation is detailed on the site, allowing you to browse options before joining online. You can also search for a travel partner, and, unusually, it also links to other companies offering women's tours.

Women's Travel Club

www.womenstravelclub.com

North America's largest travel club for women – membership, which costs $35 a year, gives you access to some thirty holidays around the world. Each trip involves around 25 women, and there are no single supplements. Non-members can read travel tips, book reviews, links and trip reports on the site; you then join by fax or phone to receive a monthly newsletter, access to password-protected areas of the site (with full trip itineraries and photos), and, of course, book the holidays.

Women Welcome Women World Wide

www.womenwelcomewomen.org.uk

"Circle the world with friendship", says the "5W" logo. It's a simple concept: a directory of some 3000 women around the world, from as far afield as Kazakhstan and Argentina, who are willing to invite other members to stay in their homes. It's not so much a hospitality exchange as a cultural one: many members are not wealthy enough to travel far, and are simply interested in meeting women from other cultures. You can download an application form and send it; there is no formal subscription fee, but it asks that members donate at least £20.

Specialist holidays

General specialist holidays

A number of operators offer country-specific special interest holidays. We've reviewed the best of these, where relevant, in our individual destination sections, which start on p.227.

ACE Study Tours

www.study-tours.org

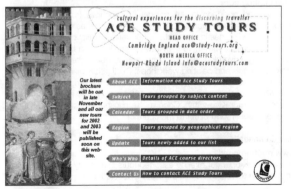

cultural experiences for the discerning traveller

ACE STUDY TOURS

HEAD OFFICE
Cambridge England ace@study-tours.org

NORTH AMERICA OFFICE
Newport Rhode Island info@acestudytours.com

Our latest brochure will be out in late November and all our new tours for 2002 and 2003 will be published soon on this website.

About ACE	Information on Ace Study Tours
Subject	Tours grouped by subject content
Calendar	Tours grouped in date order
Region	Tours grouped by geographical region
Update	Tours newly added to our list
Who's Who	Details of ACE course directors
Contact Us	How to contact ACE Study Tours

ACE (Association for Cultural Exchange) arranges very good study tours around the world, and, as an added bonus, donates part of its profits to the countries it covers. Specializing in art, architecture and history, it also covers archeology, music, natural history, houses and gardens, theatre and literature; each tour is led by expert scholars. Originally a British company (prices are quoted in sterling, and most flights, included in the cost, are from London), ACE has an American office, and the site gives details on how to book (by phone, fax or email) wherever you're travelling from. Search by subject, world region or date to read details, itineraries and costs: prices are not unreasonable considering the quality of tuition, standard of accommodation, and range of trips.

Holiday Bank

www.holidaybank.com/holcosp.asp

British one-stop holiday shop with a section devoted to specialist holidays. Here you'll find links to companies offering anything from painting in the Himalayas and rag-rolling in Umbria to golfing in Hawaii or yoga in Greece. They're arranged by destination; select from the pull-down menu to view even more choices according to activity. Companies with Websites are covered in most detail, but there are separate – very long – lists for those that you can contact by email.

Infohub

www.infohub.com

Sophisticated, good-looking US site detailing specialist holidays around the world, with pull-down menus that allow you to specify as many criteria as you like, including destination, activity, budget and travel dates. Its activity selector is superb, with more than 150 options including fashion trips, camel riding, Egyptology and tearoom tours as well as the more usual cookery schools and painting workshops. Destination-wise, it claims to have more choices than any other site – life's too short to try and prove otherwise, especially when you pull up 160 tours for Italy alone, 230 for China and 21 for Kyrgyzstan. Once you've chosen, click the link to submit an email request form direct to the operator.

Martin Randall

www.martinrandall.com

Upmarket UK operator offering escorted tours in a variety of countries, from Austria to Yemen via Lebanon and Sweden, focusing on art, architec-

ture, archeology and classical music. This is serious stuff – a Le Corbusier tour promises an "exploration of the origins of the look of the modern world", while "Heaven, Hell and Botticelli" explores the artist's work in an eschatalogical context – and prices aren't low, but you're paying for more than just a holiday on these trips … You can read details of most tours on the searchable site, but for the full list you'll need to send for a brochure. To book, download a form and send with a deposit after calling to check availability.

Shaw Guides

www.shawguides.com

It looks like a nightmare, but roll up your sleeves and get stuck in: this phenomenal directory covers every study- and hobby-based vacation imaginable. Whatever you want – arts and crafts courses, cooking schools, creative writing workshops, cultural tours, language vacations, photography, movie-making, sport – you'll find something here. Browse through lists organized by subject, then search by month, destination or keyword; reviews come with all the relevant information (type of programme, group sizes, other activities offered, costs, location and so on), plus contact details with Website where applicable.

Travel Editions

www.traveleditions.co.uk

Specialist UK operator offering short themed breaks to a range of (mostly European) destinations, at all prices. How about a weekend in Turin or Milan with tickets to a Serie A football match for £300, three nights seeing the opera in Verona for £400, or ringing in the New Year at the historic

Chateau Montebello in Niagara Falls for £900? Select by date, country or price range, or else browse the full list before faxing, calling or reserving a place online.

Voyages Jules Verne

www.vjv.co.uk

Enticing site run by upmarket UK travel operator, darling of the Sunday supplements, with a long list of options pointing you towards specialist themed trips on every continent. Steam trains, painting holidays, walking the world, exploration cruises, music and opera, art and history, scenery and landscape ... there's lots to choose from here, from a week's voyage to the court of Kubla Khan to three days admiring the King of Belgium's greenhouses. Most trips are bookable online, though for the more complex itineraries you'll need to send an email.

Cruises

Alaska's Marine Highway

www.dot.state.ak.us/external/amhs/home.html

The legendary Alaska Marine Highway System (AMHS) operates perhaps the most spectacular programme of scheduled sea voyages in the world, with its service along the "Inside Passage" complemented by trips across the Gulf of Alaska, into Prince William Sound, and out to the Aleutian Islands. The Website enables you to sketch out your itinerary between specified ports, and then submit a very detailed online reservation request. It does not, however, take payment details, and bookings remain unconfirmed until you pay by phone.

Celebrity Cruises

www.celebritycruises.com

Celebrity Cruises is a major player in the world cruise market – "Celebrity" is just a name, you don't get to share a cabin with your favourite soap star – sailing in the waters of the Caribbean, Mediterranean, South America, Alaska and Hawaii. Once you've checked out the cruise descriptions onscreen, booking via the Website is extremely easy; successive pull-down menus guide you into the relevant region, show all available dates, then offer different classes of accommodation; if you like the price, email your full details and you're done.

All the cruise lines included in these listings maintain high-quality Websites. The following other operators also run Websites, but be warned that on the whole they're nothing like as useful; most simply enable users to request printed brochures.

Bergen Line www.bergenline.com
Carnival Cruise Lines www.carnival.com
Crystal Cruises www.crystalcruises.com
Disney Cruise Line www.disneycruise.com
Fred Olsen Cruise Lines www.fredolsen.co.uk
Holland America www.hollandamerica.com
Orient Lines www.orientlines.com
P&O Cruises www.pocruises.com
Princess Cruises www.princesscruises.com
Swan Hellenic www.swanhellenic.com
Thomson Cruises www.thomson-holidays.com
Windjammer Barefoot Cruises www.windjammer.com

Cruise2.com

www.cruise2.com
Non-profit, ad-free Website that holds an unbelievable amount of cruise-related information. Search its vast database by any permutation of destination,

date, price, cabin type, cruise line or specific ship, to find exactly who's doing what; read objective reviews by journalists and comments from passengers; or use the free "Cabin Exchange" to connect with cruise companies offering specific bargains. Above all, Cruise2 is a wide-ranging portal, with links to an endless array of cruising sites arranged as responses to questions such as "Where can I find Discount Prices for Cruises to a particular Destination?" and "Where can I find Websites that have Auctions on Cruises?"

Cruise Information Service

www.cruiseinformationservice.co.uk
Information resource set up by the UK's Passenger Shipping Association, providing helpful onscreen "fact sheets" for would-be cruise passengers, and covering topics like family cruising, river cruising, and which companies offer which destinations, with contact details and active links to the relevant cruise lines.

The Cruise Marketplace

www.thecruisemarketplace.com
Californian discount travel agency that advertises itself as reducing cruise fares by up to eighty percent, with a promise to match or beat any written quote. Its Website is extremely simple; just search by cruise line and destination, and it offers you a rough price, with the invitation to call if you're interested. This isn't the place to find any useful information, so you'll have to do your research elsewhere, but once you know what you want there's no harm in doing a bit of comparison shopping here.

CruiseOpinion

www.cruiseopinion.com
Though it's basically a promotional tool for a Michigan-based travel agency that specializes in selling cruise vacations – call the phone number if you want to make an actual reservation – the CruiseOpinion Website is a valuable tool for anyone researching a cruise trip, holding five thousand lengthy, personal customer reviews of cruises taken with all the major lines. If you have a specific ship in mind, there's almost certainly a warts-and-all report here written by someone who's already done it.

The Cruise People

www.cruisepeople.co.uk
Shipping agency, with offices in London and Toronto, which takes the whole

concept of cruising considerably further than you may ever have imagined. In addition to conventional big-name cruise trips, it sells an intoxicating array of long-distance ocean voyages. Separate sections are devoted to commercial freighters and scientific research vessels that carry paying passengers, and to sailings between Europe and North America (not all of them transatlantic – some head via Suez to California). With no online booking, you have to email or call to make an enquiry; in fact there are few onscreen gimmicks here, and the Website consists mostly of endless lists ... but what fabulous lists!

Cunard

www.cunardline.com
The only cruise line that can confidently claim to have been "Advancing Civilization since 1840", Cunard continues to offer luxury cruises anywhere on the planet, or even all the way round it. Once you've specified your country of origin, you can check out full schedules (which include themed trips devoted to jazz, blues, and classical music) and ship plans. There's no online booking, but you can email a detailed request. And be sure to book early; that way you can reduce the cost of a 98-day jaunt on the *QE2* from £244,410 to a mere £195,528.

Geek Cruises

www.geekcruises.com
Geek Cruises are exactly what the name suggests: luxury cruises for computer nerds, devoted to such enticing themes as "Linux Lunacy", "PERL Whirl", and "JAVA Jam", and incorporating expert lectures and tuition. The "Convincing the Boss" section says to call it a conference, not a holiday; naturally, the ship is wired up for Internet access. Most but not all cruises are in the Caribbean, and two-thirds of the clients are said to be single females. Not everyone on board is a geek, as Geek Cruises typically lease around half the spaces on a 1500-passenger Holland America voyage. The Website offers useful links for all ports of call, and you can book and pay online by completing an endless form.

Norwegian Cruise Line

www.ncl.com (North America) and www.uk.ncl.com (UK)
Norwegian Cruise Line, which operates throughout the seven seas, is a pioneer of "freestyle cruising", a radical concept in which passengers are not required to dress up for formal dinners if they don't want to. Its sepa-

rate Websites for passengers of different nationalities are all but identical, but North American customers can email a booking request and get called back, while Europeans have to make the call themselves. Both sites offer stern-mounted Webcams for landlubbers pining for the fjords, and also a few online "special offers" that don't mention what discount, if any, they represent.

Royal Caribbean International

www.rccl.com

As the Website swiftly reveals, Royal Caribbean's activities are not restricted to the Caribbean alone; it also cruises to or around Hawaii, Alaska, Australia, Mexico and the Middle East. Assemble a "vacation folder" of any options that interest you, or simply go straight to the "Quick Reserve" page for pull-down menus of every destination and cruise. Although it is possible to reserve online, you are strongly encouraged to use a travel agent, so that you can talk the whole thing through first.

Seaview

www.seaview.co.uk

UK-based information site that covers both cruises and ferry travel, with an emphasis mainly but not exclusively on British and European waters. It offers news, features, destination guides and bulletin boards (in the "Funnel Vision" section), and most importantly of all a "Cruise Finder" facility that enables users to look for a trip by any combination of destination, price, date and company. You have to enter your name and email address to see the results, at which point you're told who to email or call to make a reservation.

Small Ship Cruises

www.smallshipcruises.com

Proclaiming itself "The biggest website in the world on small ships ...", this site sets out to cover small-boat trips of every kind, from barge rentals to diving operators. It's not exactly sophisticated (though the odd butterfly wings its way across the screen), and its reviews and listings are entirely uncritical, presumably taken from the operators' own press releases. However, there's a hell of a lot of them, with active links for most companies, and it also carries up-to-the-minute news on the latest routes and special offers. You can also book through Small Ships itself, though whatever you're enquiring about you have to complete much the same lengthy email form.

Star Clippers

www.star-clippers.com
Sailing cruises in the Mediterranean, Caribbean, and Far East on four- or five-masted clipper ships – or "mega-yachts", as the proud owner calls them. One, the *Royal Clipper*, is said to be the largest true sailing ship in the world; passengers caught up in the romance of it all can even help to haul the ropes. Though it's a ravishing memory-gobbler of a Website, however, packed with enticing images, you can't book online; you can only call, or contact a travel agent.

Eco-tourism

See p.78 for an accommodation reservation company dealing only in eco-lodges; p.216 for volunteer programmes and conservation schemes, and p.220 for wildlife and nature tours. Eco-tour operators that specialize in individual countries are reviewed with the relevant country in our "Destinations" section, which begins on p.227; for an account of Wales' Centre for Alternative Technology, the largest eco-centre in Europe, see **www.cat.org.uk** on p.409.

Ecotourism Explorer

www.ecotourism.org/travelchoice
For anyone keen to embark upon a bona-fide eco-holiday this colourful, rather laborious site – produced by the US-based International Ecotourism Society – is bursting with information and guidelines. Online factsheets deal with subjects such as how to choose an operator, while the searchable worldwide directories of eco-lodges and eco-tour operators give short reviews plus contact addresses and links to Websites. For conceptual debates, check out articles like "Find a New Viewpoint" and "Investigate Your Alternatives".

Ecotravel Center

www.ecotour.org
Produced in collaboration with Conservation International, a field-based

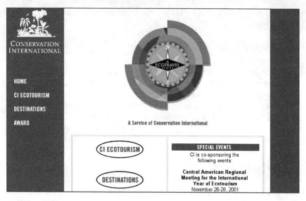

A Service of Conservation International

CI ECOTOURISM

DESTINATIONS

SPECIAL EVENTS
CI is co-sponsoring the
following events:

Central American Regional
Meeting for the International
Year of Ecotourism
November 26-28, 2001

organization with headquarters in Washington DC, the Ecotravel Center provides a number of online services. On the home page you're directed to a noticeboard detailing local (in the US) eco-travel lectures and events, plus "Resources", which includes an equipment provider search, publication reviews, and links to a wealth of green and pleasant companies. Once you're off the home page up comes another menu: "Destinations" focuses on the exotic "biodiversity hotspots" where CI concentrates its efforts, with all the information you need to plan a trip.

Field Studies Council

www.field-studies-council.org

This British educational charity runs low-impact, culturally aware environmental study holidays across the globe. Scores of choices in Britain range from the seriously specialist – "a weekend on mosses and liverworts" – to more widely appealing visions like "exploring the seashore". Some combine eco-tourism with painting, photography or arts and crafts. If you're yearning for something more exotic, however – discovering the oryx and oases of Oman, say, or meandering through the Galapagos – and have upwards of £2000 to spare, follow links to the world map. More than half of its overseas trips are in southern Europe. Read details on the site, then book using a downloadable form.

Green Travel

www.green-travel.com

Hundreds of links to green companies around the world, from research stations to responsible scuba diving operators, horseriding schools to agri-tourism associations. The site itself hasn't been updated since 2000, and some sections are better organized than others, but most of the links are still active.

Planeta.com

www.planeta.com

Though its main focus is eco-travel in Latin America, this colossal information clearing house, with hundreds of articles, official reports and links to environmental groups and tourism providers, is an indispensable read for anyone interested in eco-tourism itself. The home page details upcoming events and conferences and links to e-newsletters, forums and eco-journals across the Net. The entire site is peppered with hotlinks, sending you down intriguing alleyways at every turn – if you want to keep track of things, use the Google-powered search engine and then register for the update service to read each new article as it comes online.

Responsibletravel.com

www.responsibletravel.com

Brainchild of Body Shop magnate Anita Roddick, this searchable information site reviews and rates eco-tours and accommodation around the world. There is also a growing list of member-operators, which includes high-profile companies Sunvil, British Airways, and Abercrombie and Kent, as well as a number of grass-roots organizations around the globe. Each has to fulfil certain guidelines laid down by the site, agree to its policies being published online, and take on board any feedback posted by travellers. You can browse a full list of members, and if you sign up for a newsletter, you'll be alerted to its special deals and promotions. All this plus information on health and safety and human rights, trip reports, travellers' tips, green links, and competitions.

Tourism Concern

www.tourismconcern.org.uk

UK-based charity that lobbies governments, the industry and travellers to raise awareness of the tourism industry's impact on the planet. Quite apart from the invaluable links – covering, among other themes, eco-tourism, ethical tourism and the Third World – the resources section is worth a look: a low-tech bibliography of serious tomes, reports, research papers and magazines, some of which can be ordered online. You can also read sample articles from Tourism Concern's quarterly magazine *In Focus*, which highlights a different topic each issue – tour operators, travel guides, indigenous people and so on.

Food, drink and cookery

For a site detailing organic accommodation around the world, see p.79.

Absolute Asia

www.absoluteasia.com

A fabulous site from the upmarket New York-based tour operator, as luxurious as the gourmet tour packages it organizes throughout Asia and the South Pacific. There's a huge choice, from family-run cooking classes in remote villages to formal feasts in Japan, each one emphasizing local cuisine and culture and with good attention to all the details. Each itinerary features accommodation at top-notch hotels and resorts, sightseeing, meals, market tours, tastings, cooking classes and demonstrations. Costs, though high (from $3000 for thirteen days in Borneo or the Philippines or eight days in Korea, to $8770 for three weeks in India and $9655 for one week in Japan) include absolutely everything.

Arblaster and Clarke

www.arblasterandclarke.com

Very attractive, informative site managed by the UK specialists in wine holidays. Led by experts, all tours feature visits to top producers, chateaux and cellars, with lots of tasting along the way. "Gourmet tours", which place as much emphasis on food as drink, include a week in a seventeenth-century palazzo, a week truffle-hunting in the Loire, and a luxury cooking holiday by the beach in Bali. Champagne weekends start at around £250; those who've got more to spend should check out the long-haul trips to the US, Australia, South Africa and South America. Also walking holidays in France and Italy, picnicking and wine tasting as you go, and week-long wine cruises around remote Italian islands. Arrangements are flexible; you can book your flight separately, or opt to add on a variety of extras. No online booking; call to reserve your place.

Bike Riders Tours

www.bikeriderstours.com

Boston-based company offering small, upmarket culinary-cycling holidays for all levels of fitness (most itineraries don't exceed 35 miles a day). Tours, of Burgundy, Provence, Tuscany, Umbria and Sicily take in open-air markets, cookery demonstrations, hands-on classes and feast preparations, plus plenty of tastings. At around $2900 a go, they're not cheap, but everything is top quality, and accommodation, in inns, palaces and elegant hotels, is invariably stunning. To order online, submit the reservation form with credit card details.

Epiculinary

www.epiculinary.com

North American culinary tour company whose opening page welcomes you to "distinctive cooking journeys". It specializes in trips to France (Burgundy, Bordeaux, and Provence), Italy (Tuscany, Umbria, Venice, Sabina, the Amalfi Coast), Spain (Catalonia, Andalucia, and San Sebastian) and North America (California and the Southwest), with one trip to Mexico. All trips include classes, meals, market trips, vineyard tours and the like. Tours are arranged on the site by country, with full details of itinerary, cost, dates and everything that's included. Secure online booking.

Flavours

www.flavours-foodiehols.co.uk

UK operator offering upmarket small-group holidays in lovely old villas in Lazio; £1000 covers three hours' worth of cookery classes a day, all food including restaurant meals and wine, luxury accommodation, and visits to local food producers and places of interest. Also four-night winter cookery holidays for £500. Flights to Italy are not included, though the company can help with your travel plans. No online reservations; instead it provides a downloadable booking form.

Happy Cow's Global Guide

www.happycow.net

Aesthetically awful online guide to vegetarian restaurants and health food stores around the world. As you'd expect in an undertaking this large, the listings aren't comprehensive (three for the whole of Africa), but when it comes to Europe and North America (which includes Canada, and, rather more oddly, the Caribbean, Costa Rica, El Salvador, Guatemala, Mexico and Panama) it's not at all bad (57 in London), and each country/region offers up a couple of relevant links. There's also space for users to post their own reviews. If by chance you should land on the Happy Cow humour page (cartoons of hapless bovines) or the wisdom page (earnest chats with gurus), click your back arrow asap.

Kitty Morse

www.kittymorse.com

Every summer, cookbook author Kitty Morse organizes a two-week deluxe culinary tour of Morocco – taking in Casablanca, El Jadida, Azemmour, Essaouira, Fez, Marrakech, Meknes and Rabat, plus Ouarzazate and Tinehrir. The tour emphasizes local cuisine and culture, and includes two days of classes with Morse at her gorgeous old house south of Casablanca. You also get trips to meet local artists, culinary demonstrations, excursions to mosques, ruins and monuments, shopping trips in medinas and souks, and lots of nice dinners in restaurants, working farms and family homes. It's not cheap: $4595 includes the round-trip airfare from New York to Casablanca. Contact details are given (to a Californian travel agent) for bookings.

The Mexican Home Cooking School

http://mexicanhomecooking.com

Week-long holidays, comprising B&B and traditional cookery classes, in a

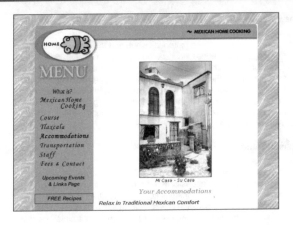

~ MEXICAN HOME COOKING

Mi Casa - Su Casa

Your Accommodations

Relax in Traditional Mexican Comfort

HOME

MENU

What is?
Mexican Home Cooking

Course
Tlaxcala
Accommodations
Transportation
Staff
Fees & Contact

Upcoming Events
& Links Page

FREE Recipes

lovely old house in the countryside near the colonial city of Tlaxcala, central Mexico. Groups are limited to one to four students (with no single supplements), and there are special vegetarian classes. The $1000 fee includes lodging, three meals a day, and five classes. Non-students pay $350. In keeping with the mom-and-pop style of the venture, there is no online ordering, and no credit card payments; all fees are received by bank-to-bank wire transfers. The site also features sample recipes, which sound very tasty indeed.

Santa Fe School of Cooking

www.santafeschoolofcooking.com
The Santa Fe School of Cooking runs regular day and weekend classes ($45–90) in traditional and contemporary Southwestern and Mexican cuisine, either hands-on or demonstration, often with market tours as well. It also leads four-day tours through northern New Mexico, which, along with gourmet meals, a Native American feast and winery tours, feature Native American dance performances and cookery lessons. You can print out a registration form and mail or fax it with payment information; you'll need to pay a $400 deposit.

Shaw Guides

http://cookforfun.shawguides.com

Get past the ugly design and cramped layout, and the Shaw Guides site is a gem. Specializing in educational and hobby-based holidays, here it offers a directory of more than seven hundred companies that run cooking classes and tours around the world. Tuscany and Provence dominate, but you can also try your skills in Papua New Guinea, Iran and Bhutan. Search by month, or cuisine, or where in the world you want to go; you're then linked to individual reviews with all the relevant informaton plus contact details with Website where appropriate.

Taste Of Culture

www.tasteofculture.com

The minimal, information-heavy site of the Taste Of Culture culinary arts centre in Tokyo gives full details of its year-round programme, which includes practical classes on themes from "a taste of summertime romance" to "decoding package labels", tasting sessions and market tours. If you're keen – and not short of a bob or two – you might prefer the more intense workshops (the four-day Peek in the Pantry, and the more advanced six-day Japanese Kitchen Workshop, which includes preparation of a multi-course feast). The centre also arranges courses for professionals – or ambitious amateurs – which combine a week of kitchen/class time with a week of independent travel. No online ordering; payment (in full) goes direct to Tokyo, and has to be in American dollars.

VegDining.com

www.vegdining.com

Slick, user-friendly guide to vegetarian restaurants around the world, with about 1000 listings and more than 750 short reviews. It's a US site, so clicking on North America (which includes Canada, the Dominican Republic, Mexico, Panama and Puerto Rico) brings most joy, and though it looks far more professional than Happy Cow (see p.200), some countries bring up fewer listings (just 31 in London), so it's as well to look at both. Send an email for details of how to buy the VegDining Card, which offers discounts at vegetarian restaurants around the world, and write a restaurant review to win serious prizes (membership of veggie organizations, holidays etc). The links page is handy, too.

History, art and archeology

If you're interested in **volunteering for a dig**, see the international archeological organizations reviewed on p.216. See also the specialist operators www.study-tours.org and www.martinrandall.co.uk reviewed on p.188 for their art history and archeology holidays. For tours in individual countries, see reviews of sites for that country.

Andante Travels

www.andantetravels.co.uk
Andante can take you to the world's archeology hotspots – southern Europe, Latin America, Syria and Jordan, North Africa, Turkey, England and Ireland – on tours led by lecturers, travel writers and active archeologists. Prices vary, but as an example you're looking at £2000 for twelve days exploring the extraordinary Roman ruins of Leptis Magna in Libya, or £2750 for a fortnight following the Ruta Maya in Mexico. Three days in prehistoric Wessex, with walks around Stonehenge and Avebury, will set you back around £275. Costs include full-board accommodation, admission fees, guides and tips, and on foreign tours include flights from the UK (which you can opt to forego). The site has all the details you need to plan a trip, though you should call to check availability.

British Museum Traveller

www.britishmuseumtraveller.co.uk
The British Museum in London organizes curator-led study tours of many of the world's most remote and mysterious places, including Sudan, Armenia, the Silk Route, Easter Island, Madagascar, Myanamar and Ethiopia. Just the names of the trips are enough to stir the imagination – "In Search of El Dorado", say, or "The Road to Timbuktu" – but you'll need a lot of money to realize your dreams (the knowledge that all profits fund museum programmes and research sweetens the pill a bit). Travellers from overseas can join tours in London or find their own way to the destination and pay land costs only.

Footprints

www.footprints-scotland.co.uk
Lively three-day tours of ancient Scotland, either on the east coast, via

part two: themes and activities

Aberdeen and Inverness (departing from Edinburgh), or around Argyll and the southwestern Highlands (from Glasgow). Tours, which take no more than six people, explore stone circles, Celtic brochs and crannogs, and even early Christian castles, emphasizing the pattern of human settlement and domestic life. They each leave twice a week and cost £360 including all travel and two nights' accommodation – overseas travellers can pay by cheque in any currency. There are plans to install online booking, but for now you need to email an availability form to reserve a place.

Holts Tours

www.battletours.co.uk
Established operator offering historical breaks and walking tours of battle sites: whether you're interested in the Hundred Years' War, the Knight Hospitallers, Napoleonic campaigns or the Western Front, you'll find a trip to suit you here. Prices vary from around £300 for two days seeing the sights in Lincoln to £2500 for ten days exploring Anglo-Zulu war sites in South Africa. The site, which you can search by battle, war, historical period or month, has full details of all the options, but no online booking. Send an email, quoting the code of the holiday you're interested in.

Plantaganet Tours

www.plantagenettours.com
Historical tours of Europe, each focusing on different figures – Eleanor of Aquitaine, Christian IV, the Medicis, and even – stretching the "historical" somewhat – King Arthur. Although they're led by a learned Dane, Peter Gravgaard, who now lives in England, prices are quoted in dollars and may seem rather high to British travellers. The quality of the research, however, and the scope of the tours, are undeniably impressive.

Stephen Ambrose Tours

www.stephenambrosetours.com
Despite charges of plagiarism, Stephen Ambrose remains one of America's key historians, and his company, managed by his son, is an admirable venture. Ambrose Sr doesn't lead the tours, but he does design the itineraries, and personally recommends the guide, and his presence is very strong on the site. The trips, naturally, reflect his areas of expertise: a Civil War tour, which starts in New Orleans and takes a week to work its way up the Mississippi via Natchez and Vicksburg into Tennessee; an outdoorsy jaunt following the pioneer footsteps of Lewis and Clark (including a canoe trip

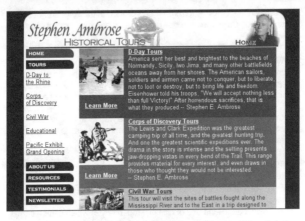

down the Missouri); and a D-Day fortnight. It's not cheap – prices start at $1250 for the Civil War tour. Links to Amazon mean that you can order Ambrose's books online.

Language holidays

All the schools below offer courses for all levels, and each one welcomes students from around the world.

AmeriSpan

www.amerispan.com

Highly rated educational travel company with a variety of immersion, volunteer and Spanish-language programmes – most of them homestays – at forty language schools throughout the Hispanic world (plus a couple of Portuguese schools in Brazil). The site couldn't be more user friendly: click a country, select a school and read no-holds-barred reviews (note that the quoted costs don't include the $100 registration fee). If you're not sure where to start, the "Choosing" search lets you specify all sorts of preferences, including safety, political stability and creature comforts, while the site recommends the best programmes for seniors, families, students or professionals. It's possible to register online, though the server is not yet secure, so you might prefer to download a form and mail it direct.

Center For Study Abroad

www.centerforstudyabroad.com
Washington-based company offering flexible, reasonably priced language programmes in Austria, France, Germany and Italy, Costa Rica, Mexico and Spain, Japan, China, Russia and Vietnam. Most are summer schools – from one to nine weeks – but you can sometimes choose to stay on for another semester or even a year. Students live with local families or in guesthouses, or are free to make their own arrangements. To apply, which costs $95, you'll need to print out the booking form.

Language Studies Abroad

www.languagestudiesabroad.com
Whether you want to learn French in Canada, Cantonese in China or Portuguese in Brazil, there are lots of countries, schools and languages to choose from here. Hundreds of classes, too, many of which can be combined with lessons in music, sports, cultural studies, cooking and even fashion history, and which range in length from one week to one year. Browse a full list or use the search, which lets you choose the size of city you wish to study in, the language, the price range and the ideal climate. Most accommodation is homestay. There's an online application form, but you'll need to phone with your credit card details. Prices vary widely, but the application fee is always $100.

Languages Abroad

www.languagesabroad.com
This Toronto-based company has a classy site detailing probably the widest selection of languages available, with all the usual destinations in western Europe and Latin America, plus places like Jordan, Morocco and Yemen, Croatia, Estonia and Ukraine. Courses last between two weeks and nine months, and accommodation is in self-catering apartments, hotels, guesthouses or with host families. The registration fee is $100. There's lots to read about each destination, school and course, and of all the sites, this is the only one geared up for secure online reservations. We could do without the occasional patronizing tone in some of the country overviews, though, and the omission of any political insight in others.

New Age, religious and spiritual

For Ayurvedic and healing holidays, see Health Breaks and Spas on p.137.

The Christian Travelers Guides

www.christian-travelers-guides.com/agents/agents.html
Contact addresses for Christian travel agents and pilgrimage operators, provided by the Christian Travelers Website. Check the travel guides page for titles of particular interest to Christians, Catholics and Jews.

Confraternity of St James

www.csj.org.uk
Based in London, the Confraternity of St James is a non-profit, non-denominational group of people who have completed the pilgrimage to the shrine of St James in Santiago de Compostela, northern Spain. Organizing conferences, lectures and "practical pilgrim days", where you can meet up with experienced pilgrims, it also runs this useful, unadorned site. Head straight for the FAQs, which cover everything, linking to relevant pages on the site and to tour operators, pilgrim stories and pilgrim associations across the Web. There's also an English-language bibliography and a secure online bookshop selling CSJ guides – and even a list of Internet cafes that you'll come across along the trail. The American pilgrims' association has a garish site at **www.geocities.com/friends_usa_santiago**, with basic information, recommended reading, and a forum.

Godserver.com

www.godserver.com
Search engine for more than 45,000 alternative health, spiritual and religious Websites. Click on "retreats" on the index page to access the top travel sites, then click again on "search engine" (*not* "search"); then scroll down to "travel" and you'll pull up another list of spiritual holidays (it claims to have 700 or so travel sites, though some of them – the directory of Native American Studies, for example – are pushing it a bit).

Heritage Tours

www.heritagetoursonline.com/jewish_heritage.html
Upmarket US operator offering cultural and adventure tours of Morocco,

South Africa, Turkey and Spain, with an emphasis on Jewish heritage. The Moroccan itineraries, in particular, are strong on the country's Jewish history and the tradition of Muslim-Jewish co-existence. Clients eat kosher meals prepared under rabbinical authority in the major cities, and fish and vegetarian meals in other places. Kosher picnics and Shabbat meals in a private home can also be arranged. No online booking; contact the company direct for more details.

Huzur Vadisi

www.huzurvadisi.com

Peaceful retreat in a mountain valley in southwest Turkey. Guests stay in traditional tents, or yurts, with beds, electricity and wooden floors (on hot nights the tip of the roof is left open, so you can stargaze from your bed), and spend their days practising yoga and swimming in the natural stone swimming pool. A full-board "relaxation week" costs just £285 per person, sharing a twin yurt (not including flight to Dalaman). It also hosts a number of courses on such things as Middle Eastern dance, yoga and T'ai Chi, for £345. The Website has lots of tempting photos of whitewashed courtyards and leafy vistas, and includes dates of courses and all costs. You'll have to make contact direct (or via Huzur Vadisi's agent in Wales) to make a booking, however, and to receive full details of the courses.

Infothai.com

www.infothai.com/itm

Information site for the International Training Institute of Thai Massage in Chiang Mai. This is one of the most highly regarded Thai massage schools, offering English-language courses for all levels, from five to ten days. Study includes yoga and meditation and the giving and receiving of supervised Thai massage. The course fee is US$50 for each five days.

International Sivananda Yoga Vedanta Centre

www.sivananda.org

Kindly faced gurus and sage quotations on the subject of bliss and inner peace dot this huge, very impressive site – lots of content, lots of links, lots of humour. Eighty or so ashrams offer retreats and yoga holidays year-round, all of them offering two yoga classes, meditation sessions and vegetarian meals per day. Costs vary, depending on whether you want to stay in a beachfront room in Nassau ($79) or in a tent in Kerala (Rs 250), but at each one guests are encouraged to participate in karma yoga (or "selfless service" – volunteering and offering donations). Click "Our Locations" on the "Om page" (it's pronounced ohhm ...) for information; and if you want to be emailed with updates, sign up for the guru grams.

Iona Community

www.iona.org.uk

Founded in 1938, the Iona Community, an ecumenical Christian fellowship marooned on a tiny island off the west coast of Scotland, works to explore inclusive approaches to worship and spirituality. The community welcomes up to 100 guests a week, along with pilgrims, to stay either in a restored medieval abbey (bunk-bedded rooms for between two and five people), a conference centre (dorms for four, six or ten), or at an adventure camp in stone-built cottages on the moors. At each centre, meals, prayer, activities, chores and social occasions are shared. Programmes include physical labour and reflections on mortality and healing; from mid-November to mid-December the abbey hosts a few individual guests simply to share meals and worship.

Kalani

www.kalani.com

Part cultural centre, part fabulously luxurious "wellness resort", Kalani Honua, on Hawaii's Big Island, offers a range of activities including yoga, lomilomi massage, watsu (water shiatsu), and Hawaiian healing. Women can commune with the goddess Pele, while men can enjoy the Pacific Men's gathering or embrace their gay spirit at the Hawaii Adventure for Naturist Gays. Nightly rates range from $20 for tent space to $240 for a gorgeous tree house with private bath.

OmPlace

www.omplace.com

Large, well-organized US directory and information site for all things alternative and spiritual. Click on "Travel" to access a searchable database – organized by destination – with links to retreats, workshops, holiday rentals and hotels, eco-tours, vegetarian vacations, adventure travel and the like. Whether you want to take a vegan tour of the rainforests of Costa Rica, stay in a Transylvanian monastery, swim with the dolphins or discover the warrior within, you can find someone to help you here.

Peng Travel & Peng France

www.pengtravel.co.uk

Anyone of the belief that "naturism is a way of life in harmony with nature, expressed by communal nudity with the aim of furthering the respect of oneself, of others and that of the environment" will want to check this site.

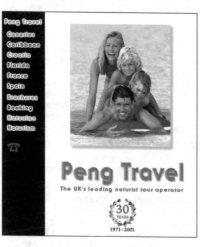

Britain's largest naturist tour operator – and the only one that is fully licensed and bonded – Peng offers naked holidays throughout the south of France, Croatia, Spain, Lanzarote, Florida and the Caribbean. You are invited to order a brochure, but it will set you back £2; in any case, the site, all happy blonde families frolicking on sandy beaches, comes up with the information you need. There's a downloadable booking form, which you can print and send off by fax.

The Retreat Company

www.retreat-co.co.uk

The Retreat Company produces a tri-annual directory of holidays, getaways and courses that promote spiritual health and wellbeing. This online version, divided into categories – Ayurveda, family, meditation, creative, and so on – lists organizations and operators (most of them, but by no means all, in the UK), with contact details and links. You can also search by destination. Bear in mind that the companies featured elect to be included on the site, and that there appears to be little vetting involved: if you want to know more, click "Focus On" to read personal reviews (always positive) of a featured retreat, venue or workshop, or call the Retreat Company direct.

Sedona Vortex Connections

www.sedonavortex.com

The small town of Sedona, in the heart of red-rock country in Arizona, has been big business for New Agers since it was found to be "the heart chakra of the planet" by psychic Page Bryant in 1981. Nowadays, people flock here to experience the five vortices, points at which, so they say, psychic and electromagnetic energies can be channelled for personal and global harmony. Michael Hamilton offers vortex tours and crystal gatherings, plus trips to Hawaii to connect with the dolphins, and jaunts to Mexico to find your inner wisdom. See **www.sedonaarizona.com/New-Age.htm** for other New Age businesses in the area.

Skyros

www.skyros.com

Best known for its two holistic holiday centres – Skyros and Atsitsa – on the eponymous Greek island, Skyros also has a winter holiday home on the Thai island of Ko Samet. Between them, they offer some 250 courses, many of them taught by big names in their field, and each one – be it yoga, writing or clowning, windsurfing, art or singing – with an emphasis on self-development. Each course runs for one week; you can take one (or, at Atsitsa, three) in the first week, choosing either to take the same one (or three), or continue with something different in the second. The Thai centre has a few special courses on fruit carving, Thai massage and the like. The message board – where you can ask questions of old Skyros hands, arrange taxi-shares and the like – is a great touch, and there's secure online booking.

Soul of India

www.soulofindia.com

Very good UK operator, run by ex-Church of England minister Kenneth Wilson, offering escorted and self-guided cultural and spiritual tours of the subcontinent. Itineraries follow the footsteps of spiritual leaders, cover themes such as Ayurveda and yoga, or are simply arranged according to religion – Hindu, Sikh, Buddhist, Jain or Christian. For an independent itinerary – which gets you car and driver, local English-speaking guides, and all hotels and trips booked in advance – you're looking at paying anything from £1465 (seventeen days following the footsteps of Gandhi) to £2170 (a fortnight from northern India into Tibet), including flights from UK. Enthusiastic without being gushing, the site gives you all the details you need, plus a handful of travel articles. To book you need to print out a form and send it with a deposit.

Painting

See also **www.industours.co.uk** (p.303) for painting tours in India, **www.filoxenia.co.uk** (p.293) for holidays in Greece and **www.skyros.com** (p.211) for holidays in Greece and Thailand.

Abruzzi Mountain Art Workshop

www.artworkshopitaly.com

Week-long drawing, painting and sculpture workshops – taught by American tutors – in a peaceful medieval village in the Abruzzi mountains, just two hours' drive from Rome. The site, all lush photos of old stone buildings and dappled golden light, certainly makes it look tempting, and each page is dotted with happy testimonials, but you'll need a lot of cash. Workshops cost $1250, including tuition and materials, unlimited studio time, accommodation in simple local apartments and a home-cooked alfresco lunch every day, but no airfare. You need Adobe Acrobat to download an application form, or you can contact the organizers direct in the US or Italy.

Art in Provence

www.artinprovence.com

American-French operation offering plein-air workshops for all abilities in that most painterly of French destinations, Provence. These are luxury trips, with accommodation in a gorgeous chateau (with its own pool), and all sorts of extra-curricular activities such as cocktail parties and trips to galleries and concerts. You're looking at $2650 for ten days, based on two sharing a room, everything included; non-painting guests are welcome for a lower rate. You can reserve online, or submit an email form and call with your credit card details.

ArtStudy

www.artstudy.com

Based in Florida, Art Study offers the chance to study painting "en plein air" in a dream of a location: Claude Monet's gardens in Giverny. You can sign up for seven or eleven days, from April through October; classes are limited to eight students, who are permitted to wander the gardens at will for one full day and six afternoons a week. The site, dotted with inspirational waterlily pictures, tells you that all instruction, lodgings and meals are included in the price, which, maddeningly, it withholds – you'll need to send off for the "free information package" to get the full low-down.

China Painting Tour

www.chinaarttours.com

Sixteen-day painting workshops, held in May and October, which double as fascinating cultural tours of China. As well as tuition from eminent Chinese watercolourists and calligraphers, students (all levels) take in a dizzying array of places, from Beijing and Shanghai to smaller villages like Zhouzhaung, Suzhou and Yangshuo, with trips to the mountains of Guilin and along the Li and Jade Dragon rivers. All this for $2850 including flight (from the west coast of the USA), accommodation, travel, tuition fees and guide. You can read the full itinerary, see examples of the tutors' work, and follow a handful of useful China links on the site.

Horizons to Go

www.horizons-art.org

True to its promise of "artistic vacations", this excellent US-based company runs intriguing small-group workshops in painting, textiles, sculpture,

ceramics, photography, glass-blowing, silver-smithing, mask-making and more. Most of the world's artistic hotspots are on offer here – Spain, France, Italy, Ireland, Nepal, Mexico and the American Southwest among them – and students are encouraged to find inspiration in local landscape, culture and history. Courses, which draw upon folk traditions and experimentation, include field trips and workshops with local craftspeople. To register, you can print out a form and mail it, or simply call direct.

Taos Institute of Arts

www.tiataos.com
One-week arts workshops in Taos, New Mexico, where for years New Agers, artists and Native Americans have lived side by side in an extraordinary desert landscape. Classes, most of which are held during spring and summer, incorporate rigorous "classical" techniques with the rich cultural traditions of the Southwest, including painting, weaving, ceramics, and jewellery-making; groups tend to be small. You can search the schedule on the site, or browse a full list of courses, clicking to see examples of tutors' works. Costs hover at around $400, but you're expected to book your own accommodation. Register by phone or email.

Photography

American Photo Mentor Series

www.mentorseries.com
Organized by the popular photography magazine *American Photo*, these holidays allow students of all abilities to join professional photographers – "mentors" – on trips around the world. The site is clear, confident and no-nonsense, telling you what to bring, what to expect, and what you'll need to pay – which is between $425 for a weekend at Annapolis to $3000 or so for ten days in China

(including airfare from LA, accommodation, most meals, local transport). Destinations change each year: 2001 offered Greece, Israel, China, Wyoming, Montana and Annapolis. All trips involve daily talks, slide presentations, and personal critiques. Check the gallery to see the impressive – very commercial – results from previous trips, and to email past participants. To book, download the form and mail it direct.

Essential India

www.essential-india.co.uk

Specialist operator (see p.301) offering a number of study tours to India, including a sixteen-day photography trip to the Himalayas tutored by a professional anthropological photographer. Emphasis is on "creative risk and cultural understanding", and as well as exploring the extraordinary local landscapes groups work with Tibetan and Gaddi communities to create individual artistic projects. The tour costs £895 (excluding flights); you'll need to send an email to book.

Photo Explorer Tours

www.photoexplorertours.com

Starting its days as a China specialist – the annual China tour, which features field trips with local professionals, is still its most popular – this US-based operator, run by award-winning travel photographer Dennis Cox, now offers trips to a stunning range of destinations. It's a long list – including Bolivia, Ethiopia, Guatemala, Iceland, India, Ireland, Irian Jaya, Myanmar, Nepal and Bhutan, New Zealand, South Africa, Thailand, Tibet, and Turkey – so browse the thumbnail details before clicking for fuller accounts. Prices vary from around $2000 for a week with the hill tribes in northern Thailand to $6500 for three weeks in Ethiopia. As well as tuition and guides, these include three/four-star accommodation, local transport, and most, if not all meals. Download a booking form and send with a deposit.

Wildshots

www.wildshots.co.uk

Nature and landscape photography trips in the Highlands of Scotland, Iceland and the US. The seven-day "highland safaris", where you can snap a wealth of wildlife, pick up fieldcraft and specialist techniques, and even learn how to build a hide or create a perfect "set", start at £450 for a week. Reckon on at least three times that for a fortnight in the astounding national parks of Arizona and Utah, or among the steaming geysers and big skies in Yellowstone, and even more if you want to photograph wild brown bears in the sub-arctic wilderness of Finland. Each trip is limited to eight to ten students. Send an email for a print brochure or to make a reservation.

Volunteering

Archaeological Institute of America

www.archaeological.org

The AIA publishes the annual *Archaeological Fieldwork Opportunities Bulletin*, which contains detailed information about three hundred excavations around the world that are open to volunteers. Each entry tells you about the excavation site, dates, costs, contact information, and summaries of work needed. You're linked from here to the publisher so you can buy the bulletin online.

Archaeology Abroad

www.britarch.ac.uk/archabroad

London-based organization that publishes a twice-yearly bulletin and a number of factsheets detailing around a thousand fieldwork opportunities outside the UK. They're available to subscribers only (£12.50 for UK citizens, $30 in the US). The site has information on how to subscribe, as well as useful general information on digging abroad.

British Trust for Conservation Volunteers

www.btcv.org

More than five hundred conservation holidays around the world. UK holidays are divided between small-group "Natural Breaks", which last from two days to two weeks – a weekend tackling drainage problems on a Pennines path, say, or dry-stone walling in the Scillies – and longer "Action Breaks" in remote parts of Scotland or the Lake District. For most projects no experience is needed, and volunteers as young as eight are accepted. International holidays, open to over-18s only, entail living and working with the local community; you might spend two weeks wolf-tracking in Slovakia, crop-planting in Nepal, or farming in Japan. You can select a project by location, month, type of work, or simply browse a full list – before booking (it's a secure server), check the offers detailed on the "Discounts" page.

Council for British Archeology

www.britarch.ac.uk

The first stop for professional archeologists and enthusiasts in the UK. Click "Fieldwork Opportunities" for a list of projects around Britain that accept volunteers; make sure to read each carefully, however, as some are open to students only.

Earthwatch Institute

www.earthwatch.org

With offices in the US, England, Australia and Japan, Earthwatch places volunteers on conservation research expeditions in more than fifty countries. Most need no skills, and whether you fancy monitoring elephant seals in the Falklands, tracking macaw activity in the Peruvian Amazon, or researching nutrition and healthcare in South India, Earthwatch has something for you. Volunteers pay something for food and lodging (which could be in anything from a mud hut or campsite to an upmarket lodge), and though prices vary, on average you're looking at around £1000/$1600 for one to three weeks, not including transport. Each Earthwatch office also has its own short "Discovery" projects; in Europe you might monitor the eagles of Mull for a week, or spend five days tracking dinosaur footprints in Yorkshire. You can search for a project by location, date or subject, or simply pull up a complete list, and reservations can be made online.

Global Service Corps

www.globalservicecorps.org

California-based organization offering community service holidays in environmental, health and education projects in Costa Rica, Tanzania and Thailand. Short-term projects (17–27 days) cost around $2000, not including flights; long-term programmes, which last up to six months (you need to have completed the short-term programme first) cost a further $600 a month. In Costa Rica, the short trip entails 17 days' organic gardening, coffee-bean-picking and light construction work, while if you stay longer you might help in local schools or assist a small start-up business. In Tanzania, projects revolve around AIDS awareness and sustainable agriculture, while Thai projects concentrate on helping students, teachers and Buddhist monks with conversational English. To apply, fill in the downloadable application form and send with a deposit. All trips are also open to non-Americans.

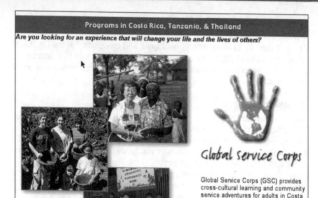

Programs in Costa Rica, Tanzania, & Thailand

Are you looking for an experience that will change your life and the lives of others?

Global service Corps

Global Service Corps (GSC) provides cross-cultural learning and community service adventures for adults in Costa Rica, Tanzania and Thailand. Short-

La Sabranenque

www.sabranenque.com

Spruce, upbeat site from a non-profit Provençal organization that restores medieval structures, paths and monuments throughout France and Italy. Taught by experienced builders, volunteers learn traditional construction techniques – stonemasonry, rubble clearing, roof-tiling – using original materials. Most of the programmes are in Provence, where volunteers live in a medieval stone village near Avignon, with time off for sightseeing and tasty home-cooked meals provided. Italian projects are in the southern region of Murgia and in a hamlet near the Swiss border. You can choose from volunteer sessions pure and simple, or combine them with sightseeing or technical training. Send an email for full details of costs, or to request a brochure.

National Trust

www.nationaltrust.org.uk/volunteers

The National Trust, which protects outstanding rural areas, houses and gardens around England, Wales and Northern Ireland, has a good-looking, flashy site detailing its working holidays at around 140 rural locations. Anyone can volunteer for a weekend, week, or fortnight – no experience necessary – to do anything from maintaining woodland paths, surveying hedgerows, clearing rhododendron bushes, rounding up goats, or restoring the gardens of stately homes. The site's search facility isn't wildly convenient: clicking an area on an interactive map pulls up an account of the geography and geology of the region – you then have to go through clicking every dot on the map to read about each place. Doing so brings you accounts of the holidays, with dates and costs and a rundown of tasks and accommodation. You can book by phone or by downloading the application form.

Sense

www.sense.org.uk

British charity that organizes about 25 holidays a year for deaf-blind people – mostly children – in England and Wales. Lasting a week each, during the school summer hoidays, they vary from stays at outdoor activity centres to farm holidays and boat trips. All accommodation and food expenses are paid for volunteers, each of whom is paired with an individual holidaymaker; training is offered, and there is support available throughout the week. For a schedule of the year's holidays you need to download an Adobe file; to apply, download another form and send it direct.

Voluntary Work Information Service

www.workingabroad.com

UK-based directory of international volunteer organizations, with opportunities in social and community projects, environmental organizations, English teaching, human rights campaigns, wildlife expeditions, health care, housing and organic farming. For anyone not sure which direction to take, click on "Voluntary Work Opportunities" to use its personalized search service. Simply fill in the form stating your interests, experience, time available, preferred countries and the like, and, for a fee, you'll be sent a report on at least twenty relevant organizations. If you'd rather do your own research, click on "Volunteer Organizations" to pull up a – very selective – list of outfits, with accounts of their programmes and contact details. "News from the Field" features trip reports and feedback from volunteers, campaign and charity news, and urgent calls for volunteers.

Volunteers for Peace

www.vfp.org

Thousands of opportunities, in more than eighty countries, for American volunteers. The work varies widely, from helping out in Palestinian refugee camps or drug recovery schemes in Portugal to tree-planting in Bangladesh. Most camps are for over-18s, though a few accept younger volunteers and some take families; the site's slightly hectoring tone – lots of directives underlined and in bold italics – perhaps reflects the fact that the average VFP volunteer is in their early 20s. There are two online directories: the searchable format is the most up to date. Choose by date, destination and camp type to see what's available, and then sort the resulting table of options by date, country, age limits or type. You can then click on each camp for details, and again to apply for a place. Volunteers from the UK should register with VFP's British partners, Youth Action for Peace (**www.yap-uk.org**), or the International Voluntary Service (**www.ivsgbn.demon.co.uk**).

Wildlife and nature

David Anderson Safari Consultants

www.davidanderson.com

Californian consultancy that offers a quite staggering array of safaris and wilderness experiences throughout Africa, ranging from the merely expensive to the positively luxurious. Most of the continent is covered, with "Hemingway" safaris in Kenya and Botswana, "flight-seeing" tours of Namibia and Tanzania, and Nile cruises in Egypt. The entire database is searchable according to both country and desired activity, and there's also a long list of game lodges; you can't book online, only submit an email enquiry.

Discover the World

www.discover-the-world.co.uk

A sister company to Iceland and Greenland specialists Arctic Experience (see p.298), this British tour operator – slogan, "where holidays come naturally" – offers 35 different wildlife- and whale-watching holidays in seven continents, including cruises from Patagonia south to Antarctica, in search of penguins and albatrosses as well as aquatic mammals, and elephant safaris in Tanzania. All tours are fully described on screen, but with no online booking you have to email to request reservation details.

Discovery Initiatives

www.discoveryinitiatives.com

The Website of this British eco-tourism operator invites users keen to take a wildlife-watching holiday to search by country, animal (ranging through pandas, tigers, rhinos and whales), habitat (from rainforest to desert) or activity (including walking, riding, cruising and rafting). It then suggests trips all over the world, setting out full itineraries and prices; email if you're interested in making a booking.

Nature Expeditions International

www.naturexp.com

Florida-based company that arranges wildlife and natural history tours in Africa, Central and South America, Asia, and Australia and New Zealand. It caters to both escorted groups and independent travellers, attracting older, more affluent participants by promising high-standard accommodation and "elective and low-intensity" adventures. Itineraries in such places as Nepal, Bali and India include conventional sightseeing as well as expeditions in pursuit of local flora and fauna, and also optional academic lectures. Choose your goal from the home page's antique world map, study complete tour details, and then call the toll-free number to discuss your trip.

Out of the Blue

www.wdcs.org

The British-based Whale and Dolphin Conservation Society is a charity that promotes the welfare of whales, dolphins and porpoises throughout the world. As well as news, information and links, its Website contains full details of the society's travel-operator offshoot, designed to set an example to less eco-sensitive operators. Out of the Blue runs a select and heavily subscribed programme of whale- and dolphin-watching trips to Scotland, Patagonia, The Azores, Canada and Nepal (yes, Nepal – you can go looking for river dolphins). Read what previous participants have said about its trips, and then send an email to sign up for any that appeal.

Safarilink

www.safarilink.com

Although its home is in the UK, the Safarilink Website serves as a comprehensive directory of British, North American, and African tour companies that offer African safaris. The site centres on what it calls "the Web's only safari search engine", **safarisearch.com**, which responds to suggested destinations or animal species by reeling off a list of suitable expeditions. Safarilink does not as yet sell holidays itself, but it does enable you to compare what's available, and then go straight to the most suitable supplier.

Vintage Africa

www.vintageafrica.com

Attractive and easy-to-use site, run by a British operator to publicize its extensive programme of African safaris, which goes well beyond the typical Botswana and Kenya itineraries to include expeditions through Ethiopia and further afield. Some of the trips are absurdly luxurious, offering for example the chance to eat fresh sushi and sip champagne cocktails as you watch chimpanzees beside Lake Tanganyika, but it does offer budget alternatives as well; if you don't want a full package, you can also just arrange accommodation in specific lodges. If anything takes your fancy, send an email.

Bird-watching

Birdquest

www.birdquest.co.uk

Promising "The Ultimate in Birding Tours", this long-established British operator offers around eighty trips each year, from a repertoire of around 150 different itineraries. All regions of the globe are covered, including cruises to Antarctica and such obscure destinations as Sakhalin and Ussuriland in Eastern Siberia. The detailed tour descriptions are packed with accounts of specific birds you might encounter, and illustrated with appealing line drawings as well as photos; there's also a substantial set of links. Although the only interactive element is a brochure-request form, you can use that to ask for a reservation.

Site designed and produced by Accent Design Group

Eagle-Eye Tours

www.eagle-eye.com

By and large, this US-based birdwatching specialist concentrates its activities in the Americas, but it caters for travellers of all nationalities (with a special toll-free number for UK customers), and also runs trips as far afield as Senegal, Morocco and Bulgaria. Tours are arranged here both by date and by region; some are even devoted to particular birds, such as Kirtland's Warbler. Specify your interests on the email form.

Footprint Adventures

www.birding-tours.co.uk

The bird-watching division of this British operator (see p.120) offers specialist tours all over the world, including a three-week "Birds of China" trip and a two-week, four-island tour of Hawaii. With flights priced separately, all are available to travellers of any nationality; you can't check availability online, but you can pay a deposit to secure your reservation.

Naturetrek

www.naturetrek.co.uk

British wildlife tour operator that takes twitchers all over the world to see birds such as the hummingbirds of Trinidad, but stresses that its clients spend more of their time on foot appreciating their chosen destination than they do scurrying off in the minibus in pursuit of the next species on the checklist. Botanists and naturalists accompany each expedition, with European regions such as the mountains of Spain figuring as prominently as exotic tropical locations. Check the Website's calendar of slide shows in the UK, and email payment details to make a reservation if anything catches your eye.

Writing

See also **www.skyros.com** (p.211) for creative writing classes in Greece and Thailand.

The Arvon Foundation

www.arvonfoundation.org

Arvon offers hugely popular week-long residential courses in lovely old houses in Devon, Shropshire, Yorkshire and Scotland. Themes run the gamut from comedy to poetry to songwriting; time is divided between workshops, private study, readings and socials. Taught by leaders in their field, most courses are open to all, and the atmosphere is relaxed, with students sharing the cooking and chores (food is provided). They cost £360 per week (£245 for untutored retreats), and there are a few grants available. You can search the site for courses by month, and use the downloadable booking form to reserve a place.

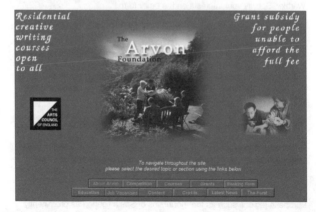

Essential India

www.essential-india.co.uk

Specialist company (see p.301) offering a nice variety of creative study tours to India. The writing course, based in Himachal Pradesh in the Himalayas, involves three-hour workshops every day, with writing trips to Tibetan monasteries, Hindu temples, street markets and mountain villages. It costs £785 for two weeks, not including flights; book by email.

Literary Traveler

www.literarytraveler.com

Patchy online magazine filled with articles about Great American Writers and the places they travelled. If you want to follow in the path of Hemingway, Twain or Melville, it has a useful directory of literary tour operators offering anything from walking tours to academic trips and custom-designed holidays, along with hotels with literary associations. "Events" lists upcoming festivals and literary events throughout the US, up to six months in advance.

Natalie Goldberg

www.nataliegoldberg.com

Minimal site from America's favourite writing guru, famed for her passionate belief in writing as a "practice" with the power to free "wild mind". Click on "Workshops" to read testimonials about her hugely popular week-long seminars at the Mabel Dodge House in Taos, New Mexico – frustratingly, you need to call the centre direct to get a schedule – and on "News" for details of other upcoming courses around the US.

Nightwriters

www.nightwriters.com

Small seminars and writers' retreats in "creative settings" – among them a sixteenth-century villa in Tuscany, a castle on the Scottish island of Mull, an antebellum inn in Virginia and a ranch house in California's wine country. The tutors, all professional American writers, each have a slightly different style – you can read about them on the site – but every course includes exercises, writing time, feedback and social events. Rates start at $650 for a week without accommodation in Virginia up to around $3000 for two weeks in Tuscany, with a hands-on cooking course thrown in. Bookings need to be made direct.

Writespace

www.writespace.co.uk

For anyone after a bit of inner peace to free the creative spirit, these writing/yoga weekends – just five students in a lovely sixteenth-century Cotswold farmhouse – could be just the ticket. You get three hours' writing time per day, along with yoga and meditation classes beneath a willow tree, and vegetarian meals are included. You'll pay £195 for a weekend (Fri–Sun), sharing a room, or £40 for a day including lunch. No online booking.

part three

destinations

Antarctica

Abercrombie and Kent

www.abercrombiekent.com

Upmarket adventure operators offering two- to three-week cruises of Antarctica and the Falkland Islands. Cruises are taken on the *Explorer*, the world's first expeditionary cruise ship, which carries 100 passengers at the most, plus 75 crew (which includes the expert guides and lecturers). You can read all about the vessel, and the various itineraries, before submitting an email form to make a provisional booking. You're looking at paying from around $6000 for an all-inclusive trip, flying from Miami.

International Association of Antarctica Tour Operators

www.iaato.org

Click on "Membership Directory – Contact Information" for links to a variety of environmentally responsible operators offering Antarctic cruises. Other pluses include the general information (including a history of tourism in the area, and guidelines for visitors), plus links to Antarctica resources, information sites and organizations.

Quark Expeditions

www.quarkexpeditions.com

Specializing in polar expedition cruises, this groundbreaking operator offers a variety of Antarctic trips, lasting from around ten days to three weeks and taking in the South Shetland, South Georgia and Falkland Islands. Prices start at around $3000, not including flights to and from Ushuaia, the world's southernmost city and the starting point for the cruises. If you've got $35,000 to spare you can join them on a full circumnavigation of Antarctica, a 13,000-mile journey that lasts two months. Itineraries of each trip are detailed on the site, along with costs. To book, however, you need to call one of their international offices (detailed on the site) or go through an agent.

Antigua

Caribbean Holidays 4 Less

www.caribbean-holidays4less.co.uk

UK-based online consolidator offering package holidays and discounted flights throughout the Caribbean, plus links to major all-inclusives such as Sandals. Holidays in Antigua start at around £700 for seven nights, including international flights. Although there are pictures and room descriptions for each hotel, the information isn't hugely detailed, so you might want to check out the newsgroup on **www.antigua-barbuda.org** (see below) to get first-hand reviews before committing yourself.

Island Inns

www.islandinns.com

Upmarket hotel and villa reservations at select properties throughout the Caribbean. The Antiguan collection includes the romantic all-inclusive Jumby Bay resort, where staff outnumber guests nine to one and nightly rates start at $650. The site has all the details you need, with long reviews, tempting photos, rates and a Specials page. Email direct to request a reservation.

Click the fish to find your ideal getaway!

Official Travel Guide to Antigua and Barbuda

www.antigua-barbuda.org

The official site of the Antigua and Barbuda Department of Tourism is well put together, packed with information and intelligent links. You can read anything you need to know about the islands here, including historical snippets, features on food, drink and cricket, and a good accommodation section complete with links to all the major properties and a handy rates comparison table. The lively message board is restricted to travel and tourism questions.

Tourscan

www.tourscan.com

North American Caribbean specialist agency that allows you to find the best offers available for packages, flights and accommodation. Use the search engine to hunt by season, price range (rates are per person including mid-week airfare from NY) and destination, refining your choice if you want to stay by the ocean, in all-inclusive or self-catering accommodation, or whatever. Options are listed in ascending order of cost, with little written information, but with links to Websites where available. If a place has no site you might find yourself wanting more details before booking (which is done via Tourscan).

Argentina

Argentina Travel Net

www.argentinatravelnet.com/indexE.htm

The major portal for Argentine tourism, featuring English translations and links to a host of small companies and adventure-tourism operators throughout the country. Search facilities enable searches by region as well as interest, and suggested Web links, to the sites of hotels and travel agencies in Buenos Aires, for example, make it clear which are available in English.

Galapagos Holidays

www.galapagosholidays.com/argentina.htm

Canadian travel agency that specializes in customized South American tours. Their four Argentine offerings range from "Cosmopolitan Buenos Aires" to "Spectacular Iguazu Falls" and trips to the country's lakes and mountains, and include accommodation in high-quality hotels. Email the lengthy form, and someone will call you back to firm up your plans.

Gobierno de la Ciudad de Buenos Aires

www.buenosaires.gov.ar

The official Buenos Aires tourism site is inconceivably dull to look at – almost entirely devoid of illustrations, it consists of long grey tracts of text – and it's entirely in Spanish, but it does carry a host of useful links to the city's hotels, restaurants, and cultural activities.

Grippo

www.grippo.com

Wide-ranging compendium, completely in Spanish, covering all matters Argentine. The tourism section is strong on destination information, with dossiers on each region that include 360° images of beautiful beaches, and there's also plenty of history, news, sports and literature; a search for cult writer Jorge Luis Borges, for example, found 326 relevant pages.

Kon-Tiki Tours and Travel

www.kontiki.org/argentina

Calling themselves "The Argentina Specialists", this Miami-based travel agency offers a wide variety of tours to South America, including several either exclusively to Argentina, or adding a visit to Buenos Aires onto trips to neighbouring countries. As you look through the site, you can assemble your own "trip planner" by adding such components as a set of tango lessons, or a tour to Iguazu Falls or Patagonia, to a basic Buenos Aires package. Then either phone or email for further information, or simply complete your booking online.

Mercotour

www.mercotour.com

Argentina-based information site, which as well as providing sections on all the country's provinces also covers Brazil, Chile, and Uruguay. Besides general listings and background for each region, including current climate conditions, it also features a large database of tourist agencies. Very little of the material is translated into English, but if you're into adventurous pursuits such as climbing, rafting, cycling or trekking, it's great for putting you in touch with on-the-spot operators.

South American Explorers

www.samexplo.org

This non-profit organization, based in upstate New York, is a member-supported clearing house for travel information and advice for South and Central America. Its Website includes personal experiences, news updates, health and safety tips, and discount offers. Sign up as a member to receive regular email and printed newsletters.

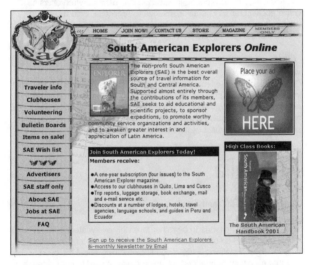

Sur del Sur

www.surdelsur.com/indexingles.html

The English version of this Argentinean Website – run by the National Department of Culture, its name translates as "The Southernmost South" – sets out to portray the country in all its "magnificence" and "idiosyncrasy". For beginners, it includes a potted history from first migrants through the Bering Strait, and a "where we are" section which bemoans isolated Argentina's position as being "too southern". Other pages cover art, the economy, literature, and of course tango. There's little of great practical use for travellers, but if you want to bone up on the basic facts, including detailed accounts of individual provinces with links to local papers and government offices, this is the place to start.

Traveland

www.traveland.com

General Latin America tour agency, based in California, which offers full online booking for short-break packages to Argentina, including a long weekend in Buenos Aires with optional excursions to tango shows and/or cattle ranches, and flights from Miami, New York or Los Angeles.

xSalir

www.xsalir.com

Cutting-edge, youth-oriented listings site for Buenos Aires; let it know what interests you, and it prides itself on telling you what you can do within the next hour in any specified district of the capital. As well as upcoming music and movie events, it also covers clubs, bars and restaurants, so you can see who has the freshest oysters and octopuses in town.

Australia

Australia Tourist Commission

www.aussie.net.au

This official Website tends to be rather feverishly overwritten, but with so much information on offer – over 10,000 pages of it – it's an essential first stop for anyone planning a trip. If you know nothing about the country, the fact that everything is arranged by region makes it hard to get started, but there's a phenomenal array of links to tour and adventure operators in every conceivable destination, as well as other government sites that offer practical advice or details on visa and health requirements.

Austravel

www.austravel.com

The Austravel company, part of Thomson International, runs package tours to Australia from both Britain and the US, though online availability checks and secure reservations from its Website are available to UK customers only. Austravel can also arrange individual components of your trip, from flights and visas to accommodation, car rental, cruises and diving excursions.

Backpack Australia

www.backpackaustralia.com.au
The best of several competing, similarly named Websites that cater for budget travellers. Its strongest feature is an online interactive booking system for over 400 hostels throughout the country, but it also offers links to travel agents, tour operators, information sites and Internet cafes, and operates its own useful "Traveller's Voice" message board for exchanging information and advice.

The Big Banana

www.bigbanana.com

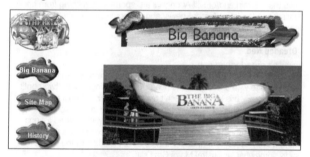

Exactly what it claims to be – a giant yellow banana – which typifies the Australian phenomenon of big garish roadside things. Unless you're planning to drive the 1000km Pacific Highway between Sydney and Brisbane – in which case you'll spot it roughly halfway along – you can visit the banana online instead. For that matter, you can also email it, while if you email the Bunyip, at Bunyip Billabong, you're promised a nice surprise.

Citysearch

www.citysearch.com.au
Although its confusing opening page might lead you to expect coverage of

the entire country, the Citysearch site provides comprehensive online guides to just four Australian cities: Sydney, Melbourne, Canberra, and, on a slightly lesser scale, Brisbane. Fortunately, the level of detail and reliability for those is first class, combining searchable databases of restaurants, clubs and other businesses coupled with reviews from local newspapers and good-quality maps. To make the most of it, it helps to know the cities well already, so it's more use for residents than for tourists, and it's also surprisingly sketchy on accommodation.

Culture and Recreation Portal

www.acn.net.au

This official government-sponsored gateway connects to around two thousand sites devoted to Australian cultural life, and a combined total of over a million pages. It holds links to every imaginable museum and gallery, from the Canberra Bicycle Museum to the Maffra Sugar Beet Museum, plus sites that explain and/or sell Aboriginal art, sports sites ranging from cricket statistics to the latest football news, and the home sites of the nation's leading authors.

Dreaded Ned

www.oz.dreadedned.com

The home page of this one-man gay guide to Australia proclaims it to be "the Website with a bucket on its head"; disappointingly, page two continues "Obviously this Website doesn't really have a bucket on its head". Once past the whimsy, however – the Dreaded Ned in question is of course folk hero Ned Kelly – it's a pretty good site, with detailed listings of gay-friendly accommodation, clubs and other services across the continent, a lively users' forum, and plenty of links, including to the official (but sadly somewhat lacklustre) Mardi Gras site.

Great Barrier Reef Visitors Bureau

www.great-barrier-reef.com

An excellent Website, on which prospective travellers can gather full information on destinations throughout the Barrier Reef region, and use a free booking service to arrange every aspect of a trip, including accommodation and car rental as well, of course, as dive trips. They even offer a special "Survivor" package, designed to reproduce the conditions "enjoyed" by the participants in the sensational US TV series. Separate self-contained sites deal with local "sub-regions", and there's also a great set of links covering the practical side of travelling to Australia, including visa and custom regulations along with airlines. The last word invites you to "send us a nice chatty booking or enquiry email because you hate using forms".

OzOutback

www.ozoutback.com.au

OzOutback deals primarily in images of Australian landscapes, wildlife, and especially Aboriginal culture, which you can email to friends as electronic postcards or buy for your own use. The captions hold some useful destination information, and you can also get a free email address to use as you travel. The main reason to visit, however, is to work your way through the full set of outback-related links, which include lots of back-country tour operators and vehicle rental agencies.

Puffing Billy

www.puffingbilly.com.au

This lovingly compiled site details schedules and fares for the century-old Puffing Billy steam train, still chugging through the scenic Dandenong mountains 40km east of Melbourne; email or phone for bookings.

Travelmate

www.travelmate.com.au

The Travelmate site belongs to the petrol company Caltex, which explains its emphasis on driving in general and petrol prices in particular, but it's one of the very best online travel guides to Australia, enabling you to select from over 20,000 hotels across the country and request reservations online. The "map Maker" facility will sketch out an itinerary between any two locations, highlighting whatever features you request (such as museums or national parks as well, of course, as Caltex petrol stations), while "Trip Talk" is a frank message board with a lengthy and much-debated "Never Go To ... " section.

TT-Line

www.tt-line.com.au

Owned by Tasmania's state government, the TT-Line operates a regular ferry service across the Bass Strait to the island from Melbourne. One vessel is a high-speed catamaran, the other more of a cruise ship. The Website provides full schedules and fares, and while you can't literally book online you can complete a detailed reservation form for a quick email response.

Wilmap

www.wilmap.com.au

Lots of maps and photos; announcing itself as the "Australian Registry of Tourism and Accommodation", the Wilmap site holds a massive database of Australian destinations. Once you've picked a spot that appeals to you, you can read about it, look at photos, search for accommodation, and – which is where they hope to make their money – ask them to mail you a large-scale map. Or, you can simply take advantage of their full set of links to get whatever information you need.

Austria

Austrian Tourism

www.austria-tourism.at

Promising "one thing you will never experience in Austria is boredom!", this official Website devotes separate sections to visitors of different nationalities. If you fail to specify your country of origin on the home page, it'll only give you generic information, but once it knows where you're from, it reels off useful practical details, including lists of operators who can arrange your Austrian vacation. Activities such as golf, fishing, hiking, cycling, horseriding and, of course, skiing are well covered. Information specifically for North Americans is also available on the associated **www.experienceaustria.com** site.

Austrian Travel Network

www.tiscover.at

Part of **www.tiscover.com**, which also covers Germany and Switzerland, in Austria itself the Austrian Travel Network enables online searches and booking for over 5000 accommodation options, categorized by region, price and facilities. It also carries details of special all-inclusive packages, as well as listings of upcoming events.

Herzerl Tours

www.herzerltours.com

Specialist Austrian operator based in the US, which offers a very wide array of themed personal tours, covering wine, music, and cuisine as well as more strenuous activities such as ballooning and cycling. Pick up full details on the Web, then phone or email to book.

Van Gogh Tours

www.vangoghtours.com

Based in Vermont, USA, Van Gogh Tours concentrates most of its operations in Holland, but its Austria programme includes six small-group cycling tours (including one based around the *Sound of Music*), and one walking tour, with accommodation in hotels and guesthouses. There's no online booking; just call or email the owner.

Virtual Vienna

www.virtualvienna.net

Aimed primarily at Vienna's English-speaking community, so its listings include rather too many plumbers and too few restaurants for most tourists' needs, Virtual Vienna nonetheless provides a good basic practical guide to the city, and holds a multitude of links to official and governmental sites for the rest of the country.

Barbados

Barbados Tourism Encyclopedia

www.barbados.org
The official site of the Barbados Tourism Authority is a great resource and lively to boot. It's particularly strong on travel information, with links to airlines, travel agents, car rental companies, and ground operators, with an extensive searchable accommodation database that lists everything from guesthouses to luxury villas, detailing rates, facilities and links to Websites where available. You can also read about restaurants, activities and shopping, with a schedule of music, theatre and carnival events.

Belgium

For tour operators offering short breaks in Brussels and other Belgian cities, see the "European City Breaks" section which starts on p.34.

All The Restaurants in Belgium

www.resto.be

The largest Belgian restaurants site may not boast every restaurant in Belgium, but it has 7000 or so to be getting on with. You can search by location, price and style (which ranges from "mussels and chips" via "from Madagascar" to "Tex-Mex"), and then take a look at menus and photos. An interactive poll section reveals that of the top hundred in the country, only three are categorized as Belgian. Sadly, although almost all the site is translated into English, the customer reviews are not.

All Travel Belgium

www.alltravelbelgium.com

The best search engine devoted to Belgian hotels, offering a fully comprehensive range of properties throughout the country, with photographs, prices and links to their individual sites.

Belgian Tourist Office

www.visitbelgium.com

The superbly detailed official Website of the Belgian Tourist Office in the Americas – slogan, "A kingdom the size of Maryland" – covers every imaginable aspect, from "Belgium for the eclectic art nut" to "Belgium for chocolate lovers", with dozens of additional links from every page. It's great for setting you up with package tour operators – a typical special offer would be a city break in Brussels from New York for just $500 – or making your own travel arrangements on Belgian railways. Rather than handling accommodation reservations online, however, it simply links you to specific hotels.

Belgium Travel Network

www.trabel.com

So long as you can put up with its consistently drab grey screens, this site provides a clear and efficient online guide to the country. Working methodically through its multitude of menus is rewarded by all the destination information you could need on Begium's monuments and churches, beers and lace, while the associated **www.hotels-belgium.com** site offers easy-to-use searches and email bookings for hotels.

Brussels 18–30

www.brussels18-30.com
This online guide to Brussels is intended primarily for travellers aged 18–30, and centres on a guide to the capital's club scene, with links to other clubbing sites. However, plenty of its features are useful whatever your age, including not only its general destination information and public transport details, but also the excellent "Bed and Brussels" section (also available on **www.bnb-brussels.be**), which enables you to find and book B&Bs anywhere in the city.

Flanders Tourism

www.belgium-tourism.com/en/intra_0_en.shtml
The English-language version of the official Flanders Website, which includes "art cities" such as Brussels, Antwerp, Ghent and Bruges as well as the sandy Channel coast. The practical information is strong, with links to international and domestic train, ferry and flight operators. By combining the hotel search facility with the connections to local sites, you can book an entire vacation online.

Belize

Belize Online

www.belize.com
This joint Belizean-US enterprise is intended as much for potential investors in the country as for tourists, but it's still a great source of travel information, with links to tour operators as well as hotels and resorts, and also plenty of background information, plus a large bibliography for further reading.

Island Expeditions Company

www.islandexpeditions.com
US tour operator that specializes in small-group adventure-travel trips to Belize from any US city, arranging kayaking and diving along the barrier reef as well as white-water rafting on the inland rivers and expeditions to ruined Maya cities. The Website holds detailed itineraries, maps and tour descriptions, but recommends you speak with someone in the office before returning the downloadable booking form.

Reef and Rainforest Tours

www.reefrainforest.co.uk

Eco-friendly British tour company that offers a choice of six tailor-made natural history Belize itineraries, ranging from the "Belize on a Budget" trip, which takes in a week's bird-watching, based in a rainforest lodge, and a week by the sea, with scuba diving available, to the three-week Grand Tour. You can pick up full information online, but to make a reservation you have to print out and mail a booking form.

Bolivia

Bolivia Web

www.boliviaweb.com

Bolivian portal with links to all manner of sites, including business, poetry, photography and food as well as travel; it even sells mouse mats and coffee mugs. A useful set of pages is devoted to hotels in each major city, with links to those that have their own Websites.

Magic of Bolivia

www.bolivia.co.uk

British company that offers a standard three-week guided tour of Bolivia –

taking in jungle, deserts and mountains – at regular intervals between March and November each year (thus avoiding the rainy season). The Website gives full itineraries, with photos and prices, and you can also customize individual trips. There's no online booking, however; call to discuss your needs.

Myths and Mountains

www.mythsandmountains.com
Worthy Nevada-based tour company that runs a fascinating array of Bolivian expeditions. They can take you out onto Lake Titicaca on a raft, or school you in the medical lore of the Kallaway people, but they can't take credit card payments online; email for further details.

Botswana

Crocodile Camp Safaris

www.botswana.com
Based in the Botswana town of Maun, Crocodile Camp specialize in wilderness photographic expeditions, travelling by jeep, horseback or in *mokoro* (traditional canoe). How much you pay depends on how much of the hard work of a back-country trip you're prepared to shoulder yourself. Trips are priced in US dollars and sold to clients of all nationalities; payments cannot be made online.

Okavango Tours and Safaris

www.okavango.com
Although enabling tourists to experience the wildlife of the world-famous Okavango Delta is the main priority for this British tour company, they can also take small groups to meet with Bushmen in the Kalahari desert, or onto the desolate Makagadikgadi salt pans. There are good descriptions on the Web, but you have to call or email with enquiries.

Brazil

A number of operators offer eco-tours to Brazil; see p.195 for a selection. And for conservation volunteer holidays, see the section starting on p.216, in particular **www.earthwatch.org**.

Amazon Adventures

www.amazonadventures.com

Texas-based operator specializing in trips to South America. They have a variety of packages to Brazil. Their cruises, which start at $500 for a week, involve activities such as jungle trekking, survival training, spear fishing and meetings with local tribes. Alternatively, you could study medicinal plants while staying at a lodge with a river family, go wildlife-viewing in the Pantanal, swimming in the crystal waters of Bonito, take cultural and historic tours of Bahia, and much more. Prices are reasonable – $2190 for a three-week package, not including flights, in the high season, or $545 for a week-long gaucho adventure. To book, fill in the email form and fax them your credit card details.

Brazilian Embassy in London

www.brazil.org.uk

Very useful, good-looking site with all the facts and figures you'd expect from an embassy site, plus fascinating cultural articles on everything from cinema and music to fashion and cuisine. The travel and tourism channel is extremely good, with informative regional guides, links to hotels all over the country, and carnival schedules and links.

Brazilinfo.net

www.brazilinfo.net

Useful Brazilian directory with general country information plus English-language links to travel operators, hotel directories, city guides and Brazilian maps.

Brazil Nuts

www.brazilnuts.com

North American Brazil specialists offering a wide range of packages throughout the country, including cultural itineraries ("Celebrate Life", for example, which explores African heritage in Rio and Salvador Da Bahia), off-the-beaten-track trips (canoe expeditions through the remote Pantanal waterways, say), Amazonian jungle lodges and city tours. You can also choose "budget" options that allow you to book flight and hotel only, leaving you free to arrange add-ons when you arrive. Most tours, though not escorted, hook you up with a guide who will take care of you for the duration of your trip; if you want to plan your own itinerary, fill in the online form and they'll suggest hotels and quote a price. Otherwise, to book, email them direct. There's also a travel forum, though more people post questions than reply.

Carnaval.com

www.carnaval.com

This gem of a carnival site, packed with information on all the great party cities, has large sections on Salvador and Rio. Quite apart from the pages of links relating to the carnivals – music files, video clips, historical background, parade schedules, samba schools and so on – you can glean huge amounts of travel information here, with links to city guides, accommodation, restaurants and bars, as well as a host of general background reading.

Insider's Guide to Rio

www.ipanema.com

There's an overwhelming amount of information on this phenomenal site, every other word, it seems, hotlinked to a useful database or a relevant cross-reference. With its straight-talking, common-sense advice, its lively tone and its palpable passion for the place, the guide gives you all the skinny on Rio's beaches, restaurants and nightlife, its drag queens and its samba parades, the thongs and the beach soccer, with maps and scores of photos. Accommodation reviews are honest and illuminating, and you can book rooms – and local tours – online. Your guide to Ipanema, incidentally, is Fred, a wisecracking dog; if you've got a spare moment you can make him bark and growl.

Journey Latin America

www.journeylatinamerica.co.uk

UK operator covering Mexico and Central and South America. While offering a handful of escorted group holidays, which they divide into "journeys" (adventurous trips, using public transport and staying in simple accommodation) and "tours" (private vehicles, posher hotels, softer adventure), they also suggest a number of independent itineraries: many of them allow you to choose between "tourist-class" hotels or more upmarket places, and you can decide whether to count your flight in, too. Click "News and Links" for late availability holidays. They also publish a chart of best-buy airfares, return and one-way, with details of passes. There's no online ordering; email them direct.

Lost World Adventures

www.lostworldadventures.com

US company organizing small-group itineraries which you can either book as is or customize to your own tastes. Their Brazil options include an adventurous ten-day Amazonian camping trip, exploring the rainforest, river islands and Lago Janauari Ecological Park, which will set you back around $1500. You can read full itineraries, and details of accommodation, on the site, but bookings, in the first instance, should be made by email.

Reef and Rainforest

www.reefrainforest.co.uk

This UK operator specializes in tailor-made natural history-oriented tours. The Brazil trip, a "natural history highlights" tour, takes in a good deal, covering Rio, whale-watching in Abrolhos National Park, rainforests, Iguacu Falls and the Pantanal wetlands. Once you've read the detailed itinerary and worked out if you can afford £2000 (not including flight), simply print off the form and send it, with a cheque, to book.

Worldwide Samba Home Page

www.worldsamba.org

Huge directory of samba links around the world, including samba schools in Rio, CD reviews, Carnaval schedules, audio and video clips and an email list.

Bulgaria

British-Bulgarian Friendship Society

www.bbfs.org.uk

As well as promoting British-Bulgarian understanding, the BBFS sells its own tours of the country, using charter flights from the UK and catering to special interests such as bird-watching, textiles, and embroidery, with wine-tasting trips to three different areas and also Black Sea beach trips. Their Website, however, doesn't give prices; you have to call to get the nitty-gritty details.

Canada

Bed & Breakfast Online Canada

www.bbcanada.com

This members' organization of Canadian B&Bs includes hundreds of properties from all over the country; each has its own page with colour photos, written descriptions in English and/or French as appropriate, and prices. Search according to specific criteria or simply work through the regional lists, then email your selection direct.

Brewster Banff Tours

www.brewster.ca

Though based in Alberta, Brewster arrange holidays in each individual region of Canada, as well as multi-destination bus, rail and Discovery Drive (self-guided) tours, and also golf and ski packages. The Great Canadian

Train Vacations section of the site includes trips starting in several major cities, with full-costed itineraries; email or call with queries or reservation requests.

British Columbia Ferry Corporation

www.bcferries.com
Based in Victoria, British Columbia, BC Ferries provide online timetable and fare information for their sailings between Vancouver and Vancouver Island and the Southern Gulf Islands, and also along the Discovery Coast, to the Queen Charlotte Islands, and up the Inside Passage to Alaska. Submitting the lengthy online reservation form does not quite guarantee your booking, however; availability will be confirmed within 48 hours.

Greyhound Canada

www.greyhound.ca
Greyhound's Canadian site works in the same way as the US version (see p.420), with a speedy fare and schedule finder, but there is no online booking facility for individual tickets as yet. Travellers who want to buy a Canadian Discovery pass, or a North American CanAm pass, are channelled through the main US site.

John Steel Rail Tours

www.johnsteel.com
Canada is one of the best countries on the planet to take a train ride, with all those vast open spaces. Canadian operator John Steel organizes rail journeys for groups and individuals throughout the country. Useful charts give basic information of each tour and links to a full description of that tour's itinerary, highlights and price details. Call or email to book.

Just America

www.justamerica.co.uk
British tour company that sells a huge assortment of rail, motorcoach and self-drive Canadian holidays in conjunction with local operators, with twin emphases on the scenic Rocky Mountain and Eastern Maritime regions. They can even arrange weekend breaks from the UK to Toronto. The Website provides full itineraries and prices, together with lots of photos; call or email to make your reservation.

Parks Canada

www.parkscanada.pch.gc.ca
Comprehensive and beautifully illustrated Website, run by Canadian Heritage and covering all Canada's national and regional parks. Find any park by name, type or just clicking on the maps, and you're given full details on fees and access as well as practical tips on hiking and camping hikes.

toronto.com

www.toronto.com
This thorough independent guide to Toronto features up-to-the-minute events listings, a searchable database of around 3000 restaurants – many with detailed reviews – and Webcam views of the city. Most useful of all, however, is its online hotel booking facility. It also offers links to similar guides for Calgary, Edmonton, Montréal, Ottawa, Quebec and Vancouver.

Tourism Whistler

www.tourismwhistler.com
Top-notch site run by the premier ski resort of Whistler, north of Vancouver, which centres on a superb "Trip Planner" that enables you to specify exactly what facilities you're looking for in your accommodation, returns a list of properties available on your chosen dates, and then lets you book the whole thing online. A separate section holds current Hot Deals, public transport is outlined in detail, there's a good interactive map of the resort, and a huge list of FAQs to round things off.

Tourisme Montréal

www.tourism-montreal.org
The official city site for Montréal covers the city in painstaking detail, antici-

pating any information a visitor might need and devoting pages on end, for example, to every permutation of public transport. Like everything else, its hotel and restaurant listings are exhaustive, and come with hyperlinks wherever possible; there's also plenty of eye-candy to keep you browsing.

Travel Canada

www.travelcanada.ca
Canada's official national tourism site offers a picture-packed "Virtual Tour" of every province, and enables you to plan your itinerary by building up your own "Travel Notebook". Every individual destination abounds with further links, including not only general overviews and recommended routes, but also specific adventure operators, with sections devoted to such activities as horse riding, canoeing, cycling, and rafting.

Vacations in Canada

www.vacationsincanada.com
Based in Ontario, this portal reels off links to operators and outfitters all over Canada, with a special affinity for outdoors activities such as fishing (a search for trout fishing throws up 38 options), skiing, dog sledding and even caribou hunting. Most of the accommodation on offer is in rural mountain lodges.

Vancouver Central Reservations

www.vancouver.com
Commercial site, devoted exclusively to Vancouver, and offering reservations for almost anything related to the city, from flight deals originating in all major US cities to car rental and hotels once you arrive, and tour companies, sightseeing attractions and even golf courses to keep you entertained. The Travel Planner facility enables users to bundle together all their requirements into a single package, though as companies pay to be included, the listings are not exhaustive.

VIA Rail Canada

www.viarail.ca
Comprehensive site of the Canadian rail network, with railroad maps, pass details, and a beautifully simple search system that details full schedules and fares for any journey you can imagine. They'll even arrange – given at least 24 hours notice – for you to be dropped off or picked up at places other than scheduled stops. The adventures section is particularly interest-

ing, listing a set of services tailor-made for outdoor enthusiasts and adventurers. Reservations are made on a simple form; your request will be confirmed by email within 48 hours. If you prefer not to book online, they list travel agents around the world that deal in VIA passes and tickets (Leisurail in the UK; see p.55). There's also a good set of links to operators who offer outdoor activities that can be reached by train.

Chile

Anglatin

www.anglatin.com

This Oregon-based operator, which arranges tours for both leisure and business travellers worldwide, has an especially extensive programme in Chile, including trips out to Easter Island, tours of the deserts and mountains, and also bird-watching, fly-fishing, skiing and golf excursions. Their Website offers full online booking.

Cascada Expediciones

www.cascada-expediciones.com

Clear, straightforward English-language site run by a Santiago-based adventure-holiday operator. Trips are arranged by both activity and region, and range through trekking and riding in Patagonia or on Easter Island, climbing in the Andes, rafting and kayaking trips on the Maipo river, and wildlife expeditions on Robinson Crusoe Island. Make your booking by printing the form and faxing it to Chile.

Chile Hotels

www.chile-hotels.com

A comprehensive hotel-booking site for the entire country, based in Chile but with an office in the US, and covering 500 hotels in 80 cities. The more upmarket properties tend to have the most detailed descriptions and photographs. Bookings are made by email rather than online; they insist that's an advantage, as it ensures reservations will not be lost. Car rental and tours are also available, and the site holds lots of general Chile links.

Chile Information Project

www.chiptravel.cl
As well as its thorough destination and cultural guide to the country, with separate sections devoted to its history and environment, CHIP offers online booking for hotels and adventure packages, from the northern Atacama Desert all the way to Antarctica. Its own sightseeing tours include a "historical memory" tour of Santiago, focusing on human rights issues.

Go Chile

www.gochile.cl

Large, well-illustrated bilingual Web guide to Chile, packed with destination information for the whole country; simply click on the relevant area for details of accommodation and packages.

Secrets of Easter Island

www.pbs.org/wgbh/nova/easter/
A fascinating interactive guide to Easter Island and its mysterious statues, presented by PBS in the US and bursting with photos, panoramas and TV footage as well as informative text and maps.

China

See also **www.chinaarttours.com** for painting holidays in China.

Access China Tours

www.chinatour.com

North American tour operator, with offices in both Canada and the US, which offers educational and special-interest China trips as well as standard big-city itineraries. Join an expedition along the Silk Road, or take the more leisurely option dedicated to the gardens of famous literary figures. While the site does offer a reservation form, sadly you have to print it out and mail it in.

Adventure World

www.adventureworld.co.nz

This New Zealand operator offers a vast array of packages in China, ranging from climbing sacred mountains to cruises on the Yangtze river. The online booking form, however, merely allows users to express an interest rather than make a firm reservation.

Asian Pacific Adventures

www.asianpacificadventures.com

Californian company that arranges a genuinely unusual programme of special-interest China tours. These include the "Ethnic Festival Explorer" itinerary, to experience the cultures of China's tribal peoples; expeditions into eastern Tibet and onto the Mongolian steppes; and also women-only trips. Complete the full online reservation form if you know what you want, or just send a basic email for enquiries.

China Direct

www.chinadirect-travel.co.uk

Independent London-based travel agency selling a wide and interesting assortment of package trips to China, to lesser-known destinations as well as the major cities, and including walking, cycling and feng shui holidays. All are priced in both pounds and US dollars to suit international customers. The Website carries full itineraries; phone, fax or email to complete your booking.

China Now

www.chinanow.com

Off-the-(Great)-wall Website that started life as an online guide to Beijing and Shanghai, and has since expanded to cover other major cities such as Chengdu, Nanjing and Kunming. Its listings and reviews, however, make dull reading compared to its large database of entertaining articles on travel and cultural themes. Best of all for travellers, though, is that it also sells an unusual assortment of packaged tours, including wilderness adventures, as well as tailor-made China Rocks Underground trips, designed to introduce musicians, artists and anyone else interested to the Chinese rock and alternative-arts scenes; participants have included Oliver Stone and Helen Reddy. You can even arrange to jam with Bad Party Secretary or the Boredom Brigade.

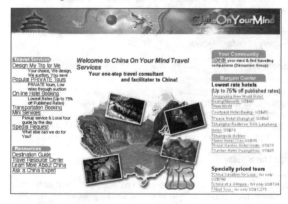

China On Your Mind

www.chinaonyourmind.com

US-based travel brokers, who invite customers planning vacations in China to state their requirements in as much or as little detail as they choose, and then negotiate direct with Chinese tour companies and hotels to come up with the best match and prices. A few standard itineraries are suggested on the Website, and you can also read other travellers' experiences or admire their photos.

China the Beautiful

www.chinapage.com

This entertaining and user-friendly site has nothing to sell, it's simply devoted to stimulating interest in all aspects of Chinese culture. Besides slide shows of painting and calligraphy, it holds translated poetry, fiction and philosophy, and a series of articles and pages exploring Chinese history from a general-interest rather than an academic perspective, with links to related sites. There's also a set of satellite photos, supposedly of the Great Wall, that finally prove you really *can't* see it from the moon.

China Travel System

www.chinats.com

Based in Beijing, the CTS makes it easy for prospective visitors to purchase well-priced tours and arrange hotel accommodation. Whether you want to use their service rather depends on whether you can stomach the propaganda on their Website, such as news stories celebrating the "50th anniversary of peaceful liberation of Tibet".

Chinaetravel

www.chinaetravel.com

The main aim of the Chinaetravel site is to sell package tours to China from Hong Kong, as well as flights, hotels and tours within the country; all are bookable online. It also provides a general introduction to visiting China, with an extensive and well-illustrated destination guide, plus good background material and vital statistics on Chinese history, culture, and geography.

Inside China Today

www.europeaninternet.com/china/

European Internet's China Website exists to provide up-to-the-minute news about China, produced by its own writers as well as gathered off the wires, for its business-traveller subscribers. However, its general-access pages are filled with links to hundreds of China-related Websites and directories, covering not only travel but also topics such as entertainment, politics, history, and popular culture.

Interchange

www.interchange.uk.com

British travel agency, which as well as offering tailor-made special-interest tours of China on such themes as a botanical programme to the mountains of the tropical southwest, can also arrange home stays with local families in major cities all over the country. Call or email for reservations.

People's Daily

http://english.peopledaily.com.cn

For the official voice of Chinese reason, check out the online version of the national newspaper, the *People's Daily*. The Website holds an archive not only of the paper's own articles, back to January 1998, but also such delights as the collected works of Deng Xiao Ping. There's also a fairly outspoken message board.

Shanghai-ed

www.shanghai-ed.com

Though the lack of a site plan makes it all a bit hard to find, this enjoyable Shanghai-based portal-cum-ezine holds plenty of useful information for anyone planning to visit, move to, or study in the city. Aimed largely at the city's expat community, it includes several interesting and amusing regular columns, horoscopes, a serialized crime novel, personal and job ads, and a useful question-and-answer feature for specific enquiries.

Vacationland

www.vacation-land.com

This San Francisco-based company offers online booking for its inexpensive package trips to China, ranging from six days in Beijing or eight days in Tibet up to eighteen-day expeditions along the "Ancient Silk Road". Standard prices are from LA or San Francisco, but you can pay a supplement to fly from elsewhere.

Costa Rica

For volunteer holidays in Costa Rica, see **www.globalservicecorps.org** (p.217), and check the other agencies reviewed in that section.

Costa Rica Accommodations

www.accommodations.co.cr

With links to more than 200 hotels, this clean, efficient site will also hook you up with car rental outfits and local tour companies. The main draw, though, is the searchable accommodation directory: you can browse the full A–Z list, click a region on the map, and search for historical hotels or for places geared towards certain activities (honeymoons, golf, fishing and so on). Reviews are short, with thumbnail photos and links to Websites, and in San José each property is grouped according to price bracket. There's a separate, far smaller, section for rental villas.

Costa Rica Naturally

www.tourism.co.cr

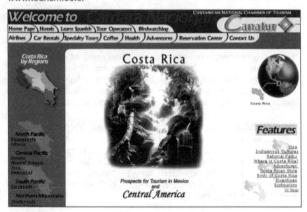

General information site brought to you by Canatur, the Costa Rica National Chamber of Tourism. It's a great place to start, not only for its detailed destination guides and articles on all the essential stuff – national parks, outdoor pursuits, indigenous cultures, eco-tourism and so on – but also the good set of links to individual hotels and jungle lodges, tour operators, language schools and travel agents.

Costa Rica Tourist Board

www.tourism-costarica.com

Though there are lots of photos and plenty of movement on Costa Rica's official tourism site, it's less sophisticated than many of its type, with little in the way of written information. Head for "Know Costa Rica" for all the practicalities – entry requirements, custom regulations and so on – or choose from the menu at the top of the screen for adventure tours and "natural attractions". The trip builder is nowhere near as exciting as it sounds: just a couple of links to local travel companies approved by the tourist board.

Costa Rica Travelweb

www.crica.com

Produced by an online travel agency in San José, this Costa Rica portal is an unabashedly commercial operation, eagerly pushing its own services while also linking to a number of ground operators and scores of hotels (click on a map to search for them by region), most of which you can then contact direct. If you want to use the agency to help custom-build a holiday, submit the detailed online booking form; if you're ready to pay, there's a printable credit card payment form.

Costa Rica's Travel Net

www.centralamerica.com

This is a very good Costa Rica one-stop shop produced by the online travel agency Travel Net. As well as offering package holidays and discounted flights (from North America), the site also provides good destination information and links. Browse the directories of hotels, car rental companies and ground operators (all of which you contact via the site), or work through the handy travel planning sheet, with its links to destination guides and accommodation options. Other features include reviews of all the national parks, detailed area maps, and domestic airline schedules.

Costa Rica Vacation Rentals

www.crvacationrentals.com

For anyone planning to self-cater in Costa Rica, this US-based agency, with a number of luxurious villas and lodges, is a good place to start. Many of the properties also offer nightly rates. Click on the property name to find descriptions and tempting photos, along with weekly rates, then email them direct with enquiries.

Costa Rica Vacations

www.costaricavacations.net

Costa Rica specialists offering flight-included packages from the US for less than $1000 – they have a good variety covering, among other things, rainforest lodges, Caribbean beaches, bird-watching and fishing. Plus links to hotels and car rental companies, late availability deals and good prices on domestic flights, along with add-on tours from San José.

Journey Latin America

www.journeylatinamerica.co.uk
This UK operator, which specializes in reasonably priced holidays to Central and South America, suggests around a dozen individual Costa Rica itineraries and offers three escorted trips (one adventurous "journey", combined with Honduras and Panamá, a "One Step Beyond" adventure trip with Panama, and a "softer" country tour). You can also check out best-buy flight deals – single and return – and air passes; email them direct to make any arrangements.

Reef and Rainforest

www.reefrainforest.co.uk
UK operators specializing in small-scale, natural history-oriented tours. You can read full itineraries and reviews of each tour on the site, and there are plenty of photos. These aren't budget holidays, starting at around £1600, without flights, for a 17-day 4WD itinerary and climbing to £2000 for two weeks "nature deluxe" – bird-watching, snorkelling, river rafting, exploring pre-Columbian ruins and jungle trekking. You could also choose a family-friendly option, a gently paced wildlife-viewing trip, or a romantic break. For scuba diving, you need to contact them direct. To book, print off the form and send a cheque.

South American Experience

www.sax.mcmail.com/costa.htm
UK specialist operator with a good range of short packages in Costa Rica. Options are clearly laid out in tables, with thumbnail descriptions of the various accommodation options available. Alhough they quote ground costs only, you can check airfares and, after registering, book flights through the company. Contact them direct to book the tours and if you want them to help you custom-design your own itinerary.

Croatia

Croatian National Tourist Board

www.htz.hr

This excellent official Website, maintained in both English and German versions, boasts a superb "Lodgingfinder" facility, which will search for hotels in any specified town or according to your chosen criteria, and come up with detailed lists plus Web links and email addresses. Other features include sections on climate and currency, and transport and activities. It also holds extensive listings of Croatia's many naturist centres – including details of where to see the well-known musical *The King is Nude*, based on a summer holiday the Prince of Wales took on the island of Rab before World War II.

Dalmatia Touristic Pages

www.dalmacija.net

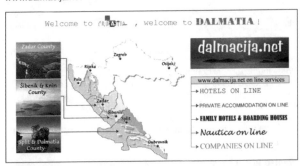

A good, well-illustrated, general site for tourists planning to visit the region of Dalmatia, along the Southern Adriatic coastline. The home page is entirely in English, but after, as you pursue the multitude of links to hotels and other local businesses, you never know whether the text will be in Croatian, English or German. Many hotels offer online booking; in fact you can even charter a yacht online. There's also plenty of background information on food, sport, history and culture.

Generalturist

www.generalturist.com

Croatia's leading travel agency runs an office in New York to cater for North American travellers. The Website promotes a wide range of detailed holiday packages, including a fourteen-day tour entitled "Croatia's Best", but they can also draw up an itinerary to suit your own requirements. Possibilities include food- and wine-themed vacations or simply short city breaks. There's no online booking, but you can email or phone to discuss your plans.

Holiday Options

www.holidayoptions.co.uk

UK package-holiday specialists who offer an extensive programme of holidays to Croatia, including week-long trips to any of ten destinations and longer combinations. Independent travellers can also simply book a seat on one of their charter flights from five UK centres to four Croatian airports (Split, Dubrovnik, Pula and Rijeka). Complete your booking by phone or email.

Istra

www.istra.com

An impressive site promoting the delights of Croatia's Istrian region, with good English translations throughout. A picture of the main local attraction – the "Episcopal Complex of the Euphrasius Basilica", in Porec – appears at the top of every page, but most of what you see is much more practically oriented. Full details of hotels include current prices in Euros and email forms to make reservations, while the food listings include some appetizing photos of the regional seafood speciality *brodet*. If you really need it, you can even pick up a rundown of petrol stations in every town.

Zagreb Tourist Board

www.zagreb-touristinfo.hr

Useful compendium of information on Croatia's capital city, which whets appetites with a couple of Virtual Walking Tours, including 360° panoramas of each successive street. It also carries detailed hotel listings, and lots of practical advice for visitors – plus an email contact for specific enquiries.

Cuba

AfroCubaWeb

www.afrocubaweb.com
An amazing compendium of anything related to Afro-Cuban history and culture, including life in modern Cuba as well as contemporary music and dance. The site also offers general advice on the legal side of travelling to the island, aimed primarily at US citizens, and links to other pages of interest.

Captivating Cuba

www.captivating-cuba.co.uk
Simple, easy-to-navigate site operated by a British company that arranges inexpensive island tours of all lengths and levels of luxury. Aided by basic destination information, you can search for holidays in any preferred location, or perhaps combine Havana with a stay by the beach. They also provide links to climate charts, currency converters, and official British government advice on travel to the region.

Casa Particular Lodging Service

www.geocities.com/casaparticular
English- and Spanish-language site designed to connect prospective visitors with private homes and apartments for rent in Havana and elsewhere on the island. Rates are very reasonable, with no agency fee; in some properties you lodge with a Cuban family, others you have to yourself. Most are fully equipped to a high standard, and all include airport pick-up and drop-off, so if you're looking for "two rooms and warm family" you can't go far wrong.

Center for Cuban Studies

www.cubaupdate.org
Site run by a New York-based non-profit organization that arranges tours for groups and individuals, including regular Cuba Update trips following a pre-planned itinerary, visits to coincide with specific festivals or events, and journeys tailored to suit particular professional interests such as health care or education. They also provide advice on all legal aspects of visiting the country.

Cuba – Consular Information Sheet

http://travel.state.gov/cuba.html

The official Consular Information Sheet, issued by the US government, provides full details on the current US attitude towards Cuba and the ongoing travel embargo; an essential update for prospective US visitors to the island.

Cuba Solidarity Campaign

www.cuba-solidarity.org

The UK's Cuba Solidarity Campaign is sufficiently devoted to the Cuban Revolution to enlist volunteers to join three-week "International Work Brigades" on the island. *Brigadistas* pay around £750, including flight, to carry out agricultural or construction work in a purpose-built camp outside Havana, and to undertake a full programme of educational and political events and visits – as well as the odd trip to the beach.

Cuba Travel Services

www.LAtoCuba.com

In itself, the CTS Website holds little of interest, with some rudimentary listings of hotels and attractions in major Cuban cities, but they do run a direct non-stop charter flight each week from Los Angeles to Havana and from Miami to Cienfuegos, tickets for which can be booked online.

Directorio Turístico de Cuba

www.dtcuba.com/esp/cuba_turistica.asp

Spanish-only site, on which you navigate via an interactive island map to obtain copious destination information and practical listings. As well as links to hundreds of hotels, it also enables you to contact car rental and other agencies, and even local music venues.

Highlife Holidays

www.highlifeholidays.co.uk/cuba/

London-based travel agency that provides assorted conventional package trips to what it calls "the most beautiful island in the Caribbean", with an emphasis on beaches rather than *brigadistas*. Their "Pearl of the Caribbean" tour takes in Havana, Trinidad, Cienfuegos and Varadero. All holidays, as well as flights and car rental, can be booked online.

Hola Sun Holidays

www.holasunholidays.com

Dual-language English and French site run by a Canadian tour company that arranges packages and flight-only deals from Montréal, Quebec or Toronto. Their most popular option is the week-long "Highlights of Cuba", based in Havana and Varadero. Call or email to book.

Marazul Charters

www.marazulcharters.com

US agency that runs charter flights from New York, Los Angeles and Miami to Havana; US citizens are of course subject to their government's regulations concerning trips to Cuba. As **www.marazultours.com** they also arrange personalized packages to the island, concentrating, for example, on professional events and conferences.

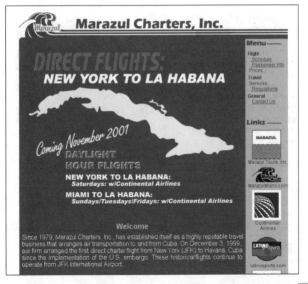

Worldwide Quest

www.worldwidequest.com

Canadian tour company that organizes cycling and hiking expeditions in Cuba each winter, with an emphasis on eco-tourism. Their ten-day "Cuba by Bike" option, using hotel accommodation, tends to be booked up way in advance. Email for details.

Cyprus

Cyprus Tourism Organization

www.cyprustourism.org

Produced by the CTO in New York, this minimal site gives short, rather bland guides to every region in southern Cyprus, with snatches of history (no mention of the Turkish invasion) and practical information on how to get here. For holidays, follow the link to **www.cyprushotdeals.com**, which offers packages, some of which include Egyptian cruises, from around $1500 for two weeks including flight.

President Holidays

www.presidentholidays.com

A UK-based operator that offers sun-and-sand packages to two resorts in Turkish-controlled northern Cyprus, plus city breaks to Istanbul. You can read details of the hotels and B&Bs on the site, check flight schedules, and search for late availabilities. To book, email them direct.

Sunvil

www.sunvil.co.uk

British company offering a range of holidays around the island, many of them off the beaten track. You need to know where you're going, however, or at least have a map in front of you, as the site is laid out on a search basis only. The safest bet is the destination search, where you select from a pull-down menu; the holiday type menu (beach, multi-centre, traditional village and so on), which asks you to specify a month, often fails to come up with a match and offers no alternatives. You can read about accommodation options, check rates and add any potential places to a personalized running list. You then email for availability and to make a provisional booking.

Czech Republic

For city breaks in Prague, see also the operators listed on p.34.

The Czech Center

www.czechcenter.com

The online Czech Center is actually the Website of the New York section of the Czech Tourist Authority, but it's a much better information resource than the authority's main site (at **www.visitczechia.cz**). As well as general destination information and advice on visiting the country, it holds several pages of well-chosen links, including to operators both in North America and in the Czech Republic, to official government sites, and also to online accommodation-booking sites.

Czech-It-Out

www.goaway.co.uk

Sister company to British Goa specialists Goaway (see p.302), handling all aspects of short-break travel to the Czech Republic from the UK, including flights, accommodation in one- to five-star hotels, Prague bus tours, and rental of cars, bikes, and even sports equipment. You can't check availability online, but email the form and they'll be in touch.

Greenways Travel Club

www.gtc.cz

Czech-American joint venture designed to promote small-group and individual travel along the Czech Greenways, a 250-mile corridor of riverside trails that stretches from Prague to Vienna through Southern Moravia and

Bohemia. The Website lists dozens of active vacation possibilities, including walking, cycling, horse riding or canoeing trips, and also guided tours focusing on art, architecture, music, folklore, or bird-watching. Full itineraries and prices are given, plus contact addresses in both Brno and Brooklyn that you can call or email to make a booking.

Lanzotic Travel

www.praguetravelbreaks.co.uk
British tour operator specializing in short-break trips to Prague from London or Manchester, though if you don't want a fully inclusive package you can also buy flights or accommodation, choosing from a long list of hotels. Phone or email to book.

Paul Laifer Tours

www.laifertours.com
New Jersey-based agency that sells all-inclusive packages from any US city to Prague and other Central and Eastern European destinations, including trips that combine the Czech capital with Berlin, Vienna and/or Budapest. Once you've settled on a flight and a hotel, complete the email form to pursue your reservation.

Romantic Czech Tours

www.romanticczechtours.com
US company, with offices in both Seattle and Prague, that runs an extensive programme of tours to the Czech Republic and beyond. Walking and hiking holidays are the twin speciality, with both rural tours and also one-way trips to Vienna or Budapest. Prices are quoted inclusive of airfares from North America, though they can also simply book accommodation. Call or email with your requests.

Travelguide

www.travelguide.cz
This Czech site suffers in parts from rather poor translations into English, but for sheer level of detail its destination guide to the entire country is unparalleled. It also offers comprehensive hotel listings, searchable by region or individual city, and complete in most cases with email addresses for reservation enquiries, plus similar databases of restaurants and Internet cafes.

Denmark

BikeDenmark

www.bikedenmark.com

With its scenic coastline and network of cycle lanes, Denmark is ideal holiday territory for bicyclists. Hence the success of BikeDenmark, a Danish company that arranges self-guided cycling tours of the country, with accommodation in inns and hotels and van transportation for your baggage. Their Website offers full details of such trips as "10 Islands in 10 days", but you can't book direct; instead it provides Web links and/or phone numbers for tour operators all over the world.

The leading tour operator for self-guided tours
Eight high quality tours in Denmark & Southern Sweden

Scandinavian American World Tours

www.scanamtours.com

Based in New Jersey, this tour company claim to have been "Traveling the world since it was flat"; their logo is a Viking longboat rocking on the open sea. As well as packaged vacations in Denmark and throughout Scandinavia, they also sell air tickets and arrange accommodation. Call or email to make your booking.

Scantours

www.scantoursuk.com

UK-based tour operator specializing in Denmark and the rest of

Scandinavia, which uses its Website to display full itineraries and rates for all sorts of Danish holidays, including short breaks to Copenhagen and/or Legoland. Customers from all over the world are welcomed, but you can only make a reservation by calling or emailing their London HQ.

Visit Denmark

www.visitdenmark.com

The home page of the Danish Tourist Board site displays twelve national flags, so you can choose your country of origin and be shown full lists of tour and transportation operators who can take you to Denmark, plus contact details for your local tourist office. Wherever you're from, the site also holds a comprehensive introduction to visiting the country, plus a destination guide to the hotels, restaurants and attractions (with Web and email addresses but not objective reviews) of Danish towns. The one snag is that you need to know the name of the region in which your chosen destination is located before you can get information about it.

Wonderful Copenhagen

www.woco.dk

The centrepiece of Copenhagen's official visitor Website is its vast alphabetical listings section, which ranges from Hans Christian Andersen and Søren Kierkegaard to Bungee Jumping and Miniature Golf. You're most likely to be looking for accommodation here, in which case you can email your requirements to take advantage of the free booking service, under which they'll find and reserve a suitable hotel; they can also arrange transportation and guides.

Dominican Republic

Condor Journeys

www.condorjourneys-adventures.com/dominican.html

With a variety of vacations in Latin America and the Caribbean, Condor have a small but interesting selection in the DR. Choose from sun-and-sand holidays, adventure breaks (including one-day trips), cultural tours based around local festivals, and windsurfing packages in Cabarete. Prices are good, with all-inclusive resorts on the Samana peninsula starting at around £85 per night. Email them for a quote.

Debbie's Dominican Republic Travel Page

www.debbiesdominicantravel.com
A personal site that's worth bookmarking? Strange, but true. Debbie's hugely impressive travel page, which invites readers to contribute their own comments, travelogues and reviews, now has more than 2600 reviews and testimonies about hundreds of Dominican hotels and resorts, with star ratings, contact information and links to Websites for each. Not only that, but diving and golfing reviews and links, a section devoted to weddings, a list of travel agents in North America and Europe, and a lively message board.

Dominican Republic Travel

www.drvacations.com/main.htm
This New York company specializes in land-only vacations, including escorted tours and all-inclusives, throughout the DR. Whether you're into hiking, diving, whale watching, biking, festivals, rubbernecking, honeymooning or just chilling out on the beach, you should find something here. Each itinerary detailed on the site gives only a starting price, however; you need to email them to get fuller details and a quote.

Hispaniola.com

www.hispaniola.com
Online travel guide produced by major Canadian travel agents Uniglobe. Maddeningly, the holiday search and booking system is too often faulty, so it's best to use this site for general travel information, including links to major all-inclusives and hotels – with at least forty in and around Cabarete – virtual tours, a language section and a superb choice of DR maps, including an interactive plan of Cabarete with links to hotels and surf schools. The message boards, on a variety of DR-related subjects, are also worth a look.

Iguana Mama

www.iguanamama.com
Highly rated DR-based adventure and eco-tour company dealing in ground-only packages. The jewels here are the mountain-biking tours, which include a twelve-day coast-to-coast itinerary, but the special family vacations ("pirates, beaches and waterfalls" for example), look great, too,

as do the exciting day-trips – biking, hiking, mule trekking, canyoning, diving and so on. Schedules, highlights and costs are laid out on the site, and you need to email them to make a reservation. If you want them to create an itinerary just for you, fill in the form detailing your interests and requirements.

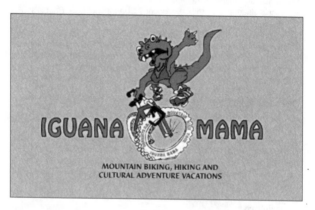

Ecuador

Adrift

www.adrift.co.uk

British white-water rafting operator that offers multi-day rafting trips on the rapids of the Rio Upano, which flows into the Amazon basin. All trips include visits to Quito and Cuenca, and you can add on a Galapagos segment too. Flights are priced separately, so any traveller in Ecuador can join any trip; email or phone for reservations.

Ecuador Explorer

www.ecuadorexplorer.com

The best overall Web guide to the country provides thorough destination information, with plenty of history and culture thrown in. It's most useful, though, for its detailed descriptions of accommodation options of all kinds, and of specialist tour operators, arranged by region and/or activity. Wherever possible, all recommendations come with links to the relevant Websites.

Galapagos Adventure Tours

www.galapagos.co.uk

British operator that arranges small-group tours of all kinds to Ecuador. Take a luxury cruise to the Galapagos Islands, or fly there and then explore on a yacht or motorboat, with diving available on some vessels. Alternatively, take a Jungle Safari or bird-watching trek into the Amazon rainforest. Booking by phone only.

Galapagos Travel

www.galapagostravel.com

California-based cruise specialist, which runs a busy programme of 11- and 14-day Galapagos tours, place an emphasis on environmentally friendly travel. Groups are accompanied by naturalists and biologists, and also given guidance with photography. Reserve via email.

Go2Ecuador

www.go2ecuador.com

Having looked through Go2Ecuador's adequate, if not expansive, destination guide to the entire country, you can use it to find and book hotels, and also arrange tours ranging from half-day sightseeing trips to multi-day packages. Reservations are by email.

Egypt

Africa Point

www.africapoint.com

Visually speaking, this travel agency site is not in the slightest bit exciting;

there's nothing here to stimulate your imagination or answer your questions. What you do get, on the other hand, is a straightforward list of dozens of well-priced Egyptian guided tours, all starting from Cairo. Choices range from three-day city stays to luxury Sun Boat cruises. Reservations can be made by email at the click of a button.

Alexandria 2000

www.alexandria2000.com

Lively site devoted to the city of Alexandria, "The Shining Pearl of the Mediterranean". As well as local news, what's on information, and cultural tips (eg "Subdued colours are best for clothes, shoes, and ties"), it provides extensive coverage of the city's monuments and the latest archeological discoveries in the offshore waters. Aimed more at city residents than visitors, however, it's short on practical help and links for tourists.

Ancient World Tours

www.ancient.co.uk

Ancient World Tours, an agent of the UK-based operator Kuoni Travel, give full details of their mouthwatering programme of attractively priced special-interest historical tours of Egypt, guided by leading archeologists and academics. Besides the obvious destinations, there are plenty of unusual and little-known alternatives, including Roman sites, early Christian monasteries, and the legendary oasis of Siwa, as visited by Alexander the Great. Sadly, you can't make bookings online, just email with enquiries.

Bible and the Mars/Egypt Connection

www.mt.net/~watcher/pyramid.html

The kind of site the Web was invented for, using VERY LARGE TYPE to spread the word of Watcher Ministries, who believe that the Great Pyramid was constructed by angels from the city of Cydonia on Mars to represent the essence of the saving work of the Messiah. All kinds of abstruse facts, figures and Biblical quotations are marshalled to explain the mysteries of ancient Egypt, such as why there aren't two more pyramids at Giza, corresponding to the stars Rigel and Betelgeuse.

Discover Egypt

www.discoveregypt.co.uk

Quick, easy-to-navigate site run by All Leisure Travel of London to promote its "Discover Egypt" tours, which include airfares from London or Manchester.

Their cruises are less high-minded than some, featuring fancy dress parties and belly dancers, while they also have a full programme of diving holidays and monument tours. The site isn't interactive, but you can submit an instant online reservation request form.

Egypt Hotel Reservation Centre

www.egyptreservation.com

A jazzy but easy-to-use site run by the EHRC, which has offices in London and Cairo, and arranges cruises and tours as well as accommodation. Check the latest special offers for bargains. The listings hold an impressive amount of detail on each hotel, but unfortunately you can only request a reservation by email, not check availability online.

Egypt Sphinx Pyramids

www.nauticom.net/users/ata/egypt.html

On first glance, this site appears to focus on the wackier side of ancient archeology. The closer you look, however, you realize that it's been forced to acknowledge "new evidence pointing to humans as the builders of the pyramids", and in fact offers a balanced view of current debates, with lots of links to different theories and conventional research.

Egypt: The Complete Guide

http://touregypt.net

The official Website of the Egyptian Ministry of Tourism makes an excellent resource for travellers. Endearingly, the accommodation listings are divided into "hotels" (with detailed prices and active links) and "hotels with little info", while there's a wealth of details on antiquities and monuments, including glimpses "behind the scenes". Colourful extras include a "virtual dive centre" and a "virtual Khan-el-Khalili" – a simulated tour through Cairo's main bazaar – plus discussion groups and recipes.

Egypt Tours

www.egypttours.com

Illinois-based agent with an extensive programme of Egypt tours, packages and cruises, mostly quite upmarket. Egypt can also be combined with other Middle-East destinations. All trips are available to customers world-wide, who submit the same detailed online booking form but simply deduct the US airfare from the usual price.

Egypt Voyager

www.egyptvoyager.com
General Egyptian site that for once is stronger on modern tourism than ancient monuments. Its superb accommodation database enables you to search over 2000 hotels by price, location, and quality, with links to those that have Websites, and there's good coverage of diving holidays too. You can also download Egyptian music and stationery. On the other hand, all it has to say about the wonderful Luxor Museum of Ancient Art is that it holds a total of 843 objects.

Egyptology Resources

www.newton.cam.ac.uk/egypt/
Massive international database maintained by the Newton Institute in Cambridge, England. As well as links to dozens of specialist archeological and historical sites, you'll find virtual reality tours of the great monuments, and a few resources for modern travellers.

Guardian's Egypt

http://guardians.net

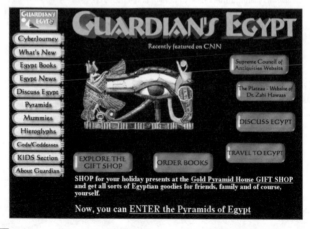

A virtual "cyberjourney" through ancient Egypt, which as well as serious-minded interviews with archeologists and the latest news of excavations, offers 360° panoramas of pyramids, temples and even individual tombs in the Valley of the Kings, to the accompaniment of sonorous booming and other sound effects. There's no practical information, but if you want to see the Sphinx "between the paws" – and buy a few souvenirs too – this is the place to come.

Ker & Downey

www.kerdowney.com

Texas tour company that offers luxurious, gourmet Nile cruises in smaller vessels than most other operators. Trips consist of either seven nights from Luxor or four from Aswan. The Website gives full prices and details, but only enables you to request brochures rather than make bookings.

Museum Tours

www.museum-tours.com

The travel section of this Colorado tour agency's Website simply offers text summaries of their relatively upmarket guided trips to Egypt. Most run for two weeks from New York; the highlight has to be the private small-group sailing trips on the Nile. You can't book online, just email for availability. The site also includes, however, an "Egypt Museum", with an interactive gallery of the Valley of the Kings.

Yallabina @ Cairo

www.yallabina.com

Under the slogan "We take your fun life seriously", the focus here is firmly on Cairo's nightlife. As well as restaurants and bars, it covers sport, movies, theatre, music (including opera and an "Online Salsa Guide"). Its more general Cairo Guide section lists hotels and attractions, but really the assumption is that you're already based in the city.

Finland

Emagine UK

www.emagine-travel.co.uk

British travel company that specializes in tours to Finland, serving as UK agent for several Finnish companies and also taking advantage of Buzz's cut-price flights to Helsinki to offer bargain package tours and city breaks. Their busiest season is midwinter, when they arrange excursions to meet Father Christmas (not the real one) in Lapland. Reservations by phone or email only.

Finnish Tourist Board

www.finland-tourism.com

Visually speaking, this official site is far from appealing, and you have to plod through some rather tedious menus to get anywhere, but there's a lot of information in there once you dig deep enough. Apart from the general destination information, it's especially useful for booking accommodation, with links to individual hotels and hostels and also to umbrella organizations and lodging chains.

The King's Road

www.thekingsroad.com

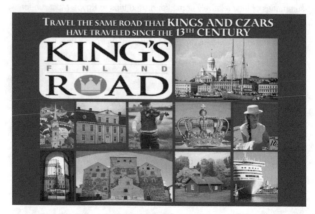

Very attractive site promoting the King's Road, a thirteenth-century route from Oslo to St Petersburg by way of the southern Finnish coast of Finland. As well as details on towns and cities along the way, including Helsinki, there's an invaluable page of links to the (surprisingly many) North American tour operators that now offer the road as an upmarket tourist itinerary.

Virtual Finland

http://virtual.finland.fi/

The Finland Information Pages, maintained by the Finnish Ministry for Foreign Affairs, provide comprehensive details on all aspects of the country's life and economy, ranging from Santa Claus to the national parks. For travellers, the best feature is a full set of tourism links.

Wild North

www.wildnorth.net

This very fancy site, run by a new eco-resort in northern Finland, uses Shockwave aplenty to dish up stunning images of the Finnish wilderness. The resort itself offers adventurous holidays, including such activities as trekking and fly-fishing.

France

Bike Tours

www.biketours.co.uk

British cycle-touring company offering an especially extensive programme of guided trips in France, graded to all levels of fitness and experience. You don't have to ride with the group if you prefer not to, but each day your luggage is carried separately ahead of you to the next evening's hotel or camp site. The Website enables you to select from all upcoming tours, and make reservations online.

Brittany Ferries

www.brittany-ferries.co.uk

As well as providing information and online booking for their cross-Channel ferry services, as detailed on p.58, Brittany Ferries' Website enables users to find and book holiday accommodation all over France. The excellent property search facility covers hotels as well as houses, cottages and chalets. Specify what type of lodging you prefer, when and where, indicate your budget and other requirements (such as being close to a beach), and it makes specific suggestions on which you can pick up further details. Ultimately, you can book the entire holiday, including ferry travel, online.

Brittany Tourist Board

www.brittanytourism.com

The English-language edition of this official site is a very high-tech affair; you can choose the heavily animated Flash version or a simpler html one, but both end up in the same places. Unless you're careful, you're liable to stray into French-language areas, but everything is translated somewhere. Although it holds plenty of information on the region as a whole, its strongest feature is the easy search facility for local hotels.

Corsican Places

www.corsica.co.uk

UK-based travel agency providing hotel, villa and apartment holidays on the rugged Mediterranean island of Corsica. A simple search throws up full details of the most relevant of 150-plus properties, and gives prices for a package that includes flights and car rental. Head first for the fine array of last-minute deals. Bookings are made by email or phone.

CybeVasion

www.cybevasion.com

General travel-related French portal, bursting with connections to hotels, campsites, agencies, and operators throughout the country. You never quite know whether a link will take you anywhere worthwhile, but there's absolutely masses of stuff here, and if you have a particular specialist interest it's well worth trying.

Discover France

www.discoverfrance.com

This US operator, based in Arizona, provides clear, succinct information on destinations throughout France, and promotes a wide range of all-inclusive cycling and walking tours, as well as simple accommodation-only deals. Prices exclude international airfares, while "booking" consists of sending an instant email without an interactive check on specific availability.

Eiffel Tower

www.tour-eiffel.fr/teiffel/tour_uk/index.html

Most of the best-known French monuments, such as the Louvre and the chateau of Versailles, run their own Websites, but the Eiffel Tower has the best. Available in English, it offers a fully illustrated history and chronology of the tower, along with practical details for visitors. The best features, however, are the memory-crunching virtual 3D tour, which enables you to explore via cross-sections, and the streaming video views from the summit. You can even send a postcard from the Tower just to prove you've really been there.

FranceDirect

www.francedirect.co.uk

With a little persistence, this rather fussy British site enables you to select from rental properties in all regions of France, ranging from half-timbered farmhouses to converted windmills. Search by date and area, and it will give you online availability, prices, and booking, including the facility to arrange cross-Channel transportation and travel insurance.

France Holiday Store

www.fr-holidaystore.co.uk

UK-based operator, claiming to be the "largest France specialist travel agency", which sells packages from a compendium of tour operators that cover everything from cycling to canal cruising, fly-drive holidays, short breaks and skiing. The Paris and regional offerings are backed up with useful destination information, while the property search holds over a thousand options, and you'll also find deals on Channel crossings. To complete your booking, email the standard form or phone.

France Tourism

www.francetourism.com

This useful complement to the main French Government Tourist Office site is run by the FGTO outpost in New York. As well as destination and practical information on France and its few remaining overseas possessions, it provides listings, and links where possible, to general and specialist US travel operators. The level of detail tends to be geared more specifically to first-time visitors to Europe, and business travellers.

France Vacations

www.francevacations.net

These Californian operators specialize in bargain travel to France from the US. The most eye-catching deals are on all-inclusive packages, with short

Paris breaks at under $700, but they can also arrange separate accommodation, car rental, and flight-only deals. The Website carries full details; email with specific queries or simply request a brochure.

French Connections

www.frenchconnections.co.uk

Attractive and user-friendly site, run by a British agency, that lists hundreds of gorgeous French holiday homes, complete with enticing pictures. Options range from fifteenth-century chateaux to picturesque stone farmhouses, and the prices too rise from the very reasonable up to £7000 for a fortnight in a chateau near Bordeaux. The easy search facility allows you to see exactly what you're getting. Each property has its own page with photos and prices, and you contact the owners directly to make your reservation. French Connections also offer painting, cookery, walking and other specialist holidays, and discounts on Channel crossings, while the site holds an illustrated bibliography of relevant books.

French Connections

Rental accommodation
Chambre's d'hotes & hotels
Châteaux and Manoirs
Long Winter Lets
Skiing accommodation
Activity holidays
Boating Holidays
Property for sale
At your service
Save on ferry travel costs
Shop direct
French products for sale

France - a world of secret delights just waiting to be discovered. In the heart of Europe its landscape, architecture, culture and history are without compare.

The French Experience

www.frenchexperience.com

New York-based travel agency that offers a full programme of vacation packages in France, including inexpensive transatlantic flights. Having chosen from a long list of budget Paris options or the good weeklong deals for Provence in the south, you can also add short self-drive or even chauffeur-driven tours in the regions, staying in hotels or chateaux. Booking requests are handled by email, phone or fax.

French Festival

www.frenchfestival.com/journeys.html

Small Californian travel agency, featuring a can-canning mademoiselle on its home page, and offering guided tours to Provence in southern France. Once there, you travel from place to place by train, staying in village hotels and hiking in the hills. There's no online booking, but service is personalized and direct.

French Home Rentals

www.frenchhomerentals.com

Oregon agency that specializes in rental properties all over France, available for periods between one week and nine months, and also runs its own French-language school in Villeneuve-sur-Lot in the southwest. Complete their online enquiry form, and you'll get a response within 24 hours.

The French Information Site

www.france.com

Colourful site, run by a Paris travel agency, but in English and featuring a toll-free phone number for US callers. As a general portal, with its own destination information complemented by links elsewhere, it enables users to read the latest French political and cultural news, access local phone directories, and even to download music by Serge Gainsbourg. Its main function, however, is to sell accommodation, minibus tours, car rental and train passes, especially for visitors to Paris. Its "French Hotel Reservation Center" selects hotels by your preferred criteria, and then provides objective guidebook and personal reviews (eg "small with a strong humidity smell, certainly not in line with the price paid") to help with the final decision. Availability can be checked, but booking is not quite interactive; confirmation takes up to three days.

Gîtes de France

www.gites-de-france.fr/eng/

The English-language version of the Website run by Gîtes de France, a government-funded agency that promotes and manages a vast array of B&B and self-catering accommodation in France. Their destination information is good, and the search facility enables you to find specific properties by region or *département*, and check their availability. To complete your booking online, however, you'll almost certainly have to negotiate a few French-only screens. They also have an online bookshop selling their own guides and directories.

Latesavers France

www.latesaversfrance.co.uk
This large searchable database of discounted French holidays from the UK, sold up to three months in advance, doesn't cover hotel accommodation, just "gîtes, cottages and villas" or camping. Search by area and cost, and it comes up with prices that include cross-Channel travel. You then submit a list of trips you'd be prepared to book, and they call you back to confirm. If you're looking for a good-value, short-notice break, this is the place to start.

Logis de France

www.logis-de-france.fr
Organization of independent French hotels, especially in smaller towns and villages, which are promoted together for their consistently good food and reasonably priced rooms. The French-only Website allows you to search out hotels by area and specific characteristics. It only takes four clicks to complete a reservation, but it also takes faith; strangely, you have to go ahead without knowing the exact price.

Maison de la France

www.franceguide.com
Using the English-language section of the French Government Tourist Office's Website enables you to get up-to-the-minute news and details of forthcoming events, and access links to local and regional tourist offices, historic monuments and the like. The practical section, "Your stay in France", is packed with destination and transport information, while asking for lodging connects you to the subsidiary site **www.resinfrance.com**. Not every French *département* is represented, but for those that are, you can specify hotels or guesthouses that meet such criteria as closeness to the beach or ski slopes. Assuming you decipher the final invitation to "see the 9 stays", you can then contact your chosen property direct.

Matthews Holidays

www.matthewsfrance.co.uk
British operator with a straightforward speciality – inexpensive self-drive

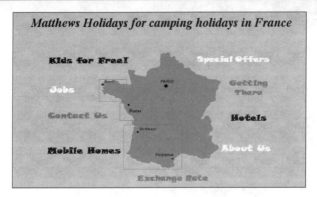

Matthews Holidays for camping holidays in France

Kids for Free!

Special Offers

Jobs

Getting There

Contact Us

Hotels

Mobile Homes

About Us

Exchange Rate

PARIS

Brest

Nantes

Bordeaux

Perpignan

mobile-home holidays in French campsites – and an equally straightforward Website. Once you've opted for one of the three available regions on the opening map – Brittany, the Vendée or Southern France – and picked your precise spot, their impressive price calculator springs into action, factoring in whatever ferry crossings you need, as well as stopovers in hotels en route. You can then complete your booking online.

Morbihan Travel

www.brittany.co.uk

Superb site run by a British agency that arranges self-catering holidays in southern Brittany, in western France. The first words you see are "click here for current availability"; for every property, you can inspect interior photos, pick up full price details, and see whether it's free for the dates you want. Actual bookings are then made by email or phone.

New Frontiers

www.newfrontiers.com/france

The France department of this general North American travel and flight agency offers lots of good-value French package trips from the US city of your choice. Paris choices are legion, with $800 for five nights from LA as a typical price, but the selection elsewhere is more limited, with only certain odd, regional cities available. Email with full details to make a reservation.

Owners in France

www.ownersinfrance.com

A somewhat slow and cumbersome site run by an organization of British owners of around 800 French vacation rentals. Once past the general destination information, search for specific properties by location, price, and facilities, then contact the relevant owner to confirm a reservation. The umbrella organization can arrange discounted rates on cross-Channel travel.

Paris Bed and Breakfast

www.parisbandb.com

California-based directory of private Parisian B&Bs, where you can either stay with a family or rent an unhosted apartment. Choose a neighbourhood via a hierarchy of small maps, and you'll eventually reach photos of specific options. Once you're decided, call the toll-free number in San Diego to finalize your reservation.

Paris Hotels

www.parishotels.com

Very plain, simple site, almost entirely devoted, as the name suggests, to finding the perfect hotel in Paris. Search by availability and/or neighbourhood (including close to the airport as well as in the city centre), click on detailed local maps to see photos and precise rates, and then email your reservation request. They also offer one or two links, to Eurostar and the like, and a handful of regional hotels, but stick to Paris and it's great.

The Paris Pages

www.paris.org

Put together by the Paris Tourist Board, this astonishingly detailed overview of all things Parisian holds links to hundreds of hotels sorted according to price and location; prices, opening hours and descriptions for all the museums and monuments; a handy French glossary; and the opportunity to send electronic postcards to your friends.

Sherpa Expeditions Online

www.sherpaexpeditions.com

Although Sherpa are based in the UK, they sell specialist walking and hiking holidays to customers worldwide. Their trips, too, take place all over the world, but their France programme is especially large and appealing, including both escorted and self-guided tours, and accommodation in tents and mountain huts as well as in village hotels. Areas covered include the Loire valley, the Dordogne, the Alps and the Pyrenees. Bookings made online are provisional, and must be confirmed by mail.

Ski France

www.skifrance.fr/welcome.htm

The English-language version of this French portal provides comprehensive links to ski resorts all over the country. It's not all that easy to use for finding general destination information, but if you have a reasonable idea of where you'd like to go, it will usually come up with an extensive list of last-minute bargains, and put you in touch with a wide range of specific hotels.

SNCF

www.sncf.com/indexe.htm

Few fancy extras on this, the English-language Website of the efficient and user-friendly French rail network – assuming you want to plan and reserve a train journey in France, however, it does the job admirably. Specify the relevant stations, and your preferred departure or arrival times, and it comes up with a bunch of alternative schedules and prices, together with advice as to which rail passes can provide useful discounts. You can complete and pay for your tickets online; they'll mail them to you if there's time, otherwise pick them up at any SNCF station.

The South France Guide

www.le-guide.com

This comprehensive list of vacation rentals in southern France, especially in Languedoc and Roussillon, is maintained by the Home France and French Affair agencies, which operate from the US and the UK. Having used the search engine to find one that appeals to you, at a suitable price, you then email the owner to complete the booking. The site also has a smaller selection of B&Bs, and connects to a database of properties for sale.

Tourist-office.org

www.tourist-office.org

A handy database of France's municipal and local tourist offices arranged by *région* and *département*. In theory, each town's listings include practical and cultural information and links to local Websites, though many of the smaller ones simply offer their address and phone number. There's also a link to the "Bookings" hotel reservations service, which is by no means comprehensive, but for the properties it does include features full online availability checks and reservations.

Voyages Ilena

www.voyagesilena.co.uk
British operator selling all-inclusive holidays to the Mediterranean island of Corsica, with accommodation in hotels, villas and cottages. Follow their detailed destination guide, and if somewhere catches your fancy you can seek out details, with prices, of specific properties. Either email them with your chosen package, or just request a brochure – and be sure to check out their cut-price last-minute offers.

Gambia

The Gambia Experience

www.gambia.co.uk
The only British operator to focus exclusively on holidays in the Gambia, with an emphasis on eco-tourism, activities including bird-watching, safaris and lazing on the beach, and weekly charter flights from Manchester and Bristol as well as London. The "10 Reasons for going to The Gambia" on their Website don't amount to much more than "it's nice and so is the weather", but then that may well be all you want from a destination. If you're interested, call to book.

Germany

For spa holidays, see the operators listed on p.137.

Brendan Tours

www.brendantours.com
US operator specializing in upmarket escorted bus tours. There's an inspiring range of German itineraries, including river cruises and combinations with many other central and eastern European countries. The site has detailed rundowns for each holiday, with weekly fare schedules (land-only

or with flight included), and names – but no photos – of hotels. If you want to book, they advise you to do so through a travel operator – a zip code search enables you to find your nearest agent.

Die Bahn

www.bahn.de

With a database of 150,000 rail stations in Germany alone, German rail network Die Bahn supplies online schedules for rail, road and sea connections all over Europe. Click "International Guests" on the home page for an English-language version.

Germany Online

www.germany-info.org/nf_index.html

Produced by the German embassy in the US, this slick site features all sorts of facts, figures and stats. The travel section is good for practical information on driving, public holidays, customs, visa regulations and so on, with links to city and regional Websites and other relevant sources. They also suggest holiday ideas and itineraries arranged thematically – gay and lesbian, cultural heritage, music, history tours and so on – with plenty of good links.

Germany Wunderbar

www.germany-tourism.de

Exhaustive, Flash-enhanced English-language version of the official tourist

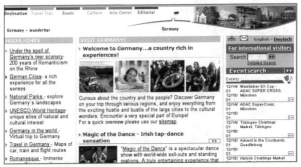

board site. If you can trawl your way through the PR hyperbole, this is a fantastic resource, with links to state tourism boards, city sites, package holidays, ski resorts, accommodation groups and so on, all grouped intelligently by subject area. While you can read about states and cities under "Destinations", "Travel Tips" is perhaps the most inspiring place to start, organized into sections including youth vacations, culinary Germany (where you'll discover "there is no end to the praise of the potato"), national parks, cultural trips, spa breaks and active travel. Each combines original content, links, and a number of suggested itineraries. You can also search the "Events" for happenings, exhibitions, concerts and festivals up to 2003.

Hotels Germany

www.lodging-germany.com
It couldn't be simpler: click on one of the 80 or so towns listed, select hotels from the chart (they're divided into three price categories), read the reviews, pore over the photos, and then use the secure server to make a reservation request.

KD River Cruises of Europe

www.rivercruises.com
US company specializing in cruises along the Rhine, Elbe and Danube rivers, lasting from a few days to two weeks. You can also take a day cruise, or combine a river cruise with a city break in Berlin or a rural touring holiday. The site gives you all the information you need, including sailing dates, itineraries, and costs, with room plans, technical details and photos of all the boats (which take between 100 and 230 passengers). There are savings if you book early, and for April and October sailings. To book, submit an online request.

Net 4 Berlin

www.net4berlin.com
Minimal but useful Berlin directory. The no-punches-pulled area guides feature links to recommended restaurants and bars, and there are separate accommodation lists with links to hostels and guesthouses. Check out, too, the general links for a selection of city guides and accommodation sites.

Rhinecastles.com

www.rhinecastles.com
Searchable information site for the castle-obsessed. Here you'll find links to

maps marking castles; castle travelogues; castle hotels, romantic hotels and country hotels with castle views; operators offering tailor-made and escorted castle tours; castles offering special "knight's meals"; companies offering castle-themed Christmas cards … and a good range of general travel links, too, including general accommodation sites, city and regional sites. Oh, and some photos of castles.

Greece

Aegean

www.agn.gr

Well-presented, visually appealing site, run by OneWorld and covering all aspects of tourism in the Aegean. Navigating through its hierarchy of inter-active maps, you can get full destination information on your chosen area, including climate details, and it's easy to find and contact hotels. Although there are plenty of links to travel agents, however, for nitty-gritty transportation, such as trains and ferries, it provides phone numbers rather than actual timetables, let alone any booking facility.

All Greek Ferries

www.ferries.gr

The best of a number of sites that aim to cover all the ferry services in Greek waters, run by the Paleologos Shipping & Travel Agency in Heraklion, Crete. As well as international connections with Italy, Cyprus, Israel, and Turkey, with useful route maps, it details all the countless domestic inter-island itineraries. Almost all the ferry companies maintain their own sites, but this is the place to choose which one suits your requirements, and offers immediate booking both online or by fax. You can also reserve train and air tickets, car rental, and accommodation.

Athens Survival Guide

www.athensguide.com

Written and maintained by American expat Matt Barrett, this very personal guide can be rather rambling at times, but it's the closest thing to having a helpful friend on the spot to give you whatever advice you need on visiting the city. "Athens is a fun place. It just looks like hell at first glance". As well as lengthy reviews of the eight hotels he recommends, he provides links to

part three: destinations

find others if necessary. He also offers comprehensive information on eating and shopping, links to recommended travel agents, and paeans of praise to the city's pristine new metro system and even to "George the Famous Taxi Driver". Once you're through with Athens, Matt's **www.greecetravel.com** site provides a less all-embracing introduction to travel in the rest of Greece.

Corfu 1

www.corfu1.com
Beneath its over-the-top abundance of flashing lights and funny noises, this frenetic site holds masses of useful information about the Ionian island of Corfu. Assuming you manage to tear yourself away from the page devoted to the Museum of the Fighters for Heptanesian Independence, you'll find links to all the businesses you might need, including the island's hotels, buried in among the rest.

Dilos Holiday World

www.dilos.com
Travel agency with offices on Crete and, for some reason, in Belgium too, which specializes in cruising the Aegean. Their site presents full itineraries and prices for various vessels, and offers online booking. They can also arrange accommodation all over Greece, or further afield, and car rental, while their destination guides are strong on Greek history and culture.

Explore Crete

www.explorecrete.com

A general destination guide to the island of Crete, which for once isn't desperate to sell you anything. Instead, it holds lots of enthusiastic articles and colourful virtual guides; there's not a lot of practical stuff in there, but it's great for firing your enthusiasm.

Filoxenia

www.filoxenia.co.uk

British tour company that runs an extensive programme of special-interest holidays in both mainland Greece and the islands, including botany, history, archeology, painting and culture. Most of their site consists of a run-through of brochures you can then order, but they do illustrate some of their options in greater details, and through their "Greco-File" consultancy they will answer queries, design tailor-made packages, and point you towards other operators who provide complementary trips.

Gogreece.com

www.gogreece.com

California-based portal, aimed primarily at first-time American visitors to Greece, which provides an overview of every destination along with links to local tourist offices, plus air, rail and ferry services, and information from the simple to the technical about the country's language, history, culture and contemporary politics.

Greek Islands Club Online

www.greekislandsclub.com

Run by upmarket British tour operator Sunvil Holidays, this site enables prospective visitors to search for their ideal holidays by island, holiday type (such as watersports, sailing or "traditional village"), or simply late availability. All prices are detailed, but rather than booking online you have to make further enquiries by email or phone.

Homeric Tours

www.homerictours.com

The largest specialist US operator to Greece, with a long and varied programme of vacations on the Greek mainland and islands, plus, of course, cruises in between. Some are geared towards ancient sights, others simply dedicated to hedonism, and the rates tend to be consistently low. Fill in the email booking form to secure the trip that interests you.

interkriti

www.interkriti.org

A comprehensive guide to Crete, the largest of the Greek islands, run by an agency in the capital Heraklion. It's most useful for providing an overview –

literally, thanks to its plethora of aerial photos. "Landing" its motorized paraglider Pegasus in any town brings access to a database of hotels, car rental and other listings, while a bulletin board carries details of other visitors' experiences.

International Chapters

www.villa-rentals.com

International Chapters, who rent upmarket villas in several worldwide locations, are represented throughout Greece, including properties on Mykonos, Crete, the Dodecanese, the Saronic islands of Spetses and Hydra, and on the mainland in Peloponnese. If money's no object and the ferries seem too slow, they can even get you there by helicopter. The Website has full details, but you can only submit a wishlist of properties rather than make online bookings.

Laskarina Holidays

www.laskarina.co.uk

A British company that specializes in high-standard apartment, villa and house stays on remote and unspoiled Greek islands. Their Website holds few photos, so it's very quick and easy to use, but fails to provide actual prices, let alone online availability or booking, and serves primarily as a brochure-request service. It's included here simply because the actual holidays are so good.

Leros

www.leros.org

A nice little site, devoted to the island of Leros in the Dodecanese, and available in four different languages. Nudging a cute donkey from page to page, you'll find detailed destination guides, plus lots of history, an atmospheric gallery of old photographs, and a helpful message board for prospective visitors. The listings are somewhat cursory, but there are enough to arrange a holiday.

Parosweb

www.parosweb.com

This exemplary little site covers the island of Paros, doubling as an online community for locals and a great source of information for would-be visitors or even residents. As well as offering virtual strolls around the island, and live Webcams from four locations, it holds busy message boards, warns you against the "stool-pigeons" who lie in wait for arriving ferry passengers, and enables you to check out restaurant menus and email a wide range of hotels. You can even mail a musical Paros postcard to your friends.

Pharos Agency

www.flypharos.com
New York agency, established in 1924, that offers a wide range of all-inclusive packages to Greece, with combinations such as a week divided between Athens and cruising the islands. While very detailed, most of their site does not offer online booking; they do, however, have an interactive search engine for finding cheap flight deals to Athens from the US.

Skiathos Island

www.skiathosinfo.com
Jazzy information site for the island of Skiathos, in which lots of pop-up menus chase you around as you track down every imaginable local business. Once you've got the destination information you need, you can link to **www.skiathos-direct.com** to contact specific hotels and travel operators. As well as arranging all-inclusive packages, you can also simply buy your ferry tickets.

Sunisle

www.sunisle.co.uk
London-based operator specializing in "Unspoiled Zakynthos", the southernmost of the Ionian islands. Their Website enables you to check online availability for a wide range of villas and apartments, and either finalize reservations or simply hold dates for a few hours while you make up your mind. They also provide links to arrange flights and car rentals.

The Symi Visitor

www.symivisitor.com
A site run by the local English-language newspaper for the lovely island of Symi in the Dodecanese that enables you to bypass the major tour operators and make your own arrangements to stay in island villas and apartments. It also features satellite photos and real-estate ads, plus local gossip and a message board.

Travel à la Carte

www.travelalacarte.co.uk

Easy-to-use site set up by a British tour operator that arranges holidays on islands in the Ionian, Sporades and Dodecanese groups. You can search for accommodation to suit your precise requirements, or just browse the late availability offers. Having checked availability by email or phone, you print your booking form from the site and mail it in.

Travelux

www.travelux.co.uk

British tour company that arranges packages both on the Ionian islands and on the mainland. As well as simple sun-and-sand holidays, you can improve your mind or your body by joining special trips devoted to painting, photography, sailing, trekking or tuition in the Alexander technique. The Website details all prices, but you have to email or phone to check on availability.

Valef Yachts

http://valefyachts.com

Valef Yachts is a US-based agency that specializes in private yacht charters and cruises around the Greek Islands. You can't literally book online, but email your choice of their set itineraries, or simply indicate how much you're prepared to spend on your own luxury voyage, and they'll take it from there, making all necessary transport arrangements.

Haiti

Haiti World

www.haitiworld.com

Somewhat dysfunctional Haitian portal, which takes an eternity to load and doesn't always take you where you want to go, but should in principle be able to connect you with hotels all over the country, and to operators such as Voyages Lumière in Port-au-Prince, which arranges trips to Voodoo festivals.

Hungary

Budapest.com

www.budapest.com

Locally based Web guide to Budapest, featuring a slide show of city attractions, listings of restaurants, shops and bars, and, most usefully, a hotel reservation service, for which you submit email requests stating three preferred options, and they get back to you once they've checked availability. Specific personal queries about visiting Hungary are also answered.

Kirker Holidays

http://kirker.ping.co.uk

UK city-break operator that offers short stays in any of seven hotels in Budapest – "the Paris of Central Europe". Complete an email reservation request to get full details on airfares.

Paul Laifer Tours

www.laifertours.com

US tour company specializing in eastern Europe (see also p.268), which offers "classic" eight-day packages to Budapest from any US city, and also twin-centre holidays to both Budapest and Prague. Choose from several alternative hotels, then send the email form to make a reservation.

Iceland

Iceland's geothermal Blue Lagoon is reviewed on p.138.

Arctic Experience

www.arctic-experience.co.uk

Environmentally-conscious British tour company that in addition to basic weekend breaks in Reykjavik offers a huge assortment of active and adventurous trips to Iceland, including hikes and jeep safaris through volcanic and geothermal wildernesses, or whale- and seal-watching in the fjords. The Website carries full itineraries, and includes an email booking form.

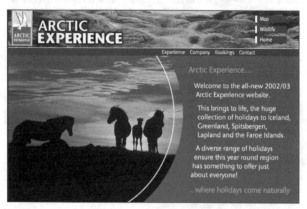

Icelandic Tourist Board

www.icetourist.is

The official Website for Iceland's tourism industry provides a colourful introduction to Europe's second largest island, with plenty of spectacular images and lots of cultural and historical information. (This includes the true story of Gudrid Thorbjarnardottir, who attempted to found a settlement on the site of modern New York during the eleventh century, and later made a pilgrimage on foot to Rome.) While its Yellow Pages section does carry listings of hotels and restaurants, with Web links where available, the lack of a good search facility, let alone detailed reviews, means that it's not all that useful for making practical travel arrangements – and thanks to the idiosyncrasies of Icelandic typography, it can also be a little hard to read.

Iceland Virgin Earth

www.icelandholidays.com

Run by a British tour operator, this site announces itself as "the one-stop Website for booking holidays in Iceland". Its bread and butter lies in long weekends or fly-drive holidays using inexpensive Icelandair flights from Heathrow, but its pull-down menus also reveal longer adventure trips into the interior, with an email form to pursue your enquiries.

Northern Lights Tours

www.randburg.com/is/nlt.html

The Iceland programme of British operator Northern Lights Tours includes inexpensive hotel breaks in Reykjavik and straightforward fly-drive packages, but also extends to cover more active options like kayaking in the fjords and even "a Holiday with the Icelandic Horse". As the name suggests, they can also ensure that you see the "northern lights" themselves, the legendary aurora borealis. Their Website welcomes customers of any nationality, with a simple email form to send if you want to make a reservation.

India

See also our section on New Age, religious and spiritual holidays, which starts on p.207.

Above The Clouds

www2.gorp.com/abvclds

Vermont-based US company who offer a wide range of high-terrain treks in the Himalayas, including a reasonably priced, three-week expedition across the Tibetan plateau through the traditional Buddhist areas of Ladakh. Sadly, once you've made your choice, you have to print off the Trek Application and use snail mail.

Business Tourism

http://businesstourism.com/train.html

This Asian tourist trade magazine provides a super-fast, very useful facility for planning journeys on India's rail network. Enter your departure point and destination to get the major trains serving that route; quick as a flash they come up with full details – departure and arrival time, frequency, facilities, stop-offs required and so on. To make a reservation, you need only to key in the first four digits of your credit card. They then contact you, giving you a reference number against which you can release the rest of the digits.

Chandertal Tours and Himalayan Folkways

www.chandertal-tours.freeserve.co.uk

In conjunction with its offshoot Himalayan Folkways, UK-based agency Chandertal Tours offers a stunning range of customized activity tours throughout India. The general trekking programme includes a 26-day budget trek and a 32-day trans-Himalayan trek, plus walks geared towards wild flowers or geological features, and even one designed to induce weight loss. Several of the same routes, such as from Manali in Himachal Pradesh to Leh in Ladakh, can also be followed by pony, mountain-bike, motorcycle, or jeep safaris. In addition, you can fish for the legendary mahseer fish in rivers in both North and South India, or tour spice and coffee plantations in the South. In fact, you're invited to suggest pretty much anything you fancy by email and they promise to do their best to arrange it. All trips are priced on a land-only basis, so participants from all countries are welcome.

Cox and Kings

www.coxandkings.co.uk

Large UK-based operator that's one of the major players in offering upmarket guided tours of India, using internal flights and staying (wherever possible) in luxury accommodation. The Website provides details and prices of their dozen or so tours, which range from the 9-day Indian Experience exploring the Golden Triangle of Delhi, Agra and Jaipur, for £695 up to the 19-day Grand Tour. You can then ask for their brochures and make your booking by phone or email. Typical prices, including return flight from Britain, are slightly over £100 per day.

Delhigate.com

www.delhigate.com

Specialist Delhi site with the added gimmick of offering a free online query service, which guarantees a personal email response to any question about the city. The site itself provides rail and air timetables, and lists rather than reviews Delhi's restaurants, hotels, and Internet cafés, with links where possible. One highlight is the section on "bad businesses", warning customers, for example, to steer clear of the restaurant that served a vegetarian kebab with a complete brass screw hidden in it. Limited coverage of the rest of the country includes online hotel bookings nationwide.

Discovery Initiatives

www.discoveryinitiatives.com
UK-based company dedicated to "Inspirational Travel to support conservation worldwide", which offers tailor-made itineraries via its very glitzy Website, such as exploring rural Rajasthan on horseback or a South Indian "Wildlife and Cultural Odyssey", visiting national parks and wildlife preserves as well as major cities. Tours are priced in both pounds and dollars.

Essential India

www.essential-india.co.uk
UK agency that offers courses of all kinds in India, such as studying painting in Goa, or learning ceramic traditions in the Himalayas. Warning that India "can be both frustratingly disappointing and breathtakingly wonderful", they aim to combine an experience of the atmosphere of India with the chance to develop new skills.

Explore the Taj Mahal

www.taj-mahal.net/
If you just want to say you've seen the Taj Mahal, this is the place to come.

As well as providing a breathtaking 360° virtual tour of India's best-known monument, it also offers a plethora of links to further information, including details of its current environmental peril.

Geographic Expeditions

www.geoex.com

Active worldwide, but based in California, Geographic Expeditions run an extensive programme of small-group India tours, including conventional sightseeing itineraries as well as trekking in Sikkim, Ladakh and Zanskar, exploring the jungles of Arunachal Pradesh, sea kayaking in the Andaman Islands, and visiting the colourful Pushkar Camel Fair in Rajasthan. They're far from cheap, but they have a high reputation. Though their Website gives extensive details, it only allows you to email for further information and brochures.

Goaway

www.goaway.co.uk

The wittily-named Goaway agency specializes in bargain packages from Britain to Goa, with options to combine the South Indian beach resort with a few days in Delhi, Mumbai or Kerala. Despite the low prices, they offer accommodation in luxury Goa hotels, and Ayurvedic treatments are also available.

Heritage Hotels of India

www.heritagehotels.com

Umbrella organization of hotels set in some of India's finest historical monuments, including magnificent forts in Rajasthan and the Himalayas, and palaces still used by Maharajahs. Most have their own Websites, offering online or email booking. The photos – and the prices – are all but irresistible, with luxurious rooms in places such as the Karni Fort in Udaipur or the Rohet Garh outside Jodhpur working out at well under £30/$40 per night.

Himalayan Travel

www.himalayantravelinc.com

US company, based in Connecticut, that arranges inexpensive tours and group treks throughout Asia. Its India programme ranges from a 16-day camel and bicycle safari through Rajasthan, culminating in a side trip to the Taj Mahal, to "the ultimate Himalayan high", a 26-day trek across "Little Tibet" to climb a 6000m peak.

Indian Railways

www.indianrail.gov.in
The official site of Indian Railways – the world's largest railway system, carrying over eleven million passengers per day. Though you can't buy tickets online, it holds full timetables, with online availability checks and fares for services up to three months in advance, and details of Indrail passes for foreign travellers. There are no destination guides, nor illustrations of any kind, but if you need to look up practical information, you'll find it here.

India Travel Portal

http://travel.indiamart.com
Among the very best of the overall India sites, this huge directory holds links to destinations throughout India. It's packed with information for prospective visitors to cities, forts, temples, museums and historic attractions all over the subcontinent, and once you've decided where you're going, you can choose from extensive links to tours and hotels.

Indus Tours

www.industours.co.uk
London-based tour company with a large programme of general-interest trips around India, covering lesser-known areas such as Orissa, Sikkim and Ladakh in addition to the well-trodden paths of Rajasthan and Goa. They also run specialist painting tours, designed to celebrate India's "perpetual feast of light, colour and atmosphere", which take artists from location to stunning location, and offer the chance to study the 5000-year traditions of Ayurvedic Medicine. Email to pursue enquiries.

Kerala.com

www.kerala.com
A colourful and exciting portal that abounds in links to all aspects of the tropical southern state of Kerala. As well as individual cities like Cochin and Trivandrumand, it has extensive coverage of the major goal for most independent travellers – the Kerala backwaters. Thanks to its long list of hotels and tour operators, it's possible to book accommodation and boat transport.

Kerala Connections

www.keralaconnect.co.uk

Small, independent British tour operator that arranges all-inclusive packages in Kerala, at India's southernmost tip and also handles bookings for resorts, hotels and self-catering villas. Their simple but attractive Website modestly calls the region "the best place in the world for a holiday". How much you pay depends on the level of luxury you prefer, but it's possible to arrange something on the tiniest of budgets.

Madhya Pradesh

www.mptourism.com

The enthusiastic official tourism Website of the central state of Madhya Pradesh holds an adequate rather than exhaustive guide to regional destinations such as the temples of Khajuraho. It comes into its own, however, in its eagerness to plan and book personalized tours. Email a request to visit Kanha National Park, for example – Asia's biggest wildlife sanctuary and Kipling's inspiration for *The Jungle Book* – and they'll arrange everything, including "ethnic dances and souvenirs".

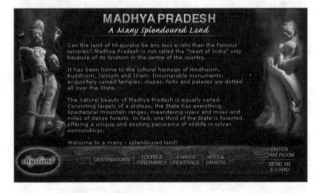

Oksana

www.oksana.co.uk

This British operator arranges adventurous expeditions worldwide, with an

Indian programme that includes hiking, pony-trekking and camping in the Himalayas of Uttar Pradesh. As well as taking in pilgrimage sites at the source of the Ganges, you also walk through the Valley of Flowers, and as a last-day treat visit the Taj Mahal. The reasonable tour prices do not include flights from your home country. Print and mail the onscreen form to book.

123India.com

www.123india.com

This specialist search engine should be able to answer any question about India you care to throw at it. Topics range widely through news, business, and pop culture, but visitors will gravitate to its Travel and Tourism page, which offers links to destination and practical information of every kind.

Orissa

www.orissa-tourism.com

Multi-coloured search clouds dance around your cursor as you explore the attractive official site of the east-coast state of Orissa. The thoughtful menu structure means you only get the information you ask for, but it's all there, with links to local tour operators and full accommodation details. Highlights include the cities of Bhubaneswar and Puri, and Konark, home of Orissan classical dance.

S D Enterprises

www.dandpani.dircon.co.uk

S D Enterprises, run from north London by the friendly Dr Dandapani, specialize in putting together complex itineraries for independent travellers wanting to explore India by rail. As well as planning and reserving all the train connections at bargain rates, and selling rail passes where they work out cheaper, they can also book accommodation. The Website has full details and schedules, including prices.

Welcome to India

www.tourindia.com

This Website, maintained by the Government of India Tourist Office in the US, is considerably easier to use, and more reliable, than the garish and very skimpy India-based equivalent. While it can provide masses of general information about destinations throughout the subcontinent, however, it's not so hot on the practical side of things, with only rather rudimentary links to hotels, tour operators and the like.

Worldwide Adventures

www.worldwidequest.com

This US company specializes in adventurous trips to remote places the world over. Most of their India programme is devoted to expensive tours of cultural and historical highlights such as the Taj Mahal and the palaces of Rajasthan, rather than more active pursuits, but they do offer trekking and cycling expeditions in the Himalayas, and also wildlife-watching trips to the national parks further south.

Indonesia

Bali Indonesia Travel Portal

www.indo.com

Although the Indonesia Travel Portal proclaims itself a resource for the entire archipelago (or "necklace of equatorial emeralds"), for the most part it concentrates on Bali, and on the upper end of the tourism market at that. Separate sections, decorated with gorgeous photos of luxury resorts, are devoted to "Bali for beauty", "Bali for lovers", and "Bali for family". That said, it does carry online hotel listings for several other islands as well, plus a reasonable guide to Jakarta; the Top 10 hotels each week offer discounts of up to sixty percent.

Bali Network

www.balinetwork.com

An appealing site, dedicated to the island of Bali – Indonesia's most popular tourist destination – and designed so that each page resembles a page of a spiral-bound notebook. From the links on the home page, you'd think its coverage was very limited, but in fact these are just paid advertisements, and if you work your way through the destination information for any of Bali's eight separate "regencies" you'll come to extensive cultural details and practical listings, including rates and photos for all the hotels.

The Bali Travel Forum

www.balitravelforum.com

A site that draws on the experiences of residents and visitors to provide information and advice for travellers to the "Ultimate Island". Polls reveal the best and the worst of Bali (in the latter category, 2.92 percent of respondents voted for "stray dogs", as opposed to 17.71 percent for "greedy or rude tourists"). If you can't find what you want in the archives, you can always just ask a direct question. The site is maintained by two associated sites, the Bali Hotel Bargain Finder and **http://balivillas.com**, which claim to offer the best available prices in a limited range of accommodation.

Darshan Tours

www.darshantours.com

Hawaii-based company specializing in eco-tourism trips to Southeast Asia, under the slogan of "Journeys to Heavenly Places". Their programme covers Bali and Lombok as well as lesser-known islands, and includes diving and wildlife tours alongside beach vacations. The Website includes plenty of serious destination information, but no online booking.

Footprint Adventures

www.footprint-adventures.co.uk

Specialist wildlife and trekking company, based in the UK, whose wide range of Indonesian trips include safaris devoted to orang-utans and komodo dragons, and five-day hikes up Mount Rinjani. Follow the site's simple hierarchy to get full details on any tour; you can then book, and pay a deposit, by emailing a form or using the secure online server. Tour prices are ground-only, so travellers from anywhere, including those already in Indonesia, are welcome to use the service. You can also buy a range of *Footprint* travel guides from here (though the two companies aren't officially linked).

Indonesia and Bali Tourism

www.indonesia-tourism.com

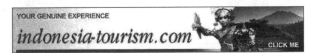

YOUR GENUINE EXPERIENCE

indonesia-tourism.com

CLICK ME

Indonesia's official tourism Website does a pretty good job of covering the whole archipelago, as opposed to just Bali. Clicking on the interactive map on the home page will take you to any island that catches your fancy, each of which holds plenty of further links exploring local history and culture. There's not all that much useful practical information, however, and it's pret-

part three: destinations

ty hard to find. Whether you're looking for hotels, restaurants or travel agents in any one region, you have to go via what at first appears to be a blank "Accommodation" page.

Komodo Tours

www.komodotours.com
An Indonesian-owned travel and tour agency, based in Denpasar on Bali, which specializes in arranging three- to nine-day guided wildlife expeditions to the three tiny islands that constitute Komodo National Park, in pursuit of the legendary ten-foot Komodo dragon and even giant crocodiles. They also offer visits, including day-trips as well as longer stays, to several other islands. Prices are quoted in US dollars to suit international customers; reservations are made by email.

Symbiosis Expedition Planning

www.symbiosis-travel.com
London-based agency that arranges all-inclusive adventure and/or special-interest expeditions to Indonesia (and other Asian destinations) from the UK. With a consistent emphasis on eco-tourism, they cover several islands, including cycling trips on Sumatra and West Java and courses in batik painting or scuba diving on Bali. Reserve by email.

Tourism Indonesia

www.tourismindonesia.com
The most comprehensive directory to all matters Indonesian, bursting with cultural, historical, and practical links. It can tell you the going rate for a block of Danish Lurpak butter in Jakarta (it's 3000 rupiah), or connect you to 25 sites about the orang-utan, including one that shows a streaming video of an orang-utan playing the piano. The "Travel Links" page can put you in touch with any number of operators, agencies and general destination guides.

Worldwalks

www.worldwalks.com
British tour company Worldwalks use their Website to advertise their small programme of guided walking tours on the island of Java, which take in active volcanoes as well as the magnificent temple of Borobudur. Ground-only rates quoted, so customers from all over the world are welcome; booking is via email.

Ireland

Dublin Tourism

www.visitdublin.com
The official visitor information Website for Dublin carries full what's-on listings for the city, along with links to places to stay or rent a car, and a huge programme of special offers ranging from musical pub crawls to speedboat rides. Detailed enquiries tend to connect you to the Irish Tourist Board's national databases, but if you're only visiting the capital you should find everything you need right here.

Family Homes of Ireland

www.family-homes.ie
Extensive listings of both B&Bs and self-catering accommodation in the towns and countryside of Ireland. The supposedly "whimsical" personal note from Irish Taoiseach (Prime Minister) Bertie Ahern with which the site opens is in fact just a straightforward endorsement, but that has to count for something. Contact individual properties via email or phone, or simply send your requirements to the co-ordinating office in Galway.

Hill-walking in Ireland

www.simonstewart.ie
Simon Stewart's enthusiastic personal site is devoted to all aspects of hill-walking in Ireland, and complements his own fully illustrated step-by-step trail guides with lots of links to commercial tour operators and other information sites.

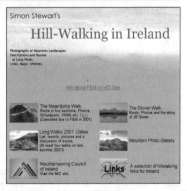

Ireland's Blue Book

www.irelands-blue-book.ie
Choose "Members" from the home page of this accommodation site to find full list-

ings of characterful (and, as they put it, "gracious") independent B&Bs, hotels and restaurants throughout Ireland. All are in scenic rural locations, and most are housed in historic buildings. Each has its own page here, with links to its own site for online reservations.

Irelandhotels.com

www.irelandhotels.com

This large database of hotels and guesthouses, searchable either by clicking on an island map or using pull-down regional and town menus, comes up with accommodation options for virtually every destination in the country, with an emphasis on fishing and golfing holidays. For most, you're given links to their own Websites, or just the phone numbers, but you can specifically request those that offer instant availability checks and online booking via Irelandhotels.

Irelandvacations.com

www.irelandvacations.com

This easily searchable Website, maintained by the Irish Tourist Board for the convenience of North American visitors, is packed with listings of, and links to, specialist tour operators in the US and Canada, and also summarizes transatlantic air services. For general destination information, however, users are automatically put through to the Board's main site (see p.311).

Irelandyes

www.irelandyes.com

In addition to promoting her *Best Little Guide to Ireland* guidebook, self-styled "Ireland expert" Michele Erdvig, who lives in Atlanta, uses her Website to sell her itinerary-planning service to prospective US visitors to the Emerald Isle. However, there's enough useful free information here, in the form of her archive of FAQs and copious links to other sites, to make it worth a few minutes of anyone's time.

Irish Farm House Holidays

www.irishfarmholidays.com

An association of farmhouses all over Ireland that offer officially approved lodging for both short- and long-stay guests, and offer genuine country cooking into the bargain. There are 31 properties in Galway alone, for example; some have their own email addresses, others just a phone, and you can also email booking requests to the Website itself.

Irish History on the Web

wwwvms.utexas.edu/~jdana/irehist.html

Carefully chosen directory of links, put together by an academic at the University of Texas, that's designed to illuminate all aspects of Irish history in a non-partisan manner, from the distant past all the way via the Famine to the Troubles. Users can inspect reproductions of original documents, find information to aid in genealogical research, check out timelines, and pick up lists of further reading. None of it is geared towards travel, but it makes a great source of background information.

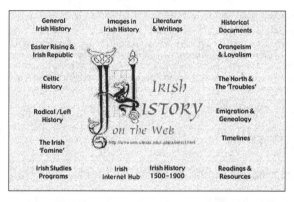

Irish Tourist Board

www.ireland.travel.ie

The official site of the Irish Tourist Board (Bord Failté) is exemplary, with masses of advice on what to see and do in every part of Ireland, complete with links to operators, photos and a good routefinder, plus very full accommodation listings – there's a selection of hotels and B&Bs in every town, including 21 hostels in central Dublin alone – and detailed background information on history, music and culture. Further links connect to the Board's top-notch subsidiary sites such as **www.golf.travel.ie**, **www.walking.travel.ie** and **www.equestrian.travel.ie**.

Ryanair

www.ryanair.com

For anyone planning a trip to Ireland from the mainland UK, the Website of budget airline Ryanair (see p.44) makes an essential first stop. Quoted one-way fares between five airports in Ireland and thirteen in the UK start as low as an amazing £1, with nothing higher than £20. True, you have to add in airport taxes, and put up with drawbacks like the lack of inflight food, but Ryanair has engineered a boom in Irish tourism, even if it has yet to offer all-inclusive packages itself.

Time Out Tours

www.timeouttours.com

Donegal-based operator that provides a huge assortment of Irish holidays. They'll schedule a detailed sightseeing or pub-crawling itinerary for you, arranging accommodation to suit your needs, or fix up an activity-based package such as a multi-day cycling trip or a tour of Ireland's narrow-gauge railways. There's an email form to request a firm booking, or you can simply ask for further advice.

Israel

AMI Travel

www.amitravel.com

North American/Israeli company specializing in inter-denominational pilgrimages to the Holy Land. Also, as the US representatives of the SPNI (Society for the Protection of Nature in Israel), they offer some great adventure trips, including desert hiking, camel trekking and snorkelling, lasting between one day and a fortnight. You can email them direct to make a provisional booking, or reserve using their downloadable enquiry form.

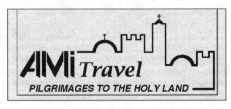

Israel Kibbutz Hotels Chain

www.kibbutz.co.il

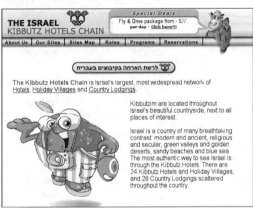

THE ISRAEL KIBBUTZ HOTELS CHAIN

Special Deals
Fly & Drive package from - $27
per day - **Click here!!!**

About Us | Our Sites | Sites Map | Rates | Programs | Reservations

לרשת האירוח בקיבוצים בעברית

The Kibbutz Hotels Chain is Israel's largest, most widespread network of <u>Hotels</u>, <u>Holiday Villages</u> and <u>Country Lodgings</u>.

Kibbutzim are located throughout Israel's beautiful countryside, next to all places of interest.

Israel is a country of many breathtaking contrast: modern and ancient, religious and secular, green valleys and golden deserts, sandy beaches and blue sea. The most authentic way to see Israel is through the Kibbutz Hotels. There are 24 Kibbutz Hotels and Holiday Villages, and 28 Country Lodgings scattered throughout the country.

The kibbutz has come a long way since 1909, when Israel's first co-operative agricultural community was established in a wave of idealism. Today many of the country's 270 kibbutzim offer accommodation for tourists for up to a few days at a time. The Kibbutz group has some fifty hotels, holiday villages and "country lodgings", most of them in lovely surroundings and many of them with upmarket resort facilities. You can click on a map to read details of each, with room photos and rate charts (look out for the special Internet-only deals), and make secure online bookings.

Israeli Internet Guide

www.iguide.co.il
Israeli links, organized by subject: if you're after a specific destination, key the city or area name into the search engine to find sites on everything from weather, maps and tourism information to religion and bibliographies.

Israel Ministry of Tourism

www.goisrael.com
With its tag line "No one belongs here more than you", Israel's North

American tourist Website, keen to emphasize the safety of travel to Israel, makes trip planning a dream. Features include links to airlines, cruise operators and hotel groups, and various search mechanisms allow you to hunt for an Israel travel specialist near you or for adventure tours, family holidays, inter-denominational tours and such like for a range of budgets.

Kibbutzim Site

www.kba.org.il/eng/welcome.htm
Links to various kibbutzim and related organizations, with details of volunteer opportunities for overseas visitors.

Longwood Holidays

www.longwoodholidays.co.uk
UK operator with a choice of holidays to Israeli resorts, including Eilat, plus Jerusalem and Galilee. There's too much distracting movement on the site, but it does cover the resorts and the hotels, along with ground tours and special packages, including PADI diving courses and kibbutz fly-drive deals. To actually make your travel arrangements, however, you need to call their hotline.

Maven Search

www.maven.co.il
Far-reaching portal with some 5000 reviewed links arranged by subject. Though it's a portal to the "Jewish World", which of course extends far beyond Israel, its "Travel and Tourism" channel pulls up local tour operators, scores of hotel groups and guesthouses, museums and galleries. To keep abreast of political matters you can click on "Israel", or sift through a variety of sources in "News and Information".

Italy

Alternative Travel Group

www.atg-oxford.co.uk
This excellent Website, run by a British operator, advertises and sells escorted walking tours, and self-guided walking and cycling tours, in several distinct Italian regions, such as Unknown Tuscany, Unknown Umbria,

Sicily, and Paths to Rome. Each tour is described in impressive detail, complete with maps, terrain guides, climate charts and instant availability checks, and priced in both pounds and US dollars for international travellers. Assuming you pass the Fitness Quiz to assess whether you're up to the challenges, you can book by completing and mailing the onscreen form.

Best of Sicily

www.bestofsicily.com

This comprehensive destination guide to the island of Sicily, written and maintained by Sicilians, makes a perfect introduction for prospective visitors. Arranged by themes as well as by region, it combines practical advice and recommendations with a wealth of information on local culture and history. While it won't help you book your holiday, its objective reviews of hotels, restaurants and rival guidebooks will certainly help you plan it.

Citalia

www.citalia.co.uk

UK company specializing in Italian holidays of all lengths and degrees of luxury, ranging from bus tours to apartment stays, and from city breaks in Rome to villa rentals in Tuscany. Contact by phone, mail or email to make a reservation; significant savings are offered on late bookings.

Florence Tourism

www.fionline.it/turismo/wel_eng.html

Offered by one of Florence's leading ISPs, this English-language site combines general city information with links to useful resources for potential travellers, including travel agencies, hotels, apartments for rent, restaurants, and discos. Following the sightseeing links soon leads you into Italian-only areas, however.

From Cottages to Castles

www.cottagestocastles.com

UK operator with a wide array of exclusive rural villas for rent, from the top to the bottom of Italy, with a gorgeous selection in the hill country of Tuscany and plenty near the sea in Sicily. You have to order a printed brochure to get a full list of their properties, and you can't make firm bookings online, but a substantial number can still be inspected on screen.

Il Chiostro

www.ilchiostro.com
Named after the Italian for "cloister", this US-based company organizes
cooking, painting, photography and writing retreats in Tuscany, Venice, and
Rome. The Website lists workshops both by date and by theme, and also
offers a Tuscan farmhouse for rent with tailor-made activities available. Call
or email to reserve, or print and mail the onscreen form.

In Italy Online

www.initaly.com
This vast US-based compendium of virtually anything to do with Italy
includes a staggering amount of background material, from detailed and
well-illustrated historical accounts to tips for travellers and feature articles
by its own team of specialists. There's also a region-by-region bibliography,
complete with online ordering, and links to tour companies of all kinds,
including hiking and biking operators. Its main *raison d'être*, however, is to
sell a wide range of accommodation, both in hotels and self-catering apartments and villas. All are fully detailed, with availability and a database of
candid appraisals from previous visitors, and online bookings can be made
from anywhere in the world.

IST Italian Breaks

www.italianbreaks.com
UK agency representing a long list of hand-picked rental properties
throughout Italy. The greatest concentration is in Rome, but they can also

offer the other major cities as well as rural locations, with photos and full descriptions. Prices are quoted exclusive of flights, which they can also arrange; phone or email to book.

The Italian Parks Portal

www.parks.it/Eindex.html
The English-language section of Italy's official natural parks site suffers somewhat from poor translations, but its images of both national and regional parks are mouthwatering. It also suggests itineraries, provides details of public transport access and guided walks once you're there, and lists hotels and campsites in the vicinity of each one.

Italian State Tourist Board

www.enit.it
Italy's official tourism site is designed as more of a portal than as an information source in its own right, although it does hold general overviews of topics such as food and drink, nature, and art (finding time to boast that "more than half the world's historical and artistic heritage is found in Italy"). Clicking on its multi-coloured maps, however, soon brings you to long sets of reviewless links, offering connections to tourism offices, tour companies, museums, monuments and individual hotels all over the country.

Stay and Visit Italy

www.stayandvisit.com
US tour company, with offices in Naples and Washington DC, that offers a programme of 13 different upscale small-group vacations in north, south and central Italy. Each tends to cover a wide area while basing itself in a succession of hotels for several nights apiece, rather than moving on every day. As well as full itineraries, the site quotes "one soup to nuts price" for each trip; email or phone to reserve.

Tourism Portal of the City of Roma

www.romaturismo.it
The very fancy, Flash-heavy, English-language official site for the "Happening City" of Rome. Once you've got used to the constantly flashing lights, and the way the various colour-coded symbols flit about the screen, it's actually extremely useful, with a huge searchable database of hotels, a "fanzine" and calendar of events, details on sightseeing and transport, and even a complaints form.

Tuscany Net

www.tuscany.net

Run by the Italy-based Charming Escapes group, primarily as a vehicle for its online accommodation booking facility, which ranges from castle and villa rentals to hotels and farmhouses, Tuscany Net covers all aspects of visiting Tuscany, from practical access details to general background information. As well as connections to local tourist offices, public transport, and attractions, it also provides links to similar sites devoted to Venice, Rome and Florence.

The Uffizi Gallery

www.uffizi.firenze.it

The English-language site of Florence's most famous art gallery provides full details of its opening hours and prices (though you can't buy tickets online) as well as a full catalogue of its contents. Selected paintings come with a text description and a full-screen reproduction. While the scans are no substitute for the real things, the QuickTime 360° tours of individual rooms are mouthwatering.

Jamaica

In the UK, most of the major travel agents offer packages to Jamaica; see p.31 for reviews of the best. For honeymoons and weddings in Jamaica, see p.181.

The Afflicted Yard

www.afflictedyard.com

Nicely designed, elegantly written, in-your-face and angry. Run by two mouthy Jamaican students – "We were those kids who laughed when the space shuttle blew up" – it certainly succeeds in its aim to be "a Jamaican-based Website that isn't operated by the Jamaican Government or a bunch of uptight romantic-minded farts in Miami". No one is exempt from their vitriol, be they tourist, politician, or Lauryn Hill, and you're going to find a *soupçon* of anti-Semitism, misogyny and homophobia here, along with the political satire, message board ("Informer Corner"), Human Rights reports, sound system audio files ("Noise in the Yard") and details of their Kingston aid project.

Airtravel

www.airtravel.com
US travel agency specializing in the Caribbean. The site is simplicity itself, with no banners, sponsor pop-ups or Flash effects: select Jamaica to pull up a list of some twenty hotels, including the major resorts. Clicking each one pulls up a very lengthy description, with everything you need to know, including room rates, amenities, meal plans and photos, plus sample air fares from the US. Email to check availability and they will contact you to make a reservation.

Beingee's Internet Negril

www.negril.com/beingee2.htm
Enthusiastic, useful site maintained by a couple of locals. Head straight for "Where to Stay", which has a list of hotels with room rates, and links to reams of information. Special deals are detailed on a separate page. There's also lots of stuff on bars and gigs. "Traveller Information" is a rag-bag, with weather forecasts and exchange rates, property to buy and a gallery of photos of boozy tourists – most useful are the "Traveller to Traveller" FAQs, which deal with such issues as drugs, driving and getting a good deal. And you can skip the Chamber of Commerce page altogether: it was last updated in 1999.

Firefly Beach Cottages/Secrets

www.jamaicalink.com
Negril's Firefly Beach Cottages (not to be confused with Firefly, Noel Coward's home) offer good value penthouse, cottage and suite accommodation in a lovely old beachside property, with four spotless "Secrets" cabins hidden among the trees, and a popular beach bar to boot. Rates start at £60/$90 at Firefly, or £26/$40 for the cabins, which have shared toilet and shower facilities and a communal hot tub. The easy-to-use site gives lots of info, with pages of enthusiastic testimonials and lots of photos of previous guests letting it all hang out. There's secure online booking, but you should email them with an availability request first, so they can offer you alternatives if necessary.

The Gleaner

www.jamaicagleaner.com
Online news site from Jamaica's leading daily paper, with all the main sto-

ries (and archives), plus weather forecasts, a chatroom, and a Webcam from downtown Kingston. There's little travel information here – "Book a Vacation" is for Jamaican travellers planning a trip abroad – but you can link to the *Gleaner*-published **www.discoverjamaica.com**, which has useful links to local tourist authority sites, plus a few individual hotels and restaurants.

Jamaicans.com

www.jamaicans.com
Lively portal with links to news, community projects, language sites, culture, music and cookery. Click on the travel channel, updated monthly, for practical information (a rundown of Jamaican public holidays, mileage charts, maps, weather forecasts) and well-written articles on the tourist destinations, with lists of hotels, restaurants and transport options. The (moderated) message boards, on subjects including politics, travel, spirituality and cooking, are superb. Some sections are less well updated than others, and there are rather too many slow-loading jumbo pop-ups, but all in all this is one to bookmark.

Jamaica Tourist Board

www.jamaicatravel.com
The general tourist information is as bland as usual on these official sites,

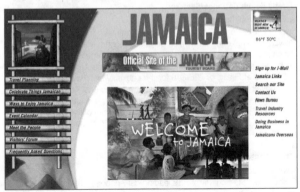

but this one is worth checking for the list of airlines and operators, the database of approved resorts, all-inclusives, guesthouses and villa representatives (some with links), and the general articles on local culture. Check the "Meet the People" programme, where they match visitors – including children – with locals with shared enthusiasms.

Jamaica Travel Net

www.jamaica-tours.com/promo.html
Managed by the hideously named US tour operator Changes in L'Attitudes, this links page is always worth a look if you're planning a resort holiday: a compilation of current last-minute and special deals offered by resorts around the island, it can save you loads of time trawling through the individual Websites. The rest of the directory isn't bad, either, divided into sections including general information, travel, resorts and weddings.

Montego Bay

www.montego-bay-jamaica.com
Bright and breezy, if ramshackle, tourist guide to Jamaica's second city. The content is upbeat without being syrupy, with news of upcoming events, quick-to-load city maps and a jumble of links to local hotels, tour operators, real estate brokers, restaurants and attractions, plus a separate links page with all sorts of Jamaica-related material.

Reggae Fusion

www.reggaefusion.com

Of the countless reggae sites out there on the Web (you can find dozens of them via **http://gemrecords.com/reggae-links.html**), this is the most intimately connected with the Jamaican scene. Although it's primarily an exhaustive encyclopedia, packed with performer biographies and background information, it also carries details of, and links to, all the island's major clubs and festivals. A separate tourism section offers reggae-oriented destination guides as well as links to airlines, tour companies and bed and breakfasts.

Sandals Resorts

www.sandals.com
The big name in all-inclusive Caribbean resorts, with six luxurious complexes, "created exclusively for couples in love", in Negril, Ocho Rios, Montego Bay and Dunn's River. Rates start at $175 per person per night (not including airfare), but the special deals detailed on the site can shave quite a bit off this. There's no online booking: North American travellers can search by their zip code for their nearest agent, while Brits are directed to www.sandals.co.uk and a list of phone numbers to call. The Sandals offshoot **Beaches**, at www.beaches.com, extends its welcome to families and groups as well as couples. Rates start at $215 per night.

Sumfest

www.reggaesumfest.com
Official site for the Jamaican music festival held every summer in Montego Bay, with news on artists, line-ups, travel tips, and links to US operators offering festival packages.

Tour-Host International

www.tourhost.com
US site offering a wide range of services for Caribbean destinations: you can book villas, apartments, packages, fly-drives, car rental and flights by emailing the onscreen form, reached either from the stand-alone Kingston section, or, if you want another resort, by choosing first from pull-down menus. Clicking "Destinations" and then "Attractions" hooks you up with various short local tours (rafting, city tours, bird-watching, reggae sites, coffee tasting, and so on) that you can book in advance.

Tourscan

www.tourscan.com
US-based Caribbean specialist agency whose nicely designed and user-friendly site is a good resource when booking a Jamaican package holiday. They've done the legwork of slogging through all the bumf from thousands of operators, airlines and resorts to come up with the best-value offers, and they guarantee not to be undersold. They have more than 1000 options in Jamaica: the speedy vacation finder allows you to search for a holiday by season rather than exact date, adding your price range (rates are per person plus airfare from NY) and destination, choosing whether you want to

be oceanfront, all-inclusive, self-catering and so on. The "further information" on each hotel is scanty, though those with Websites have links; for full details, and to book, you need to email them or call direct.

Villa Jamaica

www.villa-jamaica.com/links
Very useful links directory, categorized by subject, and with short reviews. Near on 200 for hotels alone – from guesthouses through private villas to all-inclusives – with a separate section devoted to travel (local operators, restaurants, car rental and so on).

Japan

Exodus Travels

www.exodus.co.uk
UK adventure-tour specialists offering an unstrenuous two-week tour of "Japan: Ancient and Modern", covering Kyoto, Nara, Hiroshima, Takayama, Matsumoto, Yudanaka and Tokyo, including four nights in ryokans and some meals, from £1760 land-only, £2245 with flights. Availability can be checked, and bookings made, online.

Geographic Expeditions

www.geoex.com
Californian luxury trekking and adventure-tour operator that offers several itineraries in Japan. For example, two weeks of touring and moderate hiking in the northern Alps, staying at inns along the way, will set you back from $4379 (land costs only), while a fortnight from Tokyo to Kyoto, staying at ryokans on the old Nakasendo Road and in Nikko National Park goes for around $5450 (again, land costs only). Email them for detailed itineraries. Booking, which they recommend at least four months in advance, is done over the phone.

Grand Sumo Home Page

www.sumo.or.jp/eng/index.php
Background articles, features on the great rikishi and yokozuna, and blow-by-blow accounts – and Quicktime movies – of major sumo tournaments. Also schedules, news and ticket information (you'll need some grasp of

Japanese to make the confirmation call), photos and guides to the arenas, with maps showing transport access. You can also watch a Quicktime clip of Tokyo's Ryogoku Kokugikan arena, just to whet your appetite.

The Imaginative Traveller

www.imaginative-traveller.com/japan
UK operator offering a whistlestop fifteen-day package, taking in Tokyo, the mountains, Kyoto, Okayama, Kurashiki, Nagasaki, Kyushi hot springs, Miyojima, Hiroshima and Mt Fuji. Land costs (£1995/$3185) are quoted from the UK, North America and Australasia. No online booking, although travellers from the UK can fill in a form to make reservations, which will be confirmed by email.

Jaltour

www.jaltour.co.uk
Specialist UK operator, part of the Japan Airlines group, which can arrange tours, accommodation, rail passes and flights. Their many tours include Tokyo-Kyoto and Honshu-Okinawa, as well as evocative-sounding ventures "in the footsteps of" samurai and the shogun. Prices vary, starting at around £825 for five nights in Kyoto or £900 for the same in Tokyo, but two-week tours hover at around £2000 including international flights, accommodation (often including traditional ryokans), and sightseeing. Special deals are highlighted on the home page, and you can extend your trip to cover Hawaii or Bali. They can also book accommodation, including Buddhist lodges and ryokan, but choice is limited, and no costs are quoted. No online booking; there's a downloadable form that you need to fax direct.

Japan Times

www.japantimes.co.jp
Online arm of the English-language *Japan Times*, with all the major news stories, plus features on arts and crafts, festivals and music, and the rundown on the latest sumo tournaments.

Japanese National Tourist Office

www.jnto.go.jp
Sharp, well-written content replaces the usual glossy photos and puff pieces on this official site. Intelligently designed and very engaging, it covers every aspect of travel, with country and city maps, local weather reports, and an archive of news stories. You can also search an enormous

database of tourist sights, accommodation, festivals and the like. The Travel Guide is particularly useful: under "Special Look" click on "What Interests You?", organized into "sights" (further divided into World Heritage Sites, natural areas, shrines, temples and gardens, festivals, theme parks and so on), "culture and tradition", "contemporary life", and "eating, staying, playing", to read meaty articles on topics from ryokan etiquette and cherry blossom to Japanese literature and Zen. Illustrated "looks into Japan" cover Japanese gardens, tea ceremonies, sumo, temples and ukiyo-e prints. Copious travel tips concentrate on the practical stuff, while the location guides keep it on a need-to-know basis.

Japantravelinfo.com

www.japantravelinfo.com
The North American JNTO site should be the first stop for US travellers planning a trip to Japan. It's packed with information, linking to major airlines and travel companies, detailing special tours and deals, and listing upcoming Japan-related events in the US. Plus links to relevant tourism sites, and a range of downloadable PDF files detailing walking tours, hot springs, gardens, sports, museums and annual events.

J-pop.com

www.j-pop.com
Slick and shiny US site obsessed with Japanese pop culture. Updated weekly, it's great for news, reviews and (monthly) articles on everything from Japanese fashion and pop to the newest games, with all you ever wanted to know about anime, plus lots of manga gossip.

Kabuki for Everyone

www.fix.co.jp/kabuki
Nice little site devoted to the traditional Japanese theatrical art of kabuki, with a history and a bibliography, details of upcoming shows in Japan, and links to other traditional arts including puppetry and mask-making. Plus an online theatre, with scene-by-scene accounts of popular kabuki plays, Quicktime clips of onnagatas (male actors taking on female roles), and sound files of kabuki drums and flutes.

Made in Tokyo

www.dnp.co.jp/museum/nmp/madeintokyo_e/mit.html
Beautiful, supercool architecture site focusing on fifty of Tokyo's most dis-

part three: destinations

tinctive buildings – practical, streamlined places that are really rather strange. Check out the shopping-mall-cum-driving school, the graveyard tunnel and the bus station apartments, for example. Click on the buildings for name, address, function and details, and on the red flags for surprising virtual experiences.

The Manners of the Ogasawara School

www.ogasawararyu-reihou.gr.jp/english/
Clear and concise answers to a number of tricky Japanese etiquette questions: what to do and not to do with chopsticks, where to seat yourself in a traditional room, whether it's OK to tread on the edges of a tatami mat. As the site reassures you, the Ogasawara School of Etiquette's "most important rules are thoughtful consideration and harmony of mind and soul. Also, their ideas are very rational". You can't say fairer than that.

Museum Information Japan

www.dnp.co.jp/museum/icc-e.html
Information on hundreds of museums in Japan, organized by area, and with links to home pages where appropriate.

Quirky Japan Homepage

www3.tky.3web.ne.jp/~edjacob/index.html
A mixed bag: best when directing you to off-the-beaten-track attractions and weird museums and away from overrated and "don't bother" sites; less interesting when posting music reviews. Well worth a look, though, for all sorts of intriguing snippets about Japan's fringe groups and distinctive tourist attractions, and a page of SAQs (Seldom Asked Questions).

*qUirKy jApAn hoMepAge

Are you tired of shrines and temples, reconstructed ferro-concrete castles and tea ceremonies? Do you like to get off the beaten track? Would you like to meet Japanese people who do not meet the conformist stereotype? Japan, behind the conservative grey suits and formal bows, is a country quirkier than you can ever imagine. The Quirky Japan Homepage provides information about oddities such as the The Meguro Parasitalogical Museum, the Thousand Person Bathtub, Love Hotels, temple lodging, and the *Yakumo* man (the ice cream man's evil twin).

Rei's Anime and Manga Page

www.mit.edu:8001/afs/athena/user/r/e/rei/www/Anime.html
Lively US-based fansite devoted to Japanese comic books and animation,
with links to scholarly articles, conference papers and the like.

Sake World

www.sake-world.com
Produced by the sake columnist for the *Japan Times*, this site is devoted to
the country's famed rice wine: which brand to drink, what to drink it from
and where to drink it. Also a rundown of sake events in Japan and international sake links.

See Japan

www.seejapan.co.uk
JNTO's official UK site is beautifully laid out, with visitor information (including a few useful Japanese phrases), plus pages on accommodation, eating,
and sightseeing, and loads of useful links, including to local operators that
sell the Japan Rail pass. After browsing the individual categories highlighted
on the navigator, check the FAQs, which offer more info on similar subjects.

Tokyo Food Page

www.bento.com/tokyofood.html
With listings and reviews of more
than 1000 Tokyo restaurants and
bars (searchable by cuisine, area,
name or opening days), this wonderful site offers plenty to feed the imagination. Don't miss the "Culinary
Explorer", a cornucopia of quirky
food-related travel destinations, with
photos of market stalls, weird restaurant signs, reviews of noodle museums and the like (check out the completely mad sushi sound files). Then
there's the "Speciality Cuisines", with
articles on home kitchens, menu
poetry, temple cuisine and more, the
recipes, the foodie links, the weekly

reports on restaurant openings and food events, the food shopping guides, the sake reviews …

Tokyo Q

www.nokia.co.jp/tokyoq

Tokyo Q is the hip megalopolis weekly, with news stories and feature articles (interesting enough, if you can stomach the pretentious writing), plus club, theatre and music listings and reviews. You can also read about the city's best baths, hotels, shops and restaurants, and access a selection of intriguing local links.

Virtual Okinawa

www.virtualokinawa.com

The Web guide to the subtropical archipelago of Okinawa is less than meets the eye, but it's worth a look for its tips on local bus travel, food, festivals and crafts, and its lively message board.

Weekly Post

www.weeklypost.com

Online version of Japan's best-selling news magazine, known for its sharp investigative reporting on current and economic affairs. You can read all the major news stories and editorials here, and browse or search through archives of old stories.

Kenya

For reviews of safari sites, see the "Wildlife and Nature" section, which starts on p.220.

Africa Tours

www.africasafaris.com

US safari specialist with half a dozen or so good-value Kenya itineraries costing upwards of $1500 (land only; packages with flights cost considerably more). You can join scheduled trips or take a customized tour, including the two-week "Best of Kenya", where you stay at camps in the Amboseli, Aberdares, Samburu and Masai Mara parks, among others. There are further choices under "Specials" – one-offs and seasonal migrations – and "New Programmes". To book, you need to call or email them in New York.

BZ's Kenya Travel Guide

www.bwanazulia.com/kenya
Home page of one Bwana Zulia, devoted entirely to all things Kenyan, with discussion boards, useful links, bibliography, travel tips and photos.

The Daily Nation

www.nationaudio.com/News/DailyNation/Today
Online English-language newspaper with strong, opinionated editorials on international and local news, putting a fascinating Kenyan spin on all the major stories.

Exodus

www.exodus.co.uk
Reliable British soft adventure-tour operator (see p.120) with a good choice of hiking, camping and overland safaris in Kenya. The quickest way to find them is to use the search tool: pull up a list of all holidays in Africa, click on the first Kenya trip you see, and from there you can choose to see all the Kenya options. Trips range from eleven days (the "classic safari") through longer itineraries taking in Tanzania (including a seventeen-day holiday climbing mounts Kenya and Kilimanjaro) right up to a seven-week trail following Livingston's footsteps from Kenya to Zimbabwe. There's plenty of information on each trip – though you need to download or email for really detailed notes – and online booking is fast and easy. Prices are quoted according to your country of origin, and most trips can be booked with or without flight.

Guerba

www.guerba.co.uk
UK-based adventure company offering good-value African camping and lodge safaris and a variety of overland trips. Options include four days at a tented camp in the Masai Mara National Reserve and a five-day guided Kilimanjaro trek; anyone with more time can take 23 days in the parks of Kenya and Tanzania, or even a ten-week camping trip gawping at endangered gorillas throughout eastern and southern Africa. Read thumbnail details and itineraries on the site, then click to download full tour dossiers, check dates, prices and availability, and make provisional bookings.

Kenya Web

www.kenyaweb.com

Informative portal with a variety of channels. The travel section has details on all the national parks plus links to ground operators and the like, but there's plenty more of interest elsewhere on the site. The history, in particular, is accessible and well written, and there's a handy page listing the timetables for major international and domestic airlines.

Magicalkenya.com

www.magicalkenya.com

Highly visual, interactive and informative official tourist board site, which allows you to choose an "environment" – wilderness, coast, desert, cities and so on – or a "safari" – a number of options, from wildlife to cultural safari – for general information, destination guides, and practical details on accommodation, restaurants and shopping. There's lots about Kenya's culture and its landscapes, with accounts of all the national parks and reserves and plenty to read about Kenyan music, art and cookery. Also links to safari and tour operators, 360° virtual tours and a selection of real-life travellers' tales.

2Afrika.com

www.2afrika.com

US company specializing in South African safaris, with a good range in East Africa, too, and plenty in Kenya. Choose from more than sixty itineraries, including day safaris, short excursions, camping trips and white-water safaris, perhaps incorporating golf or bird-watching into your trip. Costs are reasonable, and although they offer plenty of flight-inclusive packages from New York – from less than $2000 for ten days – you can opt for land-only options. All details are covered on the site, with itineraries, costs, accommodation details and even visa information, and you can email to reserve a place, but you should call them direct to make a booking.

Laos

Adventure Center

www.adventurecenter.com

The established Californian operator offers a creative choice of adventure holidays, around the world and throughout the year, and at competitive prices. Enter "Our World" for an interactive world map; you're then just two clicks away from the list of Laos trips, which are all included as part of longer tours through Indochina. The shortest, Bangkok to Hanoi, lasts fifteen days, while the longest is a thirty-day overland loop from Bangkok to Siem Reap. To spend the most time in Laos, plump for the Laos Adventure, a fifteen-day loop from Bangkok. Once you've read the trip summary, go to "Trip Dossier" for full details and updates, and then check the availability table. To book, you need to request a temporary hold by email or phone, then send off for a hard copy brochure that includes a booking form.

Adventures Abroad

www.adventures-abroad.com

Classy North American operator, specializing in small-group (4–21 people) cultural tours for slightly older travellers. Non-Americans can research and book trips on this site, too, as all costs and details are quoted according to where you are travelling from. Laos itineraries range from six days taking in Vientiane, Luang Prabang, the sacred Pak Ou Caves and That Luang, to trips that combine the country with Myanmar, Vietnam, Cambodia, or Thailand, or a combination of these; the longest is a 45-day trip through them all, with five days in Laos in the middle. You can download full itineraries in html or PDF formats; simply click "Book It" for secure online reservations.

Journeys International

www.journeys-intl.com

High-quality, small-group eco-tourism and cultural tours from an established US operator. They offer trips all over the world, classifying them from Grade I (relatively active, staying in lodges, with up to three miles walking per day) to demanding Grade IV wilderness travel itineraries. The two scheduled Laos tours, which both last six days, are classified as Grade I: the Laos Odyssey, which includes two days' river travel down the Mekong, and the Vientiane-Luang Prabang trip, which concentrates on Laos's major cities, taking in temples, palaces, villages and a river trip. Costs and itineraries are covered on the site, along with honest and thoughtful destination reviews. To reserve, click on "Trip Terms and Conditions", where you can either download a form with Acrobat or key in your details online, making sure to follow up with a phone call.

LaoNet's Community Homepage

www.global.lao.net

Useful Lao directory, with articles from the Australian *Lao Studies Review*, a news story archive with links to papers throughout Southeast Asia, a message board ("Announcements"), plus Laotian poems and prose. The formal Links page is often disabled, so head instead to the "virtual library", where links are arranged into categories such as art and culture, government, human rights, biographies, publications, tourism and travel. Again, too many are disabled, but persistence pays off, and you can glean useful nuggets, particularly on history and human rights issues, plus a number of interesting home pages from expat Laotians.

Steppes

www.steppeseast.co.uk

Organizing tailor-made itineraries through Indochina, central Asia and the Middle East, UK operator Steppes offers tours around Laos geared toward your desired pace and interests. Click to enter a separate site for escorted trips: those to Laos (look under Indochina) include fourteen days' learning about traditional textiles, and a river trip down the Mekong from China to Vietnam. Prices for escorted trips vary, but hover around £2000 for a group of ten, including international and domestic flights, full-board accommodation and tours. The Holiday Wizard allows you to check availability on any tour, but you need to fill in a booking form or email them direct to discuss your plans.

Symbiosis Travel

www.symbiosis-travel.co.uk
Environmentally aware travel operator, based in London, offering tailor-made itineraries and occasional small-group (four to twelve people) scheduled trips throughout Southeast Asia. Group tours to Laos rotate around special events or festivals, such as the boat race in Louang Phabang, while the custom-designed trips can emphasize adventure travel, cultural activities, or wildlife, depending upon you. Though there's lots of tantalizing copy, the site has no price information, or online booking; you can email any requests, or call them direct.

Vientiane Times

www.vientianetimes.com
This nicely designed online version of the country's one English-language newspaper should be your first stop for Laos information on the Web. Laos-related articles from around the world are posted here, along with readers' emails, usually long and impassioned political arguments from expats, and there is a page devoted to accommodation, with links. The lengthy links page itself is indispensable, directing you to everything from music sites and Hmong bookshops to embassies and travel and tourism groups. Many of the sites are rudimentary, but there's heaps of stuff out there.

Madagascar

Rainbow Tours

www.rainbowtours.co.uk
Nicely designed site from this Africa and Indian Ocean specialist, with lots of articles and background. In addition to individual itineraries (some of

which are described on the site), they organize half a dozen scheduled, small-group trips each year, including birding and wildlife tours. The bird-watching tours are phenomenal, covering rainforests, tropical dry deciduous woodlands, deserts and wetlands, where along with scores of wildlife – lemurs galore, of course – you can see hundreds of rare birds including Madagascar fish eagles and pygmy kingfishers, Chabert's, nuthatch and rufous vangas, greater and lesser vasa parrots … Tours start at around £2000 for two weeks, all in, including flight from London or Paris. No online booking; email or call.

Malaysia

Borneo Online

www.borneo-online.com.my/tourism.htm
The tourism pages of this links directory can usefully direct you to online articles, tourist offices, travel operators, hotels and domestic airlines, among other things. Most sites are specific to Borneo (with lots on Sabah and Sarawak), but many relate to the whole of Malaysia.

Exodus

www.exodus.co.uk
UK adventure-travel company with a handful of Malaysia tours, most of them including the country as part of a longer overland itinerary. The one trip that stays within Malaysia, travelling around Borneo, is a real adventure, involving remote jungle treks, mountain climbing and some very basic accommodation. You can read a daily itinerary on the site – downloading or emailing for really detailed notes if you need them – while checking avail-ability and prices. These are quoted according to where you're flying from, though most trips can be booked without flight in any case. Online booking is simple and fast.

Himalayan Travel

www.gorp.com/himtravel.htm
US adventure-tour company offering a range of experiences: some tours involve nothing more adventurous than day hikes from your comfortable hotel, while others require good levels of physical fitness. Their three

Malaysia trips, all of which leave throughout the year, focus on Borneo, culminating in a seventeen-day trip covering colonial cities, tropical jungles, cave systems and mysterious rivers, with some nights spent in traditional longhouses. Prices begin at around $850 excluding flight. There's no online booking: you need to submit a form to receive a hard copy brochure.

Malaysia Homepage

www.geographia.com/malaysia
Produced by the Malaysia Tourism Promotion Board in New York, this is an impressive, extensive online guide, with lots of meaty stuff on destinations (including the national parks), lively pieces on cultures, arts, people, myths and traditions, detailed accounts of various activities – from visiting a longhouse to spelunking – and a graphic and informative timeline. "Essentials" concerns itself mainly with North American travellers: how to get there, where to stay (a non-interactive accommodation list, organized by region), and which operator to use (another list, with full contact details, of operators on the east coast).

Malaysia My Destination.com

www.malaysiamydestination.com
The official portal of Malaysia's tourism ministry is a gruelling read (sample: "Almost anywhere you go you'll be reminded of food (as opposed to pure sustenance) in its many splendours and variation of enticements"), but efficient and useful enough, with good general destination information, a rundown on how to get there from the UK, North America, Australasia and Southeast Asia, guides to special-interest holidays, including diving and bird-watching, with hotel lists and practical information for each place cov-

ered. You can also book accommodation, though the cumbersome logging in process will deter anyone but the most determined.

Malaysia Net

www.malaysianet.net

Hotel-booking site primarily geared towards business travellers, but with plenty of inexpensive three-star options. The best deals for each region are highlighted on the home page, but if you want to do more research, choose your city and your price range to pull up a list of matches, arranged in descending order of cost and with star ratings. Click on each name for a review, rundown of facilities and photos; you can then store any potentials in a "travel cart" as you go. Online booking is swift, but while the quoted discounts are certainly impressive – many of them around 75 percent off standard rates – there is no guarantee you will get a room for these low prices on the nights you want. If you'd like to make sure of the cheapest rate, you should double-check with a couple of the accommodation sites reviewed on pp.69–73 to see what they are quoting for the same hotel on the same nights.

Malta

For diving holidays on Gozo, see **www.regal-diving.co.uk**, reviewed on p.134.

Holidays Malta

www.holidays-malta.com

This clearing house comes in useful when planning an independent Maltese holiday, with databases of hotels and guesthouses, along with self-catering apartments, villas, and farmhouses, featuring contact details and Websites for online booking. You can also book car rental and local taxi service, as well as check out the local diving schools, restaurants and clubs. Plus links to Amazon for Malta and Gozo travel guides.

Mercury Direct

www.mercury-direct.co.uk

Emphasizing the sameness and safeness of Malta for British travellers (familiar shops and road signs, driving on the left, plenty of fast food outlets), this cheap and cheerful site offers no-fuss holidays which you put together yourself. Choose from their database of hotels (from three- to five-star), pick a flight (they depart from many regional British airports), then contact them by email or phone to book and arrange car rental.

Visit Malta

www.visitmalta.com
Nicely designed, visual and varied site from the Malta Tourism Authority, with general information about Malta and the archipelago, plenty on the islands of Gozo and Comino, and a section devoted to diving, linking to courses, sites and diving holiday operators from around the world.

Mexico

For language schools in Mexico, see p.205. For cookery schools, see p.198. For art and painting vacations, see p.212.

AMTAVE

www.amtave.com/fenglish.html
AMTAVE (Mexican Association of Adventure Travel and Eco-tourism) is an umbrella organization of local companies in Mexico – anything from photo safari operators and spelunking outfits to eco-lodges – that are committed to sustainable tourism. Click the "Amtave Adventure" button at the top of the screen and choose an activity (they're divided into air, earth, water, lodges, nature and culture) – you can refine your search by adding a Mexican state if you wish – to pull up a list of AMTAVE-approved operators with links to their sites. If you prefer to choose by destination, click "Amtave By Region" and then select a state from the interactive map.

Eco-travels in Mexico

www2.planeta.com/mader/ecotravel/mexico/mexico.html
Smart design comes second to content on this useful site, a kind of information clearing house with a cornucopia of articles revolving around adventure travel and responsible tourism in Mexico, many of them from published writers. Hosted by Ron Mader, a Mexico-based travel writer and environmental journalist, it's updated regularly, and the range of content is vast, with

lots of links. To link to tour operators throughout Mexico, scroll down to "Trip Planning" and click on the directory of environmental travel providers. If you want to be more specific, look under "Featured Regions". Also book reviews and ordering (through Amazon), details of community projects and environmental reports, and an online Yahoo club for discussion and real-time chats.

Exodus Travels

www.exodus.co.uk

UK adventure-holiday operator (see p.120) with a good variety of Mexico itineraries, ranging from thirteen days visiting the volcanoes at the heart of the country to a few weeks as part of a four-month trip on the Pan-American Highway from Alaska to Panama. They also offer whale-watching in Baja, a Maya and Aztec route, and a challenging cycling trip through the Sierra Madre. You can usually choose to pay with or without flight.

Frida Kahlo

www.fridakahlo.it

Stylish site dedicated to the extraordinary artist Frida Kahlo, with critical essays, a bibliography, reviews of temporary and permanent exhibitions of her work around the world, and features relating Kahlo to contemporary culture. There's even stuff on "Frida and comics". It's produced by an Italian fan, so some of the translation is clunky, but the content is sound.

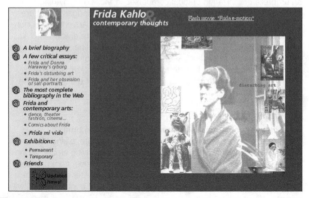

Guide2mexico

www.guide2mexico.com

Nicely put together one-stop shop, travel guide, and directory from the US. With links to farebeaters, hotel finders, package deals and tours, the home page can also direct you to destination information, feature articles, shopping sites, forums and a whole kitbag of travel tools. Click on a city name to pull up a new page, and you'll get a general overview and a host of great links, which are soundly reviewed – they include more tours, rental cars, flights and cruises, plus images, maps, hotel groups, Web guides, travellers' tales, travel guides, and so on. You're also directed towards an intelligent range of relevant historical and cultural studies that you can order from Amazon.

Hotelguide – Cancun

http://cancun.hotelguide.net

Online directory of selected Cancun hotels, divided between Cancun island, the mainland and Isla Mujeres, forty minutes away by ferry. Click on the area you're interested in and up comes a list of options with address and number of rooms; click again for contact details, rates, a brief rundown of facilities, and ways to pay. Some entries allow you to check availability and prices for the days you wish to travel, and most offer online booking.

Journey Latin America

www.journeylatinamerica.co.uk

Quality UK specialist operator with a clean and user-friendly site. Click Mexico on the interactive map to pull up an introduction, from where you can access a table of best-buy flight deals (usefully, this details return, inbound and one-way tickets); you have to email them direct for the latest quotes or to order a Mexi-pass (which is also valid on flights into the USA, Central and South America). JLA has some twenty independent itineraries for Mexico: many of them allow you to choose between "touristclass" hotels or more upmarket places, and some include flights. Two people sharing a tourist-class room on a "highlights" tour – which takes in Mexico City, Oaxaca, San Cristobal, Palenque, Merida, Chichen Itza and Cancun – costs £1134 (no flight), while a four-night train journey through the Copper Canyon (flights not included, hotel accommodation) goes for £677 for two sharing. There's no online ordering; email them direct to make a booking.

part three: destinations

Mexicanwave

www.mexicanwave.com
An online travel and lifestyle magazine based in the UK, this good-looking venture is strong on content. The home page features the main stories of the day, with well-written travelogues as well as articles on food and drink, culture (wrestling, Day of the Dead, ceramics, etc), music, art and movies. While it's particularly good on books, with reviews, author interviews (and links to Amazon), it doesn't skimp on the practicalities, with city guides – some adapted or taken from the major travel guides, others written especially for the site – plus holiday and hotel deals (some of which are also available to North American travellers), a map, currency converter and visa information.

Mexico City Guide

www.mexicocity.com.mx/mexcity.html
Useful, if scattily organized, guide to Mexico City, divided into Overview (with FAQs, maps, geographical and historical information), Activities (museums, folkloric celebrations, shows, restaurants), Attractions (by area), Facilities (restaurants, hotels) and Assistance (general orientation, communications). Before leaving, browse the archive of articles on current affairs and culture, and check the separate links page for more hotel reservations, the subway map, weather forecasts and such like.

Mexico Connect Magazine

www.mexconnect.com
Extremely good monthly online magazine, produced in the US, offering major news stories, practical travel services, and an above-average "general" forum (one of nine on the site). What makes the site stand out is its quality content – between fifteen and thirty new articles per month, on art, cookery, destinations, history, books, travel, architecture and the like. These, plus photographs, essays, reports and all sorts of useful information are available on the vast database, arranged into subject categories. Do a quick search or browse the indices to get quickly to where you want. Under "Services", you can search for a hotel, find out about local events, browse a classifieds section and access around 1500 links.

Museo Mural Diego Rivera

www.arts-history.mx/museos/mu/index2.html
A must for anyone interested in Mexican art, this Website is produced by

the Mexico City museum that houses Diego Rivera's huge, extraordinary mural *Dream of a Sunday afternoon in the Alameda*. Painted in 1948, it is a classic example of Rivera's work, and one of Mexico's greatest murals. Crammed with figures from history and from Rivera's past, it originally bore the slogan "God Does Not Exist", and was kept from the public until 1956, when the artist changed it to something utterly innocuous. The site has a history of the mural, images from it, and a fascinating section called "recognize the characters" where you can click on an individual to find out who he or she is, and why they were included at all.

S&S Tours

www.ss-tours.com
The Arizona-based company S&S Tours offers culturally and ecologically sensitive small-group trips through Mexico's Copper Canyon, including journeys on the Chihuahua Pacifico Railroad, but can also take you whale-watching in Baja, to the colonial cities, on a special Day of the Dead trip to the northern city of Alamos or birding and butterfly-watching in the Sierra Madre. Those that include flights usually depart from Tucson, Arizona. You can also read travelogues from past clients; peppered with anxieties about how to use the toilets, these are no budding Paul Therouxs, but they do give a taste of the pace and structure of the trips.

Suntrek

www.suntrek.com
Californian operator offering an inventive choice of one- to thirteen-week overland adventure tours in customized vans (see p.148). Prices are good, depending upon whether you camp or stay in hotels: Mexican itineraries include two weeks through the Yucatan starting and ending in Cancun for $799, three weeks from Mexico City to Cancun (or vice versa), or three weeks from LA through Baja to Mexico City from $1077, and six weeks from LA to Cancun (or vice versa) from $2033.

Teotihuacan Home Page

http://archaeology.la.asu.edu/teo
Accessible repository for information about Teotihuacan, the extraordinary prehistoric settlement just north of Mexico City, with lots of colour photos, maps, chronology charts, excavation reports, Quicktime movies, archeology and anthropology articles – some in Spanish – and a bibliography.

The Train Collection

www.thetraincollection.com

Puffing steam trains and jaunty mariachi music greet you to this good-looking US site, which deals exclusively in luxury rail excursions on restored vintage trains. Click on **www.southorientexpress.com** for details of five-day escorted tours through Mexico's rugged Copper Canyon, including overnight stops at luxury hotels, sightseeing and walking tours, or on **www.expressomayá.com** for five-day tours of the extraordinary archeological sites of Chichen Itza, Uxmal and Palenque and the colonial cities of Merida and Campeche. There's plenty of detail here, with itineraries and prices (you're looking at well over $1000), but no online booking – you reserve and pay via email or over the phone. They can also assist independent travellers using the first-class Chihuahua al Pacifico, which operates year round.

Tropical Adventures

www.divetropical.com

Seattle operator Tropical Adventures offers scuba diving around the world (see p.135). Their packages to the offshore Caribbean island of Cozumel, a prime dive site with its caves, tunnels, pinnacles and drop-offs, range from $200 per person double occupancy for three nights to $1050 for seven nights, with a lot of choice in between depending upon where you choose to sleep. Costs include hotel and diving, but no flights, and apply to the low season only. You need to contact them direct for more details, as there is no online booking.

Mongolia

Mongolian Tourism Board

www.mongoliatourism.gov.mn

An impressive interactive venture from a tourist board that's just a couple of years old. Head for the "fact pack" for practical information on everything from the current visa situation to how to avoid drunks (whom the site assures us "are easily recognized by a stumbling walk"); from there you can follow links to directories of restaurants, bars and discos, all with photos and short reviews. If you're after cultural snippets, this site is full of goodies,

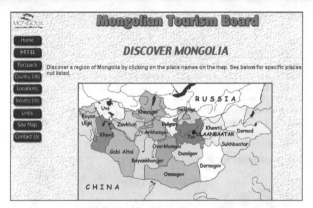

with sections on history, music, textiles, the Mongolian calendar, domestic life and so on. There are lots of photos, too, and a good set of links – a genuine pleasure to read.

Morocco

For walking holidays in Morocco, see **www.sherpaexpeditions.com** (p.154), for bird-watching see **www.eagle-eye.com** (p.223), and if you fancy learning a language in Marrakech, check out **www.languagesabroad.com** (p.206).

Best of Morocco

www.morocco-travel.com

Clunky-looking site from this UK-based Moroccan specialist. Ignore the typos, bad writing and poor design and concentrate on the very good custom-designed holidays – they can fix up anything, from beach holidays to city breaks, hiking in the High Atlas, camel trekking in the Sahara, golfing holidays, bird-watching, surfing, skiing … You can create your own holiday by moving a mouse over a map, adding nights in hotels as you go (they have a great choice, from riads in Marrakech to simple desert inns).

Email them for a quote, by all means, but call direct to discuss the finer details.

Dragoman

www.dragoman.co.uk

The stalwart UK-based overland operator (see p.146) includes Morocco on a handful of physically challenging trans-Africa camping itineraries, ranging in length from five to thirty weeks. Use the advanced search to track them down. Costs aren't always that low – this isn't a budget backpacker outfit – but the special offers can sometimes shave fifteen percent or so off the price. No online booking; email a form to request a detailed brochure or make enquiries.

Encounter

www.encounter-overland.com

Though we could do without the yoof posturing ("r u wild?" "y encounter?"), the youth-oriented division of Dragoman (see above) organizes interesting overland trips. Morocco, as well as being included on longer African itineraries, has its own fortnight-long tour – a Casablanca loop via Fes, the Atlas Mountains and Marrakech – that encounters "oceans, deserts, mountains and markets"; prices are low as can be, as entry fees, permits and adventure activities are paid from a group kitty while on the road. It's worth knowing, though, that your tour leaders "are NOT tour guides, because you are not a tourist." Extraordinarily, the only way to book a trip is by snail mail.

Exodus

www.exodus.co.uk

Soft adventure-travel company (see p.120) with more than a dozen holidays in Morocco – including camel treks in the Sahara, off-road bike journeys through the Atlas Mountains, and day-hikes around Marrakech based in a lovely old gîte – lasting from 8 to 22 days. Though initially ugly and off-putting, with underlined text throughout, the site does provide the salient details of each trip (use the advanced search to find them). If you're happy to forego the detailed trip notes, which you need to download or email for separately, you can book online immediately.

Guerba

www.guerba.co.uk

British soft adventure company offering good-value tours of Morocco, including treks, accommodated safaris, and escorted cultural tours, some of which are exclusive to the Website. The eight-day "Essential Morocco", which covers Fes, Marrakech, Rabat, the holy town of Moulay Idriss, the Roman ruins at Volubilis and the walled town of Essaouira, costs less than £200, while a twelve-day trek in the High Atlas, including accommodation in a Berber village, goes for around £100 more, not including flights. Read thumbnail details and itineraries on the site, then click to download full tour dossiers, check dates, prices and availability, and make provisional bookings.

La Maison du Maroc

www.maroc.net

Many sections of this information site are in French, though you can read English-language news and subscribe to receive email news bulletins. In addition to the links to a variety of cultural sites including magazines and ezines, the site has hundreds of music files from Radio Casablanca, which also beams out a live daily news broadcast.

Naturally Morocco

www.naturallymorocco.co.uk

Small independent company offering "eco-holidays" based in a lovely old house in the elegant walled city of Taroudant. As well as holding the offices of two environmental organizations, the house sleeps up to 30 guests in twin, double or family rooms, with a couple of self-catering apartments. One-week packages, which include the assistance of on-site staff, who cook, lead excursions to the mountains, oases and the ocean, and generally look after you, cost around £195 per person exclusive of flights. There are discounts on longer stays, for children and for groups, and they can make provision for budget travellers. Email to check availability.

Tourism in Morocco

www.tourism-in-morocco.com
Moroccan travel portal. While there are a few useful features listed on the home page – a "news group" (message board), links to Amazon, and an email form to receive details of special offers – you need to click on the waving palm tree to get to the body of the site. Here you'll find links to everything from airlines and car rental to accommodation, restaurants, museums and online travel operators, some of them in French.

Nepal

Aaha Nepal

www.aahanepal.com
Although this Nepalese Web portal is especially good for links to NGO associations and local tour operators, the sections on handicrafts, health,

hotels, news and media are also worth a look. The home page foregrounds a selection of short features (on local festivals, national parks, etc), news stories and specialist travel sites; you can then fast-track to a trekking company, Kathmandu hotel, or a weather report.

Footprint Adventures

www.footprint-adventures.co.uk

While this popular UK tour company (see p.120) runs small-group adventure and wildlife tours in most regions of the world, their Nepal programme is especially appetizing. As well as high-altitude treks in all the major destinations – priced according to whether you stay in basic local lodges (which work out cheaper) or carry camping equipment – they offer bird-watching and whitewater rafting expeditions. All itineraries are fully described and priced, and there's secure online booking for US and UK customers.

Green Lotus Trekking

www.green-lotus-trekking.com

Exemplary site from a small, high-quality Kathmandu operator. They can arrange as much or as little as you need, from trekking, mountaineering, rafting and jungle safaris, to city tours, domestic flights and hotel rooms. The site is packed with background information on each trip, with maps, itineraries, altitude graphs, photos and costs (quoted in US$), plus full details on their nice selection of hotels, from one- to five-star, with links to sites where available. Online reservations – but not bookings – are simple; submit the form to receive an email invoice, then fax them with credit card details to secure a non-refundable deposit. The balance is paid on your arrival in Kathmandu. The message board is a good place to find trekking partners.

Himalayan Explorers Club

www.hec.org

Join the HEC online (it's based in Boulder, Colorado, and charges $30 a year) to get such perks as use of clubhouses in Kathmandu and Pakistan (free luggage storage, email/Web access, phone and fax, use of trip reports, etc), a downloadable version of the *Nepal Volunteer Handbook*, access to HEC homestay programmes, hard copy and online newsletters (also available to non-members), and discounts in Kathmandu hotels and shops. There's plenty on the site for non-members, too, with links to discussion groups, trek operators and so on, an online catalogue of books and maps (no secure server yet, and they only ship international orders to members), plus a good list of FAQs, answered by David Reed, author of the *Rough Guide to Nepal*. The HEC also leads treks around Everest and the Annapurna circuit (from $1800 for 24 days from the US); email to book direct.

International Porter Protection Group

www.ippg.net
The IPPG works to improve health and safety for trekking porters around the world by raising awareness of the issue of porter exploitation. There's a useful list of endorsed trekking companies in Nepal, the UK and the US.

Malla Treks

www.mallatreks.com
Very good Nepali trekking operator partnered with US adventure-travel specialists Mountain Travel Sobek. The site is good, too, with itineraries and costs for a nice variety of treks, from a tea-house trek with guide, porter, meals and lodge accommodation to a 23-day pilgrimage to Tibet's holy Mount Kailas for around $4000. Online ordering is secure, and US bank account holders can use the failsafe Internet-cheque system.

Mountain Spirits

www.mountainspirits.com
Reputable US operator, run by an Idaho couple and a Nepali family, specializing in adventure travel to Nepal. Dotted with quotes from the Buddha, the simple, pared-down site details their scheduled trips, including easy two-week tea-house treks (around $1350, land costs only), moderate to strenuous tent treks (around $1950 for two or three weeks) and strenuous mountaineering trips (three to four weeks), along with volunteering opportunities at a school they are building in the Khumbu area. No online booking; email them direct.

Muir's Tours

www.nkf-mt.org.uk
Owned by the Nepal Kingdom Foundation, Muir's Tours is a UK-based,

Buddhist-run operator promising eco-friendly small-group travel with all profits going to good causes in the places they visit. Their tailor-made and fixed options combine outdoor travel with immersion in local conservation efforts and time spent with locals. Sadly, the site is a mess, however laudable the organization. But it does provide enough detail to be going on with, describing treks that range from a ten-day jaunt with three days in Kathmandu to a month-long trip into the Makalu-Barun region southeast of Everest. The last-minute deals are well worth a look, and you may want to check out their volunteer programme.

Nepal Home Page

www.nepalhomepage.com
Extremely useful resource site, a cornucopia of discussion forums, directories of trekking agencies, domestic flight schedules, and a detailed festival calendar. Plus general country information, trip reports, feature articles, news stories, weather reports, a bibliography, travel FAQs and a travel bulletin board – everything, in fact that you could ask for.

Nepal Information Directory

www.catmando.com/nepal.htm
Nepalese directory with links to diplomatic missions and organizations, hotels and guesthouses, trekking companies and jungle resorts, restaurants, travel agents and newspapers. Best of all, though, is the entire section devoted to biscuits, sadly lacking from most directories of this type.

Snow Lion Expeditions

www.snowlion.com
Flexible small-group tours from this reputable US operator specializing in adventure travel throughout Asia. The site is image heavy and slow to load, but it's worth waiting for details of their many trekking and cultural tours (which coincide with pilgrimages or local festivals), along with the articles, features and bibliographies that burst out of the home page. They have six Everest itineraries (including ten days' moderate trekking or 27 days' challenging mountaineering), four Annapurna expeditions (check the trekking/rafting/jungle safari combination), and a gem of a trek through the forbidden kingdom of Mustang. To book, download the application form, print it and fax it direct. They can also put you in touch with past clients for recommendations and advice.

Tiger Mountain

www.tigermountain.com

Slick site from one of the more upmarket local operators (clients, they claim, include Jimmy Carter and Diana Ross), who also bring you the famed Tiger Tops jungle lodges and tented camps in Chitwan and Bardia national parks. They deal with everything, from trekking, river-running trips and safaris to booking cars, buses and accommodation in hotels, lodges and tented camps. It's a copious site, and can be confusing: head first for their schedule of treks and tours, which includes tea-house treks from $685, a rhododendron trek from $950 and a Mustang/white-water combination from $2740 (land costs only). Click on the buttons on the right to check out the jungle camps and lodges or to book a rafting trip. You can make real-time online bookings with Acteva, or email Tiger Mountain direct if you want a tailor-made trip.

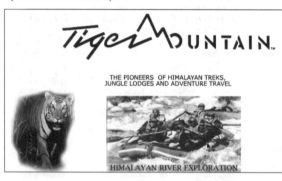

THE PIONEERS OF HIMALAYAN TREKS, JUNGLE LODGES AND ADVENTURE TRAVEL

HIMALAYAN RIVER EXPLORATION

Trekking In the Nepal Himalaya

www.trekinfo.com

The first stop for anyone considering trekking in Nepal, this invaluable site provides all you need to prepare yourself: sensible country information, health advice, up-to-date news on permit requirements and fees, and a downloadable visa application form. Bonuses include Nepali news stories and feature articles, and, best of all, a really good bunch of links to trekking companies, bookstores and trekking gear outfitters. There's also a handy message board for anyone seeking a trekking partner.

The Netherlands

Amsterdam Travel Service

www.amsterdamtravel.co.uk

A division of the British agency Bridge Travel (see p.34), the Amsterdam Travel Service specializes in weekend and short-break trips from London to Amsterdam, offering a selection of fifty fully-detailed hotels ranging from one to five stars. Both all-inclusive packages and individual nights' accommodation can be booked via email.

Bookings NL

www.bookings.nl

Hotel-booking site, developed in and dedicated to the Netherlands, that centres on a gazetteer of over a hundred Dutch cities, from Aalsmeer to Zwolle. For each destination, it produces a lengthy list of accommodation options of all standards, the majority of which offer both availability checks and real-time booking online. If you're wary about security, you can choose to fax your details instead.

Cannabis Café

www.cannabis-cafe.com

Dedicated to "over-indulgence, decadence and self-abuse", this unabashed, in-your-face Website not only provides full directions and encouragement to help you find its sponsor – one of Amsterdam's legendary "coffee shops" – but also provides a jokey guide to "Alternative Amsterdam".

4Winds Tours

www.4windstours.com

Washington-based operator that offers inexpensive small-group barge tours of Holland and neighbouring countries, on which participants use bicycles to explore beyond the canals; self-drive barge rentals are also available. Spring, when the tulips are in bloom, is the busiest season. Reservations can only be made by printing and mailing the onscreen form.

Holland Bicycling Tours

www.hollandbicyclingtours.com

Californian company specializing in well-priced cycling tours of Holland, which it loquaciously calls "ideally suited to this mode of transportation". Both the main itineraries – the (Spring-only) Tulip Tour and the Highlights of Holland Tour – start and finish in Amsterdam and take in several lesser-known destinations. Air travel is not included, and add-ons are easy to arrange. To complete a booking, either mail or email the onscreen form together with a deposit.

The Official Holland Website

www.visitholland.com

The excellent official Website for the Netherlands holds tell-it-like-it-is details on all the towns and cities – in the virtual tour of Amsterdam, it tells you to avoid the alleyways "riddled with miserable-looking junkies" – as well as good links to make hotel reservations wherever you choose to go. You can even buy Dutch cheese online.

Radio Netherlands

www.rnw.nl

The best single online source of information on what's going on in contemporary Holland, with well-written English-language reporting on news and current affairs, together with reviews, previews and feature articles on cultural events and activities, all peppered with audio clips.

New Zealand

100% Pure New Zealand

www.purenz.com

With a clean interface and easy navigation, New Zealand's official tourism site offers far more than the usual glossy illustrations and puff pieces. Head first for the searchable "Experience Themes" – with names like thrill zone, heartland, chill out and kiwi spirit – where, beyond the slick copy about snow-capped peaks, emerald lakes and revitalized senses, there's a wealth of useful stuff. The "wilderness" area, for example, has a long list of activity operators – everything from overlanding, canyoning and diving to fishing and hot air ballooning – to guided tours, national parks, and regional tourist offices, linking up to sites where available. "Heartland" directs you towards the "real people", linking to backpackers' sites and hundreds of privately owned hostels and B&Bs. There's a lot of useful cross-referencing and heaps of general information about the islands.

AA New Zealand Accommodation Guide

www.nz-accommodation.co.nz

Good all-round site, quick to load and easy to use. To find somewhere to stay, search by destination and by accommodation type, then refine your search by tapping in any special needs. You'll get a review, rates, and reservation details, with links where applicable. The same site also holds links to leading museums, wildlife tours, cruises, adventure operators, shops, tour groups and transport companies. You can do a simple search by activity or region, perhaps adding details of your budget and your interests. There's also useful general destination information and an events guide, with menus that allow you to search according to where you're planning to be and when.

A J Hackett Bungy

www.ajhackett.com

A J Hackett, the original bungy jump operator, now has five NZ sites, including Kawarau, Queenstown, the first bungy bridge in the world; a "wilderness

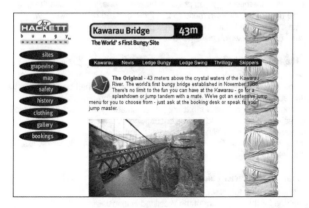

jump" 71m above the Shotover River in Skippers Canyon; and Nevis canyon, which at 134m is the highest jump in the world. You can read breathless accounts, view scary photos and book any of the trips online, and then you can buy rugged and sensible fleeces and sweats from the online store.

Best of NZ Pass

www.bestpass.co.nz

Easy-to-use travel pass, which combines trains, ferries and buses and lets you travel for up to six months with unlimited stopovers. You can save as much as 31 percent on standard adult fares for every journey you make, and gain discounts on accommodation and sightseeing. There are three versions, ranging from a simple one-island pass for $462 (saving $132) to a luxury pass that allows you to explore both islands thoroughly ($725, which saves you $320). Email them direct to buy.

Budget Backpacker Hostels

www.backpack.co.nz

Low on design, and high on information, this online version of New Zealand's BBHs directory is really useful. The easily downloadable "Quick Reference" section gives prices for each hostel (there are 280 of them) plus their BPPs, or "Backpacker Perception Percentages", awarded by hostellers themselves. If you prefer to browse online, you can use the clickable map or a pull-down menu to find more detailed hostel reviews with rates, BPPs and enlargable thumbnail pictures. You can also email to order their BBH card, which gives good discounts on buses and flights.

The Flying Fox

www.theflyingfox.co.nz

The kind of thing that New Zealand does so well. Reached by jet boat or the eponymous aerial tramway, this remote little "eco-resort", set by the Wanganui River on the North Island, is remarkably good value. The site features lots of sun-dappled photos of sparkling streams, freshly brewing coffee and simple, cosy cabins (just two of them), and tempts with accounts of delicious organic food, total peace and quiet, and possible bushwalks, horsetreks, and canoe trips. Email them to book.

Franz Josef Glacier Guides

www.franzjosefglacier.com

Named for the focal point of the Westland National Park on the South

Island – the world's steepest and fastest-flowing glacier open to tours – this outfit can take you to places normally only accessible to experienced mountaineers. Options range from half-day treks to challenging overnight trips, with safety equipment and professional guides included. Online bookings are not secure, but you can supply credit card details by fax or phone; your card is not debited until you take your trip, and cancellations can be made up to 24 hours in advance.

Guest in New Zealand

www.ginz.com

Christchurch-based travel shop specializing in tailor-made itineraries throughout Australasia. Their accommodation-booking service is simple: view lodges, B&Bs and farmstays in each region – choose a location, get a list, select a name, get a photo and full details – or simply browse through full listings. A secure server allows safe online booking; written confirmation and vouchers are mailed, faxed or emailed to you. They can also fix you up with rental cars (plus motorbikes and camper vans), domestic flights, train and ferry tickets and guided tours (divided into categories such as walking, nature, special interest and adventure).

Holiday Accommodation Parks of New Zealand

www.holidayparks.co.nz

Formerly known as the Camp and Cabin Association, New Zealand's Holiday Parks offer more than 270 camps, ranging from simple tented sites to comfortable complexes with motels and backpacker lodges. The rather joyless-looking site, an online version of their directory, is divided into geographical zones, with a map showing the locations of the parks on each island. Clicking the map will bring up a brief description of that area, with a list of all the parks in that zone: click again for maps, descriptions, facilities, average costs, contact details and home pages.

Māori Resources Online

www.culture.co.nz

Busy Maori site, updated daily, packed with high-quality content. The recipe section, for example, details the history and spiritual significance of traditional dishes, while message boards include cultural discussion and politics, with links to newsgroups. Te Karere Ipurangi, a full listing of Maori news, is worth a look, and you'll want to browse through the reviews, biographies, and weighty research articles. Links are well chosen and intelligently placed.

part three: destinations

New Zealand Bed and Breakfast Book Online

www.bnb.co.nz

The online version of Moonshine Press's handbook is a handy and user-friendly list of more than 1500 B&Bs all over New Zealand. Searching by criteria (homestay, farmstay, etc), perhaps refining your search with cost and preferred bathroom details, brings up a list of options with rates; you then click for pictures, reviews, guest books and contact details (bookings are made direct with hosts). You can also browse the guest book separately, but avoid the map search facility, which tends to lead to computer crash. The site is updated daily and new B&Bs are inspected to ensure that they meet required standards.

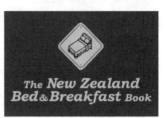

The **New Zealand Bed & Breakfast Book**

New Zealand Lodge Association

www.lodgesofnz.co.nz

Simple, pared-down site run by an umbrella organization of the country's rather fabulous full-board boutique hotels, which are invariably set in stunning locations. Just click on a map to find reviews and contact details for every lodge in New Zealand; from there you'll be sent to individual home pages (though these do not always have online booking). Also some general information about outdoor activities throughout the islands.

New Zealand Sites

www.newzealandsites.com

Superfast, very well organized directory of NZ Websites, with more than 5000 reviewed links for travel alone. Divided into subsections including accommodation, attractions, destinations, information, maps, tour operators, transportation and travel agents, categories are further subdivided as necessary, with a running tally of links for each one. The design and interface is soothing, despite its huge volume, which is a boon on a directory like this.

New Zealand Wine

www.nzwine.com

Official site of New Zealand's wine industry, with background details, history, a directory of vineyards and relevant links. You'll probably want to skip the news section – it's geared towards the business side of things – but if you're thirsty for knowledge about cabernet and merlot, including what to eat with them and which wineries produce the best, this is the place to come. You can also search for contact details of every winery on the islands.

NZCity

http://home.nzcity.co.nz

Customizable, varied portal with daily links to New Zealand's news, weather, travel and sports stories. The site takes a while to load, partly because of their database of news links, but it's worth the wait, and they don't overdo the images. Setting up a personal page and removing all the features you don't need helps save time.

Pedallers' Paradise

www.voyager.co.nz/~dabhand/ppguides.html

Bearing all the clunky design hallmarks of a lovingly put-together amateur site, this is the online companion to *Pedallers' Paradise*, the best cycling guides to New Zealand. The guides, which look almost as rudimentary as the site, are useful and lively, updated annually, with route descriptions and profiles, distances between main centres, and information on local attractions and services (including places to stay, eat and mend your bike). The site includes full details – including online updates – and contact details for international stockists. They've also come up with a good introduction to the perils and pleasures of cycling in New Zealand, and handy backpackers' links.

Wellington NZ

www.wellingtonnz.com

The official tourism site of New Zealand's capital takes a while to load, but digs deeper than the gushing home page suggests, featuring searchable databases of acccommodation in all budgets (with secure online booking) and restaurants, along with lots of bumf on restaurants and bars, shops, events and festivals, and even a couple of suggested itineraries. You can buy ferry tickets and make travel plans at their online travel centre. The links, related to Wellington and New Zealand, are well chosen.

part three: destinations

Whale Watch Kaikoura

www.whalewatch.co.nz

The waters around the Maori village of Kaikoura, on the South Island, attract more than a dozen species of whales, which come closer to shore here than anywhere else in the world. Whale Watch organizes boat trips out to see the colossal Sperm Whale along with (in summer) migratory species including Humpbacks and Orca. New Zealand Fur Seals and the Royal Albatross also make an appearance, and you can even arrange to swim with dolphins. Book your tour online (at least a few days in advance) – they'll refund eighty percent of your fare if you don't spot a cetacean. You can also book local accommodation on the site, and read about local restaurants and attractions.

YHA New Zealand

www.yha.org.nz

Although the cartoonish interface, all clashing colours and jazzy fonts, is off-putting, the official New Zealand YHA site is handy enough and simple to use. It provides full details on membership, and of all the hostels (fewer than sixty in NZ); you can apply to join and book a bed up to 48 hours in advance. Read here about discounts available to card holders, and of YHA's various packages and travel passes. Less successful is the Events Calendar, which consistently fails to come up with anything interesting, and the peculiar section on glamour backpacking for girls, complete with make-up and outfit tips.

Zorb Online

www.zorb.com

It's whacky! It's crazy! And that's just the Website! New Zealand (Rorotura, to be precise) is the home of Zorbing (that's where grown-ups climb into big inflated bouncing balls and hurl themselves down hills), and on this site its inventors tell you everything you need to know about this adrenalin-pumping hobby of madmen. In Rorotura, by the way, you can hydro-Zorb: they add a bucket of water to the ball so you can slide about and get drenched, with the Zorb rotating wildly and the water churning like rapids around you.

Norway

Borton Overseas

www.bortonoverseas.com
Based in North America's Nordic heartland, Minneapolis, Borton sell their Scandinavian tour packages to US residents only. As well as all-inclusive trips, they can also arrange hotel passes or simply book accommodation for specific nights. Booking requests are handled via email.

Hotell.org

www.hotell.org
Although it also includes a few restaurants, this Norwegian directory is largely devoted to accommodation options of all kinds. Skip straight past the massive opening list of hotels by searching for your specific destination. Not all the individual hotel sites remain active, but there are still plenty to choose from, and contact direct. A separate page features a huge range of

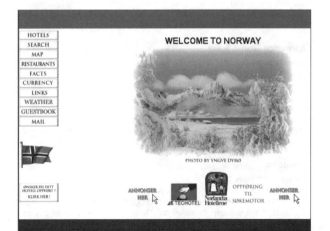

WELCOME TO NORWAY

HOTELS
SEARCH
MAP
RESTAURANTS
FACTS
CURRENCY
LINKS
WEATHER
GUESTBOOK
MAIL

ØNSKER DU DITT
HOTELL OPPFØRT ?
KLIKK HER !

PHOTO BY YNGVE DYRØ

ANNONSER
HER.

TECHOTEL

Norlandia
Hotellene

OPPFØRING
TIL
SØKEMOTOR

ANNONSER
HER.

links to governmental, tourist board, and transportation sites, but in the absence of tour operators and private companies it's better for gathering information than for making concrete arrangements.

Nordique Tours

www.nordiquetours.com
Californian operator whose Norwegian tours range from the one-day "Norway in a Nutshell" rail excursion from Oslo, via two-, three- and four-day "Mystic Fjords" trips, up to the full two-week Nordique Adventure, which takes in Denmark and Sweden into the bargain. Email the onscreen form to register your interest.

Norway.com

www.norway.com
Massive portal whose concern with Norway extends to offering links to businesses, tour companies, and even newspapers, all over Scandinavia. The best feature for prospective visitors, however, is the ability to create personalized guides to major Norwegian cities; **www.virtualoslo.com**, for example, invites you to specify your interests, travel dates, and practical needs, takes you on a "virtual walk" if you so desire, and returns your own detailed, printable document.

Norwegian Tourist Board

www.visitnorway.com
This official tourism site – itself a subsection of the all-encompassing Norwegian government site **www.norway.org** – lists and links to information offices all over the world, holds a zoomable map of the country, and provides both a general introduction and detailed advice for travellers. It makes an excellent first port of call, though once you work your way through to a specific hotel, you may find the English text gives way to Norwegian.

Scantours

www.scantoursuk.com
London agency that sells its extensive range of Scandinavian vacations to US as well as British travellers. Norwegian offerings include the three-day "Taste of a Glacier", the less appetizing five-day "Taste of Flam", and longer cruises up to the remote Arctic island of Spitsbergen. To ensure customers know exactly what they're getting, all bookings are arranged by phone or email.

Peru

Andean Trails

www.andeantrails.co.uk

British adventure specialists, based in Edinburgh, whose programme of Peru trips takes in relatively obscure regions of the country, such as the Huayhuash mountains in the north, and the Tambopata rainforest reserve in the southeast, as well as trekking and mountain-bike expeditions along the Inca Trail. Full itineraries and prices are detailed on screen; email any further questions, or download and mail a booking form.

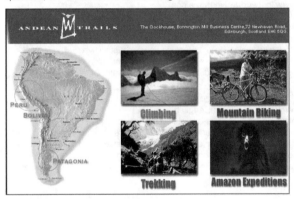

Destination South America

www.dsatravel.co.uk

British tour operator, part of the large Steppes Travel Group, which custom-designs all-inclusive package trips to Peru for travellers on all budgets. Their basic standard itineraries can be supplemented with activities such as para-gliding, white-water rafting or bird-watching. Set out your needs by email, print and mail the online booking form when you're ready, and they'll handle all the arrangements.

The Inca Trail

www.ex.ac.uk/~RDavies/inca/

If your interest in Peru stems from its pre-Columbian heritage, and the "lost city" of Machu Picchu in particular, this exuberant fan site, run by British traveller Ron Davies, will certainly whet your appetite. In addition to his own journals and photos, it features a massive set of links to other sites, covering all aspects of South American history, travel, and archeology, and also includes lists of tour operators both Peruvian and international.

Lost World Adventures

www.lostworldadventures.com

US company, based outside Atlanta, whose extensive range of South American tours includes a truly mouthwatering array of Peruvian expeditions. Most centre on archeological wonders, but potential add-ons include staying in jungle lodges and rafting down mountain rivers; all trips can be customized to meet your needs. Talk your plans through by email or phone, then mail your details to make a reservation.

Peru.com

www.peru.com/index_english.asp

Although run by a Lima-based travel agency primarily in order to sell its customized tours and adventure trips, the Peru.com portal features a great deal of useful general information, news, and statistics about the country. To negotiate its hotel-booking facility online, you'll need to read Spanish, but you can always simply email the company and they'll make all arrangements for you.

Poland

New Millennium Holidays

www.newmillennium-holidays.co.uk

UK operator offering bus travel and flights to central Europe and Italy. Ten-day bus trips to Poland – Krakow Zakopane, at the foot of the High Tatra mountains, or Krynica in the "land of sunny meadows"– cost from £120 half-board, with the possibility of a number of two-centre combinations.

They can also arrange day excursions from each of the three destinations. Travellers from outside the UK are encouraged to meet the tours on site and to contact the company about price reductions.

Poland Home Page

http://poland.pl

Links directory divided into useful categories – environment, sports, information and so on. The vast majority of sites are in Polish, but there are enough English-language options to make it worth a look. Under "Tourism and Recreation" you'll find sections on hotels, "most interesting regions", "holidays in Poland for foreigners", and even "holidays on a horseback". You can't say fairer than that.

Sophisticated Traveler

www.affordablepoland.com

Californian travel agency and tour operator specializing in good-value trips to Central and Eastern Europe from a variety of US cities. Independent packages start at $599 for a week – if you book a flight with them they can fix up hotels, guided tours, car rental and train travel. They also arrange half a dozen escorted tours, which start at around $1300 for an eight-day "Gems of the North" trip, rising to $2700 for the three-week "Grand Heritage", which takes in a string of the country's most atmospheric old towns and resorts. "Folklore and Leisure" is a nicely conceived ten-day package which combines the best of the two themes. No online booking; email them for more.

Travel to Poland

www.visit.pl

Poland-based online travel service with a database of hotels, castles and guesthouses in a variety of major destinations; click to read reviews, see photos and check availability. Prices are quoted in US dollars. Package details – Jewish culture in Krakow, say, or weekend breaks in Warsaw – are laid out in the same way: click on a destination, then the accommodation name, to read all about the excursions and activities included in the price of a stay. There's also the option to fill in a form detailing your interests so they can tailor an itinerary for you.

Portugal

Algarve Home Page

www.algarvenet.com

Algarve portal, with regional information, practical details, links to hotels and guesthouses, a villa rental section (and lots more in the classified ads) and a bibliography. You can use the searchable database to find anything from accountants to watersports.

Association of Tour Operators to Portugal

www.atop.org

ATOP is an organization of twenty or so major US tour operators with established Portugal programmes. Each listing comes with a brief review and contact details, including email addresses, but frustratingly they fail to provide links to Websites.

Magellan Tours

www.magellantours.com

US operator specializing in custom-designed travel to Portugal, with a wide range of options including the Azores and Madeira, Douro river cruises, golf holidays, biking tours, wine-tasting trips, fly-drives and accommodation-only deals. Their "discover weeks", for two to six people, allow you to explore off-the-beaten-track places while staying in luxury pousadas and manor houses, while "green weeks" combine sightseeing with bird-watching and dolphin-spotting. There are few indications of costs on the site; submit a form, stating all requirements including your budget, to receive a quote.

Oporto.com

www.oporto.com

Though ostensibly about Oporto, this portal is actually more general. The home page hits you with every figure and statistic you'd ever need to know about Portugal, while links – not all of which work – direct you to travel guides, maps and local tour operators. Under accommodation, you're linked to the relevant pages of a number of general accommodation sites. For restaurants and cuisine, you're better off looking at Virtual Portugal (see p.366).

Portugal Hotel Guide

www.maisturismo.pt
Searchable database of hotels; hunt by name, star rating, type of accommodation, or area to pull up a list of names and addresses. It's all rather patchy, but there are enough links to Websites to make it worthwhile.

Portugal InSite

www.portugal-insite.pt
The Website of the Portuguese tourist board is bursting with detail, including a searchable database of hotels and restaurants, with lists of ground operators, travel agents and car rental companies. You can also read some suggested short itineraries and historical notes about all the regions.

Portugal Post

www.portugalpost.com
The main news stories from a variety of press and online sources, along with links to all Portugal's key newspapers, including *The News*, the country's largest English-language weekly. There are also links to travel guides, portals, and general country information.

Portugal Travel and Tourism

www.portugal.org/tourism
Official government site, geared around business and investment, with a tourism channel that's of most use to North American travellers. The lodging section needs some beefing up, but click on "Before You Go" for all sorts of practical information, including flight schedules from the US, and, best of all, a table of operators leading tours to Portugal, organized by theme (adventure, nature, golf, religious, river cruises and so on).

Pousadas de Portugal

www.pousadas.pt
Though occasionally slow, this fabulous site, which entreats you to "Discover Pousadas Land", is worth a bit of patience for its wealth of detail on the country's forty or so distinctive hotels, many of them in historic buildings. Search for regional or historical *pousadas*, by facilities or environment, or simply click icons on a map. There's lots of background stuff, plus reviews of each, with photos and virtual tours, prices, details of facilities

and sample menus, and accounts of local festivals and sights. Anyone on a touring holiday will find the themed itineraries useful, and there are discounts for honeymooners, young people, over-60s and so on. To book, either contact the *pousada* direct, call the reservation centre in Lisbon, email the site, or submit a booking form. They also provide contact details for *pousada* agents around the world.

Simply Portugal

www.simplyportugal.co.uk

Recommended British Portugal specialists with a great range of places to stay throughout the country. Click on a map to search by destination, or choose by property type (from rustic cottages and beachside apartments to luxurious *pousadas*), checking the local weather as you go. Many holidays include car rental, and they also offer self-drive "wandering holidays", where you can book a couple of nights each in a string of places. There are enough details here for you to confidently make a booking: fill in the online enquiry form and they'll call you direct. The late availabilities page, incidentally, has good prices on holidays up to six weeks in advance.

Virtual Portugal

www.portugalvirtual.pt

Admirably clear and no-nonsense, this portal displays all its contents on the home page, where you click into channels such as transport, food, leisure and tourism, to find a mixture of links and original content. The links directories are laid out in user-friendly tables, with lots of good stuff on food and drink and a handy directory of restaurants (the vast majority of them in Lisbon) grouped by cuisine.

Russia

Beetroot Bus

www.beetroot.org

Backpacker tours around Russia on (non-Russian) minibuses. Weekly departures from Moscow or St Petersburg during the summer, stopping at a range of places on a ten-day, one-way trip or a sixteen-day loop. They'll pick you up before the tour, fix your visa (for a fee) and organize budget accommodation (in hotels, camps or lodges) along the way. If you want them to book accommodation before or after the trip they can do that, too, charging you £15 per night. Prices start at around £300 for ten days. To book, download a form and fax or email it to the specialist UK operator, The Russia Experience (see below).

Regent Holidays

www.regent-holidays.co.uk

Specializing in Russia, Eastern Europe and the former Soviet bloc states, this worthy operator – "holidays for thinking people" – offers a number of suggested itineraries and customized tours, including city breaks in Moscow and St Petersburg. A seven-day tour of the Golden Ring, a string of ancient towns northeast of Moscow, costs around £350, excluding flight. Download the brochures with Acrobat, and then contact them direct.

The Russia Experience

www.trans-siberian.co.uk

Excellent British company providing exciting itineraries for independent travellers. Most trips involve at least some time in the company of a "buddy" – a local who will show you the ropes and lead you to little-known sights – and they'll fix you up with as many experiences as you choose: trekking in Siberia, horse riding in Kyrgyzstan, rafting in the Altai Mountains, jeep trekking in the Mongolian Gobi … Along with bus tours (see www.beetroot.org, above), overland trips, language schools in Moscow and city breaks, Russia Experience specializes in Trans-Siberian train jour-

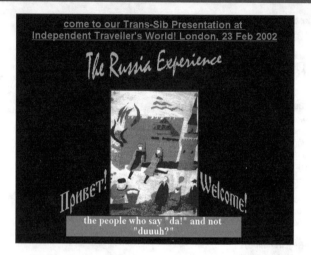

neys. Costs are extremely reasonable: around £1000 for the "Big Trans-Sib", for example, a fifteen-day trip from Moscow to Beijng via Lake Baikal and Ulan Bator, including Siberian saunas, and time with the nomads of Mongolia. There's also a message board full of advice and questions, and a set of lively links. Download the brochure to read full trip details and background information; then email, fax or post the booking form with a deposit. Travellers from North America should log onto **www.sunvalleytravel.com**, their US agents.

Russia Tourism Pages

www.russia-tourism.com
Well-organized links directory devoted to travel and tourism and divided into 24 sections including regions, museums, eco-tourism, hotels (including hostels and home stays), weather, women and money.

Russian National Tourist Office

www.russia-travel.com
Idiosyncratic site where you can fill in a visa application form, use the track-

ing system to check how much longer you're going to have to wait for it to be processed, read about a handful of hotels, check out the river cruises and tours (great if you yearn to hunt wood birds or attend an aviation show), or even book a berth on the Trans-Siberian railway from Moscow to Vladivostok.

Russian Travel Bureau

www.russiantravelbureau.com
US company offering small-group escorted tours of Russia, among them a one week "Bargain Tour", which costs $950 including flight and takes in Moscow and St Petersburg with a stop in Helsinki. At the other end of the spectrum, "Peter the Great's Grandeur" is an all-inclusive luxury trip staying at posh hotels in Moscow, Novgorod, and St Petersburg. You can also take a river cruise, or piece together your own holiday, booking hotel rooms in Moscow and St Petersburg and choosing between a variety of day tours. No online booking.

Singapore

Asia Cyber Holidays

www.asiacyberholidays.com/singapore/singapore_hotels.htm
Though the background information provided by this online travel marketing company – based in Switzerland and Bangkok – isn't bad, with thumbnail sketches of all Singapore's most interesting neighbourhoods, the site is most useful for anyone wanting to book accommodation online. They've got a choice of around fifty hotels in the city, ranging from $50 per night to $400 (but that's a one-off, for the swanky Raffles Hotel). Click on the name to see photos and brochure blurb, and submit an online availability form – then double-check with the general accommodation booking sites listed on pp.71–73 to compare rates at your chosen hotels. It's also possible to reserve day tours online, from walking tours of Chinatown to junk cruises around the harbour.

Makan Time – Singapore Unofficial Food Page

www.makantime.com
Lively dining guide to one of the world's great foodie cities, with a huge

Makan Time in Singapore !

the quest for the "Shiokest" continues ...

database of restaurant reviews and restaurant home pages, readers' reviews (with a "hall of shame" for complaints), lots of background information, a host of intriguing articles and plenty of links (look under "Magazine" and "Directory").

South Africa

For a handful of good safari sites, see "Wildlife and Nature", which starts on p.220.

Africa Tours

www.africasafaris.com

US Africa specialist with scheduled and customized safaris and tours of South Africa, including three- or four-day packages to Kruger National Park, Sun City, Cape Town and so on, with options to travel on the luxurious Blue Train. There are further choices under "Specials" – one-offs and seasonal migrations – and "New Programmes". To book, you need to call or email them in New York.

Africa Travel Centre

www.africatravel.co.uk

An impressive list of tours – some scheduled, others customized – is offered by this culturally sensitive British Africa specialist. Choose from cricket and rugby holidays (combining matches with tours of key areas such as Kruger Park, the Mpumalanga region and the Cape vineyards); a "South Africa in Depth" fly-drive itinerary; luxury tours – including a trip on the Blue Railway; short city breaks from Johannesburg, and a host of other options. Costs, upwards of £1500, include international flights. Email to book.

African Adrenalin

www.africanadrenalin.co.za

Nicely organized clearing house for a variety of South Africa-based companies offering accommodation, safaris, train journeys and adventure holidays. Speedy links take you to the company concerned, many of which offer online booking.

African Odyssey

www.africanodyssey.co.uk

British southern and eastern Africa specialists. Alhough you can request a quote for any of their accommodation options (they have a good choice throughout the country, from guesthouses through safari lodges to luxury towers), and book any of the specials (usually themed holidays – family adventures, sun and sand, wine-tasting and so on) through the site, you'll need to contact them for a brochure to get details of their escorted tours and tailor-made itineraries.

Ananzi Search Engine

www.ananzi.co.za

Useful South African links directory with a speedy search engine. The "Travel" section – divided into geographic regions – covers subjects as varied as backpacking, hunting and fishing, time shares, travel operators and vineyards, and it's also worth taking a look at "Entertainment" (cybercafes, bars, music sites, restaurants) and "Reference" (newspapers, city guides, magazines).

Ecoafrica.com

www.ecoafrica.com

Ecoafrica acts as an agent for a South Africa-based operator specializing in scheduled and customized cultural and nature tours. From the home page you can link to overland expeditions, game lodges, safaris, adventure tours and national parks, along with a selection of special deals and promotions. There's lots of choice, from backpackers' safaris to cultural history tours and dinosaur tracking, canoe trips and long-term overlanding, with plenty of detail on each. Email them to check availability and make a provisional booking.

Global Exchange

www.globalexchange.org

San Francisco-based non-profit organization offering political and cultural

"reality tours" around the world, examining how US economic and foreign policies impact on other countries. Trips are one-offs, so it varies what's on offer, but there are always a handful of South Africa itineraries, focusing on women's history, maybe, or giving an overview of the work of the Truth and Reconciliation Commission. Tours include meetings with grass-roots workers and community leaders, as well as sightseeing and nights out. They cost around $2500 for two weeks, with everything included but flights. To book, fill in the online form and fax or send by snail mail.

Travel Southern Africa

www.travelsa.com

More than 3000 pages on this drab information site (as they admit, they've made it "fast rather than pretty"), most of them relating to South Africa. Whether you're looking for canoeing and caving operators, tented safari camps, city guides, houseboats or luxury rail services, you'll find it here. All listings come with contact details including Websites where available.

Spain

Anyone intending to walk the Camino de Santiago pilgrimage trail should turn to the review of the Confraternity of St James Website on p.207.

Abreu Tours

www.abreu-tours.com
Large US agency, whose densely packed Website holds reams of details
on its varied programme of Spanish vacations, which include city breaks,
escorted tours, villa rentals, and hotel stays. Visits to mainland Spain can
be combined with add-ons in Portugal or the Canary Islands. Wade
through the endless charts to cost your itinerary for yourself, or simply
email the form and they'll do it for you.

Alternative Mallorca

www.alternativemallorca.com
Independent British company which offers roughly seventy rental properties
and thirty hotels in the obscurer, less frenetic regions of the Balearic island
of Mallorca. Search for your ideal villa using such criteria as sea view,
degree of peacefulness, pool, or nearby restaurants. They can also arrange
walking holidays in the Soller valley. Call or email for reservations.

Andalucia Com

www.andalucia.com
Privately run Web portal, based in Andalucia and designed to promote
regional businesses in general, and tourism in particular. As well as its own
introductory overviews, including excellent details and illustrations of local
natural parks, it holds masses of links to rental properties, hotels, adventure-tour operators and the like.

Andalucian Adventures

www.andalucian-adventures.co.uk
Full details of idyllic walking and painting holidays in the hills of southern
Spain, such as the Alpujarra range in the Sierra Nevada National Park.
Guides include best-selling author and *Rough Guide* stalwart Chris
Stewart. There's no online booking, but at least the "Useful Links" really
are useful.

Barcelona On Line

www.barcelona-on-line.es/eng/
A handy independently run guide to Barcelona, with up-to-the-minute listings as well as general practical information. Searching for hotels or rental
apartments, by area, price, or other criteria, enables you both to access

properties' Websites, or to submit an email request to Barcelona On Line's own discount booking service.

Magical Spain

www.magicalspain.com

Small-scale operation, run by American expatriates in Seville, that offers walking tours of that city as well as nearby Cordoba and Granada, day trips in the Andalucian countryside, and multi-day tours in the region that focus on themes such as the Moorish heritage or local cuisine. Call or email to create your own personalized itinerary.

On Foot in Spain

www.onfootinspain.com

US operator specializing in small-group walks and hikes across northern Spain – along the pilgrim route of the Camino de Santiago (see p.207), in the Picos de Europa, and in the Basque country. The emphasis is less on clocking up the miles than in appreciating your surroundings. As well as introducing the flora and fauna, guides attempt to bring to life regional culture, folklore and history. Accommodation is in rural inns, monasteries, and small hotels. Email to book.

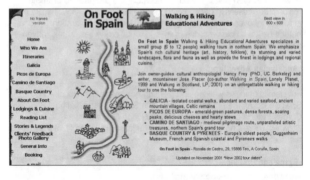

Paradores

www.parador.es

The concept of Spain's *parador* hotels, set in beautifully converted historic buildings, has been copied worldwide, but the originals remain as irresistible as ever. Once you've found photos, rates and other details of each one – under the far-from-obvious heading "Spain in 86 Clicks"– you can email direct for reservations. The home page also lists special offers and multi-night discounts.

Rustic Blue

www.rusticblue.com

Appealing, nicely illustrated site, filled with testimonials from happy clients, promoting a small Granada-based company that arranges both guided walking and horse-riding holidays, and also villa and apartment rentals, in rural Andalucia; they can even put you up in a furnished cave. They don't sell flights, but have good deals on rental cars. Full details are available on screen, but you have to call Spain to book.

Si Spain

www.sispain.org

Created and maintained by the Spanish embassy in Ottawa, this excellent English-language directory site has mushroomed to become perhaps the best overall online Spanish resource, featuring links to cultural, political, linguistic and historical sites of all kinds. Though its focus is not primarily on tourism, the "Travelling to Spain" section makes a useful introduction for visitors, and lists assorted Canadian operators.

Spanish Harbour Holidays

www.spanish-harbour.co.uk

This UK operator concentrates on the quieter, family-oriented areas of Catalunya, offering hotels and self-catering accommodation both along the Costa Blanca and in the more remote mountain villages. All prices and details are provided on screen, but bookings can only be made by phone.

Spanish Heritage

www.shtours.com

New York-based tour agency, linked to the massive Far and Wide operation, which offers a huge array of package trips to Spain, from the mainland cities to the islands. To each basic tour, clients can add on their own selection of components such as flights and car rental. Complete the lengthy email form to state your needs.

Spanish Steps

www.spanishsteps.com
North American operator that leads small-group walking and photography tours of varying lengths, including inn-to-inn pilgrimages along northern Spain's Camino de Santiago, and multi-day adventures in Andalucia's Cabo de Gato National Park. They can also create customized bike tours on request; call or email to book.

Tourist Office of Spain

www.tourspain.es
Although lumbering English translations make this huge official site less user-friendly than it could have been, it's still a great resource for anyone planning a trip to Spain. A searchable database provides listings – though not availability or booking – for accommodation of all kinds, and you can also find operators for a wide range of adventurous activities, plus calendars of upcoming events, suggested itineraries, useful contacts, and much more.

typicallyspanish.com

www.typicallyspanish.com
This Spanish-run directory site may be horrendously cluttered and fussy, with a barrage of new menus popping into view at the slightest twitch of a mouse, but it's worth persevering to reach its many thousands of links to all matters Hispanic, from bullfighting to history to property for sale.

Sweden

Hotels in Sweden

www.hotelsinsweden.net
This searchable database of Swedish accommodation is efficient and clean. Search by name, place, province, hotel chain affiliation, or by special needs to pull up a list of matches, with icons denoting facilities and rates, along with full contact details and links to individual Websites.

Sweden Information Smorgasbord

www.sverigeturism.se/smorgasbord
Huge English-language information site with well-written articles on every

aspect of the culture, and loads of links (many of them to Swedish sites) so you can pursue your interest in anything from youth hostels to the fiddler company of Falun. The tourism section includes links to all the regional tourist boards.

Sweden Tourist Information

www.visit-sweden.com
Glossy site from the Swedish Travel and Tourism Council, with destination guides and articles, pretty pictures, and intelligently organized links for each section. There's little chance for interactive activity, but it's a good start as an information source.

Swedish Touring Club

www.meravsverige.nu/STF_INT/bo.asp
A voluntary organization promoting hearty holidays in the great outdoors, the Swedish Touring Club has 315 IYHF-affiliated youth hostels, 8 mountain stations, and 40 or so mountain huts, all set in gorgeous countryside. You can search the site for any accommodation that takes your fancy, using the "special selection" menu to refine your search if you want such things as disabled access or good fishing nearby. Matches come with photos (except in the case of the mountain huts), a rundown of facilities and daily rates. You can't book in advance for the mountain huts or stations, but there are online reservation forms for the hostels.

Switzerland

Camping.ch

www.camping.ch

Searchable database of Swiss campsites with three search criteria (type of site, site facilities, facilities within 2km) and an incredibly detailed set of refinements – no trees, numerous trees, drain connections, washing facilities … Unfortunately you can only pick one category from each pull-down menu, which leads to a few difficult choices (footsink or hot shower? children's playground or children's swimming pool?). When the results appear on the screen, click to read full details of each site, with tempting photos. Many have their own Web pages, to which you are directed for online booking.

Ski Switzerland

www.skiswitzerland.com

Dull to look at but does the job: click on a resort name to read an overview of conditions and facilities, see photos, and peruse skiing and summer maps. You can also search for hotels in a number of resorts, find relevant online maps, and, using Adobe Acrobat, print a variety of brochures produced by hotels and resorts.

Switzerland Tourism

www.myswitzerland.com

If you can get past the purple prose (though it's always good to know that "mountains, lakes and valleys will put forward their best foot"), Switzerland's official tourism site is a sophisticated operation, with lots of interactive city and resort information, and online booking for hotels, holidays, excursions and special events. Choose from a pull-down menu of categories such as art and culture, city breaks or scenic tours to read about special offers, or use the search facility to hunt down attractions and holidays geared towards special interests (cycling, skiing, gastronomy, "water fun"), refining the search if you want a family holiday, or to go at a particular time of year, or if you have a certain region in mind. With a database of more than 1800 hotels, this is also a good place to search for accommodation.

Tanzania

For safari sites, see "Wildlife and Nature", on p.220.

Another Land

www.anotherland.com

US-based operator specializing in small-group cultural holidays to Tanzania, Zanzibar and Uganda. Scheduled trips change regularly, but as an example, their "folklore safari", in northern Tanzania, has you staying in luxury lodges and tented camps while experiencing the traditions, crafts and culture of the Chagga people. Their customized "family and friends" expeditions include a "Tanzania for Two" itinerary which gets you to off-the-beaten-track destinations inaccessible to larger groups. They also custom-design trips, and provide a form with a list as long as your arm. So whether you're into banana fibre craft or tinga tinga, initiation rites or scuba diving, they can fix something up. There's lots of interesting background material, and plenty to tempt you – but you'll need serious money (around $4000 for a fortnight) if you succumb. Submit an online form to make a reservation.

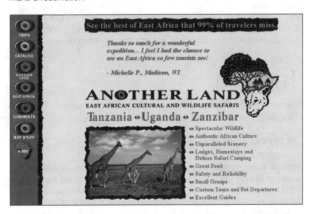

Simply Tanzania

www.simplytanzania.co.uk

Headed by an ex-VSO programme director and study tour leader for the Britain-Tanzania Society, this company organizes quality customized tours. You can choose from a selection of tried and trusted two-week itineraries – including Serengeti safaris, beach stays in Zanzibar, sojourns with the Chagga people of Kilimanjaro, and game-viewing in the Selous wilderness – or get them to design one for you. Accommodation varies from tourist lodges, tented camps and farms to simple guesthouses. No online booking; email for full details.

Tanzania Tourist Board

www.tanzania-web.com/home2.htm

The official Website is sleek and impressive, with destination guides, reviews of the national parks, and links to lodges and recommended operators in Tanzania and the UK. The message boards are useful for making contacts.

Zanzibar Travel Network

www.zanzibar.net

Very thorough online guide, boasting destination overviews (including hotlinks to hotels, restaurants and dive centres), along with a detailed history, getting there information, and a list of links to some seriously obscure sites.

Thailand

See p.198 for more companies that offer cooking holidays in Thailand.

All Thailand Experiences

www.all-thailand-exp.com

Reputable, eco-conscious US tour company, based in Oregon but with offices in Chiang Mai and specializing in northern Thailand. Via the Website, you can custom-design Thai holidays of all kinds, incorporating such components as hill-tribe treks, dive courses, white-water rafting, and bird-watching – or just sitting on the beach. Once you've agreed an itinerary by email, you can confirm your booking and pay online.

Bangkok Metro

http://bkkmetro.com
Online version of Bangkok's monthly listings magazine, with feature articles, restaurant and club listings, reviews of arts and sports events and a travel section with offers from guesthouses, local operators and the like. You can also print out coupons to get discounts at various bars and restaurants.

Chiang Mai Thai Cookery School

www.thaicookeryschool.com
Highly recommended cookery school offering a range of one- to five-day courses, some of which involve extras such as vegetable carving, market visits, and curry-paste making. You can choose either to be taught at the chef's restaurant or at his family home just outside Chiang Mai, and places can be reserved online.

Chiva Som

www.chivasom.net
Voted the best spa resort in the world by readers of *Condé Nast Traveler* magazine, the luxurious Chiva Som, south of Hua Hin, has space for just 57 people in a seven-acre beachfront setting dotted with lagoons and waterfalls. The twenty treatment rooms offer such delights as sound healing, chakra balancing, floatation therapy and no-knife face lifts. Rates start at $315 per person for one night's full board with a health and beauty consultation, massage and use of the facilities, rising to $10,458 for two weeks in the palatial "Golden Bo" suite. Packages start at $1240 for a five-night holistic retreat. Email a reservation form to check availability, and they'll contact you direct.

Dreaded Ned

www.dreadedned.com
The site that claims, like namesake Ned Kelly, to have "a bucket on its head" is in fact a gay guide to Thailand, with good general information about what it means to be gay in Thailand, and what it's like for gay visitors, with contact details for gay groups, a bibliography, legal details, etiquette tips and a good set of links to related sites. The gay venue guide makes up the core of the site, covering hotels, bars, clubs, restaurants, businesses and commercial sex venues, with reviews, full contact details and links. It's strongest on Bangkok, but has good stuff for other areas including Chiang Mai, Phuket and Pattaya, and even the more remote regions. Most pages are regularly updated (for details see under "New"),

though the "In the News" section, under "Explore Gay Thailand" goes only up to mid-1999. For current local gossip, click on "Scene and Heard" under the Gay Venue Guide.

Exodus

www.exodus.co.uk

Reliable UK adventure travel company (see p.120) offering half a dozen tours of Thailand. The only one to concentrate exclusively on the country involves sixteen days' trekking, bussing, train-riding, rafting, elephant-riding and island-hopping for £710 (excluding flight). All the others include Thailand as part of a longer Southeast Asia itinerary, climaxing with the thirty-week trans-Asia overland marathon, which will set you back a cool £5000 (again, not including flight).

Footprint Adventures

www.footprint-adventures.co.uk

Eco-friendly UK company (see p.120) offering a really nice range of small-group adventure, birding and wildlife tours around the world. The Thailand adventure holidays – including jungle safaris, trekking and a diving/canoeing/caving combo – start at £105/$160 for six days' jungle trekking, not including flight. The priciest, at £285/$430, gets you twelve days exploring northern Thailand and the Golden Triangle, and includes a three-night trek, an overnight in a hill-tribe village, elephant rides and a rafting trip. Bird-watching holidays range from four days with the rare Gurney's Pitta near Krabi to a trip that takes in Khao Yai, Kaeng Krachan, Doi Inthanon and Doi Suthep national parks. You can email a reservation form or use the secure online booking system, and you can also buy a range of *Footprint* travel guides (though the two companies aren't officially linked).

Himalayan Travel

www.himalayantravelinc.com

North American company organizing a good range of group trekking, cycling, wildlife and mountaineering trips around the world. Thailand trips start at around $500 for an eight-day hill-tribe trek, rising to nearly $1000 for "the highlights of Siam" tour. They also offer customized tours including three days staying among the hill tribes of Mae Hong Son or elephant safaris in the jungles of Chiang Rai (both around $250 per person based on two sharing). No online booking; you need to submit a form requesting a hard copy brochure.

Infothai.com

www.infothai.com

Wide-ranging directory of Thai Websites with an on-site Bangkok magazine (with lots of tourist information and articles). You can also access **welcome-to.chiangmai-chiangrai.com** and its useful Travel Help facility (see p.384). The links ("Customer Sites") are arranged alphabetically rather than by subject, which can mean a bit of a trawl, but throws up a few unexpected gems among the restaurants, guesthouses, shops and NGOs, including Chiang Mai's International Training Institute of Thai Massage, reviewed on p.208. Check out, too, the site devoted "to a very talented man who happens to be King", HM Norodom Sihanouk of Cambodia, who has directed, produced and scored music for 28 films.

Journeys International

www.journeys-intl.com

High-quality, small-group eco-tourism and cultural tours from an established US operator. They offer trips all over the world, classifying them from Grade I (relatively active, staying in lodges) to demanding Grade IV wilderness travel itineraries. The three scheduled Thailand tours – including a hill-tribe trek and a rainforest safari – go up to Grade II. Land costs, starting at $650 for five days, are reasonable, though a couple of the trips can only be booked as an extension to another tour. To reserve, click on "Trip Terms and Conditions", where you can either download a form with Acrobat or key in your details online, making sure to follow up with a phone call.

Magic of the Orient

www.magic-of-the-orient.com

Upmarket UK operator specializing in scheduled and custom-made packages to Asia. Choose Thailand in the Destination Information section, then use the search facility to find the Tour Modules (private tours). There's a good choice here, from a simple car plus driver and a variety of diving packages to cruises aboard a converted rice barge and a five-day Northern hill tribes/Golden Triangle combination. Searching for Hotel Information brings up a list of accommodation – all rather swanky, even the quirky beach-hut style places – complete with reviews and photos, and there's also a full set of packages from cooking courses to beach holidays. Add anything that catches your eye to the travel planner, a kind of as-you-go shoppng basket. To book, email the details from your travel planner, and they'll send you a quote within 24 hours.

Myths and Mountains

www.mythsandmountains.com

Nevada-based operator specializing in cultural, educational and eco-tours of Asia and South America (for US travellers only). Trips concentrate on cultures and crafts, holy sites, traditional healing, or wildlife and the environment. Their fixed Thailand itineraries, which take only four to six people, include sea canoeing (3–7 days from $650 without airfare), and a Thai massage and hill-tribe villages combination (18 days from $2395). The site holds brief details, but to see a detailed itinerary, or to request a custom-designed tour, you'll need to submit an enquiry form. And when it comes to booking a scheduled trip you'll need to fill in yet more forms, either online or downloaded, and send them hard copy, along with a deposit.

Tourist Authority of Thailand

www.tat.or.th

Thailand's official tourism authority bids you "welcome to the land of smiles", with a site chock-full of sensible, useful content. There's masses on each region and all sorts of odds and ends including audio files of basic phrases, weather reports, and Thai horoscopes. You can read guides to individual areas online, or download the Adobe Acrobat mini-brochures under "Things to See and Do". Look for "Experience Thailand" (also "Things to See and Do") for good stuff on where to seek tuition in Buddhism, the martial art of Muay Thai, and Thai cooking.

Welcome to Chiang Mai and Chiang Rai

http://welcome-to.chiangmai-chiangrai.com

Online magazine full of information about north Thailand, with lists of recommended accommodation, restaurants and activities, plus articles on everything from elephants, festivals and hill tribes to fortune-telling and carrot-carving. The site design leaves a lot to be desired, but the content can't be

bettered: their Travel Help (also accessible at **www.infothai.com** – see p.383) is particularly useful. Simply fill in an email form outlining your interests, and you'll get an automatic response full of detail about relevant accommodation, operators and activities. They're happy to give even more detailed advice if you email them direct.

Trinidad and Tobago

Welcome to Trinidad and Tobago

www.visittnt.com

Produced by TIDCO, the islands' tourism authority, this official site isn't flashy, but it's gratifyingly easy to use, and genuinely useful, with a searchable accommodation database featuring guesthouses, host homes and hotels, many of which offer online booking; you can search on each island. The background information on carnival is superb, with histo-

ries, food reviews, mas camp listings, audio tapes and more, and there's a lively section on the islands' other main festivals, with a good account of Divali, the Hindu "festival of lights". You can even check flights to and between the islands, using Travelocity (see p.33) to book online, and there are links to charter and ferry companies.

Turkey

For relaxation weeks at a mountain retreat in southwest Turkey, see **www.huzurvadisi.com** on p.208.

Aka Kurdistan

www.akakurdistan.com

An offshoot of the book *Kurdistan, in the Shadow of History*, by Susan Meiselas, this stunning, emotive site calls itself a "borderless space ... to build a collective memory with a people that have no national archive". The ongoing timeline uses old photographs and testimony from Kurds and colonial administrators, anthropologists, missionaries and journalists to create a personal impression of Kurdistan's history and culture; you can also check the bibliography and follow links to relevant sites.

Bodrum Guide

www.bodrum4u.com

Local guide with information on Bodrum's history, cuisine, local customs and the like, and some links to local tour operators. There's a lot to read about the extensive nightlife, though more for a general impression than anything particular.

Bora Özkök Tours

www.boraozkok.com

San Diego agency specializing in cultural tours of Turkey and the "Stans", stressing history, folklore, and archeology, with a few adventure trips and explorations of remote regions. Bora himself leads eight or so 18–30-day tours per year, providing flute and dance accompaniment along the way (you can buy his CDs on the site), and there are plenty more options, ranging from 15–21 days in length. There's also a twelve-day "mini tour" covering Istanbul and the western and central regions. Accommodation is in luxury hotels – or as close as possible – and prices, at around a grand for a fortnight (land costs only), aren't bad. You can submit an online booking form, but the server isn't secure, so it's best to call.

Cagaloglu Hammam

www.cagalogluhamami.com.tr

A guide to Istanbul's glorious three-hundred-year-old marble hammam (Turkish baths) with lots of pictures, a history, opening hours and directions.

Explore Turkey

www.exploreturkey.com

Information portal that is especially strong on Turkey's history. Although there are brief destination guides and patchy links to hotels, it's of most use for its thorough, well-written cultural information, covering subjects such as historical figures, architecture, archeological sites and folk traditions.

HiTiT

www.hitit.co.uk

For once the term "alternative guide" just about hits the mark: this site tells it like it is about Turkey's most popular destinations, giving a balanced overview and spicing it all up with travellers' tales. There are also plenty of photos, links to local news sources, feature articles and details on outdoor activities and shopping. You can search by region, destination or subject.

Kalkan Region

www.kalkan.org.tr

Useful guide to the southwestern resort town of Kalkan and its surroundings, with lots of photos, links to hotels and restaurants, and a limited amount of practical information, including addresses of local health providers.

Pacha Tours

www.pachatours.com

New York-based Turkey specialists offering a wide range of holiday options. Their escorted tours, which have a cultural emphasis, range in length from 8 to 32 days and come suited to a variety of budgets. The popular seventeen-day Cultural Heritage, which includes in-depth museum trips, folkloric performances, and lectures throughout the west and central regions, starts at $2500 (land costs only), staying in luxury hotels; the Super Value Western Turkey, which emphasizes art and archeology, goes at a faster pace, uses simpler hotels and starts at $800. You could also choose to follow the footsteps of St Paul, trace the country's Jewish heritage, or explore the remote east, among other options. The drawbacks are that groups aren't small, and there is no online booking; download a form or call them direct.

Tapestry Holidays

www.tapestryholidays.com

At pains to distance themselves from the "package holiday" concept, promising an entrée into the "real Turkey", this classy UK operator provides a nice range of holidays – including special-interest breaks – to the less commercial Turquoise coast resorts around Dalaman, along with short jaunts to Istanbul and Cappadocia. You can read full, refreshingly honest reviews of the accommodation options, which range from boutique hotels to cave houses and rustic cottages, along with dates, costs, flight details and tempting photos. Prices are good, and there is usually a happy selection of late availabilities. To make a provisional booking you can either call them, submit an online form, or get them to call you, when, unusually, you can discuss the finer details of every room available, and choose the one you prefer. They can also provide childcare facilities.

Turkey.com

www.turkey.com

Sophisticated portal with reviewed links grouped into channels for business, news, travel, culture, sport and shopping. Plus a wide range of forums (you need to register to post) on history, politics, cuisine, human rights, music, literature, travel – many of them, even those that would seem to be totally innocent, are aflame with political debate.

TWARP

www.twarp.com

Online clearing house for a variety of Turkish travel services from hotels to tour guides to cruises, most of them in the major resorts and cities. Information is variable; if you're happy that you've got a good picture of that pension in Cappadocia or that bareboat yacht charter, you can book online (benefiting in some cases from special Web rates), or at least make email enquiries. The hot deals section often comes up with late availabilities.

UK

UK tourist boards

The official tourist board sites for England, Scotland, Wales and Northern Ireland are reviewed under the relevant country headings.

Travel Britain

www.travelbritain.org

This tourist board site, designed specifically for visitors from North America, bears a strong resemblance to **www.visitbritain.com** (see below), with the added bonus of lots of travel details. Here you'll find agents who specialize in British vacations, along with special deals from airlines, hotels, and tour operators, and a variety of discounts on passes and admission fees. There are sections on speciality travel – mature, family, student and gay – plus a great selection of links to everything from Eastenders to Webcams.

Visit Britain

www.visitbritain.com

One of the best tourist board sites on the Web – efficient, intelligently laid out, and very nicely designed. Among its many useful features, the travel information pages do a great job of picking their way through Britain's confusing tangle of bus, train and ferry lines, highlighting various money-saving passes and linking to the major travel-planning sites. The comprehensive accommodation database runs the gamut from castles to hostels, more of which are featured in "Britain for Less", where you're directed to good-value hotels and restaurants, free events and attractions. "Before You Go" includes a searchable database of all Britain's tourist offices with contact details and opening hours.

Tour operators

British Travel International

www.britishtravel.com

This garish one-stop US travel agent might look like a nightmare, but it can offer all sorts of help with independent arrangements. Come here for deals on apartments, cottages and hotels, plus national rail and bus passes, admission tickets and cellphone rental, but because of the volume of business, don't come expecting a lot of detail – the hotels they deal with, for example, are simply listed with name, address and price. They provide more information for self-catering; London apartments and country cottages, organized by region, come with photos and reviews as well as a price chart. Only a selection of self-catering options are on view here; for the full list, you need to send off, and pay, for their catalogues. It's possible to book online, but the server isn't secure, so you may prefer to call the toll-free number.

CIE Tours

www.cietours.com

This US operator has been organizing escorted bus tours around the UK and Ireland for more than seventy years. All you need to know about the many tours – which have soggily evasive names like "Scottish Dream", "British Elegance", "Irish Charm" and so on – including daily itineraries, price (with or without flight) and hotel information is detailed on the site. They can also arrange self-drive itineraries (including "London at Leisure"). To book, you need to fill in a detailed online form and, if paying by card, download a printable payment form.

The English Experience

www.english-experience.com

Somewhat misleadingly named, this specialist US operator arranges small-group and independent tours all over the UK, including Scotland, Ireland and – unusually – Guernsey, as well as Sussex, Shropshire, the Cotswolds and the Lake District. You can choose from escorted, fixed-departure tours, tours with driver/guides, or custom-designed trips. They also offer day-trips – including from London to Paris – and door-to-door airport pick-up service. Call to make reservations.

Historic Homes of Britain

www.specialtytraveluk.com

If your vision of the UK is all turrets, moats and Old Masters, this is the site for you. Offering customized tours of castles, country houses, stately homes and gardens, they can also design trips around special interests – as long as they're of the antiques, architecture, cathedrals and literature kind. You stay in manor houses and country estates, and in many cases eat lunch and dinner with the owners. The site also details a couple of scheduled tours per year, often timed to coincide with the Chelsea Flower Show, which are geared towards American travellers and go for around $2000 for ten days, excluding flight. Email them for more details.

Home At First

www.homeatfirst.com

Specializing in independent self-catering holidays throughout the UK and Ireland, US company Home At First can book your entire trip, arrange accommodation only, or organize all ground arrangements – lodging, transportation, guide services and so on. While the accommodation is undeniably top-notch, featuring the kinds of places that send anglophiles weak at the knees – an abbey cottage in Shropshire, riverside flats in London, apartments on a country estate in the Lake District – you should bear in mind that only the best are shown on the site. Each place can be booked for a week minimum, and you can combine as many as you wish.

Lord Addison Travel

www.lordaddison.com

A city gent with a cane and bowler – presumably his lordship himself – welcomes you to this US site, which offers a wide range of small-group escorted tours around the UK. You can search for trips for every

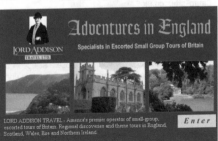

Adventures in England

Specialists in Escorted Small Group Tours of Britain

LORD ADDISON TRAVEL – America's premier operator of small-group, escorted tours of Britain. Regional discoveries and theme tours in England, Scotland, Wales, Eire and Northern Ireland.

Enter

month up to a year ahead: tours may revolve around stately homes and gardens, castles and cathedrals, battlefields, maritime history or a host of other themes. They also have a two-week "Grand Tour", covering London, Salisbury and the New Forest, Bath and the Cotswolds, North Wales, Chester, the Lake District, York and Edinburgh. Clicking on the tour name brings a detailed itinerary plus costs from all the major US airports. There are separate forms should you wish for further information or to make a booking request.

Sterling Tours

www.sterlingtours.com
US operator offering a variety of UK experiences: package tours on more than fifty themes from antique collecting to gardens; custom-designed itineraries with a driver/guide; serviced apartments in London; weekly cottage rentals; car rental, and train passes. They can also fix barge cruises, trips oriented around festivals, walking vacations and other activity holidays. There are a couple of sample itineraries on the site, plus details of their escorted tours (eleven people max) to tourist hot-spots including the Scottish Highlands, the West Country, Ireland and London. To book, fill out the email request form.

UK accommodation

For more on lodgings in the UK, look also at the tourist board Websites reviewed for each country and the general accommodation sites detailed on pp.66–84.

Camp-sites.co.uk

www.camp-sites.co.uk
Searchable directory of campsites and caravan parks around the UK. Choose your country – England, Scotland or Wales – to pull up a list of matches with contact details and links to Websites. Links highlighted on the home page also allow you to choose a selection of hotels in England and Wales, discounted weekend breaks at certain chains, and self-catering apartments in London or Edinburgh.

Country Holidays

www.country-holidays.co.uk
More than 5000 self-catering options throughout the UK, from farmhouses

through urban studios to barn conversions. You have the reassurance of knowing that the properties are all vetted and regularly inspected, and many offer a "short break" two- or three-night option, which saves having to book for a full week. Use the search mechanism to specify your needs, and then browse the list of results, clicking the photo for more details and to book.

Farm Stay UK

www.farm-holidays.co.uk

A co-operative of more than 1000 inspected and vetted working farms providing guest accommodation throughout the UK – some even offer camping pitches. Searching by region brings up sophisticated zoomable maps showing the precise location of each farm, and at this point you can choose between self-catering or B&B. Each review comes with photos, star ratings, a rundown of facilities and contact details. To book, you need to call or email the farm direct.

Great Inns of Britain

www.greatinns.co.uk

Neat little Website representing sixteen classy, independently owned inns. In pretty villages in England and Scotland, all are chosen for their friendly, local atmosphere, their good food and drink, and their welcoming hosts. There's plenty of information on the site, including tariffs, with photos and vaguely irreverent reviews, but bookings must be made with the owners direct.

The Landmark Trust

www.landmarktrust.co.uk

The Landmark Trust snaps up intriguing properties – follies, forts, manor houses, mills, cottages, castles, gatehouses, towers – on the point of falling down, restores them and rents them out. Today they have more than 160

"Landmarks" across Britain, all of them available for rent by the week, providing peaceful retreats with no TV, radio, phone, or microwave. To see the full range, and to make a reservation, you need to order the handbook, which you can do online (they refund the cost if you book a stay). To whet your appetite, the site also features price and availability charts, gushing guest book testimonials, and photos of a number of the most popular properties.

The National Trust

www.nationaltrust.org.uk/cottages/nt.asp

A charity established in 1895 to buy and protect threatened buildings, coastal stretches and areas of countryside, the National Trust now offers more than 300 holiday properties in England, Wales and Northern Ireland. Many of them stand in the grounds of historic homes, and would originally have housed estate workers. You can search by location and party size, or browse a full list organized by geographic region: each cottage is described in full with photos, a rate tariff and availability check. You can also read visitors' comments on individual properties before filling in an email form, or calling, to book. The **National Trust in Scotland (www.nts.org.uk)** has about thirty properties.

The Vivat Trust

www.vivat.org.uk

Like the Landmark Trust (see p.393), Vivat rescues important listed buildings, spruces them up, and rents them out as luxurious holiday lets. Though it has fewer properties than Landmark – and many of them are smaller – the site is more immediately satisfying in that you can see everything, check availability, and book online. It's also possible to arrange mini-breaks of three to five nights rather than stay a whole week. Prices aren't low, but these places, from medieval chantries to follies, are special, and ideally suited to romantic breaks.

UK public transport

National Express

www.gobycoach.com

The site of the British intercity bus network, National Express, features information on all its passes and ticket options and an online booking service. You can also buy Student, Young Persons and 50-plus passes. Tickets are mailed out if you book more than four days in advance, otherwise you have to collect them. If you do a lot of travelling by bus you might want to register: it speeds up the booking process by storing your contact information, gives you priority when it comes to special offers, and for each journey you make adds points to a loyalty card.

Public Transport Information (UK)

www.pti.org.uk
A great example of intelligent, user-friendly Web design, this site offers links to every public transport service – rail, air, coach, bus, ferry, metro and tram – in the UK, and between the UK and Ireland. You can also look up all rail, ferry and coach routes between the UK and mainland Europe. It's beautifully organized, and whatever you're looking for, it gives clear and concise tips on how to find it.

The Trainline

www.thetrainline.com
This site allows you to book any train journey within the UK – though not a sleeper. You need to register, and to have a specific journey in mind, and can then search according to whether you want to get to your destination quickly, or pay as little as possible.

Traintaxi

www.traintaxi.co.uk
It couldn't be simpler: click on the name of a national rail station or underground stop to find out if and when there will be taxis waiting and whether advance booking is necessary. If there is no rank they list at least three local minicab numbers and/or suggest alternative stations.

UK Railways on the Net

www.rail.co.uk
UK portal with links to Railtrack timetables, National Rail's daily train information, and all the Websites of British train networks. The travel bureau sets its sights higher, with links to international train companies, along with British regional tourist information, travel operators and accommodation sites.

UK information

@UK

www.atuk.co.uk
You'll find everything relating to travel and tourism in the UK in this directo-

ry, arranged by region: operators offering all-in holidays or day tours; restaurants, pubs, accommodation; public transport sites; local events listings, and so on. Bear in mind, though, that businesses can add their entry to any section, so looking up "shops in Shropshire", for example, rather than highlighting cute craft stores in Gobowen, will bring up the same lot of e-commerce sites found in every other shopping section.

Curry House

www.curryhouse.co.uk

Online guide to Britain's most popular cuisine with links, arranged by geographic region, to the hundreds of curry restaurant guides out there on the Web. Plus curry recipes from around the world, cooking tips, news on the UK curry scene, and links to crazy curry fan sites.

Good Beach Guide

www.goodbeachguide.co.uk

Check out Britain's best and worst beaches with information from the Marine Conservation Society, who grade water quality according to EC guidelines (which are available to peruse on the site). Search by region to read about recommended beaches, with a general overview including details on water quality, litter, facilities, tourist information and such like – or click "Beach Results" to discover which ones have proved to be dismal, filthy failures.

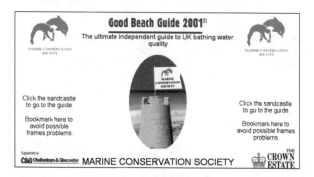

Holidays in the UK

www.holidayuk.co.uk

Links to ground operators offering activity breaks throughout the UK, including walking, cycling, boating and so on, with a special section for self-catering cottages in England and Wales and another for specialist activities (from classic car rental to sea kayaking). For each category you can choose operators by picking them from a map or browsing a full list with short reviews – clicking the company name brings up details. To make an enquiry or provisional booking, you need to fill in their email form.

The Knowhere Guide

www.knowhere.co.uk

Unedited reports, reviews and information written by site users about their local area. Often the information is contradictory – there's usually more than one contributor for any one place – it's generally poorly written, and it may well be out of date. In effect it reads like a big newsgroup, a free-for-all which will appeal most to anyone under 25. Anyone over 35, however, should enter with caution.

UK The Guide

www.uktheguide.com

"Your survival guide to Britain", they call it – a links directory for travellers on a budget, organized into areas including countryside, food and drink, gay, sport, history, accommodation and bands. The site consistently comes up with interesting selections, and there's a separate section for practicalities such as itineraries, offers (anything from clubbing breaks to hostel discounts) and getting to Britain, with links to relevant operators depending upon your country of departure.

England

English tourist boards

Travel England

www.travelengland.org.uk

Boasting few flourishes and little flair, this official site nonetheless does its job. With searchable databases for accommodation, attractions and events, plus regional guides with links to local tourist offices, it's a useful starting point, and the "What's New" pages, updated monthly, invariably come up with intriguing snippets on new attractions, promotions and products. Good links page, too.

East of England www.eastofenglandtouristboard.com
Heart of England www.visitheartofengland.com
Isle of Wight www.isle-of-wight-tourism.gov.uk
The Lake District www.cumbria-the-lake-district.co.uk
London www.londontouristboard.com
Northumbria www.ntb.org.uk
The Northwest www.visitnorthwest.com
Southeast England www.seetb.org.uk and
   www.southeastengland.uk.com
West Country www.wctb.co.uk
Yorkshire www.ytb.org.uk

London

London Free List

www.londonfreelist.com
Directory of more than 1500 things to do in London for £3 or less, from comedy clubs to exhibitions, cinemas and yard sales.

Londontown.com

www.londontown.com
The best thing about this London guide is the hotel-booking facility, where

you can reserve rooms in chains such as Radisson, Thistle and Millennium – either in central London or near an airport – at discounted rates. The home page also highlights special deals on everything from souvenirs to airport transfers. Elsewhere, there's an events calendar giving background on all the major events and festivals – with links where available – while seasonal articles highlight the best upcoming exhibitions, concerts and happenings. "London Town Direct" is a links directory divided into areas including travel (tour operators, ground operators and so on) and "going

Top London attractions

British Museum www.thebritishmuseum.ac.uk
Buckingham Palace www.royal.gov.uk
Cabinet War Rooms www.iwm.org.uk
Chessington World of Adventure www.chessington.co.uk
Hampton Court Palace www.hrp.org.uk
HMS Belfast www.iwm.org.uk
Houses of Parliament www.parliament.uk
Imperial War Museum www.iwm.org.uk
Kensington Palace www.hrp.org.uk
London Aquarium www.londonaquarium.co.uk
London Eye www.ba-londoneye.com
London Zoo www.londonzoo.co.uk
Madame Tussaud's www.madame-tussauds.com
National Gallery www.nationalgallery.org.uk
National Maritime Museum www.nmm.ac.uk
National Portrait Gallery www.npg.org.uk
Natural History Museum www.nhm.ac.uk
Royal Academy www.royalacademy.org.uk
St Paul's Cathedral www.stpauls.co.uk
Science Museum www.nmsi.ac.uk
Tate Gallery www.tate.org.uk
Tower of London www.hrp.org.uk
Victoria and Albert Museum www.vam.ac.uk
Wallace Collection www.the-wallace-collection.org.uk
Westminster Abbey www.westminster-abbey.org
Windsor Castle www.royal.gov.uk

out" (shopping, bars, clubs), but it's a patchy affair – the restaurant directory, for example, consists only of an "essential" Top 10, the pub guide is useless, and there's only one cinema listed.

This Is London

www.thisislondon.co.uk

The Website of London's daily, the *Evening Standard*, not only has all the headlines and stories featured in the paper, but its "Hot Tickets" section is a great place for comprehensive and up-to-date entertainment listings. "Tourist Information" features links to all the main attractions and general information on the complexities of the transport system and so on, and there's a handy "Days Out Guide", full of snippets about artists and events, with museum reviews and schedules. The children's section is well worth a look for anyone with kids in tow.

English attractions

The Eden Project

www.edenproject.com

Colourful and informative site from the wildly successful Cornish ecology centre – "a living theatre of plants and people". With all the practical information you need for a visit, and lots of luscious photos, the site also affords glimpses into the project's huge conservatories – or biomes – and their

recreated habitats, where they grow plants from places as diverse as the Brazilian rainforests, Oceanic Islands, West Africa, and California.

English Heritage

www.english-heritage.org.uk

Responsible for protecting England's historic buildings, natural features and archeological sites, EH has some 400 properties open to the public. The site allows you to search for them by name, region and feature (romantic ruins? Humps and bumps?) or theme (countryside? Artistic passion? Haunted heritage?). Each entry comes with a brief review, access information, opening hours and rundown of facilities, along with news of special events. Overseas visitors can order a money-saving EH pass (valid for a week) by fax or phone – there are plans to install an online ordering facility – while UK residents have the option of becoming a member (again, not yet online) to get free admission to all sites.

Longleat House and Safari Park

www.longleat.co.uk

This magnificent Elizabethan house, with its landscaped grounds designed by Capability Brown, was the first stately home in the UK to establish a safari park on site. Since the 1960s Longleat has become synonymous with "seeing the lions", while its owner, the Marquess of Bath – not your typical aristocrat (songwriter, creator of erotic murals, liberal democrat, old hippie) – is a constant source of fascination. The house itself comes with a host of tourist experiences – a menu as long as your arm lets you read about them all, from the library of medieval documents through the Dr Who museum to the longest hedge maze in the world, along with photos and brief overviews of the major rooms in the house. Links lead you to the marquess' own Website, which is a compelling read in itself, filled with his erotic poetry and lyrics, photographs of his murals – which you can see at the house – and six books of his ongoing autobiography.

National Museum of Photography, Film and Television

www.nmpft.org.uk

Bradford's hugely successful media museum has an efficient, stimulating Website, with all relevant visitor details, special events listings, and an interactive floor plan detailing the permanent galleries and temporary exhibitions. You can read about the museum's star artefacts, including the world's first negative, first television footage and first moving picture – an 1888 film of

Leeds Bridge – and read film schedules for the towering IMAX cinema and the only Cinerama cinema in the world that's open to the public.

The Shakespeare Birthplace Trust

www.shakespeare.org.uk
Visitor information on the five Shakespeare houses in or near Stratford-upon-Avon, a calendar of Shakespeare-related events, and general information about the Bard. For RSC performances in Stratford, check **www.albemarle-london.com/rsc-stratford.html**.

Stonehenge and Avebury Stone Circles

www.stonehenge-avebury.net
Clumsy-looking but informative site, which covers Stonehenge, probably the most famous Megalithic monument in the world, and the nearby Avebury, where the standing stones are even bigger. A simple chart runs through opening times, costs, history, new discoveries, theories, and research news for each, and you can click a link for Quicktime movies of the sites, including one from Stonehenge's interior, which is normally closed to visitors. The Website is brought to you by the Megalithic Society, who also lead free, own-car tours to ancient sites around Britain – email them for details.

WELCOME TO

www.stonehenge-avebury.net
QTVR G-Tour Pages

----the web site offering the most reliable and useful information on Wiltshire's Stonehenge and Avebury, the world's most famous stone circles and henges These World Heritage monuments, under the care of English Heritage and the National Trust, are over 4000 years old and the most visible surviving signs of an advanced early-British culture in Wessex in Southern England

What is Stonehenge?
When was it built? And by whom?
What did it represent?
Why was it built?
How did it function?

And what is known about nearby Avebury, which has the world's biggest stone circles and whose broadly-similar mysteries are being solved by multi-disciplinary scholars in archaeology, science and ancient religion?

Treasurehouses

www.treasurehouses.co.uk
Umbrella organization for ten of England's most important palaces, stately homes and castles, including Blenheim Palace, Castle Howard,

Chatsworth, Leeds Castle, Longleat and Woburn Abbey. Click on the thumbnail photos for overviews, practical details, and links to Websites.

English city sites

For each major city listed below we've chosen two sources of Web information: an **official** site, produced by the local tourist board, city council or other such civic body, and an "**unofficial**" site – perhaps an online guide, home page, local listings magazine or newspaper site. These, while they may not necessarily be particularly "alternative", all have something to offer visitors over and above the official sources.

Bath
official www.visitbath.co.uk
unofficial www.thisisbath.com

Blackpool
official www.blackpooltourism.com
unofficial website.lineone.net/~johnfinlay/blacpool/blakpool.htm

Brighton
official www.brighton.co.uk
unofficial www.theinsight.co.uk

Cambridge
official www.cambridge.gov.uk/leisure/tourism.htm
unofficial www.adhoc.co.uk

Durham
official www.countydurham.com
unofficial www.durhamsearch.co.uk/citypages/durham.html

Liverpool
official www.visitliverpool.com
unofficial www.pool-of-life.co.uk

Manchester
official www.manchester.gov.uk/visitorcentre
unofficial www.manchester.com

Newcastle-upon-Tyne
official www.newcastle.gov.uk
unofficial www.tyne-online.com

Norwich
official www.norwich.gov.uk
unofficial www.ubooty.co.uk
Oxford
official www.visitoxford.org
unofficial www.oxfordcity.co.uk
York
official www.york-tourism.co.uk
unofficial www.thisisyork.co.uk

Scotland

Scottish tourist boards

Scottish Tourist Board

www.visitscotland.com
Scotland's official tourism site is a fine example of its kind, attractively designed, packed with information and easy to navigate by means of the interactive map and menus. The searchable accommodation database, with more than 8500 places to stay, provides all the information you need to research your hotel, B&B, hostel, campsite or self-catering apartment, and in many cases you can book online. They've also gathered contact details for a range of travel operators from mainland Europe and the USA, and, along with a database of thousands of activities, compiled events calendars with listings for music, art and festivals. The itinerary ideas (including a "malts and monarchs" castles/whisky distillery combo) are a nice touch, too, and there are scores of good links.

Aberdeen and Grampian **www.agtb.org**
Angus and City of Dundee **www.angusanddundee.co.uk**
Argyll, the Isles, Loch Lomond, Stirling and Trossachs
  www.scottish.heartlands.org
Aviemore and the Cairngorms **http://aviemore.org**
Ayrshire and Arran **www.ayrshire-arran.com**
Dumfries and Galloway **www.galloway.co.uk**
Edinburgh and the Lothians **www.edinburgh.org**

Kingdom of Fife www.standrews.co.uk
Greater Glasgow and Clyde Valley http://seeglasgow.com
Highlands of Scotland www.host.co.uk
Orkney www.visitorkney.com
Perthshire www.perthshire.co.uk
Scottish Borders www.scot-borders.co.uk
Shetland Islands www.visitshetland.com
Western Isles www.witb.co.uk

Scottish information and attractions

For short tours of ancient Scotland, see
www.footprints-scotland.co.uk reviewed on p.203 in the
"History, Art and Archeology" section.

About Scotland

www.aboutscotland.co.uk
Lively, nicely illustrated guide with a changing roster of articles on major
features or landmarks, historical essays, and a regular "letter from Argyll" –
all wildlife sightings, local lore and dramatic weather – from a local B&B
owner. The accommodation listings are superb – each place has been
approved and reviewed by the About Scotland team – with lots of photos
and details for each hotel, B&B or self-catering cottage.

Caledonian Castles

www.caledoniancastles.co.uk
One of the best of many such sites on the Web – labours of love, all of
them, produced by misty-eyed castle fans from around the world. This one
has pictures and information on more than a hundred Scottish castles,
including lesser-known places not found on other sites. It's easy to navigate, searching by region or castle name, with lovely photos, location maps
and ground plans, and plenty of historic background on each place. Those
that are open to the public have links to their official site.

Caledonian MacBrayne

www.calmac.co.uk
Caledonian MacBrayne is the main ferry operator serving such Scottish
islands as Arran, Bute, Harris, Iona, Lewis, Mull and Skye. You can check

out their schedules on the site, or download the full timetable in PDF format, but actual online booking is available for the busier and more expensive routes only, and even then for travellers with cars only, and for straightforward single or return journeys only. It is also possible, however, to buy Island Rover tickets, which offer unlimited travel for eight or fifteen days, and in any case availability for foot passengers is not a problem.

Edinburgh Festivals

www.edinburghfestivals.com
Really useful venture, pulling together information on all Edinburgh's major festivals, including *the* Edinburgh festival, the fringe, the film festival, the military tattoo, the jazz and blues festival, and Hogmanay, with contact details and programme information for each, along with highlights of all current and forthcoming festivals, schedules of related events, and links to the official Websites.

Edinburgh Galleries Association

www.edinburgh-galleries.co.uk
Don't expect any bells and whistles on this worthy site, just monthly updates on exhibitions at the major private and public galleries, with photos, locator maps, admission fees, opening hours, contact details and links to Web sites.

Lochness Live!

www.lochness.scotland.net
Daft as a brush, with two Webcams – one of them underwater – set up for potential Nessie sightings, a "sightings file" (from 1998 only, sadly, though it does include a shot of the "fast-moving black object" spotted on the Webcam by a Texas couple), plus links to local accommodation and to the Loch Ness shop, with its "spectacular range of gifts and toys".

Rampant Scotland

www.rampantscotland.com
This is the kind of links directory that makes you want to kiss the screen – huge, functioning, searchable and genuinely useful, linking you to anything and everything from hotels, haunted castles, folklore sites, city guides, poetry sites, magazines and newspapers – even the Big Page of Bagpipe Humour (**http://users.aol.com/wgority/jokes.html**) – what more could you ask for?

Scotland's Malt Whisky Trail

www.maltwhiskytrail.com
The Highland region of Speyside has seven malt whisky distilleries – more than half of Scotland's total – and a tourist industry geared up to appeal to anyone partial to a wee dram. The site's interactive map allows you to click on distillery icons to discover more details about each, and pop-up windows advertise recommended local accommodation.

Scottish Highlands Online Travel Guide

www.wannabethere.com
So the Highlands got trendy all of a sudden, if this yoof site – aimed at under-35s – is to be believed. You'll need to opt out of the multimedia extravaganza that is Flash 4 – lots of bagpipes, lots of morphing buzzwords, lots of broken links – and go instead to the pared-down version. It'll make you cringe – "Wanna set the heather on fire?" – but once you get over that, it's a clean, efficient site, which does a good job. The partying section, in particular, is an unusual resource, with lively details on local pubs, clubs and festivals with photos, interactive maps, and comprehensive events listings. You can also book activity breaks ("Wanna do it in the great outdoors?"), snap up a range of hostel, bus and train deals – and even splash out on "romantic" weekends – though those candlelit dining rooms and four poster beds come at a price.

Walk Scotland

www.walkscotland.com

Whether you're into munro bagging or simply fancy a day's hiking somewhere pretty, this impressive site – which extends its scope to all sorts of activity holidays, including canoeing and kayaking – is a gem. As well as the database of routes (anything from two miles up), which is updated weekly, come here for walking news and mountain reports, gear reviews, weather forecasts and live Webcam images for Ben Nevis, Aonach Mor and the Cairngorms. The online bookshop sells used outdoor and travel books, which are also offered on the message board (a good place to find walking companions). The links page is a volume in itself.

Wales

Welsh tourist boards

TravelWales.org

www.travelwales.org

Official tourist board site designed specifically for travellers from North America, with lots of practical information including details of operators offering escorted and independent tours or adventure holidays, complete with contact details and Websites. The accommodation section details special deals offered by the bigger, more upmarket hotels.

Visit Wales

www.visitwales.com

Wales' official tourism site features seasonal news and offers on the home page, plus a searchable directory of more than 600 Welsh links, an accommodation database and an events calendar. Separate sections deal with activity holidays, cycling, walking and golf, with links to accommodation, operators and routes relevant to each.

Isle of Anglesey www.anglesey.gov.uk
Cardiff www.cardiffmarketing.co.uk
Mid- and west coast Wales www.mid-wales-tourism.org.uk
North Wales www.nwt.co.uk

South Wales www.southernwales.com
South Wales valleys www.valleyswelcome.org.uk
Southwest Wales www.pembrokeshire-holidays.com
Swansea www.want2getaway.net

Welsh information and attractions

Castles of Wales

www.castlewales.com

Labour of love from American castle enthusiast Jeff Thomas, with information and photographs on more than four hundred medieval castles. It's a
good read, with learned accounts of Welsh medieval history, biographies of
all the great castle builders, locator maps and a bibliography, plus a small
section on Welsh abbeys and religious sites. You can also follow links to
castles offering accommodation.

Centre for Alternative Technology

www.cat.org.uk

This self-sufficient 40-acre eco-community was established in Powys during
the oil crisis of 1974. Six families now live on the site, which has become
one of Wales' major tourist attractions. Using wind, water and solar power,
self-built environmentally sound buildings, organic farming and alternative
sewage systems, the centre has seven acres open to the public; entrance
is via a water-powered cliff railway. Along with displays on conservation,
recycling and organic farming, a smallholding and loads of kids' activities,
CAT offers courses on anything from blacksmithing to the art of compost-
ing. There's an email form if you want to book online, plus all the practical
details for anyone hoping to visit and stay nearby.

Every Celtic Thing on the Web

http://og-man.net/angwels.htm

No-fuss directory of links to all manner of Welsh sites including home
pages, crafts and bookshops, rock bands, local councils, accommodation
agencies, festivals, theme parks, newsgroups and much more.

Portmeirion

www.portmeirion-village.com

Most famous for being the other-worldly village in the cult 1960s TV series The

Prisoner, the surreal coastal settlement of Portmeirion is one of Wales' major attractions. The site offers an informative guide to the whole village, with snippets on the writers and actors who've spent time here, the local pottery and Prisoner connections, and the very particular look of the place, dreamed up by maverick architect Clough Williams-Ellis. You can also check out the accommodation in the swanky Hotel Portmeirion, along with a number of quirky self-catering cottages, and fill out an availability request form online.

Welsh Rarebits Hotels of Distinction

www.welsh.rarebits.co.uk
More than forty hand-selected quality hotels – country houses, inns, spas – with maps, reviews, photos, tariffs and links to Websites. Though prices in the main aren't low – these are luxurious, award-winning places – most properties offer special short-break deals. Bookings are made direct with the hotel.

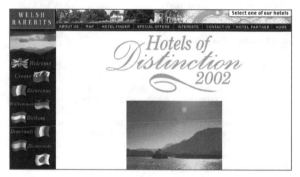

Northern Ireland

Northern Irish tourist boards

Northern Ireland Tourist Board

www.discovernorthernireland.com
This fully searchable site has lots of good features, including a database of

local information centres. Many tourist offices, including those for Down and Belfast, have their own pages here. Pull-down menus allow you to view lists of attractions, activities, hotels (bookable online) and restaurants by region. Once you've selected something from any of these you can go on to search for nearby features in all sorts of categories. There's a genealogy section, too, for anyone yearning to trace their Ulster roots.

Derry www.derryvisitor.com
Fermanagh www.fermanagh-online.com
Lisburn www.lisburn.gov.uk
Newcastle www.newcastletic.org
North Antrim (Giants Causeway) www.northantrim.com

Northern Irish tours and attractions

Belfast Black Taxi Tours

www.belfasttours.com
Lively taxi tours of Belfast, taking in all the historical and political sights – including the murals on the Shankill and Falls roads – as well as longer excursions to the north Antrim Coast. The site features contact details, photos and testimonials; you can book by email or phone.

Federation of Retail Licence Trade

www.ulsterpubs.com
Searchable database of Northern Irish pubs, with opening hours, a run-down of facilities, contact details and photos for each. You can hunt for your tavern of choice by clicking on a map, refining your search by specifying places with gardens, places that welcome kids, or places that offer food and music.

Wild Ulster Jeep Tours

www.wildulster.com
Based in Hillsborough, this inventive company runs jeep tours of Fermanagh, the Antrim coast, and off-the-beaten-track destinations in the rugged Mourne Mountains. They'll also arrange activity tours or trips timed to coincide with National Trust events and festivals. Their "wild weekends", designed for small groups, have themes from Belfast nightlife to falcony and walking. Email them to make a booking request.

The Channel Islands

Guernsey Tourist Board

www.guernseytouristboard.com

Attractive and user-friendly site linking to all carriers with flights to the island, along with operators from the UK and mainland Europe. The searchable accommodation database features photos, reviews and contact details (including Websites) for every place it lists, and there's a rundown of sites and attractions organized by subject area.

Jersey Tourism

www.jersey.com

Jersey's official tourist site links to all the other main Jersey sites on the Web, making it pretty comprehensive. You can hook up with a variety of accommodation sites, most of them with online booking, along with ferry companies and airlines, and there's a searchable database of specialist operators for holidays and short breaks. Travellers from North America have their own separate sections.

Sark Tourism

www.sark-tourism.com

The smallest of the Channel Islands – just three miles by one and a half – has a rather sophisticated site, with an events schedule and a directory listing all the accommodation, including self-catering and campsites. You can even book flights and ferries. The front-page news story, updated weekly, gives the site a homely, local feel.

Isle Of Man

Isle of Man Government

www.gov.im/tourism

Good information about this fiercely independent island enclave, just sixty miles off the northwest coast of England. The official site provides details on how to get there, where to stay (with a searchable accommodation database) and a special offers page covering deals offered by airlines, ferry companies and hotels.

USA

This section is primarily intended to point readers towards the official tourism Websites for all US states and major cities, as well as selected high-profile attractions and national transportation operators.

Bear in mind that other sites of use to anyone hoping to travel within the USA are scattered throughout this book. See, for example, the online travel agents, airlines and accommodation sites detailed in Part One, and the many operators specializing in specific activities and interests who are included in Part Two.

State tourism sites

Every US state runs its own Website to promote local tourism. As all follow very much the same formula, there's no point reviewing each one in detail here. Suffice it to say that all offer descriptions and photographs of regional attractions, listings and links for accommodation, and provide email addresses and toll-free numbers for specific enquiries. You'll also find details of free maps and brochures, mailed out on request.

Alabama www.touralabama.org
Alaska www.dced.state.ak.us/tourism
Arizona www.arizonaguide.com
Arkansas www.arkansas.com
California www.gocalif.com
Colorado www.colorado.com
Connecticut www.ctbound.org
Delaware www.visitdelaware.net
Florida www.flausa.com
Georgia www.georgia.org
Hawaii www.gohawaii.com
Idaho www.visitid.org
Illinois www.enjoyillinois.com
Indiana www.enjoyindiana.com
Iowa www.state.ia.us/tourism
Kansas www.travelKS.com
Kentucky www.kentuckytourism.com
Louisiana www.louisianatravel.com
Maine www.visitmaine.com
Maryland www.mdisfun.org
Massachusetts www.massvacation.com
Michigan www. michigan.org
Minnesota www.exploreminnesota.com
Mississippi www.visitmississippi.org
Missouri www.missouritourism.org
Montana www.visitmt.org
Nebraska www.visitnebraska.org

Nevada www.travelnevada.com
New Hampshire www.visitnh.gov
New Jersey www.state.nj.us/travel
New Mexico www.newmexico.org
New York State www.iloveny.com
North Carolina www.visitnc.com
North Dakota www.ndtourism.com
Ohio www.ohiotourism.com
Oklahoma www.travelok.com
Oregon www.traveloregon.com
Pennsylvania www.state.pa.us
Rhode Island www.visitrhodeisland.com
South Carolina www.discoversouthcarolina.com
South Dakota www.travelsd.com
Tennessee www.tnvacation.com
Texas www.traveltex.com
Utah www.utah.com
Vermont www.1-800-vermont.com
Virginia www.virginia.org
Washington www.tourism.wa.gov
West Virginia www.callwva.com
Wisconsin www.travelwisconsin.com
Wyoming www.wyomingtourism.org

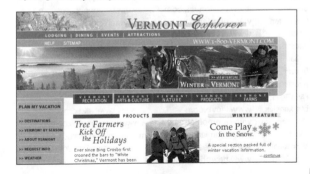

part three: destinations

City sites

Many of the Websites listed in our "Finding What You Need" section (see p.3) provide detailed online guides to specific US destinations. Full listings for all major US cities, for example, can be found both on guidebook sites such as **Rough Guides** and **Frommers**, and via the online-only services of **about.com** and **away.com**. Similarly, accommodation throughout the United States can be booked using the general lodging sites reviewed on p.68 onwards. In addition, however, every city and destination has its own official site, usually run by the local Convention and Visitors Bureau. All the official sites listed below facilitate online accommodation reservations, and most also hold thorough guides to dining, sightseeing, activities and forthcoming events. Many regional newspapers and magazines also offer good online destination guides, which tend to concentrate on restaurant and entertainment listings rather than accommodation. For each city below we've listed the most useful local media Website for prospective visitors.

	Official city site	Local media
Atlanta	www.atlanta.com	www.creativeloafing.com
Baltimore	www.baltconvstr.com	www.sunspot.net
Boston	www.bostonusa.com	www.bostonphoenix.com
Charleston	www.charlestoncvb.com	www.charleston.net
Chicago	www.chicago.il.org	www.chicagotribune.com
Cincinnati	www.cincyusa.com	www.citybeat.com
Dallas	www.dallascvb.com	www.dallasobserver.com
Denver	www.denver.org	www.denverpost.com
Houston	www.houston-guide.com	www.houston-press.com
Las Vegas	www.lasvegas24hours.com	www.lvrj.com
Los Angeles	www.lacvb.com	www.laweekly.com
Memphis	www.memphistravel.com	www.gomemphis.com
Miami	www.miamiandbeaches.com	www.miaminewtimes.com
Minneapolis	www.minneapolis.org	www.startribune.com
New Orleans	www.neworleanscvb.com	www.bestofneworleans.com

New York	www.nycvisit.com	www.villagevoice.com
Orlando	www.orlandoinfo.com	www.orlandoweekly.com
Philadelphia	www.pcvb.org	www.cpcn.com
Phoenix	www.phoenixcvb.com	www.phoenixnewtimes.com
Salt Lake City	www.saltlake.org	www.avenews.com
San Antonio	www.sanantoniocvb.com	www.mysanantonio.com
San Diego	www.sandiego.org	www.sdreader.com
San Francisco	www.sfvisitor.org	www.bestofthebay.com
Santa Fe	www.santafe.org	www.santafenewmexican.com
Savannah	www.savcvb.com	www.savannahnow.com
Seattle	www.seeseattle.org	http://seattlep-i.nwsource.com
St Louis	www.st-louis-cvc.com	http://home.post-dispatch.com
Washington DC	www.washington.org	www.washingtoncitypaper.com

Major attractions

Crazy Horse Memorial

www.crazyhorse.org

An extraordinary monument to one man's obsession, the Crazy Horse Memorial is an equestrian figure of the Sioux leader that has been whittled from a mountainside in the Black Hills of South Dakota ever since 1948. On completion it will, at 563ft high and 641ft long, be the largest statue in the world, larger even than the Great Pyramid. Use the Website to find out about visiting, follow the work in progress, make a donation, or even apply for a job.

Disney Vacations Online

www.disney.com

Despite all the resources at its disposal, the travel section of the Disney Website is surprisingly concise. Eschewing interactive games and animations, it simply provides a basic rundown of the various "lands" and "towns" in both Walt Disney World and Disneyland, plus overviews of the resort hotels and a bit of general travel information (weather charts, driving distances, park hours, etc). When you're ready to book, things couldn't be simpler. Simply choose the most popular package (hotel of your choice, park passes and various perks) or piece together one of your own (adding car rental, maybe). A quick availability check will come up with an alternative if your preferred hotel is full. Links facilitate booking at Disney parks elsewhere in the world, but flights to or from the US are not available online. Stern warnings admonish users not to suggest or encourage illegal activity, or even post recipes.

Graceland

www.elvis.com

Twenty-five years since Elvis left the building, his official Website is still largely dedicated to encouraging visits to his former Memphis home of Graceland. Assuming that a virtual tour of the mansion persuades you to buy a ticket for the real thing, you can also book a room at the nearby Heartbreak Hotel, as well, of course, as shopping for souvenirs and ingesting reams of online trivia.

Mardi Gras, New Orleans

www.mardigrasneworleans.com

America's greatest street party is celebrated in all its mind-boggling detail by this privately run fan site. As well as tips on how to get the most out of Carnival, and fascinating historical links, it enables users to buy costumes, accessories, and grandstand seats online – or simply to watch the parades on streaming video.

Rock and Roll Hall of Fame

www.rockhall.com

Cleveland's premier tourist attraction maintains an entertaining online presence with a Website that's devoted as much to the many legendary inductees into the hall as to practical advice for visitors. Highlights include

the daily "Today In Rock History" feature (holding such gems as "Billy J. Kramer appears on the Ed Sullivan Show") and a Top 10 of the greatest songs ever (Stairway to Heaven ranks at #1).

Smithsonian Institution

www.si.edu

The Smithsonian Website celebrates sixteen US national museums and its National Zoo, most but not quite of all of which are in Washington DC. The collection of the National Air and Space Museum, in particular, lends itself to being displayed online, but all the museums are covered well, with full practical details for visitors plus news of current and forthcoming temporary exhibitions. To get the best of the "Virtual Smithsonian" section you'll need a high bandwidth connection.

Universal Studios

www.universalstudios.com

Universal Studios make a bit more effort than Disney to provide lively online guides to their Florida and California theme parks, though all that Flash animation can be a strain on an ordinary modem. If you feel the urge to turn your virtual visit into an actual one, Woody Woodpecker will guide you through making the necessary arrangements, from simply buying park tickets to reserving a fully inclusive package.

Transportation sites

Alaska Railroad

www.akrr.com

The Alaska Railroad, the last full-service railroad in the US, offers short train tours through Alaska's amazing scenery. Options range from a two-day excursion from Anchorage to Talkeetna, including a night in Talkeetna, a tour of McKinley Glacier, and a river trip, for $400, to an eight-night tour, including a night in Anchorage, for around $1500 (excluding flight to Alaska). Email the reservation form, or print it and fax it direct; they will confirm by phone, fax, or mail.

Amtrak

www.amtrak.com

The wordy Website of the US national rail network allows users to browse schedules, route maps, timetables and fares. However, you need to register to buy tickets and find out about discounted fares, exclusive to the site, while sadly, their good-value train passes for foreign travellers are not available online (though they do provide a mailing address and telephone number for international sales representatives).

Green Tortoise Adventure Travel

www.greentortoise.com
This much-loved, vaguely counter-cultural, long-distance bus company, based in San Francisco, has been running transcontinental "adventure trips" in buses kitted out with bunks, fridges and music systems for nearly thirty years. The site is clumsy to look at but assured in tone, featuring full schedules – destinations include the national parks, New Orleans, and Alaska, with special trips to festivals such as Burning Man and Mardi Gras – and last-minute discounts, with a downloadable booking form. There's also a chat room and bulletin board, plus news of the "frequent crawler" scheme, which earns users points towards a free trip.

Greyhound

www.greyhound.com
The quick, slick site of the US intercity bus network features a route map and pull-down menus for travel planning and buying tickets (check "Discounts" for special fares, and "Terminals" for contact details for every bus terminal in the USA). A handy table displays a rundown of Greyhound's Discovery pass (for North American travellers), and the Ameripass and regional passes (for non-US travellers), which offer unlimited stopovers from anything from four to sixty days. To search for individual fares or check schedules simply key in dates, departure point and destination. US citizens can buy tickets online up to ten days in advance. International travellers, however, are only able to go through the server to buy passes, and then only up to 21 days in advance.

Train Hoppers Space

http://catalog.com/hop
The lovingly prepared Train Hoppers Space isn't exactly high-tech, but it's got everything the twenty-first century hobo – or armchair hobo – could desire. Perhaps the history of train brake systems isn't for you, but the train-hoppers' slang is a treat: so now you know that a Reefer is a refrigerated box car and that a Bull is a railroad security person, "usually driving white American trucks around the yard". Links connect to the National Hobo Association and *The Hobo Times* as well as lots of rail fan sites and train-related newsgroups.

The great outdoors

Americansouthwest.net

www.americansouthwest.net
A privately run fan site devoted to the national parks and wilderness areas of the desert Southwest, featuring some great photos, masses of links, and an especially copious section on the region's little-known, but stunningly beautiful, slot canyons.

GORP

www.gorp.com
As detailed on p.121, the GORP (Great Outdoors Recreation Pages) Website makes an invaluable tool for adventurous travellers the world over, but it's strongest of all on its home territory of the USA. It offers step-by-step practical guides to all the major national parks and wilderness areas, and also sells its own programme of adventurous tours. All trips are bookable online, though prices are seldom cheap.

National Park Service

www.nps.gov
This invaluable Website covers every component of the wonderful national park system, with full practical details for the whole gamut of National Monuments, National Historic Sites, National Seashores and so on, as well as for the parks themselves. For big names, such as the Grand Canyon, Yellowstone and Yosemite, the range of information is breathtaking, covering camping, hiking, wildlife and lodging, with full links to private accommodation options and activity operators in the vicinity.

National Scenic Byways Online

www.byways.org
Sponsored by the Federal Highway Administration, this luscious site honours America's most beautiful driving routes, detailing highly illustrated itineraries across the length and breadth of the country.

Roadside America

www.roadsideamerica.com
An online version of the book of the same name, this entertaining compendium of wayside oddities includes such highlights as the world's only life-size Chocolate Moose, and the rival towns that boast populations of all-white and all-black squirrels.

Sierra Club

www.sierraclub.org
The veteran environmental organization uses its Website to promote awareness of issues and events throughout the US, with links to "chapters" in each individual state for coverage of local activities. For travellers, however, its most useful feature is the "Outings" section, as described on p.122, which details the club's lengthy list of adventure-travel expeditions, all of which can be booked online.

UK tour operators

America As You Like It

www.america-as-you-like-it.com
While the speciality on this UK Website is on booking accommodation in prime resort areas such as New York, Florida, California, and New England (from hotels and national-park lodges to rental apartments and ski-chalets), they can also arrange entire fly-drive itineraries. Call or email to book.

AmeriCan Adventures

www.americanadventures.com
UK company operating budget-oriented small-group tours in all regions of the US, including coast-to-coast trips, and with an emphasis on outdoor

adventures. Accommodation is in hotels and camp sites as well as in independent Roadrunner youth hostels. Complete the email form to check availability and request a reservation.

Complete North America

www.completenorthamerica.com
Helpful and informative Website run by UK operator that offers tailor-made itineraries throughout the US, including fly-drives, bus trips, and city breaks. Flights and car or RV rental can also be arranged separately. Prices are not the cheapest; the focus instead is on guaranteeing a problem-free holiday, with accommodation in high-standard hotels. They claim to have so many special offers that they can't even show any on screen; email for the latest deals or with specific enquiries.

Just America

www.justamerica.co.uk
This thorough and comprehensive site outlines the full US programme offered by a British agency that specializes in both self-guided trips (travelling either in a rental car or by rail) and escorted coach tours, and also features ranch holidays and weekend breaks. Use the interactive map to get full details, including dates and prices, but only send the email form once you've called and been given an invoice number.

Titan Travel

www.titantravel.co.uk
UK operator Titan's extensive list of guided bus and rail tours of the US are intended primarily for older and more sedate travellers, but they provide comprehensive coverage of the country's natural splendours as well as its most historic cities, and enjoy a reputation for efficiency. Availability can be checked via email. If you're more interested in a fly-drive, follow the homepage link to Connections Worldwide instead.

Vietnam

Exodus

www.exodus.co.uk

This stalwart UK adventure-travel company (see p.120) organizes a nice choice of Vietnam holidays. To find them, type Asia into the holiday search, then click on the first Vietnam trip you see. From there you can choose to view all the Vietnam itineraries, including a hill-tribe tour and a nineteen-day Saigon to Hanoi trip travelling by bike, boat and train. Vietnam also features on a combined overland and train trip with Laos, Cambodia and Thailand, and on an unusual south Indochina trip with Kampuchea and Thailand. The site provides itineraries for each – though you need to download or email for really detailed notes – and online booking is straightforward. Prices are quoted according to where you're flying from, though most trips can be booked without flight.

Himalayan Travel

www.gorp.com/himtravel.htm

North American company organizing scheduled adventure tours, from the relatively unchallenging – comfortable hotels, gentle day hikes – to hard-going mountaineering expeditions. Their Vietnam itineraries run the gamut from gentle "highlights" tours, through a fifteen-day Central Highlands Explorer, with beach camping and trekking in the northern hills, to an eighteen-day cycling trip (only ten days are spent actually on a bike). There's no online booking: you need to submit a form to receive a hard copy brochure.

Journeys International

www.journeys-intl.com

This US operator organizes small-group eco and cultural tours, classified from Grade I (relatively active, staying in lodges) to Grade IV (demanding wilderness travel). Each of the three Vietnam tours, which start at around $1000, counts as a grade I–II. Though they offer a couple of general country tours by road, train, and boat, most intriguing is the Grand Vietnam Explorer, which includes a trek into the hill tribes of the north where you stay in a simple village longhouse. You can read daily itineraries on the site, along with trip reviews from past clients. To reserve, click on "Trip Terms and Conditions", where there's a downloadable application form and an online booking facility.

Myths and Mountains

www.mythsandmountains.com

Nevada-based operator offering an unusual selection of cultural tours. Their ten or so Vietnam trips are varied and creative: "Ancient Medicines in Modern Vietnam", for example, includes lakeside Tai Chi, a visit to a traditional hospital, medicinal herb and tree walks, while a twelve-day folk art tour combines gallery trips with the chance to watch craftspeople at work, travelling from the hill communities of the north, through Hanoi, and down to Hue, Hoi An and Danang. They

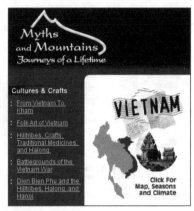

Myths and Mountains
Journeys of a Lifetime

Cultures & Crafts
: From Vietnam To Kham
: Folk Art of Vietnam
: Hilltribes, Crafts, Traditional Medicines, and Halong
: Battlegrounds of the Vietnam War
: Dien Bien Phu and the Hilltribes, Halong, and Hanoi

VIETNAM

Click For Map, Seasons and Climate

can also arrange biking holidays, sea canoeing, and tours of Vietnam War battlegrounds. Each is described tantalizingly on the site, but to see a detailed itinerary, or to request a custom-designed tour, you'll need to submit a form. And when it comes to booking a scheduled trip you have to fill in yet more forms, either online or downloaded, and send them with your deposit.

Vietnam Adventures

www.vietnamadventures.com

With its combination of travelogue, articles and practical detail, this US-produced site can save you a lot of time trawling around the Web. The "adventures" themselves are short travel features, most of them written by sitemaster Martin Wilson. And they're not all adventures, exactly – among the obligatory travellers' tales you'll also find plenty about local delicacies and cultural phenomena. More useful, however, is the hotel booking facility – click the name of a city on a map to read about a selection of hotels, with photos and readers' reviews. Vietnam Adventures offers discounted rates on most of them, and you can book a room online. The site also details up-to-date flight deals from North America, with an online enquiry form.

Visit Vietnam

www.visitvietnam.co.uk

Indochina specialists, based in London, with a nice selection of tailor-made holidays, independent itineraries and escorted tours. If you're going it alone, you're looking at around £600 for ten days, flight included, with a few days in a posh hotel; small-group tours, including flight, accommodation and all sightseeing, cost £400 more. They also do a fifteen-day train journey which includes stops at Hue and a Tay village, a boat trip on the Perfume River, and a couple of days in Hanoi and Halong Bay. Active types should check out the "eco-tour", a relatively gentle affair involving short forest treks, cycling and wildlife spotting, or the cycling holiday – with some car pick-ups and train journeys – which stops at Hanoi, Hue, Hoi An, Danang and Saigon. Submit an email form to check availability.

Zimbabwe

For safari sites, see "Wildlife and Nature", which starts on p.220.

Africa Tours

www.africasafaris.com

Though it specializes in custom-designing independent itineraries, this US-based Africa specialist has a handful of scheduled safaris and tours of Zimbabwe, including short packages to Victoria Falls, Matopos, the Eastern Highlands and the Great Zimbabwe Ruins, which leave any day of the week and can be taken in any combination. The longer tours cost upwards of $4000 with international flight, though you can book without airfare too – there's no online booking, so you should call or email them in New York.

Africa Travel Centre

www.africatravel.co.uk

Culturally sensitive Africa specialist offering a really good range of scheduled and customized tours. Click "Itineraries" to see the full rundown: Zimbabwe trips include the ten-day "Zimbabwe Special", visiting Hwange National Park, Victoria Falls and the Matobos Hills, or the shorter "Snapshot of Zimbabwe", which covers all the major sites in just one week.

If you want to get off the beaten track, go for "Eastern Delights", which combines a trip to Victoria Falls with the more remote areas of the east. You can also choose a two-centre holiday, with Zanzibar, Mauritius or South Africa. Costs, upwards of £1300, include international flights. Email them to book.

African Adrenalin

www.africanadrenalin.co.za
Clearing house for a variety of travel operators in southern Africa, offering anything from accommodation, train journeys and adventure holidays to elephant, horseback and overland safaris. Click Zimbabwe on the list of countries and then choose a theme from the menu; up pops a list of relevant companies with links. Many of them offer online booking.

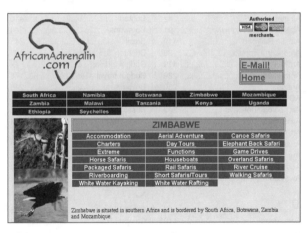

Index

index

index

Around the World

Alaska ★ Algarve ★ Amsterdam ★ Andalucía ★ Antigua & Barbuda ★ Argentina ★ Auckland Restaurants ★ Australia ★ Austria ★ Bahamas ★ Bali & Lombok ★ Bangkok ★ Barbados ★ Barcelona ★ Beijing ★ Belgium & Luxembourg ★ Belize ★ Berlin ★ Big Island of Hawaii ★ Bolivia ★ Boston ★ Brazil ★ Britain ★ Brittany & Normandy ★ Bruges & Ghent ★ Brussels ★ Budapest ★ Bulgaria ★ California ★ Cambodia ★ Canada ★ Cape Town ★ Caribbean Islands ★ Central America ★ Chile ★ China ★ Copenhagen ★ Corsica ★ Costa Brava ★ Costa Rica ★ Crete ★ Croatia ★ Cuba ★ Cyprus ★ Czech & Slovak Republics ★ Devon & Cornwall ★ Dodecanese & East Aegean ★ Dominican Republic ★ The Dordogne & the Lot ★ Dublin ★ Ecuador ★ Edinburgh ★ Egypt ★ England ★ Europe ★ First-time Asia ★ First-time Europe ★ Florence ★ Florida ★ France ★ French Hotels & Restaurants ★ Gay & Lesbian Australia ★ Germany ★ Goa ★ Greece ★ Greek Islands ★ Guatemala ★ Hawaii ★ Holland ★ Hong Kong & Macau ★ Honolulu ★ Hungary ★ Ibiza & Formentera ★ Iceland ★ India ★ Indonesia ★ Ionian Islands ★ Ireland ★ Israel & the Palestinian Territories ★ Italy ★ Jamaica ★ Japan ★ Jerusalem ★ Jordan ★ Kenya ★ The Lake District ★ Languedoc & Roussillon ★ Laos ★ Las Vegas ★ Lisbon ★ London ★

in Twenty Years

London Mini Guide ★ London Restaurants ★ Los Angeles ★ Madeira ★ Madrid ★ Malaysia, Singapore & Brunei ★ Mallorca ★ Malta & Gozo ★ Maui ★ Maya World ★ Melbourne ★ Menorca ★ Mexico ★ Miami & the Florida Keys ★ Montréal ★ Morocco ★ Moscow ★ Nepal ★ New England ★ New Orleans ★ New York City ★ New York Mini Guide ★ New York Restaurants ★ New Zealand ★ Norway ★ Pacific Northwest ★ Paris ★ Paris Mini Guide ★ Peru ★ Poland ★ Portugal ★ Prague ★ Provence & the Côte d'Azur ★ Pyrenees ★ The Rocky Mountains ★ Romania ★ Rome ★ San Francisco ★ San Francisco Restaurants ★ Sardinia ★ Scandinavia ★ Scotland ★ Scottish Highlands & Islands ★ Seattle ★ Sicily ★ Singapore ★ South Africa, Lesotho & Swaziland ★ South India ★ Southeast Asia ★ Southwest USA ★ Spain ★ St Lucia ★ St Petersburg ★ Sweden ★ Switzerland ★ Sydney ★ Syria ★ Tanzania ★ Tenerife and La Gomera ★ Thailand ★ Thailand's Beaches & Islands ★ Tokyo ★ Toronto ★ Travel Health ★ Trinidad & Tobago ★ Tunisia ★ Turkey ★ Tuscany & Umbria ★ USA ★ Vancouver ★ Venice & the Veneto ★ Vienna ★ Vietnam ★ Wales ★ West Africa ★ Washington DC ★ Women Travel ★ Yosemite ★ Zanzibar ★ Zimbabwe

also lookout for our phrasebooks, music guides and reference books

Informed, independent advice
on the major gaming platforms

Punchy reviews
of the top games in every genre

Hints, tips and cheats
to crack each game

Directories
of the best Web sites and gaming resources

Sorted

ROUGH GUIDES